THE WORLD'S CLASSICS

LEAVES OF GRASS

WALT WHITMAN had recently turned 36 years of age when he published the first edition of *Leaves of Grass* in July 1855. If the date was not the Fourth of July, America's Independence Day, it should have been and was probably intended as the day of publication because Whitman declared not only independence from his past as a journalist, freelance writer, and poetaster but his literary independence from the conventions that made 'Literature' something of an anachronism in the democracy he celebrated. Answering Ralph Waldo Emerson's call in his essay 'The Poet' for 'metre-making argument,' Whitman wrote poetry whose expansive form and theme reflected the lives and occupations of Americans who did not have the leisure time to read 'poetry.' *Leaves of Grass* also departed from the 'standard of the evening lamp' in defining the significance of sex in the poetic exploration of experience. By celebrating his own 'personal nature', Whitman celebrated the American (and human) nature in practically all its aspects. His book went through six editions and several more printings in the next thirty-five years—in the face of disapproving reviews, repeated attempts at censorship, and even one 'banning' in Boston (in 1882). Yet it was from that declining literary center, in nearby Concord, that *Leaves of Grass* received its strongest and most enduring endorsement. After reading his complimentary copy, Emerson called Whitman's bold experiment in literature 'the most extraordinary piece of wit and wisdom that America has yet contributed'—a critical assessment that remains true today.

JEROME LOVING is Professor of English at Texas A&M University. His books include *Emerson, Whitman, and the American Muse* and *Emily Dickinson: The Poet on the Second Story*.

THE WORLD'S CLASSICS

WALT WHITMAN

Leaves of Grass

Edited with an Introduction by
JEROME LOVING

Oxford   New York
OXFORD UNIVERSITY PRESS

Oxford University Press, Walton Street, Oxford OX2 6DP

Oxford New York
Athens Auckland Bangkok Bombay
Calcutta Cape Town Dar es Salaam Delhi
Florence Hong Kong Istanbul Karachi
Kuala Lumpur Madras Madrid Melbourne
Mexico City Nairobi Paris Singapore
Taipei Tokyo Toronto

and associated companies in
Berlin Ibadan

Oxford is a trade mark of Oxford University Press

Introduction, Note on the Text, Select Bibliography,
Chronology, Explanatory Notes © Jerome Loving 1990

First published as a World's Classics paperback 1990

British Library Cataloguing in Publication Data

Data available

Library of Congress Cataloging in Publication Data
Whitman, Walt, 1819-1892.
Leaves of grass/Walt Whitman: edited with an introduction by
Jerome Loving.
p. cm.—(The World's classics)
Includes bibliographical references.
I. Loving, Jerome, 1941- . II. Title. III. Series.
PS3201 1990 811'3—dc20 89-22859

ISBN 0-19-282675-1

9 10

Printed in Great Britain by
BPC Paperbacks Ltd
Aylesbury, Bucks

CONTENTS

CONTENTS

INTRODUCTION

On the copyright page to the present edition of *Leaves of Grass* (the last one prepared by the poet), it is stated that the second annex, 'Good-Bye My Fancy,' enjoys the same protection as that of the eight 'editions' of the book published between 1855 and 1891. Technically, only six editions were published during the poet's lifetime, and actually none of them was safe from pirating before 1891, the year of the first international copyright agreement. Not that *Leaves of Grass* was ever in much danger of being stolen by one of the European publishing houses. The first foreign edition—prepared in 1868 by the British critic William Michael Rossetti with Whitman's cooperation—had to be 'selected,' meaning expurgated. Now the whole of *Leaves of Grass*, plus two appendices and a retrospective essay, was safely published, if still not acceptable to the genteel standards of the time, in either the United States or Great Britain. The irony of the copyright protection is underscored by the fact that the Librarian of Congress, whose name appears on the copyright page, was A. R. Spofford, long suspected by Whitman and his friends to have been 'Sigma,' the anonymous author of an attack on the poet and his book in 1882. Calling Whitman's work 'a glorification of the animal man' in the *New York Tribune*, 'Sigma' attempted to qualify, if not deny, the assertion by Ralph Waldo Emerson in 1855 that *Leaves of Grass* was 'the most extraordinary piece of wit and wisdom that America had yet contributed' to world literature. Rather, 'Sigma' argued, Emerson ultimately had come to view the book as fatally flawed by what he called a 'disgusting priapism.'

Although today it is Whitman's probable homosexuality that is often emphasized, in the nineteenth century it was largely his frank allusions to heterosexuality—'libidinous joys only' in the 'Children of Adam' sequence—that tended to focus the reader's attention on part instead of the whole of *Leaves of Grass*. For Whitman, sex was an important part of the human experience celebrated in many of his poems. Yet it was also the part that got him into the most trouble with the critics of Victorian America who defended the 'standard of the evening lamp'—what used to be called the 'TV family viewing hour' in twentieth-century America. When Emerson first read *Leaves* in 1855, he chose to ignore the problem posed by the sexual references in such poems eventually entitled 'Song of Myself'and 'The Sleepers,' no doubt because sex was implicitly part of the nature he had praised in his own prose-poems, or essays, as 'part or parcel of God.' By 1860, however, when Whitman had travelled from New York to Boston to supervise the publication of the third, expanded, edition of his book, Emerson thought Whitman ought to censor himself a little in order to give the book a 'chance to be popularly seen, apprehended.' In response to this, Whitman asked as the two walked on Boston Common: 'You think that if I cut the book there would be a book left?' Whitman remembered the grave look on Emerson's face: 'This seemed to disturb him just a bit. Then he smiled at me and said, "I did not say as good a book—I said a good book." '[1]

Emerson had more than a literary interest in the fortunes of *Leaves of Grass*. Immediately after reading his complimentary copy in 1855, he had written Whitman a letter in which he greeted the poet 'at the beginning of a great career.' Without securing Emerson's permission, Whitman in turn published his letter in the *New York Tribune* of 10 October 1855. The poet also included a copy of the letter as an appendix to his 1856 edition and adorned the spine of the book in gold letters with a prominent phrase from the letter, including Emerson's name. When Whitman ignored Emerson's advice in 1860 and went ahead with the publication of the third (unexpurgated) edition of his book, neither Emerson nor Whitman could have been surprised by the critical reaction. For example, the *Boston Post*, noting Emerson's association with the book, wrote: 'The most

[1] Horace Traubel, *With Walt Whitman in Camden* (New York, 1914), III, p. 439.

charitable conclusion at which we can arrive is that both
Whitman's *Leaves* and Emerson's laudation had a common
origin in temporary insanity.' It was not, however, the
allusions to physiology and sex alone that disturbed
Whitman's critics but his bold departure in general from
the rules of conventional poetry. He broke open the
standard metered line, discarded the obligatory rhyme
scheme, and freely expressed himself in the living vernacular
of American speech:

> I celebrate myself, and sing myself,
> And what I assume you shall assume,
> For every atom belonging to me as good belongs to you.
>
> I loafe and invite my soul,
> I lean and loafe at my ease observing a spear of summer
>   grass.

In the original (1855) version of 'Song of Myself,' the first
line read simply, 'I celebrate myself' and the untitled poem
was called 'Walt Whitman' in most of the successive
editions of *Leaves of Grass* until 1881, when the poet finally
decided on the definitive arrangement and titles of his
poems. In celebrating himself, '*a Person*, a human being . . .
in the latter half of the Nineteenth Century,' he spoke
of all mankind as emblems of God. And the 'mankind'
he celebrated specifically included women. Apparently,
Whitman did not, like other writers before him, trust the
utility of such general terms but insisted that the woman be
named in his catalogs of what he called the 'divine average':

> I am the poet of the woman the same as the man,
> And I say it is as great to be a woman as to be a man.

A number of women of the poet's day responded with
enthusiasm, including, the Englishwoman Anne Gilchrist.
The widow of Blake's biographer (who finished her
husband's book and wrote several of her own as well)
described Whitman in 'A Woman's Estimate of Walt
Whitman' (1870) as 'the beloved friend of all [who]
initiated for them a "new and superb friendship"; [he]
whispered that secret of a god-like pride in a man's self, and

a perfect trust in woman, whereby their love for each other, no longer poisoned and stifled, but basking in the light of God's smile, and sending up to Him a perfume of gratitude, attains at last a divine and tender completeness.'

Part of Mrs Gilchrist's enthusiasm for *Leaves of Grass*, as the reader may suspect from the lushness of her prose, stemmed from the fact that she fell passionately in love with Whitman upon reading his book, immediately began what was at first a one-sided correspondence with the poet, and finally announced in 1876 her plan to come to America. Whitman hastily replied that he did not approve of her 'American trans-settlement.' Never personally (only poetically) comfortable with women outside their maternal roles, he had earlier tried to discourage her connubial affections by saying, 'You must not construct such an unauthorized and imaginary ideal Figure, and call it W. W. . . . The actual W. W. is a very plain personage, and entirely unworthy [of] such devotion.' Mrs Gilchrist ignored the distinction and relocated to Philadelphia, just across the river from Camden, New Jersey, where the poet was then living, only to discover the dramatic difference between the lusty poet of *Leaves of Grass* and the aging, semi-invalid author who had suffered his first paralytic stroke in 1873. They nevertheless became good friends during Gilchrist's stay in the United States, and by the time of her departure in 1879 she had no doubt understood the deeper meaning of Whitman's candor about himself. The personality dramatized in *Leaves of Grass* is best appreciated when we realize that Whitman wrote not exclusively about present actuality but about the Emersonian state of *becoming*. In the case of women, this meant their sexuality and ultimately their fecundity. What apparently attracted such female readers as Mrs Gilchrist was the poet's lifting of the veil of ladyhood to reveal their womanly vitality, their desire to become co-equal lovers (and partners) of man instead of objects of male sexual (and social) utility. 'Walt Whitman, the effeminate world needed thee,' wrote Sara Willis Parton, the American author of such popular books as *Fern Leaves from Fanny's Portfolio* (1853) and *Ruth Hall* (1855). 'I confess

I extract no poison from these "Leaves"—to me they have brought only healing.'

Whitman's egalitarian attitude towards women stemmed from his Jacksonian background in politics, yet he was never radical in his love for democracy, or what he called the 'good cause.' He would have never told the 'workers of the world' to unite but rather to preserve their identity as artisans in the New World of endless possibility. 'I have allow'd the stress of my poems from the beginning to end,' he declared in 'A Backward Glance O'er Travel'd Roads,' 'to bear upon American individuality and assist it—not only because that is a great lesson in Nature, amid all her generalizing laws, but as counterpoise to the leveling tendencies of Democracy.' Whitman far preferred its *leavening* tendencies that produced an average that was 'divine' in its sense of Personality:

> The pure contralto sings in the organ loft,
> The carpenter dresses his plank, the tongue of his
>   foreplane whistles its wild ascending lisp,
> The married and unmarried children ride home to their
>   Thanks-giving dinner,
> The pilot seizes the king-pin, he heaves down with a
>   strong arm,
> The mate stands braced in the whale-boat, lance and
>   harpoon are ready,
> The duck-shooter walks by silent and cautious stretches,
> The deacons are ordain'd with cross'd hands at the altar,
> The spinning-girl retreats and advances to the hum of
>   the big wheel,
> The farmer stops by the bars as he walks on a First-day
>   loafe and looks at the oats and rye . . .

And so the catalog goes for more than fifty additional lines to conclude: 'And of these one and all I weave the song of myself.' Americans were identified not only by what they did for a living but by the national consensus that they were bound together by their individuality as 'simple, separate' persons. To this contradiction, which still lies at the heart of American ideology, Whitman added the revised role of the poet as the most representative person—'Walt Whitman, a kosmos, of Manhattan the son.'

Whitman's poetic vision, of course, was not limited to Americans but extended to men, women, and children around the globe. This is seen more clearly in later poems, such as 'Passage to India' in which technological progress is the ostensible reason to celebrate the common cause of humanity on its 'Passage to more than India!' The poet's logocentrism, however, is tempered by the realistic detail of the nature he observes. Writing about his native city of New York as the 22-year-old editor of the *Aurora*, he was already aware of his country's representative reality: 'Here are people of all classes and stages of rank—from all countries on the globe—engaged in all the varieties of avocations—of every grade, every hue of ignorance and learning, morality and vice, wealth and want, fashion and coarseness, breeding and brutality, elevation and degradation, impudence and modesty.' Thirteen years later as the poet of *Leaves of Grass*, he envisaged himself as the macrocosm of the life he surveyed so tellingly:

> Of every hue and caste am I, of every rank and religion,
> A farmer, mechanic, artist, gentleman, sailor, quaker,
> Prisoner, fancy-man, rowdy, lawyer, physician, priest.

The message here is that the poet is totally American and America is totally representative of the divinity and humanity of men and women in countries around the world.

It was an audacious act to declare oneself so egotistically, to write—as Whitman did in 'Song of Myself'—that not only is he 'not curious about God' (because he beholds 'God in every object'), but he is not even curious about how there can be someone 'more wonderful than myself.' To try to understand Whitman's confidence, we must return to its source—to what Emerson called the 'long foreground' to *Leaves of Grass*. It might be said that Whitman had nothing *but* himself to celebrate in 1855. When Emerson wrote to him at the 'beginning' of his career as a poet, Whitman had already concluded—often unsuccessfully—careers as a carpenter, 'jour' (journeyman) printer, school teacher, journalist, and construction speculator. The second of eight children born to an alcoholic father and a whining but loving mother, he had finished his formal schooling at the sixth grade (12–13 years). The family was often in economic difficulty and moved several times between the city of Brooklyn and the country around Huntington, Long Island. Whitman joined the work force early, no doubt to assist the care and feeding of his large family. Not long out of adolescence, he gradually replaced his father as the family patriarch. Ersatz though he was in the years preceding his father's death in 1855, he was apparently far superior to his father in the capacity to care. In an allegorical sketch published when Whitman was 25 but whose internal evidence suggests it was first drafted when he was 16, the future poet wrote: 'Though a bachelor, I have several girls and boys that I consider my own.' Although he calls the first girl Louisa, she is probably based on his older sister Mary Elizabeth, who, like her mother, grew up to marry an alcoholic. The other 'daughter' is more easily identified as his younger sister because his sketch of her anticipates the instability of her adult life, mainly as a hypochrondriac. Describing Hannah Louisa as 'a very beautiful girl, in her fourteenth year,' Whitman notes that 'Flattery comes too often to her ears. From the depths of her soul I now and then see misty revealings of thought and wish, that are not well.' He continues the sketch by musing on the 'dreary thought' of 'what may happen, in the future years, to a handsome, merry child.' Unhappy as she was in her adult life, Hannah managed to outlive all her brothers and sisters—though Whitman was often distracted by reports about his sister's ill-fated marriage to an unsuccessful landscape painter.

Whitman's family of siblings was a microcosm of the society he would celebrate in his famous catalogs where, in democratic fashion, the president is named alongside the prostitute. The poet's eldest brother spent his last years in an asylum. The youngest brother spent his life mentally retarded and physically handicapped. A third brother died early of alcoholism and tuberculosis. Yet another Whitman 'son' became a successful civil engineer, a fifth brother became a Civil War hero, and of course the 'Elder Brother' himself became a famous poet. 'Elder Brother' is one of the poet's appellations for God. Another is 'camerado,' Whitman's own coinage. His relationship to God was of the same kind he bore to his own brothers and sisters. Not the Heavenly Father that Emily Dickinson addressed so ironically, God was 'In the faces of men and women . . . and in my own face in the glass.' Indeed, the poet addresses God as a big brother who is always approachable:

> Listener up there! what have you to confide to me?
> Look in my face while I snuff the sidle of evening,
> (Talk honestly, no one else hears you, and I stay only a
>   minute longer.)

Like God, the poet was 'both in and out of the game and watching and wondering at it'—the 'Father' who was also the brother.

Whitman was, as he declared himself, 'the poet of the Body' and 'the poet of the Soul.' He contradicted the Transcendentalist or American Romantic concept of nature as the 'Not-me'—that is, in the Neoplatonic sense of nature as merely the emblem of God. It might be said that Whitman's 'transcendentalism' was less discursive than Emerson's, more mystical, because the persona of 'Song of Myself' never sacrifices the body for the soul but always wakes up to the sense of both. His transcendental experience began *and ended* with the mating of Body and Soul, best exemplified in the often-noted Section Five of 'Song of Myself.' 'Loafe with me on the grass,' beckons the flesh to the spirit,

> . . . loose the stop from your throat,
> Not words, not music or rhyme I want, not custom or
>   lecture, not even the best,
> Only the lull I like, the hum of your valvèd voice.

> I mind how once we lay such a transparent summer
>   morning,
> How you settled your head athwart my hips and gently
>   turn'd over upon me,

    And parted the shirt from my bosom-bone, and plunged
            your tongue to my bare-stript heart,
    And reach'd till you felt my beard, and reach'd till you
            held my feet.

The conclusion to this dream of God in the flesh is that the
poet now knows 'that the hand of God is the promise of my
own' and 'the spirit of God is the brother of my own.'

In *Nature* (1836) Emerson had called the Understanding,
or empirical reasoning, 'the Hand of the mind' to distinguish
it from Reason, which he considered intuitive and tran-
scendent of material objects. In calling the 'hand of God'
the 'promise' of his own existence in the mind of God,
Whitman undermines his own contradiction to Transcend-
entalism with regard to the equality of Body and Soul.
Caught in the inconsistency, he might have said—as he
does at the close of 'Song of Myself'—that he is 'large' and
contains 'multitudes' of contrary beliefs which are them-
selves resolved in the Final Analysis. Yet Whitman does
contradict himself here, and it may be the first sign of his
gradual coming into line with the logocentrism that
characterizes much of American literature in the nineteenth
century. Whitman's most original poetry (and thought),
therefore, is to be found largely in the first three editions of
Leaves of Grass (1855, 1856, 1860). The poet no doubt
suspected as much when he established his definitive
arrangement, which attempts to distribute the strongest
poems somewhat evenly throughout the 422 pages of
poetry. The edition opens with 'Inscriptions,' which consists
of many post-1860 poems, then moves into the 'Paumanok'
poems of 1860, which in turn take us into the heart of his
book, 'Song of Myself.' This long poem, America's first in
terms of Yankee originality, is followed mainly by poems
first published in 1860 but written during Whitman's five-
year period of greatest creativity, 1855–60.

Leaves of Grass in its final rendering is structured to reflect
the poet's life. In old age he likened the book to a carefully
constructed cathedral, but of course it developed by the fits
and starts of a life that was naturally episodical. It is the

rearrangement of such episodes that gives the book its thematic balance. Beginning with 'One's-Self I Sing' and ending with 'Good-Bye My Fancy,' the final ordering paces the life through its many climaxes and convulsions—through the heights of 'Song of Myself' to the crisis poems of 'Out of the Cradle Endlessly Rocking' and 'As I Ebb'd with the Ocean of Life.' It is in these latter seashore poems that Whitman begins to question the poet's ability to use language to break through to God (though in later poems still he resumes the Emersonian confidence in poetry but without the earlier, Whitmanian, originality). They are strategically placed between poems reflecting two traumatic periods in Whitman's personal life, the loneliness of the years 1857–60 when he sought personal love, and the Civil War, when the poet witnessed the carnage of his 'divine average.' In 'Calamus' he tells of 'the secret of my nights and days' as a frequently unrequited lover. These poems speak of Adhesiveness, a phrenological term Whitman employed to describe male relationships (whereas the 'Children of Adam' sequence, which precedes them, celebrates Amativeness, or heterosexual relationships). The 'Calamus' poems are deeply personal and are the most frequently cited evidence of Whitman's homoerotic tendencies. It is in *Drum-Taps*, however, that we find poems that reflect more directly on the poet's interaction with men, generally younger men whom he would come to as he did his siblings—as father and brother. Indeed, few of the numberless wounded and sick soldiers Whitman visited daily in the Washington hospitals during and after the war were aware that the prematurely gray man (called 'The Good Gray Poet' in a pamphlet defending *Leaves of Grass* against censorship in the 1860s) was a poet. Poets in those days dressed like other gentlemen, in black suits; whereas Whitman's casual western attire suggested a retired sea captain or frontier scout. Yet 'wound dresser' (and government worker) by day, Whitman was a poet at night and produced his volume of war poems in 1866. In poems from 'Beat! Beat! Drums!' to 'Vigil Strange I Kept on the Field One Night' and 'A Sight in Camp in the Daybreak Gray and Dim,' he reflects on both the war's early excitement and its ultimate pathos.

It is often noted, however, that *Drum-Taps* (first published separately) lacks the spontaneity and personal involvement of the earlier poetry. Whitman had been involved in the war, but he had not witnessed any battles. Actually, he visited only two battlefields after the events, Fredericksburg and Chancellorsville; his experience came through the war's bloody consequences, which he mainly encountered in the wartime hospitals. As a result, the 'Drum-Taps' poems are perhaps the work of a (somewhat) distanced observer—of someone who comes to the experience after the fact and must somehow make a new sense of it. This detachment, however, tends to vanish in the 'Sequel' to the volume, a series written and hastily added to the book after the assassination of President Abraham Lincoln on 14 April 1865. In the poem which makes the 'Sequel' so memorable, 'When Lilacs Last in the Dooryard Bloom'd,' Whitman attained the rank of Milton and Shelley as master of the elegy. Unlike his British precursors in *Lycidas* and *Adonais*, Whitman did not personally know the subject of his poetic lament; yet he had long admired Lincoln (who had been a reader of *Leaves of Grass*) and immediately grasped the symbolic importance for America of his sudden passing. Indeed, in death Lincoln came alive to signify the terrific cost the American people had paid for the institution of slavery:

> I saw battle-corpses, myriads of them,
> And the white skeletons of young men, I saw them,
> I saw the debris and debris of all the slain soldiers of the
>   war.

As in any great elegy, the poet reconciles the personal death of Lincoln with the public life his subject now represents. Yet Whitman's *personal* regard for the slain president is what makes the poem almost as compelling as the earlier, more egocentric poems.

Whitman may have viewed Lincoln as the political equivalent of the American Poet he had both invented and sought to personify. In any event, he wrote three other poems on the slain president and, beginning in 1879, delivered a public lecture every year on the anniversary of the assassination. The most famous of these poems—and still Whitman's best-known poem—is 'O Captain! My Captain!' Written in conventional meter and rhyme, it is uncharacteristic of the poet's style. It was also the favorite of his family members (none of whom ever fully appreciated the originality of Whitman's 'language experiment'), and Whitman ultimately regretted having written it because it took attention away from his more original work. If the Lincoln lecture was also popular, it must have been for its content and not for its delivery. It has been said of the poet that he wrote 'barrels' of lectures in his early manhood and thought later in his career of becoming a professional lecturer. The reality, however, is that Whitman was a mediocre public speaker at best. A close friend recorded that whenever Whitman read or spoke in public, he gave an artificial delivery in a high-pitched voice not characteristic of his more natural, conversational style. This is surprising when we consider the strong oratorical element in the poetry. What distinguishes Whitman's verse from that of his precursors, even from Emerson, whose octosyllabic line reflected Oliver Wendell Holmes's theory that periodicity in poetry is determined by human respiration, is that its speech-act breaks free of the convention of formal writing, or literature, altogether. The colloquial nature allows for a freedom that transcends even Emerson's call in 'The Poet' for an American bard who 'is inflamed and carried away by his thought.' But Whitman put it best in an anonymous puff for the 1855 *Leaves*. He called himself 'An American bard at last! One of the roughs, large, proud, affectionate, eating, drinking, and breeding, his costume manly and free, his face sunburnt and bearded, his postures strong and erect, his *voice* bringing hope and prophecy to the generous races of young and old' (my italics).

Speech was the 'twin' of his vision, and thus the poetry is best appreciated when read aloud—out loud, if not out of doors. As a character out of the tradition of the American Tall Tale, the narrator is half-body, half-soul; but it is the body that animates the soul, not vice-versa. Before Whitman, American poetry had cherished too much the soul. From Anne Bradstreet's 'The Flesh and the Spirit' to Henry Wadsworth Longfellow's 'Nature', as well as Emerson's *Nature*, the body was the 'unregenerate' part, at best the child of Mother Nature and not God the Father. It was more than a Transcendentalist emblem to Whitman, whose poetry transcends the metaphysical, as it were, to come full circle in the fashion of the life cycle he celebrates. It is the *spoken* word that Whitman writes, 'Only the lull I like, the hum of your valvèd voice.' As noted earlier, this line is addressed to the soul, but the narrator insists that the spirit become as physical as the flesh. 'Lack one lacks both,' he announces. 'The unseen is proved by the seen, / Till that becomes unseen and receives proof in its turn.' Although many of his poems underwent several title changes, the name of his book never changed. The grass was not only the emblem, or 'handkerchief of the Lord,' but also evidence of the never-ending cycle of nature:

> What do you think has become of the young and old
> men?
> And what do you think has become of the women and
> children?
>
> They are alive and well somewhere,
> The smallest sprout shows there is really no death.

His book, then, literally *leaves* of grass, was a physical object in a sense that perhaps only a former printer could so appreciate. Whitman not only wrote the poems but set the type for part of the first edition. The manuscript, as he told a friend in old age, went to the 'ragman,' but the book went into the cycle of successive editions throughout his lifetime. Every time it went out of print, Whitman put out another, sometimes to cancel out the previous edition whose cycle was ready for renewal.

Whitman intended *Leaves of Grass* as a gift to the reader, something physical (and sensual) as well as thoughtful. Whereas the 1855 edition was a thin quarto, the 1856 edition was a smaller, 16mo volume, if also thicker, perhaps to allow the ideal reader to carry the volume around, to read it while pausing from work, or to take it to the seashore where Whitman claimed to have first read Emerson. Largely self-taught, the poet did not want the cultural veil of 'book learning' to come between himself and his reader. 'Take off your hat to nothing known or unknown or to any man or number of men,' he advised in his 1855 Preface. 'Go freely with powerful uneducated persons and with the young and with the mothers of families, read these leaves in the open air every season of every year of your life.' Whitman himself did not much enjoy the company of literary people (and in some circles the feeling was mutual because of the seemingly brash, untutored language and style of *Leaves of Grass*). His friends were not exclusively the 'roughs' he wrote about but included educated people who loved literature more than literary matters. Yet the intimate associations were with the 'powerful uneducated persons'— omnibus drivers, Civil War veterans (from both sides), and printers' 'devils.' Mainly, these individuals were men younger than himself and unmarried, but the relationships often extended to their relatives, whose familial associations simulated his own large family background. This affinity to the family that Whitman, a lifelong bachelor, never had for himself may account for the fact that he addressed his readers as siblings:

> Do you see O my brothers and sisters?
> It is not chaos or death—it is form, union, plan—it is
>   eternal life—it is Happiness.

Although the detail in *Leaves of Grass* is realistic, its message is highly idealistic, expressing the Cartesian duality that fades in the twentieth century with American modernism and certainly postmodernism. Today critics prefer to emphasize his demographic pluralism, which included African-Americans (a topic virtually ignored by every other major American writer of the period, with the exception of Herman Melville and Mark Twain). While some of Whitman's lines have been 'deconstructed' into statements relating to race, class, and gender, the whole of his work remains stubbornly apolitical. Yet it is 'political' in the sense that he reached out to a new breed of reader—the average American, for whom 'Literature' was previously a cultural menace and a threat. Whitman made it lower-case and 'lower-class'.

> Have you practis'd so long to learn to read?
> Have you felt so proud to get at the meaning of poems?
>
> Stop this day and night with me and you shall possess
>   the origin of all poems,
> You shall possess the good of the earth and sun, (there
>   are millions of suns left,)
> You shall no longer take things at second or third hand,
>   nor look through the eyes of the dead, nor feed on
>   the spectres in books,
> You shall not look through my eyes either, nor take
>   things from me.
> You shall listen to all sides and filter them from your self.

The idea about books is Emersonian—that books are for 'the scholar's' idle times. 'When he can read God directly,' Emerson said in his American Scholar Address, 'the hour is too precious to be wasted in other men's transcripts of their readings.' Both writers are advocating self-reliance, but the important difference is that by 'scholar' Emerson probably meant the American intelligentsia, whereas by 'reader' Whitman surely meant everybody. 'The proof of a poet,' he wrote in his Preface, 'is that his country absorbs him as affectionately as he has absorbed it.' It is important to note that this final sentence of the introduction to his work does not employ the subjunctive. *Leaves of Grass* was anything but theoretical in its desire to embrace America.

Whitman thought that Americans probably had 'the fullest poetical nature'—that America itself was a poem, 'essentially the greatest poem.' For all that, his fellow citizens were slow to accept *Leaves of Grass* as American literature. Mainly, they were persuaded by hostile critics—as even Emily Dickinson was—that Whitman's book was 'disgraceful'. Whitman came to view the book as his alter ego that would be better understood in the twentieth century:

> My book and I—what a period we have presumed to span! those thirty years from 1850 to '80—and America in them! Proud, proud indeed may we be, if we have cull'd enough of that period in its own spirit to worthily waft a few live breaths of it to the future!

Had it not been for a band of disciples who kept his name alive, Whitman may well have been forgotten in the early part of this century (as Melville was). When American literature became an academic subject in schools and universities in the 1920s, Whitman's reputation was still obscured by the New Critic preference for the well-made, rigorously impersonal poem. As late as the 1940s Gay Wilson Allen, who would produce in the next decade the first definitive biography of the poet, had difficulty finding a publisher for his comprehensively researched *Walt Whitman Handbook* (1946). Hence, it took almost a century for *Leaves of Grass* to fulfill its critical potential, if not its popular one. Today, Whitman is viewed as America's Homer or its Dante, his work as the touchstone for literary originality in the New World and worlds he celebrated. Yet to the end Whitman insisted that no one could fully appreciate his verses as a 'literary performance.' Rather, they were an 'outcropping' of his own 'emotional and other personal nature.' *Leaves of Grass* in this sense is autobiography but one whose interior landscape reflects the psyche of a nation that had in the nineteenth century finally added a body of great poetry to its other, more practical achievements.

NOTE ON THE TEXT

THE text for *Leaves of Grass* reprinted here is the so-called Death-bed edition published by David McKay, Publisher, dated 1891–2 on the title-page. The actual 'death-bed' edition was a book hastily gathered together from the unbound sheets of an 1889 reprint of *Leaves of Grass*, when Whitman's literary executors thought that the poet was about to die in December 1891. Strictly speaking, the main body of the 1891–2 edition is an 'issue' reprinted from the 1881 definitive edition (Whitman's final arrangement of poems appearing in all subsequent editions of *Leaves of Grass*). To this were added the appendices 'Sands at Seventy' and 'Good-Bye My Fancy' as well as the retrospective essay 'A Backward Glance O'er Travel'd Roads.' The present Oxford World's Classics edition has added the Preface to the 1855 (1st) Edition of *Leaves of Grass* and Ralph Waldo Emerson's letter of greeting to the poet upon reading the 1855 edition.

I would like to thank Roger Asselineau, Ed Folsom, Justin Kaplan, and Edwin Haviland Miller for their advice in preparing this volume. As the saying goes, all the mistakes are my own.

SELECT BIBLIOGRAPHY

Gay Wilson Allen, *The New Walt Whitman Handbook* (New York University Press, 1975).

——, *The Solitary Singer: A Critical Biography of Walt Whitman* (New York University Press, 1955).

Harold Aspiz, *Walt Whitman and the Body Beautiful* (University of Illinois Press, 1980).

Roger Asselineau, *The Evolution of Walt Whitman* (Harvard University Press, 2 vols., 1960, 1962).

Critical Essays on Walt Whitman, ed. James Woodress (G. K. Hall, 1983).

Betsy Erkkila, *Whitman the Political Poet* (Oxford University Press, 1988).

C. Carroll Hollis, *Language and Style in Leaves of Grass* (Louisiana State University Press, 1983).

George B. Hutchinson, *The Ecstatic Whitman: Literary Shamanism and the Crisis of the Union* (Ohio State University Press, 1986).

Justin Kaplan, *Walt Whitman: A Life* (Simon and Shuster, 1980).

M. Jimmie Killingsworth, *Whitman's Poetry of the Body: Sexuality, Politics, and the Text* (University of North Carolina Press, 1989).

Jerome Loving, *Emerson, Whitman, and the American Muse* (University of North Carolina Press, 1982).

Ivan Marki, *The Trial of the Poet: An Interpretation of the First Edition of Leaves of Grass* (Columbia University Press, 1976).

James E. Miller, Jr., *The American Quest for a Supreme Fiction: Whitman's Legacy in the Personal Epic* (University of Chicago Press, 1979).

——, *A Critical Guide to Leaves of Grass* (University of Chicago Press, 1957).

Edwin Haviland Miller, *Walt Whitman's Poetry: A Psychological Journey* (Houghton Mifflin, 1968).

——, *Walt Whitman's 'Song of Myself': A Mosaic of Interpretations* (University of Iowa Press, 1989).

Floyd Stovall, *The Foreground of Leaves of Grass* (University Press of Virginia, 1974).

M. Wynn Thomas, *The Lunar Light of Whitman's Poetry* (Harvard University Press, 1987).

Walt Whitman: The Early Poems and the Fiction, ed. Thomas L. Brasher (New York University Press, 1963).

Walt Whitman: The Correspondence, ed. Edwin Haviland Miller (New York University Press, 6 vols., 1961–77).

Walt Whitman. The Measure of His Song, ed. Ed Folsom and Dan Campion (Holy Cow! Press, 1981).

A CHRONOLOGY OF
WALT WHITMAN

1819   Born 31 May at West Hills near the township of Huntington, Long Island, to Walter Whitman and Louisa Van Velsor.

1823   Whitman family moves to Brooklyn.

1830   Completes formal education. Works as an office boy, first for a lawyer, then for a doctor.

1831–4   Works as an apprentice in various printing firms and on the *Long Island Patriot*, then as a compositor for the *Long Island Star*. Whitman family moves back to the country during this period.

1835   Works in various printing offices in New York City until the great fire of 12 August.

1836–8   Teaches in several schools on Long Island and participates in debating societies.

1838–9   Founds and edits the *Long-Islander* in Huntington.

1839–41   Returns to teaching and campaigns for Van Buren.

1841   Moves back to New York City to work as a printer for the *New World*. Begins to write short fiction and poetry for the *Democratic Review* and other publications.

1842   Becomes editor of the *Aurora*; writes about hearing Emerson deliver a lecture on 'Nature and the Powers of the Poet.' Edits the *Evening Tattler*. Serializes *Franklin Evans*, a temperance novel, in the *New World*.

1843   Edits *The Statesman*.

1844   Edits the *New York Democrat* and works for the *New York Mirror*.

1845–6   Returns to Brooklyn; works for the *Long Island Star*.

1846–8   Edits the *Brooklyn Daily Eagle*. Writes about Emerson's 'Spiritual Laws.'

1848   Fired from the editorship of the *Brooklyn Daily Eagle*. Moves to New Orleans and edits the *Crescent*.

1848–9   Returns to Brooklyn and edits the *Freeman*, a 'free soil' newspaper.

1850–4   Operates printing office; builds and speculates in house construction in Brooklyn. Begins writing the political essay, 'The Eighteenth Presidency!'

1855   Publishes first edition of *Leaves of Grass* possibly on the Fourth of July; sends complimentary copies to the literary lights of the day, including Emerson, who sends the author his famous 'letter of thanks' for 'the wonderful gift of *Leaves of Grass*.' Father dies on 11 July.

1856   Prints second edition of *Leaves of Grass*, which includes Emerson's letter, an 'open letter' to Emerson, and (on the spine of the volume) the words, 'I greet you at the beginning of a great career   R. W. Emerson.' Completes 'The Eighteenth Presidency!' and places into proof. Writes for *Life Illustrated*, the magazine of the phrenological concern which 'published' the second edition of *Leaves of Grass*. Receives visit from Emerson.

1857–9   Edits the *Brooklyn Times*. Receives visit from Henry David Thoreau and Amos Bronson Alcott. Writes the 'Calamus' sequence and other poems.

1860   Publishes the third edition of *Leaves of Grass* with the Boston firm of Thayer and Eldridge, whose house list otherwise consists of abolitionist literature. Meeting with Emerson, who urges Whitman to omit the 'Children of Adam' poems from the 1860 edition.

1861   12 April, Civil War commences; publishes his recruiting poem, 'Beat! Beat! Drums!'; brother George enlists in the Union Army.

1862   George Whitman slightly wounded at the Battle of Fredericksburg (13 December); travels to the battle site and remains in camp for two weeks.

1863   Establishes residence in Washington, DC, where he secures a part-time job as a clerk in the Army Paymaster's Office and devotes himself to hospital work. Forms close associations with William Douglas O'Connor and the naturalist John Burroughs.

1864   Returns to Brooklyn for six months because of ill health.

1865   Appointed clerk in the Department of the Interior; subsequently dismissed in an efficiency move by the

Secretary but also for being the author of an indecent book. Issues *Drum-Taps* in the summer, *Sequel to Drum-Taps* in the autumn following the assassination of President Lincoln. The latter includes 'When Lilacs Last in the Dooryard Bloom'd.' Hired as a clerk in the Attorney General's office. Meets Peter Doyle, ex-Confederate soldier and streetcar conductor, who becomes the poet's intimate friend.

1866 O'Connor publishes *The Good Gray Poet*, which extols Whitman and attacks Secretary of the Interior James Harlan.

1867 John Burroughs publishes *Notes on Walt Whitman as Poet and Person*, partially written or revised by Whitman. Fourth edition of *Leaves of Grass*.

1868 A 'selected' edition of *Leaves of Grass* published in England, edited by William Michael Rossetti. O'Connor's short story, 'The Carpenter,' published in *Putnam's Monthly Magazine*, beginning the increasingly common association of Whitman with Christ.

1869–70 Anne Gilchrist reads *Leaves of Grass* and publishes the highly favorable 'An Englishwoman's Estimate of Walt Whitman' in the Boston *Radical*. Prints fifth edition of *Leaves of Grass*, plus *Democratic Vistas* and *Passage to India*

1871 Reads 'After All, Not to Create Only' (later called 'Song of the Exposition') at the opening of the American Institute of New York.

1872 Delivers 'As a Strong Bird on Pinions Free' ('Thou Mother with Thy Equal Brood') at Dartmouth College commencement.

1873 23 January, suffers first paralytic stroke. Mother dies 23 May. Moves to Camden, New Jersey, and lives with the George Whitman family.

1876 British-American newspaper debate over Whitman's neglect by US critics, precipitated in part by the poet's anonymous *West Jersey Press* article. Mrs Gilchrist comes to America.

1877 Gives lecture on Thomas Paine in Philadelphia.

1879 Delivers the first of the Lincoln lectures. Mrs Gilchrist returns to England. Tours the American West.

1880   Edmund Clarence Stedman's article on 'Walt Whitman'
        published in *Scribner's*, the first non-partisan and
        generally favorable appraisal of the poet's work.

1881   Sixth and final edition of *Leaves of Grass* published in
        Boston; visits the ailing Emerson in Concord,
        Massachusetts.

1882   Meets Oscar Wilde in Camden. Boston District Attorney
        Oliver Stevens (at the urging of Anthony Comstock's
        Society for the Suppression of Vice) threatens
        Whitman's Boston publisher, James R. Osgood, with
        prosecution. Osgood, after unsuccessfully persuading
        Whitman to accept any of the District Attorney's
        required expurgations, ceases publication. Sixth edition
        is reissued by Philadelphia publisher Rees Welsh
        (succeeded by David McKay). Probably as a result of
        the Boston controversy, Whitman realizes a substantial
        profit from the sale of his book—for the first and only
        time in his life.

1883   Richard Maurice Bucke publishes his biography of
        Whitman, closely supervised by the poet.

1884   Profits from the 1882 sale of *Leaves of Grass* allow the poet
        to purchase his own house on Mickle Street in Camden.

1885   Suffers sun stroke.

1888   Second paralytic stroke. Horace Traubel raises money
        for medical care and begins his conversations with
        Whitman, which will be the basis for the multi-volume
        With Walt Whitman in Camden, some of which remains un-
        published. *November Boughs* printed.

1890   Denies in a letter to John Addington Symonds the homo-
        sexual interpretation of the 'Calamus' poems; claims to
        have sired six illegitimate children.

1891   Publishes the 'Death-bed Edition' of *Leaves of Grass*
        (dated 1891–2).

1892   Dies 26 March; buried in Harleigh Cemetery in
        Camden.

Leaves of Grass

Including

SANDS AT SEVENTY ... *1st Annex*,

GOOD-BYE MY FANCY ... *2d Annex*,

A BACKWARD GLANCE O'ER TRAVEL'D ROADS,

and Portrait from Life.

COME, said my Soul,
Such verses for my Body let us write, (for we are one,)
That should I after death invisibly return,
Or, long, long hence, in other spheres,
There to some group of mates the chants resuming,
(Tallying Earth's soil, trees, winds, tumultuous waves,)
Ever with pleas'd smile I may keep on,
Ever and ever yet the verses owning—as, first, I here and now,
Signing for Soul and Body, set to them my name,

Walt Whitman

PHILADELPHIA

DAVID McKAY, PUBLISHER

23 SOUTH NINTH STREET

1891-'2

COPYRIGHTS, &c.

1st ed'n 1855, Brooklyn (N. Y., South District)—renew'd (1883) 14 yrs.
2d ed'n 1856, Brooklyn—renew'd (1884) 14 yrs.
3d ed'n 1860, Boston, Thayer & Eldridge Pub'rs.
4th ed'n 1867, N. Y., So. Dist.: Pub'd New York.
5th ed'n 1871, Washington, D. C.
6th ed'n 1876—Centennial issue—inc'd'g TWO RIVULETS: two vols.
7th ed'n 1881, Boston, Mass.: Osgood Pub.: [This includes in the present
    vol. pages 1 to 382.]
8th ed'n 1882, Philadelphia: McKay Pub'r.
Sands at Seventy: Annex, 1888—November Boughs—Philadelphia.
A Backward Glance, &c.: November Boughs, 1888—Philadelphia.
Good-Bye my Fancy: 2d Annex, 1891—Philadelphia.

[Which last-named copyright (holding good to 1919—then, on application, continued 14 years further) expires May 19, 1933.]

☞ As there are now several editions of L. of G., different texts and dates, I wish to say that I prefer and recommend this present one, complete, for future printing, if there should be any; a copy and fac-simile, indeed, of the text of these 438 pages. The subsequent adjusting interval which is so important to form'd and launch'd work, books especially, has pass'd; and waiting till fully after that, I have given (pages 423–438) my concluding words.   W. W.

CONTENTS.

3

CONTENTS.

CONTENTS.

INSCRIPTIONS.

ONE'S–SELF I SING.

ONE'S-SELF I sing, a simple separate person,
Yet utter the word Democratic, the word En-Masse.

Of physiology from top to toe I sing,
Not physiognomy alone nor brain alone is worthy for the Muse, I
    say the Form complete is worthier far,
The Female equally with the Male I sing.

Of Life immense in passion, pulse, and power,
Cheerful, for freest action form'd under the laws divine,
The Modern Man I sing.

AS I PONDER'D IN SILENCE.

As I ponder'd in silence,
Returning upon my poems, considering, lingering long,
A Phantom arose before me with distrustful aspect,
Terrible in beauty, age, and power,
The genius of poets of old lands,
As to me directing like flame its eyes,
With finger pointing to many immortal songs,
And menacing voice, *What singest thou?* it said,
Know'st thou not there is but one theme for ever-enduring bards?
And that is the theme of War, the fortune of battles,
The making of perfect soldiers.

Be it so, then I answer'd,
I too haughty Shade also sing war, and a longer and greater one
    than any,
Waged in my book with varying fortune, with flight, advance and
    retreat, victory deferr'd and wavering,

(*Yet methinks certain, or as good as certain, at the last,*) *the field
       the world,*
For life and death, for the Body and for the eternal Soul,
Lo, I too am come, chanting the chant of battles,
I above all promote brave soldiers.

IN CABIN'D SHIPS AT SEA.

In cabin'd ships at sea,
The boundless blue on every side expanding,
With whistling winds and music of the waves, the large imperious
       waves,
Or some lone bark buoy'd on the dense marine,
Where joyous full of faith, spreading white sails,
She cleaves the ether mid the sparkle and the foam of day, or
       under many a star at night,
By sailors young and old haply will I, a reminiscence of the land,
       be read,
In full rapport at last.

Here are our thoughts, voyagers' thoughts,
Here not the land, firm land, alone appears, may then by them be
       said,
*The sky o'erarches here, we feel the undulating deck beneath our
       feet,*
We feel the long pulsation, ebb and flow of endless motion,
*The tones of unseen mystery, the vague and vast suggestions of the
       briny world, the liquid-flowing syllables,*
*The perfume, the faint creaking of the cordage, the melancholy
       rhythm,*
The boundless vista and the horizon far and dim are all here,
And this is ocean's poem.

Then falter not O book, fulfil your destiny,
You not a reminiscence of the land alone,
You too as a lone bark cleaving the ether, purpos'd I know not
       whither, yet ever full of faith,
Consort to every ship that sails, sail you !
Bear forth to them folded my love, (dear mariners, for you I fold
       it here in every leaf ;)
Speed on my book ! spread your white sails my little bark athwart
       the imperious waves,
Chant on, sail on, bear o'er the boundless blue from me to every
       sea,
This song for mariners and all their ships.

TO FOREIGN LANDS.

I HEARD that you ask'd for something to prove this puzzle the New
World,
And to define America, her athletic Democracy,
Therefore I send you my poems that you behold in them what you
wanted.

TO A HISTORIAN.

You who celebrate bygones,
Who have explored the outward, the surfaces of the races, the life
that has exhibited itself,
Who have treated of man as the creature of politics, aggregates,
rulers and priests,
I, habitan of the Alleghanies, treating of him as he is in himself
in his own rights,
Pressing the pulse of the life that has seldom exhibited itself, (the
great pride of man in himself,)
Chanter of Personality, outlining what is yet to be,
I project the history of the future.

TO THEE OLD CAUSE.

To thee old cause !*
Thou peerless, passionate, good cause,
Thou stern, remorseless, sweet idea,
Deathless throughout the ages, races, lands,
After a strange sad war, great war for thee,
(I think all war through time was really fought, and ever will be
really fought, for thee,)
These chants for thee, the eternal march of thee.

(A war O soldiers not for itself alone,
Far, far more stood silently waiting behind, now to advance in
this book.)

Thou orb of many orbs !
Thou seething principle ! thou well-kept, latent germ ! thou centre !
Around the idea of thee the war revolving,
With all its angry and vehement play of causes,
(With vast results to come for thrice a thousand years,)
These recitatives for thee, — my book and the war are one,
Merged in its spirit I and mine, as the contest hinged on thee,
As a wheel on its axis turns, this book unwitting to itself,
Around the idea of thee.

EIDÓLONS.

I MET a seer,
Passing the hues and objects of the world,
The fields of art and learning, pleasure, sense,
    To glean eidólons.*

Put in thy chants said he,
No more the puzzling hour nor day, nor segments, parts, put in,
Put first before the rest as light for all and entrance-song of all,
    That of eidólons.

Ever the dim beginning,
Ever the growth, the rounding of the circle,
Ever the summit and the merge at last, (to surely start again,)
    Eidólons! eidólons!

Ever the mutable,
Ever materials, changing, crumbling, re-cohering,
Ever the ateliers, the factories divine,
    Issuing eidólons.

Lo, I or you,
Or woman, man, or state, known or unknown,
We seeming solid wealth, strength, beauty build,
    But really build eidólons.

The ostent evanescent,
The substance of an artist's mood or savan's studies long,
Or warrior's, martyr's, hero's toils,
    To fashion his eidólon.

Of every human life,
(The units gather'd, posted, not a thought, emotion, deed, left out,)
The whole or large or small summ'd, added up,
    In its eidólon.

The old, old urge,
Based on the ancient pinnacles, lo, newer, higher pinnacles,
From science and the modern still impell'd,
    The old, old urge, eidólons.

The present now and here,
America's busy, teeming, intricate whirl,
Of aggregate and segregate for only thence releasing,
    To-day's eidólons.

These with the past,
Of vanish'd lands, of all the reigns of kings across the sea,
Old conquerors, old campaigns, old sailors' voyages,
      Joining eidólons.

Densities, growth, façades,
Strata of mountains, soils, rocks, giant trees,
Far-born, far-dying, living long, to leave,
      Eidólons everlasting.

Exaltè, rapt, ecstatic,
The visible but their womb of birth,
Of orbic tendencies to shape and shape and shape,
      The mighty earth-eidólon.

All space, all time,
(The stars, the terrible perturbations of the suns,
Swelling, collapsing, ending, serving their longer, shorter use,)
      Fill'd with eidólons only.

The noiseless myriads,
The infinite oceans where the rivers empty,
The separate countless free identities, like eyesight,
      The true realities, eidólons.

Not this the world,
Nor these the universes, they the universes,
Purport and end, ever the permanent life of life,
      Eidólons, eidólons.

Beyond thy lectures learn'd professor,
Beyond thy telescope or spectroscope observer keen, beyond all
      mathematics,
Beyond the doctor's surgery, anatomy, beyond the chemist with
      his chemistry,
      The entities of entities, eidólons.

Unfix'd yet fix'd,
Ever shall be, ever have been and are,
Sweeping the present to the infinite future,
      Eidólons, eidólons, eidólons.

The prophet and the bard,
Shall yet maintain themselves, in higher stages yet,
Shall mediate to the Modern, to Democracy, interpret yet to them,
      God and eidólons.

And thee my soul,
Joys, ceaseless exercises, exaltations,
Thy yearning amply fed at last, prepared to meet,
　　　Thy mates, eidólons.

Thy body permanent,
The body lurking there within thy body,
The only purport of the form thou art, the real I myself,
　　　An image, an eidólon.

Thy very songs not in thy songs,
No special strains to sing, none for itself,
But from the whole resulting, rising at last and floating,
　　　A round full-orb'd eidólon.

FOR HIM I SING.

FOR him I sing,*
I raise the present on the past,
(As some perennial tree out of its roots, the present on the past,)
With time and space I him dilate and fuse the immortal laws,
To make himself by them the law unto himself.

WHEN I READ THE BOOK.

WHEN I read the book, the biography famous,
And is this then (said I) what the author calls a man's life?
And so will some one when I am dead and gone write my life?
(As if any man really knew aught of my life,
Why even I myself I often think know little or nothing of my real
　　　life,
Only a few hints, a few diffused faint clews and indirections
I seek for my own use to trace out here.)

BEGINNING MY STUDIES.

BEGINNING my studies the first step pleas'd me so much,
The mere fact consciousness, these forms, the power of motion,
The least insect or animal, the senses, eyesight, love,
The first step I say awed me and pleas'd me so much,
I have hardly gone and hardly wish'd to go any farther,
But stop and loiter all the time to sing it in ecstatic songs.

BEGINNERS.*

How they are provided for upon the earth, (appearing at intervals,)
How dear and dreadful they are to the earth,
How they inure to themselves as much as to any — what a paradox appears their age,
How people respond to them, yet know them not,
How there is something relentless in their fate all times,
How all times mischoose the objects of their adulation and reward,
And how the same inexorable price must still be paid for the same great purchase.

TO THE STATES.

To the States or any one of them, or any city of the States, *Resist much, obey little,*
Once unquestioning obedience, once fully enslaved,
Once fully enslaved, no nation, state, city of this earth, ever afterward resumes its liberty.

ON JOURNEYS THROUGH THE STATES.

ON journeys through the States we start,
(Ay through the world, urged by these songs,
Sailing henceforth to every land, to every sea,)
We willing learners of all, teachers of all, and lovers of all.

We have watch'd the seasons dispensing themselves and passing on,
And have said, Why should not a man or woman do as much as the seasons, and effuse as much?

We dwell a while in every city and town,
We pass through Kanada, the North-east, the vast valley of the Mississippi, and the Southern States,
We confer on equal terms with each of the States,
We make trial of ourselves and invite men and women to hear,
We say to ourselves, Remember, fear not, be candid, promulge the body and the soul,
Dwell a while and pass on, be copious, temperate, chaste, magnetic,
And what you effuse may then return as the seasons return,
And may be just as much as the seasons.

TO A CERTAIN CANTATRICE.

HERE, take this gift,
I was reserving it for some hero, speaker, or general,
One who should serve the good old cause, the great idea, the prog-
 ress and freedom of the race,
Some brave confronter of despots, some daring rebel ;
But I see that what I was reserving belongs to you just as much as
 to any.

ME IMPERTURBE.

ME imperturbe, standing at ease in Nature,
Master of all or mistress of all, aplomb in the midst of irrational
 things,
Imbued as they, passive, receptive, silent as they,
Finding my occupation, poverty, notoriety, foibles, crimes, less im-
 portant than I thought,
Me toward the Mexican sea, or in the Mannahatta or the Tennes-
 see, or far north or inland,
A river man, or a man of the woods or of any farm-life of these
 States or of the coast, or the lakes or Kanada,*
Me wherever my life is lived, O to be self-balanced for contingen-
 cies,
To confront night, storms, hunger, ridicule, accidents, rebuffs, as
 the trees and animals do.

SAVANTISM.

THITHER as I look I see each result and glory retracing itself and
 nestling close, always obligated,
Thither hours, months, years — thither trades, compacts, establish-
 ments, even the most minute,
Thither every-day life, speech, utensils, politics, persons, estates ;
Thither we also, I with my leaves and songs, trustful, admirant,
As a father to his father going takes his children along with him.

THE SHIP STARTING.

LO, the unbounded sea,
On its breast a ship starting, spreading all sails, carrying even her
 moonsails,
The pennant is flying aloft as she speeds she speeds so stately
 below emulous waves press forward,
They surround the ship with shining curving motions and foam.

I HEAR AMERICA SINGING.

I HEAR America singing, the varied carols I hear,
Those of mechanics, each one singing his as it should be blithe
     and strong,
The carpenter singing his as he measures his plank or beam,
The mason singing his as he makes ready for work, or leaves off
     work,
The boatman singing what belongs to him in his boat, the deck-
     hand singing on the steamboat deck,
The shoemaker singing as he sits on his bench, the hatter singing
     as he stands,
The wood-cutter's song, the ploughboy's on his way in the morn-
     ing, or at noon intermission or at sundown,
The delicious singing of the mother, or of the young wife at work,
     or of the girl sewing or washing,
Each singing what belongs to him or her and to none else,
The day what belongs to the day — at night the party of young
     fellows, robust, friendly,
Singing with open mouths their strong melodious songs.

WHAT PLACE IS BESIEGED?

WHAT place is besieged, and vainly tries to raise the siege?
Lo, I send to that place a commander, swift, brave, immortal,
And with him horse and foot, and parks of artillery,
And artillery-men, the deadliest that ever fired gun.

STILL THOUGH THE ONE I SING.

STILL though the one I sing,*
(One, yet of contradictions made,) I dedicate to Nationality,
I leave in him revolt, (O latent right of insurrection ! O quench-
     less, indispensable fire !)

SHUT NOT YOUR DOORS.

SHUT not your doors to me proud libraries,
For that which was lacking on all your well-fill'd shelves, yet
     needed most, I bring,
Forth from the war emerging, a book I have made,
The words of my book nothing, the drift of it every thing,
A book separate, not link'd with the rest nor felt by the intellect,
But you ye untold latencies will thrill to every page.

POETS TO COME.

Poets to come ! orators, singers, musicians to come !
Not to-day is to justify me and answer what I am for,
But you, a new brood, native, athletic, continental, greater than
   before known,
Arouse ! for you must justify me.

I myself but write one or two indicative words for the future,
I but advance a moment only to wheel and hurry back in the
   darkness.

I am a man who, sauntering along without fully stopping, turns a
   casual look upon you and then averts his face,
Leaving it to you to prove and define it,
Expecting the main things from you.

TO YOU.

Stranger, if you passing meet me and desire to speak to me, why
   should you not speak to me?
And why should I not speak to you?

THOU READER.

Thou reader throbbest life and pride and love the same as I,
Therefore for thee the following chants.

STARTING FROM PAUMANOK.

1

Starting from fish-shape Paumanok*where I was born,
Well-begotten, and rais'd by a perfect mother,
After roaming many lands, lover of populous pavements,
Dweller in Mannahatta my city, or on southern savannas,
Or a soldier camp'd or carrying my knapsack and gun, or a miner
   in California,
Or rude in my home in Dakota's woods, my diet meat, my drink
   from the spring,
Or withdrawn to muse and meditate in some deep recess,
Far from the clank of crowds intervals passing rapt and happy,

Aware of the fresh free giver the flowing Missouri, aware of mighty
 Niagara,
Aware of the buffalo herds grazing the plains, the hirsute and
 strong-breasted bull,
Of earth, rocks, Fifth-month* flowers experienced, stars, rain, snow,
 my amaze,
Having studied the mocking-bird's tones and the flight of the
 mountain-hawk,
And heard at dawn the unrivall'd one, the hermit thrush from the
 swamp-cedars,
Solitary, singing in the West, I strike up for a New World.

2

Victory, union, faith, identity, time,
The indissoluble compacts, riches, mystery,
Eternal progress, the kosmos, and the modern reports.

This then is life,
Here is what has come to the surface after so many throes and
 convulsions.

How curious! how real!
Underfoot the divine soil, overhead the sun.

See revolving the globe,
The ancestor-continents away group'd together,
The present and future continents north and south, with the
 isthmus between.

See, vast trackless spaces,
As in a dream they change, they swiftly fill,
Countless masses debouch upon them,
They are now cover'd with the foremost people, arts, institutions,
 known.

See, projected through time,
For me an audience interminable.

With firm and regular step they wend, they never stop,
Successions of men, Americanos, a hundred millions,
One generation playing its part and passing on,
Another generation playing its part and passing on in its turn,
With faces turn'd sideways or backward towards me to listen,
With eyes retrospective towards me.

3

Americanos! conquerors! marches humanitarian!
Foremost! century marches! Libertad! masses!
For you a programme of chants.

Chants of the prairies,
Chants of the long-running Mississippi, and down to the Mexican
        sea,
Chants of Ohio, Indiana, Illinois, Iowa, Wisconsin and Minnesota,
Chants going forth from the centre from Kansas, and thence equi-
        distant,
Shooting in pulses of fire ceaseless to vivify all.

4

Take my leaves America, take them South and take them North,
Make welcome for them everywhere, for they are your own off-
        spring,
Surround them East and West, for they would surround you,
And you precedents, connect lovingly with them, for they connect
        lovingly with you.

I conn'd old times,
I sat studying at the feet of the great masters,
Now if eligible O that the great masters might return and study me.

In the name of these States shall I scorn the antique?
Why these are the children of the antique to justify it.

5

Dead poets, philosophs, priests,
Martyrs, artists, inventors, governments long since,
Language-shapers on other shores,
Nations once powerful, now reduced, withdrawn, or desolate,
I dare not proceed till I respectfully credit what you have left
        wafted hither,
I have perused it, own it is admirable, (moving awhile among it,)
Think nothing can ever be greater, nothing can ever deserve more
        than it deserves,
Regarding it all intently a long while, then dismissing it,
I stand in my place with my own day here.

Here lands female and male,
Here the heir-ship and heiress-ship of the world, here the flame of
        materials,

Here spirituality the translatress, the openly-avow'd,
The ever-tending, the finalè of visible forms,
The satisfier, after due long-waiting now advancing,
Yes here comes my mistress the soul.

6

The soul,
Forever and forever — longer than soil is brown and solid — longer
    than water ebbs and flows.

I will make the poems of materials, for I think they are to be the
    most spiritual poems,
And I will make the poems of my body and of mortality,
For I think I shall then supply myself with the poems of my soul
    and of immortality.

I will make a song for these States that no one State may under
    any circumstances be subjected to another State,
And I will make a song that there shall be comity by day and by
    night between all the States, and between any two of them,
And I will make a song for the ears of the President, full of weap-
    ons with menacing points,
And behind the weapons countless dissatisfied faces;
And a song make I of the One form'd out of all,
The fang'd and glittering One whose head is over all,
Resolute warlike One including and over all,
(However high the head of any else that head is over all.)

I will acknowledge contemporary lands,
I will trail the whole geography of the globe and salute courte-
    ously every city large and small,
And employments! I will put in my poems that with you is hero-
    ism upon land and sea,
And I will report all heroism from an American point of view.

I will sing the song of companionship,
I will show what alone must finally compact these,
I believe these are to found their own ideal of manly love, indi-
    cating it in me,
I will therefore let flame from me the burning fires that were
    threatening to consume me,
I will lift what has too long kept down those smouldering fires,
I will give them complete abandonment,
I will write the evangel-poem of comrades and of love,
For who but I should understand love with all its sorrow and joy?
And who but I should be the poet of comrades?

7

I am the credulous man of qualities, ages, races,
I advance from the people in their own spirit,
Here is what sings unrestricted faith.

Omnes ! omnes ! let others ignore what they may,
I make the poem of evil also, I commemorate that part also,
I am myself just as much evil as good, and my nation is — and I
    say there is in fact no evil,
(Or if there is I say it is just as important to you, to the land or
    to me, as any thing else.)

I too, following many and follow'd by many, inaugurate a religion,
    I descend into the arena,
(It may be I am destin'd to utter the loudest cries there, the win-
    ner's pealing shouts,
Who knows ? they may rise from me yet, and soar above every thing.)

Each is not for its own sake,
I say the whole earth and all the stars in the sky are for religion's
    sake.

I say no man has ever yet been half devout enough,
None has ever yet adored or worship'd half enough,
None has begun to think how divine he himself is, and how cer-
    tain the future is.

I say that the real and permanent grandeur of these States must
    be their religion,
Otherwise there is no real and permanent grandeur ;
(Nor character nor life worthy the name without religion,
Nor land nor man or woman without religion.)

8

What are you doing young man ?
Are you so earnest, so given up to literature, science, art, amours ?
These ostensible realities, politics, points ?
Your ambition or business whatever it may be ?

It is well — against such I say not a word, I am their poet also,
But behold ! such swiftly subside, burnt up for religion's sake,
For not all matter is fuel to heat, impalpable flame, the essential
    life of the earth,
Any more than such are to religion.

9

What do you seek so pensive and silent?
What do you need camerado?*
Dear son do you think it is love?

Listen dear son — listen America, daughter or son,
It is a painful thing to love a man or woman to excess, and yet it
    satisfies, it is great,
But there is something else very great, it makes the whole coin-
    cide,
It, magnificent,* beyond materials, with continuous hands sweeps
    and provides for all.

10

Know you, solely to drop in the earth the germs of a greater
    religion,
The following chants each for its kind I sing.

My comrade!
For you to share with me two greatnesses, and a third one rising
    inclusive and more resplendent,
The greatness of Love and Democracy, and the greatness of Reli-
    gion.

Melange mine own, the unseen and the seen,
Mysterious ocean where the streams empty,
Prophetic spirit of materials shifting and flickering around me,
Living beings, identities now doubtless near us in the air that we
    know not of,
Contact daily and hourly that will not release me,
These selecting, these in hints demanded of me.

Not he with a daily kiss onward from childhood kissing me,
Has winded and twisted around me that which holds me to him,
Any more than I am held to the heavens and all the spiritual
    world,
After what they have done to me, suggesting themes.

O such themes — equalities! O divine average!
Warblings under the sun, usher'd as now, or at noon, or set-
    ting,
Strains musical flowing through ages, now reaching hither,
I take to your reckless and composite chords, add to them, and
    cheerfully pass them forward.

11

As I have walk'd in Alabama my morning walk,
I have seen where the she-bird the mocking-bird sat on her nest
    in the briers hatching her brood.

I have seen the he-bird also,
I have paus'd to hear him near at hand inflating his throat and
    joyfully singing.

And while I paus'd it came to me that what he really sang for was
    not there only,
Nor for his mate nor himself only, nor all sent back by the echoes,
But subtle, clandestine, away beyond,
A charge transmitted and gift occult for those being born.

12

Democracy! near at hand to you a throat is now inflating itself
    and joyfully singing.

Ma femme! for the brood beyond us and of us,
For those who belong here and those to come,
I exultant to be ready for them will now shake out carols stronger
    and haughtier than have ever yet been heard upon earth.

I will make the songs of passion to give them their way,
And your songs outlaw'd offenders, for I scan you with kindred
    eyes, and carry you with me the same as any.

I will make the true poem of riches,
To earn for the body and the mind whatever adheres and goes
    forward and is not dropt by death;
I will effuse egotism and show it underlying all, and I will be the
    bard of personality,
And I will show of male and female that either is but the equal
    of the other,
And sexual organs and acts! do you concentrate in me, for I am
    determin'd to tell you with courageous clear voice to prove
    you illustrious,
And I will show that there is no imperfection in the present, and
    can be none in the future,
And I will show that whatever happens to anybody it may be
    turn'd to beautiful results,
And I will show that nothing can happen more beautiful than
    death,

And I will thread a thread through my poems that time and events
are compact,
And that all the things of the universe are perfect miracles, each
as profound as any.

I will not make poems with reference to parts,
But I will make poems, songs, thoughts, with reference to ensemble,
And I will not sing with reference to a day, but with reference to
all days,
And I will not make a poem nor the least part of a poem but has
reference to the soul,
Because having look'd at the objects of the universe, I find there
is no one nor any particle of one but has reference to the
soul.

13

Was somebody asking to see the soul?
See, your own shape and countenance, persons, substances, beasts,
the trees, the running rivers, the rocks and sands.

All hold spiritual joys and afterwards loosen them;
How can the real body ever die and be buried?

Of your real body and any man's or woman's real body,
Item for item it will elude the hands of the corpse-cleaners and
pass to fitting spheres,
Carrying what has accrued to it from the moment of birth to the
moment of death.

Not the types set up by the printer return their impression, the
meaning, the main concern,
Any more than a man's substance and life or a woman's substance
and life return in the body and the soul,
Indifferently before death and after death.

Behold, the body includes and is the meaning, the main concern,
and includes and is the soul;
Whoever you are, how superb and how divine is your body, or any
part of it!

14

Whoever you are, to you endless announcements!

Daughter of the lands did you wait for your poet?
Did you wait for one with a flowing mouth and indicative hand?

Toward the male of the States, and toward the female of the States,
Exulting words, words to Democracy's lands.

Interlink'd, food-yielding lands !
Land of coal and iron ! land of gold ! land of cotton, sugar, rice !
Land of wheat, beef, pork ! land of wool and hemp ! land of the
    apple and the grape !
Land of the pastoral plains, the grass-fields of the world ! land of
    those sweet-air'd interminable plateaus !
Land of the herd, the garden, the healthy house of adobie !
Lands where the north-west Columbia winds, and where the south-
    west Colorado winds !
Land of the eastern Chesapeake ! land of the Delaware !
Land of Ontario, Erie, Huron, Michigan !
Land of the Old Thirteen ! Massachusetts land ! land of Vermont
    and Connecticut !
Land of the ocean shores ! land of sierras and peaks !
Land of boatmen and sailors ! fishermen's land !
Inextricable lands ! the clutch'd together ! the passionate ones !
The side by side ! the elder and younger brothers ! the bony-
    limb'd !
The great women's land ! the feminine ! the experienced sisters
    and the inexperienced sisters !
Far breath'd land ! Arctic braced ! Mexican breez'd ! the diverse !
    the compact !
The Pennsylvanian ! the Virginian ! the double Carolinian !
O all and each well-loved by me ! my intrepid nations ! O I at
    any rate include you all with perfect love !
I cannot be discharged from you ! not from one any sooner than
    another !
O death ! O for all that, I am yet of you unseen this hour with
    irrepressible love,
Walking New England, a friend, a traveler,
Splashing my bare feet in the edge of the summer ripples on Pau-
    manok's sands,
Crossing the prairies, dwelling again in Chicago, dwelling in every
    town,
Observing shows, births, improvements, structures, arts,
Listening to orators and oratresses in public halls,
Of and through the States as during life, each man and woman
    my neighbor,
The Louisianian, the Georgian, as near to me, and I as near to
    him and her,
The Mississippian and Arkansian yet with me, and I yet with any
    of them,

Yet upon the plains west of the spinal river, yet in my house of
    adobie,
Yet returning eastward, yet in the Seaside State or in Maryland,
Yet Kanadian cheerily braving the winter, the snow and ice wel-
    come to me,
Yet a true son either of Maine or of the Granite State, or the
    Narragansett Bay State, or the Empire State,
Yet sailing to other shores to annex the same, yet welcoming every
    new brother,
Hereby applying these leaves to the new ones from the hour they
    unite with the old ones,
Coming among the new ones myself to be their companion and
    equal, coming personally to you now,
Enjoining you to acts, characters, spectacles, with me.

15

With me with firm holding, yet haste, haste on.

For your life adhere to me,
(I may have to be persuaded many times before I consent to give
    myself really to you, but what of that?
Must not Nature be persuaded many times?)

No dainty dolce affettuoso I,
Bearded, sun-burnt, gray-neck'd, forbidding, I have arrived,
To be wrestled with as I pass for the solid prizes of the universe,
For such I afford whoever can persevere to win them.

16

On my way a moment I pause,
Here for you! and here for America!
Still the present I raise aloft, still the future of the States I
    harbinge glad and sublime,
And for the past I pronounce what the air holds of the red
    aborigines.

The red aborigines,
Leaving natural breaths, sounds of rain and winds, calls as of birds
    and animals in the woods, syllabled to us for names,
Okonee, Koosa, Ottawa, Monongahela, Sauk, Natchez, Chatta-
    hoochee, Kaqueta, Oronoco,
Wabash, Miami, Saginaw, Chippewa, Oshkosh, Walla-Walla,
Leaving such to the States they melt, they depart, charging the
    water and the land with names.

17

Expanding and swift, henceforth,
Elements, breeds, adjustments, turbulent, quick and audacious,
A world primal again, vistas of glory incessant and branching,
A new race dominating previous ones and grander far, with new
    contests,
New politics, new literatures and religions, new inventions and arts.

These, my voice announcing — I will sleep no more but arise,
You oceans that have been calm within me ! how I feel you, fathom-
    less, stirring, preparing unprecedented waves and storms.

18

See, steamers steaming through my poems,
See, in my poems immigrants continually coming and landing,
See, in arriere, the wigwam, the trail, the hunter's hut, the flat-boat,
    the maize-leaf, the claim, the rude fence, and the backwoods
    village,
See, on the one side the Western Sea and on the other the Eastern
    Sea, how they advance and retreat upon my poems as upon
    their own shores,
See, pastures and forests in my poems — see, animals wild and
    tame — see, beyond the Kaw,* countless herds of buffalo
    feeding on short curly grass,
See, in my poems, cities, solid, vast, inland, with paved streets,
    with iron and stone edifices, ceaseless vehicles, and com-
    merce,
See, the many-cylinder'd steam printing-press — see, the electric
    telegraph stretching across the continent,
See, through Atlantica's depths pulses American Europe reaching,
    pulses of Europe duly return'd,
See, the strong and quick locomotive as it departs, panting, blowing
    the steam-whistle,
See, ploughmen ploughing farms — see, miners digging mines —
    see, the numberless factories,
See, mechanics busy at their benches with tools — see from among
    them superior judges, philosophs, Presidents, emerge, drest
    in working dresses,
See, lounging through the shops and fields of the States, me well-
    belov'd, close-held by day and night,
Hear the loud echoes of my songs there — read the hints come at
    last.

19

O camerado close ! O you and me at last, and us two only.

O a word to clear one's path ahead endlessly !
O something ecstatic and undemonstrable ! O music wild !
O now I triumph — and you shall also ;
O hand in hand — O wholesome pleasure — O one more desirer
and lover !
O to haste firm holding — to haste, haste on with me.

SONG OF MYSELF.

I

I CELEBRATE myself, and sing myself,
And what I assume you shall assume,
For every atom belonging to me as good belongs to you.

I loafe and invite my soul,
I lean and loafe at my ease observing a spear of summer grass.

My tongue, every atom of my blood, form'd from this soil, this
air,
Born here of parents born here from parents the same, and their
parents the same,
I, now thirty-seven years old in perfect health begin,
Hoping to cease not till death.

Creeds and schools in abeyance,
Retiring back a while sufficed at what they are, but never forgotten,
I harbor for good or bad, I permit to speak at every hazard,
Nature without check with original energy.

Houses and rooms are full of perfumes, the shelves are crowded
with perfumes,
I breathe the fragrance myself and know it and like it,
The distillation would intoxicate me also, but I shall not let it.

The atmosphere is not a perfume, it has no taste of the distillation,
it is odorless,
It is for my mouth forever, I am in love with it,
I will go to the bank by the wood and become undisguised and
naked,
I am mad for it to be in contact with me.

The smoke of my own breath,
Echoes, ripples, buzz'd whispers, love-root, silk-thread, crotch and
    vine,
My respiration and inspiration, the beating of my heart, the pass-
    ing of blood and air through my lungs,
The sniff of green leaves and dry leaves, and of the shore and
    dark-color'd sea-rocks, and of hay in the barn,
The sound of the belch'd words of my voice loos'd to the eddies
    of the wind,
A few light kisses, a few embraces, a reaching around of arms,
The play of shine and shade on the trees as the supple boughs
    wag,
The delight alone or in the rush of the streets, or along the fields
    and hill-sides,
The feeling of health, the full-noon trill, the song of me rising from
    bed and meeting the sun.

Have you reckon'd a thousand acres much? have you reckon'd
    the earth much?
Have you practis'd so long to learn to read?
Have you felt so proud to get at the meaning of poems?

Stop this day and night with me and you shall possess the origin
    of all poems,
You shall possess the good of the earth and sun, (there are millions
    of suns left,)
You shall no longer take things at second or third hand, nor look
    through the eyes of the dead, nor feed on the spectres in
    books,
You shall not look through my eyes either, nor take things from me,
You shall listen to all sides and filter them from your self.

3

I have heard what the talkers were talking, the talk of the begin-
    ning and the end,
But I do not talk of the beginning or the end.

There was never any more inception than there is now,
Nor any more youth or age than there is now,
And will never be any more perfection than there is now,
Nor any more heaven or hell than there is now.

Urge and urge and urge,
Always the procreant urge of the world.

Out of the dimness opposite equals advance, always substance and
    increase, always sex,
Always a knit of identity, always distinction, always a breed of life.

To elaborate is no avail, learn'd and unlearn'd feel that it is so.

Sure as the most certain sure, plumb in the uprights, well entretied,
    braced in the beams,
Stout as a horse, affectionate, haughty, electrical,
I and this mystery here we stand.

Clear and sweet is my soul, and clear and sweet is all that is not
    my soul.

Lack one lacks both, and the unseen is proved by the seen,
Till that becomes unseen and receives proof in its turn.

Showing the best and dividing it from the worst age vexes age,
Knowing the perfect fitness and equanimity of things, while they
    discuss I am silent, and go bathe and admire myself.

Welcome is every organ and attribute of me, and of any man
    hearty and clean,
Not an inch nor a particle of an inch is vile, and none shall be
    less familiar than the rest.

I am satisfied — I see, dance, laugh, sing;
As the hugging and loving bed-fellow*sleeps at my side through
    the night, and withdraws at the peep of the day with
    stealthy tread,
Leaving me baskets cover'd with white towels swelling the house
    with their plenty,
Shall I postpone my acceptation and realization and scream at my
    eyes,
That they turn from gazing after and down the road,
And forthwith cipher and show me to a cent,
Exactly the value of one and exactly the value of two, and which
    is ahead?

4

Trippers and askers surround me,
People I meet, the effect upon me of my early life or the ward
    and city I live in, or the nation,
The latest dates, discoveries, inventions, societies, authors old and
    new,

My dinner, dress, associates, looks, compliments, dues,
The real or fancied indifference of some man or woman I love,
The sickness of one of my folks or of myself, or ill-doing or loss or
    lack of money, or depressions or exaltations,
Battles, the horrors of fratricidal war, the fever of doubtful news,
    the fitful events;
These come to me days and nights and go from me again,
But they are not the Me myself.

Apart from the pulling and hauling stands what I am,
Stands amused, complacent, compassionating, idle, unitary,
Looks down, is erect, or bends an arm on an impalpable certain
    rest,
Looking with side-curved head curious what will come next,
Both in and out of the game and watching and wondering at it.

Backward I see in my own days where I sweated through fog with
    linguists and contenders,
I have no mockings or arguments, I witness and wait.

5

I believe in you my soul, the other I am must not abase itself to you,
And you must not be abased to the other.

Loafe with me on the grass, loose the stop from your throat,
Not words, not music or rhyme I want, not custom or lecture, not
    even the best,
Only the lull I like, the hum of your valvèd voice.

I mind how once we lay such a transparent summer morning,
How you settled your head athwart my hips and gently turn'd over
    upon me,
And parted the shirt from my bosom-bone, and plunged your
    tongue to my bare-stript heart,
And reach'd till you felt my beard, and reach'd till you held my
    feet.

Swiftly arose and spread around me the peace and knowledge that
    pass all the argument of the earth,
And I know that the hand of God is the promise of my own,
And I know that the spirit of God is the brother of my own,
And that all the men ever born are also my brothers, and the
    women my sisters and lovers,
And that a kelson of the creation is love,
And limitless are leaves stiff or drooping in the fields,

And brown ants in the little wells beneath them,
And mossy scabs of the worm fence, heap'd stones, elder, mullein
and poke-weed.

6

A child said *What is the grass ?* fetching it to me with full hands ;
How could I answer the child? I do not know what it is any
more than he.

I guess it must be the flag of my disposition, out of hopeful green
stuff woven.

Or I guess it is the handkerchief of the Lord,
A scented gift and remembrancer designedly dropt,
Bearing the owner's name someway in the corners, that we may
see and remark, and say *Whose ?*

Or I guess the grass is itself a child, the produced babe of the
vegetation.

Or I guess it is a uniform hieroglyphic,
And it means, Sprouting alike in broad zones and narrow zones,
Growing among black folks as among white,
Kanuck, Tuckahoe, Congressman, Cuff,*I give them the same, I
receive them the same.

And now it seems to me the beautiful uncut hair of graves.

Tenderly will I use you curling grass,
It may be you transpire from the breasts of young men,
It may be if I had known them I would have loved them,
It may be you are from old people, or from offspring taken soon
out of their mothers' laps,
And here you are the mothers' laps.

This grass is very dark to be from the white heads of old mothers,
Darker than the colorless beards of old men,
Dark to come from under the faint red roofs of mouths.

O I perceive after all so many uttering tongues,
And I perceive they do not come from the roofs of mouths for
nothing.

I wish I could translate the hints about the dead young men and
women,

And the hints about old men and mothers, and the offspring taken
　　soon out of their laps.

What do you think has become of the young and old men?
And what do you think has become of the women and chil-
　　dren?

They are alive and well somewhere,
The smallest sprout shows there is really no death,
And if ever there was it led forward life, and does not wait at the
　　end to arrest it,
And ceas'd the moment life appear'd.

All goes onward and outward, nothing collapses,
And to die is different from what any one supposed, and luckier.

7

Has any one supposed it lucky to be born?
I hasten to inform him or her it is just as lucky to die, and I
　　know it.

I pass death with the dying and birth with the new-wash'd babe,
　　and am not contain'd between my hat and boots,
And peruse manifold objects, no two alike and every one good,
The earth good and the stars good, and their adjuncts all good.

I am not an earth nor an adjunct of an earth,
I am the mate and companion of people, all just as immortal and
　　fathomless as myself,
(They do not know how immortal, but I know.)

Every kind for itself and its own, for me mine male and female,
For me those that have been boys and that love women,
For me the man that is proud and feels how it stings to be
　　slighted,
For me the sweet-heart and the old maid, for me mothers and the
　　mothers of mothers,
For me lips that have smiled, eyes that have shed tears,
For me children and the begetters of children.

Undrape! you are not guilty to me, nor stale nor discarded,
I see through the broadcloth and gingham whether or no,
And am around, tenacious, acquisitive, tireless, and cannot be
　　shaken away.

8

The little one sleeps in its cradle,
I lift the gauze and look a long time, and silently brush away flies
  with my hand.

The youngster and the red-faced girl turn aside up the bushy hill,
I peeringly view them from the top.

The suicide sprawls on the bloody floor of the bedroom,
I witness the corpse with its dabbled hair, I note where the pistol
  has fallen.

The blab of the pave, tires of carts, sluff of boot-soles, talk of the
  promenaders,
The heavy omnibus, the driver with his interrogating thumb, the
  clank of the shod horses on the granite floor,
The snow-sleighs, clinking, shouted jokes, pelts of snow-balls,
The hurrahs for popular favorites, the fury of rous'd mobs,
The flap of the curtain'd litter, a sick man inside borne to the
  hospital,
The meeting of enemies, the sudden oath, the blows and fall,
The excited crowd, the policeman with his star quickly working
  his passage to the centre of the crowd,
The impassive stones that receive and return so many echoes,
What groans of over-fed or half-starv'd who fall sunstruck or in
  fits,
What exclamations of women taken suddenly who hurry home and
  give birth to babes,
What living and buried speech is always vibrating here, what howls
  restrain'd by decorum,
Arrests of criminals, slights, adulterous offers made, acceptances,
  rejections with convex lips,
I mind them or the show or resonance of them — I come and I
  depart.

9

The big doors of the country barn stand open and ready,
The dried grass of the harvest-time loads the slow-drawn wagon,
The clear light plays on the brown gray and green intertinged,
The armfuls are pack'd to the sagging mow.

I am there, I help, I came stretch'd atop of the load,
I felt its soft jolts, one leg reclined on the other,
I jump from the cross-beams and seize the clover and timothy,
And roll head over heels and tangle my hair full of wisps.

10

Alone far in the wilds and mountains I hunt,
Wandering amazed at my own lightness and glee,
In the late afternoon choosing a safe spot to pass the night,
Kindling a fire and broiling the fresh-kill'd game,
Falling asleep on the gather'd leaves with my dog and gun by my
          side.

The Yankee clipper is under her sky-sails, she cuts the sparkle and
          scud,
My eyes settle the land, I bend at her prow or shout joyously from
          the deck.

The boatmen and clam-diggers arose early and stopt for me,
I tuck'd my trowser-ends in my boots and went and had a good
          time ;
You should have been with us that day round the chowder-kettle.

I saw the marriage of the trapper in the open air in the far west,
          the bride was a red girl,
Her father and his friends sat near cross-legged and dumbly
          smoking, they had moccasins to their feet and large thick
          blankets hanging from their shoulders,
On a bank lounged the trapper, he was drest mostly in skins, his
          luxuriant beard and curls protected his neck, he held his
          bride by the hand,
She had long eyelashes, her head was bare, her coarse straight
          locks descended upon her voluptuous limbs and reach'd to
          her feet.

The runaway slave came to my house and stopt outside,
I heard his motions crackling the twigs of the woodpile,
Through the swung half-door of the kitchen I saw him limpsy and
          weak,
And went where he sat on a log and led him in and assured him,
And brought water and fill'd a tub for his sweated body and bruis'd
          feet,
And gave him a room that enter'd from my own, and gave him
          some coarse clean clothes,
And remember perfectly well his revolving eyes and his awkwardness,
And remember putting plasters on the galls of his neck and ankles ;
He staid with me a week before he was recuperated and pass'd
          north,
I had him sit next me at table, my fire-lock lean'd in the corner.

11

Twenty-eight young men bathe by the shore,
Twenty-eight young men and all so friendly;
Twenty-eight years of womanly life and all so lonesome.

She owns the fine house by the rise of the bank,
She hides handsome and richly drest aft the blinds of the window.

Which of the young men does she like the best?
Ah the homeliest of them is beautiful to her.

Where are you off to, lady? for I see you,
You splash in the water there, yet stay stock still in your room.

Dancing and laughing along the beach came the twenty-ninth bather,
The rest did not see her, but she saw them and loved them.

The beards of the young men glisten'd with wet, it ran from their
        long hair,
Little streams pass'd all over their bodies.

An unseen hand also pass'd over their bodies,
It descended tremblingly from their temples and ribs.

The young men float on their backs, their white bellies bulge to
        the sun, they do not ask who seizes fast to them,
They do not know who puffs and declines with pendant and bend-
        ing arch,
They do not think whom they souse with spray.

12

The butcher-boy puts off his killing-clothes, or sharpens his knife
        at the stall in the market,
I loiter enjoying his repartee and his shuffle and break-down.

Blacksmiths with grimed and hairy chests environ the anvil,
Each has his main-sledge, they are all out, there is a great heat in
        the fire.

From the cinder-strew'd threshold I follow their movements,
The lithe sheer of their waists plays even with their massive arms,
Overhand the hammers swing, overhand so slow, overhand so
        sure,
They do not hasten, each man hits in his place.

13

The negro holds firmly the reins of his four horses, the block swags
    underneath on its tied-over chain,
The negro that drives the long dray of the stone-yard, steady and
    tall he stands pois'd on one leg on the string-piece,
His blue shirt exposes his ample neck and breast and loosens over
    his hip-band,
His glance is calm and commanding, he tosses the slouch of his
    hat away from his forehead,
The sun falls on his crispy hair and mustache, falls on the black
    of his polish'd and perfect limbs.

I behold the picturesque giant and love him, and I do not stop
    there,
I go with the team also.

In me the caresser of life wherever moving, backward as well as
    forward sluing,
To niches aside and junior bending, not a person or object miss-
    ing,
Absorbing all to myself and for this song.

Oxen that rattle the yoke and chain or halt in the leafy shade,
    what is that you express in your eyes?
It seems to me more than all the print I have read in my life.

My tread scares the wood-drake and wood-duck on my distant and
    day-long ramble,
They rise together, they slowly circle around.

I believe in those wing'd purposes,
And acknowledge red, yellow, white, playing within me,
And consider green and violet and the tufted crown intentional,
And do not call the tortoise unworthy because she is not something
    else,
And the jay in the woods never studied the gamut, yet trills pretty
    well to me,
And the look of the bay mare shames silliness out of me.

14

The wild gander leads his flock through the cool night,
Ya-honk he says, and sounds it down to me like an invitation,
The pert may suppose it meaningless, but I listening close,
Find its purpose and place up there toward the wintry sky.

The sharp-hoof'd moose of the north, the cat on the house-sill,
    the chickadee, the prairie-dog,
The litter of the grunting sow as they tug at her teats,
The brood of the turkey-hen and she with her half-spread wings,
I see in them and myself the same old law.

The press of my foot to the earth springs a hundred affections,
They scorn the best I can do to relate them.

I am enamour'd of growing out-doors,
Of men that live among cattle or taste of the ocean or woods,
Of the builders and steerers of ships and the wielders of axes and
    mauls, and the drivers of horses,
I can eat and sleep with them week in and week out.

What is commonest, cheapest, nearest, easiest, is Me,
Me going in for my chances, spending for vast returns,
Adorning myself to bestow myself on the first that will take me,
Not asking the sky to come down to my good will,
Scattering it freely forever.

15

The pure contralto sings in the organ loft,
The carpenter dresses his plank, the tongue of his foreplane whistles
    its wild ascending lisp,
The married and unmarried children ride home to their Thanks-
    giving dinner,
The pilot seizes the king-pin, he heaves down with a strong arm,
The mate stands braced in the whale-boat, lance and harpoon are
    ready,
The duck-shooter walks by silent and cautious stretches,
The deacons are ordain'd with cross'd hands at the altar,
The spinning-girl retreats and advances to the hum of the big
    wheel,
The farmer stops by the bars as he walks on a First-day loafe and
    looks at the oats and rye,
The lunatic is carried at last to the asylum a confirm'd case,
(He will never sleep any more as he did in the cot in his mother's
    bed-room ;)
The jour printer with gray head and gaunt jaws works at his case,
He turns his quid of tobacco while his eyes blurr with the manu-
    script ;
The malform'd limbs are tied to the surgeon's table,
What is removed drops horribly in a pail ;

The quadroon girl is sold at the auction-stand, the drunkard nods
       by the bar-room stove,
The machinist rolls up his sleeves, the policeman travels his beat,
       the gate-keeper marks who pass,
The young fellow drives the express-wagon, (I love him, though
       I do not know him ;)
The half-breed straps on his light boots to compete in the race,
The western turkey-shooting draws old and young, some lean on
       their rifles, some sit on logs,
Out from the crowd steps the marksman, takes his position, levels
       his piece ;
The groups of newly-come immigrants cover the wharf or levee,
As the woolly-pates hoe in the sugar-field, the overseer views them
       from his saddle,
The bugle calls in the ball-room, the gentlemen run for their part-
       ners, the dancers bow to each other,
The youth lies awake in the cedar-roof'd garret and harks to the
       musical rain,
The Wolverine*sets traps on the creek that helps fill the Huron,
The squaw wrapt in her yellow-hemm'd cloth is offering moccasins
       and bead-bags for sale,
The connoisseur peers along the exhibition-gallery with half-shut
       eyes bent sideways,
As the deck-hands make fast the steamboat the plank is thrown for
       the shore-going passengers,
The young sister holds out the skein while the elder sister winds it
       off in a ball, and stops now and then for the knots,
The one-year wife is recovering and happy having a week ago
       borne her first child,
The clean-hair'd Yankee girl works with her sewing-machine or in
       the factory or mill,
The paving-man leans on his two-handed rammer, the reporter's
       lead flies swiftly over the note-book, the sign-painter is
       lettering with blue and gold,
The canal boy trots on the tow-path, the book-keeper counts at
       his desk, the shoemaker waxes his thread,
The conductor beats time for the band and all the performers
       follow him,
The child is baptized, the convert is making his first professions,
The regatta is spread on the bay, the race is begun, (how the
       white sails sparkle !)
The drover watching his drove sings out to them that would
       stray,
The pedler sweats with his pack on his back, (the purchaser hig-
       gling about the odd cent ;)

The bride unrumples her white dress, the minute-hand of the clock
     moves slowly,
The opium-eater reclines with rigid head and just-open'd lips,
The prostitute draggles her shawl, her bonnet bobs on her tipsy
     and pimpled neck,
The crowd laugh at her blackguard oaths, the men jeer and wink
     to each other,
(Miserable ! I do not laugh at your oaths nor jeer you ;)
The President holding a cabinet council is surrounded by the great
     Secretaries,
On the piazza walk three matrons stately and friendly with twined
     arms,
The crew of the fish-smack pack repeated layers of halibut in the
     hold,
The Missourian crosses the plains toting his wares and his cattle,
As the fare-collector goes through the train he gives notice by the
     jingling of loose change,
The floor-men are laying the floor, the tinners are tinning the roof,
     the masons are calling for mortar,
In single file each shouldering his hod pass onward the laborers ;
Seasons pursuing each other the indescribable crowd is gather'd,
     it is the fourth of Seventh-month,* (what salutes of cannon
     and small arms !)
Seasons pursuing each other the plougher ploughs, the mower
     mows, and the winter-grain falls in the ground ;
Off on the lakes the pike-fisher watches and waits by the hole in
     the frozen surface,
The stumps stand thick round the clearing, the squatter strikes
     deep with his axe,
Flatboatmen make fast towards dusk near the cotton-wood or
     pecan-trees,
Coon-seekers go through the regions of the Red river or through
     those drain'd by the Tennessee, or through those of the
     Arkansas,
Torches shine in the dark that hangs on the Chattahooche or
     Altamahaw,*
Patriarchs sit at supper with sons and grandsons and great-grand-
     sons around them,
In walls of adobie, in canvas tents, rest hunters and trappers after
     their day's sport,
The city sleeps and the country sleeps,
The living sleep for their time, the dead sleep for their time,
The old husband sleeps by his wife and the young husband sleeps
     by his wife ;
And these tend inward to me, and I tend outward to them,

And such as it is to be of these more or less I am,
And of these one and all I weave the song of myself.

16

I am of old and young, of the foolish as much as the wise,
Regardless of others, ever regardful of others,
Maternal as well as paternal, a child as well as a man,
Stuff'd with the stuff that is coarse and stuff'd with the stuff that
　　is fine,
One of the Nation of many nations,* the smallest the same and the
　　largest the same,
A Southerner soon as a Northerner, a planter nonchalant and
　　hospitable down by the Oconee I live,
A Yankee bound my own way ready for trade, my joints the
　　limberest joints on earth and the sternest joints on
　　earth,
A Kentuckian walking the vale of the Elkhorn in my deer-skin
　　leggings, a Louisianian or Georgian,
A boatman over lakes or bays or along coasts, a Hoosier, Badger,
　　Buckeye ;*
At home on Kanadian snow-shoes or up in the bush, or with
　　fishermen off Newfoundland,
At home in the fleet of ice-boats, sailing with the rest and tack-
　　ing,
At home on the hills of Vermont or in the woods of Maine, or the
　　Texan ranch,
Comrade of Californians, comrade of free North-Westerners, (lov-
　　ing their big proportions,)
Comrade of raftsmen and coalmen, comrade of all who shake
　　hands and welcome to drink and meat,
A learner with the simplest, a teacher of the thoughtfullest,
A novice beginning yet experient of myriads of seasons,
Of every hue and caste am I, of every rank and religion,
A farmer, mechanic, artist, gentleman, sailor, quaker,
Prisoner, fancy-man,* rowdy, lawyer, physician, priest.

I resist any thing better than my own diversity,
Breathe the air but leave plenty after me,
And am not stuck up, and am in my place.

(The moth and the fish-eggs are in their place,
The bright suns I see and the dark suns I cannot see are in their
　　place,
The palpable is in its place and the impalpable is in its place.)

17

These are really the thoughts of all men in all ages and lands, they
are not original with me,
If they are not yours as much as mine they are nothing, or next
to nothing,
If they are not the riddle and the untying of the riddle they are
nothing,
If they are not just as close as they are distant they are nothing.

This is the grass that grows wherever the land is and the water is,
This the common air that bathes the globe.

18

With music strong I come, with my cornets and my drums,
I play not marches for accepted victors only, I play marches for
conquer'd and slain persons.

Have you heard that it was good to gain the day?
I also say it is good to fall, battles are lost in the same spirit in
which they are won.

I beat and pound for the dead,
I blow through my embouchures my loudest and gayest for them.

Vivas to those who have fail'd!
And to those whose war-vessels sank in the sea!
And to those themselves who sank in the sea!
And to all generals that lost engagements, and all overcome heroes!
And the numberless unknown heroes equal to the greatest heroes
known!

19

This is the meal equally set, this the meat for natural hunger,
It is for the wicked just the same as the righteous, I make appoint-
ments with all,
I will not have a single person slighted or left away,
The kept-woman, sponger, thief, are hereby invited,
The heavy-lipp'd slave is invited, the venerealee is invited;
There shall be no difference between them and the rest.

This is the press of a bashful hand, this the float and odor of hair,
This the touch of my lips to yours, this the murmur of yearning,
This the far-off depth and height reflecting my own face,
This the thoughtful merge of myself, and the outlet again.

Do you guess I have some intricate purpose?
Well I have, for the Fourth-month showers*have, and the mica on
    the side of a rock has.

Do you take it I would astonish?
Does the daylight astonish? does the early redstart twittering
    through the woods?
Do I astonish more than they?

This hour I tell things in confidence,
I might not tell everybody, but I will tell you.

20

Who goes there? hankering, gross, mystical, nude;
How is it I extract strength from the beef I eat?

What is a man anyhow? what am I? what are you?

All I mark as my own you shall offset it with your own,
Else it were time lost listening to me.

I do not snivel that snivel the world over,
That months are vacuums and the ground but wallow and filth.

Whimpering and truckling fold with powders for invalids, con-
    formity goes to the fourth-remov'd,
I wear my hat as I please indoors or out.

Why should I pray? why should I venerate and be ceremonious?

Having pried through the strata, analyzed to a hair, counsel'd with
    doctors and calculated close,
I find no sweeter fat than sticks to my own bones.

In all people I see myself, none more and not one a barley-corn
    less,
And the good or bad I say of myself I say of them.

I know I am solid and sound,
To me the converging objects of the universe perpetually flow,
All are written to me, and I must get what the writing means.

I know I am deathless,
I know this orbit of mine cannot be swept by a carpenter's
    compass,

I know I shall not pass like a child's carlacue* cut with a burnt
    stick at night.

I know I am august,
I do not trouble my spirit to vindicate itself or be understood,
I see that the elementary laws never apologize,
(I reckon I behave no prouder than the level I plant my house by,
    after all.)

I exist as I am, that is enough,
If no other in the world be aware I sit content,
And if each and all be aware I sit content.

One world is aware and by far the largest to me, and that is my-
    self,
And whether I come to my own to-day or in ten thousand or ten
    million years,
I can cheerfully take it now, or with equal cheerfulness I can wait.

My foothold is tenon'd and mortis'd in granite,
I laugh at what you call dissolution,
And I know the amplitude of time.

21

I am the poet of the Body and I am the poet of the Soul,
The pleasures of heaven are with me and the pains of hell are
    with me,
The first I graft and increase upon myself, the latter I translate
    into a new tongue.

I am the poet of the woman the same as the man,
And I say it is as great to be a woman as to be a man,
And I say there is nothing greater than the mother of men.

I chant the chant of dilation or pride,
We have had ducking and deprecating about enough,
I show that size is only development.

Have you outstript the rest? are you the President?
It is a trifle, they will more than arrive there every one, and still
    pass on.

I am he that walks with the tender and growing night,
I call to the earth and sea half-held by the night.

Press close bare-bosom'd night—press close magnetic nourishing
    night !
Night of south winds — night of the large few stars !
Still nodding night—mad naked summer night.

Smile O voluptuous cool-breath'd earth !
Earth of the slumbering and liquid trees !
Earth of departed sunset—earth of the mountains misty-topt !
Earth of the vitreous pour of the full moon just tinged with blue !
Earth of shine and dark mottling the tide of the river !
Earth of the limpid gray of clouds brighter and clearer for my
    sake !
Far-swooping elbow'd earth — rich apple-blossom'd earth !
Smile, for your lover comes.

Prodigal, you have given me love—therefore I to you give love !
O unspeakable passionate love.

22

You sea ! I resign myself to you also—I guess what you mean,
I behold from the beach your crooked inviting fingers,
I believe you refuse to go back without feeling of me,
We must have a turn together, I undress, hurry me out of sight of
    the land,
Cushion me soft, rock me in billowy drowse,
Dash me with amorous wet, I can repay you.

Sea of stretch'd ground-swells,
Sea breathing broad and convulsive breaths,
Sea of the brine of life and of unshovell'd yet always-ready graves,
Howler and scooper of storms, capricious and dainty sea,
I am integral with you, I too am of one phase and of all phases.

Partaker of influx and efflux I, extoller of hate and conciliation,
Extoller of amies and those that sleep in each others' arms.

I am he attesting sympathy,
(Shall I make my list of things in the house and skip the house
    that supports them?)

I am not the poet of goodness only, I do not decline to be the
    poet of wickedness also.

What blurt is this about virtue and about vice?
Evil propels me and reform of evil propels me, I stand indifferent,

My gait is no fault-finder's or rejecter's gait,
I moisten the roots of all that has grown.

Did you fear some scrofula out of the unflagging pregnancy?
Did you guess the celestial laws are yet to be work'd over and
rectified?

I find one side a balance and the antipodal side a balance,
Soft doctrine as steady help as stable doctrine,
Thoughts and deeds of the present our rouse and early start.

This minute that comes to me over the past decillions,
There is no better than it and now.

What behaved well in the past or behaves well to-day is not such
a wonder,
The wonder is always and always how there can be a mean man
or an infidel.

23

Endless unfolding of words of ages!
And mine a word of the modern, the word En-Masse.

A word of the faith that never balks,
Here or henceforward it is all the same to me, I accept Time abso-
lutely.

It alone is without flaw, it alone rounds and completes all,
That mystic baffling wonder alone completes all.

I accept Reality and dare not question it,
Materialism first and last imbuing.

Hurrah for positive science! long live exact demonstration!
Fetch stonecrop mixt with cedar and branches of lilac,
This is the lexicographer, this the chemist, this made a grammar
of the old cartouches,*
These mariners put the ship through dangerous unknown seas.
This is the geologist, this works with the scalpel, and this is a
mathematician.

Gentlemen, to you the first honors always!
Your facts are useful, and yet they are not my dwelling,
I but enter by them to an area of my dwelling.

Less the reminders of properties told my words,
And more the reminders they of life untold, and of freedom and
    extrication,
And make short account of neuters and geldings, and favor men
    and women fully equipt,
And beat the gong of revolt, and stop with fugitives and them that
    plot and conspire.

24

Walt Whitman, a kosmos, of Manhattan the son,
Turbulent, fleshy, sensual, eating, drinking and breeding,
No sentimentalist, no stander above men and women or apart from
    them,
No more modest than immodest.

Unscrew the locks from the doors!
Unscrew the doors themselves from their jambs!

Whoever degrades another degrades me,
And whatever is done or said returns at last to me.

Through me the afflatus surging and surging, through me the cur-
    rent and index.

I speak the pass-word primeval, I give the sign of democracy,
By God! I will accept nothing which all cannot have their coun-
    terpart of on the same terms.

Through me many long dumb voices,
Voices of the interminable generations of prisoners and slaves,
Voices of the diseas'd and despairing and of thieves and dwarfs,
Voices of cycles of preparation and accretion,
And of the threads that connect the stars, and of wombs and of
    the father-stuff,
And of the rights of them the others are down upon,
Of the deform'd, trivial, flat, foolish, despised,
Fog in the air, beetles rolling balls of dung.

Through me forbidden voices,
Voices of sexes and lusts, voices veil'd and I remove the veil,
Voices indecent by me clarified and transfigur'd.

I do not press my fingers across my mouth,
I keep as delicate around the bowels as around the head and heart,
Copulation is no more rank to me than death is.

I believe in the flesh and the appetites,
Seeing, hearing, feeling, are miracles, and each part and tag of me
    is a miracle.

Divine am I inside and out, and I make holy whatever I touch or
    am touch'd from,
The scent of these arm-pits aroma finer than prayer,
This head more than churches, bibles, and all the creeds.

If I worship one thing more than another it shall be the spread of
    my own body, or any part of it,
Translucent mould of me it shall be you !
Shaded ledges and rests it shall be you !
Firm masculine colter it shall be you !
Whatever goes to the tilth of me it shall be you !
You my rich blood ! your milky stream pale strippings of my life !
Breast that presses against other breasts it shall be you !
My brain it shall be your occult convolutions !
Root of wash'd sweet-flag ! timorous pond-snipe ! nest of guarded
    duplicate eggs ! it shall be you !
Mix'd tussled hay of head, beard, brawn, it shall be you !
Trickling sap of maple, fibre of manly wheat, it shall be you !
Sun so generous it shall be you !
Vapors lighting and shading my face it shall be you !
You sweaty brooks and dews it shall be you !
Winds whose soft-tickling genitals rub against me it shall be you !
Broad muscular fields, branches of live oak, loving lounger in my
    winding paths, it shall be you !
Hands I have taken, face I have kiss'd, mortal I have ever
    touch'd, it shall be you.

I dote on myself, there is that lot of me and all so luscious,
Each moment and whatever happens thrills me with joy,
I cannot tell how my ankles bend, nor whence the cause of my
    faintest wish,
Nor the cause of the friendship I emit, nor the cause of the friend-
    ship I take again.

That I walk up my stoop, I pause to consider if it really be,
A morning-glory at my window satisfies me more than the meta-
    physics of books.

To behold the day-break !
The little light fades the immense and diaphanous shadows,
The air tastes good to my palate.

Hefts of the moving world at innocent gambols silently rising
    freshly exuding,
Scooting obliquely high and low.

Something I cannot see puts upward libidinous prongs,
Seas of bright juice suffuse heaven.

The earth by the sky staid with, the daily close of their junction,
The heav'd challenge from the east that moment over my head,
The mocking taunt, See then whether you shall be master !

25

Dazzling and tremendous how quick the sun-rise would kill me,
If I could not now and always send sun-rise out of me.

We also ascend dazzling and tremendous as the sun,
We found our own O my soul in the calm and cool of the day-
    break.

My voice goes after what my eyes cannot reach,
With the twirl of my tongue I encompass worlds and volumes of
    worlds.

Speech is the twin of my vision, it is unequal to measure itself,
It provokes me forever, it says sarcastically,
Walt you contain enough, why don't you let it out then ?

Come now I will not be tantalized, you conceive too much of
    articulation,
Do you not know O speech how the buds beneath you are folded?
Waiting in gloom, protected by frost,
The dirt receding before my prophetical screams,
I underlying causes to balance them at last,
My knowledge my live parts, it keeping tally with the meaning of
    all things,
Happiness, (which whoever hears me let him or her set out in
    search of this day.)

My final merit I refuse you, I refuse putting from me what I really
    am,
Encompass worlds, but never try to encompass me,
I crowd your sleekest and best by simply looking toward you.

Writing and talk do not prove me,
I carry the plenum*of proof and every thing else in my face,
With the hush of my lips I wholly confound the skeptic.

26

Now I will do nothing but listen,
To accrue what I hear into this song, to let sounds contribute
    toward it.

I hear bravuras of birds, bustle of growing wheat, gossip of flames,
    clack of sticks cooking my meals,
I hear the sound I love, the sound of the human voice,
I hear all sounds running together, combined, fused or following,
Sounds of the city and sounds out of the city, sounds of the day
    and night,
Talkative young ones to those that like them, the loud laugh of
    work-people at their meals,
The angry base of disjointed friendship, the faint tones of the sick,
The judge with hands tight to the desk, his pallid lips pronoun-
    cing a death-sentence,
The heave'e'yo of stevedores unlading ships by the wharves, the
    refrain of the anchor-lifters,
The ring of alarm-bells, the cry of fire, the whirr of swift-streak-
    ing engines and hose-carts with premonitory tinkles and
    color'd lights,
The steam-whistle, the solid roll of the train of approaching cars,
The slow march play'd at the head of the association marching
    two and two,
(They go to guard some corpse, the flag-tops are draped with
    black muslin.)

I hear the violoncello, ('tis the young man's heart's complaint,)
I hear the key'd cornet, it glides quickly in through my ears,
It shakes mad-sweet pangs through my belly and breast.

I hear the chorus, it is a grand opera,
Ah this indeed is music — this suits me.

A tenor large and fresh as the creation fills me,
The orbic flex of his mouth is pouring and filling me full.

I hear the train'd soprano (what work with hers is this?)
The orchestra whirls me wider than Uranus flies,
It wrenches such ardors from me I did not know I possess'd
    them,
It sails me, I dab with bare feet, they are lick'd by the indolent
    waves,
I am cut by bitter and angry hail, I lose my breath,

Steep'd amid honey'd morphine, my windpipe throttled in fakes
    of death,
At length let up again to feel the puzzle of puzzles,
And that we call Being.

27

To be in any form, what is that?
(Round and round we go, all of us, and ever come back thither,)
If nothing lay more develop'd the quahaug*in its callous shell were
    enough.

Mine is no callous shell,
I have instant conductors all over me whether I pass or stop,
They seize every object and lead it harmlessly through me.

I merely stir, press, feel with my fingers, and am happy,
To touch my person to some one else's is about as much as I can
    stand.

28

Is this then a touch? quivering me to a new identity,
Flames and ether making a rush for my veins,
Treacherous tip of me reaching and crowding to help them,
My flesh and blood playing out lightning to strike what is hardly
    different from myself,
On all sides prurient provokers stiffening my limbs,
Straining the udder of my heart for its withheld drip,
Behaving licentious toward me, taking no denial,
Depriving me of my best as for a purpose,
Unbuttoning my clothes, holding me by the bare waist,
Deluding my confusion with the calm of the sunlight and pasture-
    fields,
Immodestly sliding the fellow-senses away,
They bribed to swap off with touch and go and graze at the edges
    of me,
No consideration, no regard for my draining strength or my anger,
Fetching the rest of the herd around to enjoy them a while,
Then all uniting to stand on a headland and worry me.

The sentries desert every other part of me,
They have left me helpless to a red marauder,
They all come to the headland to witness and assist against me.

I am given up by traitors,
I talk wildly, I have lost my wits, I and nobody else am the
    greatest traitor,

I went myself first to the headland, my own hands carried me
there.

You villain touch! what are you doing? my breath is tight in its
throat,
Unclench your floodgates, you are too much for me.

29

Blind loving wrestling touch, sheath'd hooded sharp-tooth'd
touch!
Did it make you ache so, leaving me?

Parting track'd by arriving, perpetual payment of perpetual loan,
Rich showering rain, and recompense richer afterward.

Sprouts take and accumulate, stand by the curb prolific and vital,
Landscapes projected masculine, full-sized and golden.

30

All truths wait in all things,
They neither hasten their own delivery nor resist it,
They do not need the obstetric forceps of the surgeon,
The insignificant is as big to me as any,
(What is less or more than a touch?)

Logic and sermons never convince,
The damp of the night drives deeper into my soul.

(Only what proves itself to every man and woman is so,
Only what nobody denies is so.)

A minute and a drop of me settle my brain,
I believe the soggy clods shall become lovers and lamps,
And a compend of compends is the meat of a man or woman,
And a summit and flower there is the feeling they have for each
other,
And they are to branch boundlessly out of that lesson until it
becomes omnific,
And until one and all shall delight us, and we them.

31

I believe a leaf of grass is no less than the journey-work of the stars,
And the pismire is equally perfect, and a grain of sand, and the
egg of the wren,

And the tree-toad is a chef-d'œuvre for the highest,
And the running blackberry would adorn the parlors of heaven,
And the narrowest hinge in my hand puts to scorn all machinery,
And the cow crunching with depress'd head surpasses any statue,
And a mouse is miracle enough to stagger sextillions of infidels.

I find I incorporate gneiss, coal, long-threaded moss, fruits, grains,
    esculent roots,
And am stucco'd with quadrupeds and birds all over,
And have distanced what is behind me for good reasons,
But call any thing back again when I desire it.

In vain the speeding or shyness,
In vain the plutonic rocks send their old heat against my approach,
In vain the mastodon retreats beneath its own powder'd bones,
In vain objects stand leagues off and assume manifold shapes,
In vain the ocean settling in hollows and the great monsters lying
    low,
In vain the buzzard houses herself with the sky,
In vain the snake slides through the creepers and logs,
In vain the elk takes to the inner passes of the woods,
In vain the razor-bill'd auk sails far north to Labrador,
I follow quickly, I ascend to the nest in the fissure of the cliff.

32

I think I could turn and live with animals, they are so placid and
    self-contain'd,
I stand and look at them long and long.

They do not sweat and whine about their condition,
They do not lie awake in the dark and weep for their sins,
They do not make me sick discussing their duty to God,
Not one is dissatisfied, not one is demented with the mania of
    owning things,
Not one kneels to another, nor to his kind that lived thousands of
    years ago,
Not one is respectable or unhappy over the whole earth.

So they show their relations to me and I accept them,
They bring me tokens of myself, they evince them plainly in their
    possession.

I wonder where they get those tokens,
Did I pass that way huge times ago and negligently drop them?

Myself moving forward then and now and forever,
Gathering and showing more always and with velocity,
Infinite and omnigenous, and the like of these among them,
Not too exclusive toward the reachers of my remembrancers,
Picking out here one that I love, and now go with him on brotherly
     terms.

A gigantic beauty of a stallion, fresh and responsive to my caresses,
Head high in the forehead, wide between the ears,
Limbs glossy and supple, tail dusting the ground,
Eyes full of sparkling wickedness, ears finely cut, flexibly moving.

His nostrils dilate as my heels embrace him,
His well-built limbs tremble with pleasure as we race around and
     return.

I but use you a minute, then I resign you, stallion,
Why do I need your paces when I myself out-gallop them?
Even as I stand or sit passing faster than you.

33

Space and Time! now I see it is true, what I guess'd at,
What I guess'd when I loaf'd on the grass,
What I guess'd while I lay alone in my bed,
And again as I walk'd the beach under the paling stars of the
     morning.

My ties and ballasts leave me, my elbows rest in sea-gaps,
I skirt sierras, my palms cover continents,
I am afoot with my vision.

By the city's quadrangular houses — in log huts, camping with
     lumbermen,
Along the ruts of the turnpike, along the dry gulch and rivulet bed,
Weeding my onion-patch or hoeing rows of carrots and parsnips,
     crossing savannas, trailing in forests,
Prospecting, gold-digging, girdling the trees of a new purchase,
Scorch'd ankle-deep by the hot sand, hauling my boat down the
     shallow river,
Where the panther walks to and fro on a limb overhead, where
     the buck turns furiously at the hunter,
Where the rattlesnake suns his flabby length on a rock, where the
     otter is feeding on fish,
Where the alligator in his tough pimples sleeps by the bayou,

Where the black bear is searching for roots or honey, where the
　　beaver pats the mud with his paddle-shaped tail ;
Over the growing sugar, over the yellow-flower'd cotton plant, over
　　the rice in its low moist field,
Over the sharp-peak'd farm house, with its scallop'd scum and
　　slender shoots from the gutters,
Over the western persimmon, over the long-leav'd corn, over the
　　delicate blue-flower flax,
Over the white and brown buckwheat, a hummer and buzzer there
　　with the rest,
Over the dusky green of the rye as it ripples and shades in the
　　breeze ;
Scaling mountains, pulling myself cautiously up, holding on by low
　　scragged limbs,
Walking the path worn in the grass and beat through the leaves of
　　the brush,
Where the quail is whistling betwixt the woods and the wheat-lot,
Where the bat flies in the Seventh-month eve, where the great gold-
　　bug drops through the dark,
Where the brook puts out of the roots of the old tree and flows to
　　the meadow,
Where cattle stand and shake away flies with the tremulous shud-
　　dering of their hides,
Where the cheese-cloth hangs in the kitchen, where andirons
　　straddle the hearth-slab, where cobwebs fall in festoons
　　from the rafters ;
Where trip-hammers crash, where the press is whirling its cylinders,
Wherever the human heart beats with terrible throes under its
　　ribs,
Where the pear-shaped balloon is floating aloft, (floating in it my-
　　self and looking composedly down,)
Where the life-car is drawn on the slip-noose, where the heat
　　hatches pale-green eggs in the dented sand,
Where the she-whale swims with her calf and never forsakes it,
Where the steam-ship trails hind-ways its long pennant of smoke,
Where the fin of the shark cuts like a black chip out of the water,
Where the half-burn'd brig is riding on unknown currents,
Where shells grow to her slimy deck, where the dead are corrupt-
　　ing below ;
Where the dense-starr'd flag is borne at the head of the regiments,
Approaching Manhattan up by the long-stretching island,
Under Niagara, the cataract falling like a veil over my countenance,
Upon a door-step, upon the horse-block of hard wood outside,
Upon the race-course, or enjoying picnics or jigs or a good game
　　of base-ball,

At he-festivals, with blackguard gibes, ironical license, bull-dances,
    drinking, laughter,
At the cider-mill tasting the sweets of the brown mash, sucking
    the juice through a straw,
At apple-peelings wanting kisses for all the red fruit I find,
At musters, beach-parties, friendly bees, huskings, house-raisings ;
Where the mocking-bird sounds his delicious gurgles, cackles,
    screams, weeps,
Where the hay-rick stands in the barn-yard, where the dry-stalks
    are scatter'd, where the brood-cow waits in the hovel,
Where the bull advances to do his masculine work, where the stud
    to the mare, where the cock is treading the hen,
Where the heifers browse, where geese nip their food with short
    jerks,
Where sun-down shadows lengthen over the limitless and lonesome
    prairie,
Where herds of buffalo make a crawling spread of the square
    miles far and near,
Where the humming-bird shimmers, where the neck of the long-
    lived swan is curving and winding,
Where the laughing-gull scoots by the shore, where she laughs her
    near-human laugh,
Where bee-hives range on a gray bench in the garden half hid by
    the high weeds,
Where band-neck'd partridges roost in a ring on the ground with
    their heads out,
Where burial coaches enter the arch'd gates of a cemetery,
Where winter wolves bark amid wastes of snow and icicled trees,
Where the yellow-crown'd heron comes to the edge of the marsh
    at night and feeds upon small crabs,
Where the splash of swimmers and divers cools the warm noon,
Where the katy-did*works her chromatic reed on the walnut-tree
    over the well,
Through patches of citrons and cucumbers with silver-wired leaves,
Through the salt-lick or orange glade, or under conical firs,
Through the gymnasium, through the curtain'd saloon, through the
    office or public hall ;
Pleas'd with the native and pleas'd with the foreign, pleas'd with
    the new and old,
Pleas'd with the homely woman as well as the handsome,
Pleas'd with the quakeress as she puts off her bonnet and talks
    melodiously,
Pleas'd with the tune of the choir of the whitewash'd church,
Pleas'd with the earnest words of the sweating Methodist preach-
    er, impress'd seriously at the camp-meeting ;

Looking in at the shop-windows of Broadway the whole forenoon,
    flatting the flesh of my nose on the thick plate glass,
Wandering the same afternoon with my face turn'd up to the
    clouds, or down a lane or along the beach,
My right and left arms round the sides of two friends, and I in the
    middle ;
Coming home with the silent and dark-cheek'd bush-boy, (behind
    me he rides at the drape of the day,)
Far from the settlements studying the print of animals' feet, or
    the moccasin print,
By the cot in the hospital reaching lemonade to a feverish patient,
Nigh the coffin'd corpse when all is still, examining with a candle ;
Voyaging to every port to dicker and adventure,
Hurrying with the modern crowd as eager and fickle as any,
Hot toward one I hate, ready in my madness to knife him,
Solitary at midnight in my back yard, my thoughts gone from me
    a long while,
Walking the old hills of Judæa with the beautiful gentle God by
    my side,
Speeding through space, speeding through heaven and the stars,
Speeding amid the seven satellites and the broad ring, and the
    diameter of eighty thousand miles,
Speeding with tail'd meteors, throwing fire-balls like the rest,
Carrying the crescent child that carries its own full mother in
    its belly,
Storming, enjoying, planning, loving, cautioning,
Backing and filling, appearing and disappearing,
I tread day and night such roads.

I visit the orchards of spheres and look at the product,
And look at quintillions ripen'd and look at quintillions green.

I fly those flights of a fluid and swallowing soul,
My course runs below the soundings of plummets.

I help myself to material and immaterial,
No guard can shut me off, no law prevent me.

I anchor my ship for a little while only,
My messengers continually cruise away or bring their returns to me.

I go hunting polar furs and the seal, leaping chasms with a pike-
    pointed staff, clinging to topples of brittle and blue.

I ascend to the foretruck,

I take my place late at night in the crow's-nest,
We sail the arctic sea, it is plenty light enough,
Through the clear atmosphere I stretch around on the wonderful
    beauty,
The enormous masses of ice pass me and I pass them, the scenery
    is plain in all directions,
The white-topt mountains show in the distance, I fling out my
    fancies toward them,
We are approaching some great battle-field in which we are soon
    to be engaged,
We pass the colossal outposts of the encampment, we pass with
    still feet and caution,
Or we are entering by the suburbs some vast and ruin'd city,
The blocks and fallen architecture more than all the living cities
    of the globe.

I am a free companion, I bivouac by invading watchfires,
I turn the bridegroom out of bed and stay with the bride myself,
I tighten her all night to my thighs and lips.

My voice is the wife's voice, the screech by the rail of the stairs,
They fetch my man's body up dripping and drown'd.

I understand the large hearts of heroes,
The courage of present times and all times,
How the skipper saw the crowded and rudderless wreck of the
    steam-ship, and Death chasing it up and down the storm,
How he knuckled tight and gave not back an inch, and was faith-
    ful of days and faithful of nights,
And chalk'd in large letters on a board, *Be of good cheer, we will
    not desert you;*
How he follow'd with them and tack'd with them three days and
    would not give it up,
How he saved the drifting company at last,
How the lank loose-gown'd women look'd when boated from the
    side of their prepared graves,
How the silent old-faced infants and the lifted sick, and the sharp-
    lipp'd unshaved men;
All this I swallow, it tastes good, I like it well, it becomes mine,
I am the man, I suffer'd, I was there.

The disdain and calmness of martyrs,
The mother of old, condemn'd for a witch, burnt with dry wood,
    her children gazing on,
The hounded slave that flags in the race, leans by the fence, blow-
    ing, cover'd with sweat,

The twinges that sting like needles his legs and neck, the mur-
    derous buckshot and the bullets,
All these I feel or am.

I am the hounded slave, I wince at the bite of the dogs,
Hell and despair are upon me, crack and again crack the marks-
    men,
I clutch the rails of the fence, my gore dribs, thinn'd with the
    ooze of my skin,
I fall on the weeds and stones,
The riders spur their unwilling horses, haul close,
Taunt my dizzy ears and beat me violently over the head with
    whip-stocks.

Agonies are one of my changes of garments,
I do not ask the wounded person how he feels, I myself become
    the wounded person,
My hurts turn livid upon me as I lean on a cane and observe.

I am the mash'd fireman with breast-bone broken,
Tumbling walls buried me in their debris,
Heat and smoke I inspired, I heard the yelling shouts of my com-
    rades,
I heard the distant click of their picks and shovels,
They have clear'd the beams away, they tenderly lift me forth.

I lie in the night air in my red shirt, the pervading hush is for my
    sake,
Painless after all I lie exhausted but not so unhappy,
White and beautiful are the faces around me, the heads are bared
    of their fire-caps,
The kneeling crowd fades with the light of the torches.

Distant and dead resuscitate,
They show as the dial or move as the hands of me, I am the clock
    myself.

I am an old artillerist, I tell of my fort's bombardment,
I am there again.

Again the long roll of the drummers,
Again the attacking cannon, mortars,
Again to my listening ears the cannon responsive.

I take part, I see and hear the whole,

The cries, curses, roar, the plaudits for well-aim'd shots,
The ambulanza slowly passing trailing its red drip,
Workmen searching after damages, making indispensable repairs,
The fall of grenades through the rent roof, the fan-shaped explosion,
The whizz of limbs, heads, stone, wood, iron, high in the air.

Again gurgles the mouth of my dying general, he furiously waves
    with his hand,
He gasps through the clot *Mind not me — mind — the entrenchments.*

34

Now I tell what I knew in Texas in my early youth,
(I tell not the fall of Alamo,
Not one escaped to tell the fall of Alamo,*
The hundred and fifty are dumb yet at Alamo,)
'Tis the tale of the murder in cold blood of four hundred and
    twelve young men.

Retreating they had form'd in a hollow square with their baggage
    for breastworks,
Nine hundred lives out of the surrounding enemy's, nine times
    their number, was the price they took in advance,
Their colonel was wounded and their ammunition gone,
They treated for an honorable capitulation, receiv'd writing and
    seal, gave up their arms and march'd back prisoners of war.

They were the glory of the race of rangers,
Matchless with horse, rifle, song, supper, courtship,
Large, turbulent, generous, handsome, proud, and affectionate,
Bearded, sunburnt, drest in the free costume of hunters,
Not a single one over thirty years of age.

The second First-day morning* they were brought out in squads
    and massacred, it was beautiful early summer,
The work commenced about five o'clock and was over by eight.

None obey'd the command to kneel,
Some made a mad and helpless rush, some stood stark and
    straight,
A few fell at once, shot in the temple or heart, the living and dead
    lay together,
The maim'd and mangled dug in the dirt, the new-comers saw
    them there,

Some half-kill'd attempted to crawl away,
These were despatch'd with bayonets or batter'd with the blunts
    of muskets,
A youth not seventeen years old seiz'd his assassin till two more
    came to release him,
The three were all torn and cover'd with the boy's blood.

At eleven o'clock began the burning of the bodies;
That is the tale of the murder of the four hundred and twelve
    young men.

35

Would you hear of an old-time sea-fight?*
Would you learn who won by the light of the moon and stars?
List to the yarn, as my grandmother's father the sailor told it to me.

Our foe was no skulk in his ship I tell you, (said he,)
His was the surly English pluck, and there is no tougher or truer,
    and never was, and never will be;
Along the lower'd eve he came horribly raking us.

We closed with him, the yards entangled, the cannon touch'd,
My captain lash'd fast with his own hands.

We had receiv'd some eighteen pound shots under the water,
On our lower-gun-deck two large pieces had burst at the first fire,
    killing all around and blowing up overhead.

Fighting at sun-down, fighting at dark,
Ten o'clock at night, the full moon well up, our leaks on the gain,
    and five feet of water reported,
The master-at-arms loosing the prisoners confined in the after-hold
    to give them a chance for themselves.

The transit to and from the magazine is now stopt by the sentinels,
They see so many strange faces they do not know whom to trust.

Our frigate takes fire,
The other asks if we demand quarter?
If our colors are struck and the fighting done?

Now I laugh content, for I hear the voice of my little captain,
We have not struck, he composedly cries, *we have just begun our
    part of the fighting.*

Only three guns are in use,
One is directed by the captain himself against the enemy's main-
mast,
Two well serv'd with grape and canister silence his musketry and
clear his decks.

The tops alone second the fire of this little battery, especially the
main-top,
They hold out bravely during the whole of the action.

Not a moment's cease,
The leaks gain fast on the pumps, the fire eats toward the powder-
magazine.

One of the pumps has been shot away, it is generally thought we
are sinking.

Serene stands the little captain,
He is not hurried, his voice is neither high nor low,
His eyes give more light to us than our battle-lanterns.

Toward twelve there in the beams of the moon they surrender to
us.

36

Stretch'd and still lies the midnight,
Two great hulls motionless on the breast of the darkness,
Our vessel riddled and slowly sinking, preparations to pass to the
one we have conquer'd,
The captain on the quarter-deck coldly giving his orders through
a countenance white as a sheet,
Near by the corpse of the child that serv'd in the cabin,
The dead face of an old salt with long white hair and carefully
curl'd whiskers,
The flames spite of all that can be done flickering aloft and below,
The husky voices of the two or three officers yet fit for duty,
Formless stacks of bodies and bodies by themselves, dabs of flesh
upon the masts and spars,
Cut of cordage, dangle of rigging, slight shock of the soothe of
waves,
Black and impassive guns, litter of powder-parcels, strong scent,
A few large stars overhead, silent and mournful shining,
Delicate sniffs of sea-breeze, smells of sedgy grass and fields by the
shore, death-messages given in charge to survivors,
The hiss of the surgeon's knife, the gnawing teeth of his saw,

Wheeze, cluck, swash of falling blood, short wild scream, and long, dull, tapering groan,
These so, these irretrievable.

37

You laggards there on guard ! look to your arms !
In at the conquer'd doors they crowd ! I am possess'd !
Embody all presences outlaw'd or suffering,
See myself in prison shaped like another man,
And feel the dull unintermitted pain.

For me the keepers of convicts shoulder their carbines and keep watch,
It is I let out in the morning and barr'd at night.

Not a mutineer walks handcuff'd to jail but I am handcuff'd to him and walk by his side,
(I am less the jolly one there, and more the silent one with sweat on my twitching lips.)

Not a youngster is taken for larceny but I go up too, and am tried and sentenced.

Not a cholera patient lies at the last gasp but I also lie at the last gasp,
My face is ash-color'd, my sinews gnarl, away from me people retreat.

Askers embody themselves in me and I am embodied in them,
I project my hat, sit shame-faced, and beg.

38

Enough ! enough ! enough !
Somehow I have been stunn'd.　Stand back !
Give me a little time beyond my cuff'd head, slumbers, dreams, gaping,
I discover myself on the verge of a usual mistake.

That I could forget the mockers and insults !
That I could forget the trickling tears and the blows of the bludgeons and hammers !
That I could look with a separate look on my own crucifixion and bloody crowning.

I remember now,
I resume the overstaid fraction,
The grave of rock multiplies what has been confided to it, or to
    any graves,
Corpses rise, gashes heal, fastenings roll from me.

I troop forth replenish'd with supreme power, one of an average
    unending procession,
Inland and sea-coast we go, and pass all boundary lines,
Our swift ordinances on their way over the whole earth,
The blossoms we wear in our hats the growth of thousands of
    years.

Eleves, I salute you! come forward!
Continue your annotations, continue your questionings.

39

The friendly and flowing savage, who is he?
Is he waiting for civilization, or past it and mastering it?

Is he some Southwesterner rais'd out-doors? is he Kanadian?
Is he from the Mississippi country? Iowa, Oregon, California?
The mountains? prairie-life, bush-life? or sailor from the sea?

Wherever he goes men and women accept and desire him,
They desire he should like them, touch them, speak to them, stay
    with them.

Behavior lawless as snow-flakes, words simple as grass, uncomb'd
    head, laughter, and naivetè,
Slow-stepping feet, common features, common modes and ema-
    nations,
They descend in new forms from the tips of his fingers,
They are wafted with the odor of his body or breath, they fly out
    of the glance of his eyes.

40

Flaunt of the sunshine I need not your bask — lie over!
You light surfaces only, I force surfaces and depths also.

Earth! you seem to look for something at my hands,
Say, old top-knot, what do you want?

Man or woman, I might tell how I like you, but cannot,

And might tell what it is in me and what it is in you, but cannot,
And might tell that pining I have, that pulse of my nights and
    days.

Behold, I do not give lectures or a little charity,
When I give I give myself.

You there, impotent, loose in the knees,
Open your scarf'd chops till I blow grit within you,
Spread your palms and lift the flaps of your pockets,
I am not to be denied, I compel, I have stores plenty and to spare,
And any thing I have I bestow.

I do not ask who you are, that is not important to me,
You can do nothing and be nothing but what I will infold you.

To cotton-field drudge or cleaner of privies I lean,
On his right cheek I put the family kiss,
And in my soul I swear I never will deny him.

On women fit for conception I start bigger and nimbler babes,
(This day I am jetting the stuff of far more arrogant republics.)

To any one dying, thither I speed and twist the knob of the door,
Turn the bed-clothes toward the foot of the bed,
Let the physician and the priest go home.

I seize the descending man and raise him with resistless will,
O despairer, here is my neck,
By God, you shall not go down! hang your whole weight upon me.

I dilate you with tremendous breath, I buoy you up,
Every room of the house do I fill with an arm'd force,
Lovers of me, bafflers of graves.

Sleep — I and they keep guard all night,
Not doubt, not decease shall dare to lay finger upon you,
I have embraced you, and henceforth possess you to myself,
And when you rise in the morning you will find what I tell you is so.

41

I am he bringing help for the sick as they pant on their backs,
And for strong upright men I bring yet more needed help.

I heard what was said of the universe,
Heard it and heard it of several thousand years;
It is middling well as far as it goes — but is that all?

Magnifying and applying come I,
Outbidding at the start the old cautious hucksters,
Taking myself the exact dimensions of Jehovah,
Lithographing Kronos, Zeus his son, and Hercules his grandson,
Buying drafts of Osiris, Isis, Belus, Brahma, Buddha,
In my portfolio placing Manito loose, Allah on a leaf, the crucifix
    engraved,
With Odin and the hideous-faced Mexitli and every idol and image,
Taking them all for what they are worth and not a cent more,
Admitting they were alive and did the work of their days,
(They bore mites as for unfledg'd birds who have now to rise and
    fly and sing for themselves,)
Accepting the rough deific sketches to fill out better in myself,
    bestowing them freely on each man and woman I see,
Discovering as much or more in a framer framing a house,
Putting higher claims for him there with his roll'd-up sleeves driving
    the mallet and chisel,
Not objecting to special revelations, considering a curl of smoke
    or a hair on the back of my hand just as curious as any
    revelation,
Lads ahold of fire-engines and hook-and-ladder ropes no less to
    me than the gods of the antique wars,
Minding their voices peal through the crash of destruction,
Their brawny limbs passing safe over charr'd laths, their white
    foreheads whole and unhurt out of the flames;
By the mechanic's wife with her babe at her nipple interceding for
    every person born,
Three scythes at harvest whizzing in a row from three lusty angels
    with shirts bagg'd out at their waists,
The snag-tooth'd hostler with red hair redeeming sins past and to
    come,
Selling all he possesses, traveling on foot to fee lawyers for his
    brother and sit by him while he is tried for forgery;
What was strewn in the amplest strewing the square rod about
    me, and not filling the square rod then,
The bull and the bug never worshipp'd half enough,
Dung and dirt more admirable than was dream'd,
The supernatural of no account, myself waiting my time to be one
    of the supremes,
The day getting ready for me when I shall do as much good as
    the best, and be as prodigious;

By my life-lumps ! becoming already a creator,
Putting myself here and now to the ambush'd womb of the shadows.

42

A call in the midst of the crowd,
My own voice, orotund sweeping and final.

Come my children,
Come my boys and girls, my women, household and intimates,
Now the performer launches his nerve, he has pass'd his prelude
    on the reeds within.

Easily written loose-finger'd chords — I feel the thrum of your
    climax and close.

My head slues round on my neck,
Music rolls, but not from the organ,
Folks are around me, but they are no household of mine.

Ever the hard unsunk ground,
Ever the eaters and drinkers, ever the upward and downward sun,
    ever the air and the ceaseless tides,
Ever myself and my neighbors, refreshing, wicked, real,
Ever the old inexplicable query, ever that thorn'd thumb, that
    breath of itches and thirsts,
Ever the vexer's *hoot! hoot!* till we find where the sly one hides
    and bring him forth,
Ever love, ever the sobbing liquid of life,
Ever the bandage under the chin, ever the trestles of death.

Here and there with dimes on the eyes walking,
To feed the greed of the belly the brains liberally spooning,
Tickets buying, taking, selling, but in to the feast never once going,
Many sweating, ploughing, thrashing, and then the chaff for pay-
    ment receiving,
A few idly owning, and they the wheat continually claiming.

This is the city and I am one of the citizens,
Whatever interests the rest interests me, politics, wars, markets,
    newspapers, schools,
The mayor and councils, banks, tariffs, steamships, factories, stocks,
    stores, real estate and personal estate.

The little plentiful manikins skipping around in collars and tail'd
    coats,

I am aware who they are, (they are positively not worms or fleas,)
I acknowledge the duplicates of myself, the weakest and shallowest
    is deathless with me,
What I do and say the same waits for them,
Every thought that flounders in me the same flounders in them.

I know perfectly well my own egotism,
Know my omnivorous lines and must not write any less,
And would fetch you whoever you are flush with myself.

Not words of routine this song of mine,
But abruptly to question, to leap beyond yet nearer bring ;
This printed and bound book — but the printer and the printing-
    office boy ?
The well-taken photographs — but your wife or friend close and
    solid in your arms ?
The black ship mail'd with iron, her mighty guns in her turrets —
    but the pluck of the captain and engineers ?
In the houses the dishes and fare and furniture — but the host and
    hostess, and the look out of their eyes ?
The sky up there — yet here or next door, or across the way ?
The saints and sages in history — but you yourself ?
Sermons, creeds, theology — but the fathomless human brain,
And what is reason ? and what is love ? and what is life ?

43

I do not despise you priests, all time, the world over,
My faith is the greatest of faiths and the least of faiths,
Enclosing worship ancient and modern and all between ancient
    and modern,
Believing I shall come again upon the earth after five thousand
    years,
Waiting responses from oracles, honoring the gods, saluting the
    sun,
Making a fetich* of the first rock or stump, powowing with sticks. in
    the circle of obis,*
Helping the llama or brahmin as he trims the lamps of the idols,
Dancing yet through the streets in a phallic procession, rapt and
    austere in the woods a gymnosophist,*
Drinking mead from the skull-cup,* to Shastas and Vedas admirant,
    minding the Koran,
Walking the teokallis, spotted with gore from the stone and knife,
    beating the serpent-skin drum,
Accepting the Gospels, accepting him that was crucified, knowing
    assuredly that he is divine,

To the mass kneeling or the puritan's prayer rising, or sitting
    patiently in a pew,*
Ranting and frothing in my insane crisis,* or waiting dead-like* till
    my spirit arouses me,
Looking forth on pavement and land, or outside of pavement and
    land,
Belonging to the winders of the circuit of circuits.*

One of that centripetal and centrifugal gang I turn and talk like a
    man leaving charges before a journey.

Down-hearted doubters dull and excluded,
Frivolous, sullen, moping, angry, affected, dishearten'd, atheistical,
I know every one of you, I know the sea of torment, doubt,
    despair and unbelief.

How the flukes splash !
How they contort rapid as lightning, with spasms and spouts of
    blood !

Be at peace bloody flukes* of doubters and sullen mopers,
I take my place among you as much as among any,
The past is the push of you, me, all, precisely the same,
And what is yet untried and afterward is for you, me, all, precisely
    the same.

I do not know what is untried and afterward,
But I know it will in its turn prove sufficient, and cannot fail.

Each who passes is consider'd, each who stops is consider'd, not
    a single one can it fail.

It cannot fail the young man who died and was buried,
Nor the young woman who died and was put by his side,
Nor the little child that peep'd in at the door, and then drew back
    and was never seen again,
Nor the old man who has lived without purpose, and feels it with
    bitterness worse than gall,
Nor him in the poor house tubercled by rum and the bad dis-
    order,*
Nor the numberless slaughter'd and wreck'd, nor the brutish koboo
    call'd the ordure of humanity,
Nor the sacs merely floating with open mouths for food to slip in,
Nor any thing in the earth, or down in the oldest graves of the
    earth,

Nor any thing in the myriads of spheres, nor the myriads of
      myriads that inhabit them,
Nor the present, nor the least wisp that is known.

44

It is time to explain myself — let us stand up.

What is known I strip away,
I launch all men and women forward with me into the Unknown.

The clock indicates the moment — but what does eternity indicate?

We have thus far exhausted trillions of winters and summers,
There are trillions ahead, and trillions ahead of them.

Births have brought us richness and variety,
And other births will bring us richness and variety.

I do not call one greater and one smaller,
That which fills its period and place is equal to any.

Were mankind murderous or jealous upon you, my brother, my
      sister?
I am sorry for you, they are not murderous or jealous upon me,
All has been gentle with me, I keep no account with lamentation,
(What have I to do with lamentation?)

I am an acme of things accomplish'd, and I an encloser of things
      to be.

My feet strike an apex of the apices of the stairs,
On every step bunches of ages, and larger bunches between the
      steps,
All below duly travel'd, and still I mount and mount.

Rise after rise bow the phantoms behind me,
Afar down I see the huge first Nothing, I know I was even there,
I waited unseen and always, and slept through the lethargic mist,
And took my time, and took no hurt from the fetid carbon.

Long I was hugg'd close — long and long.

Immense have been the preparations for me,
Faithful and friendly the arms that have help'd me.

Cycles ferried my cradle, rowing and rowing like cheerful boatmen,
For room to me stars kept aside in their own rings,
They sent influences to look after what was to hold me.

Before I was born out of my mother generations guided me,
My embryo has never been torpid, nothing could overlay it.

For it the nebula cohered to an orb,
The long slow strata piled to rest it on,
Vast vegetables gave it sustenance,
Monstrous sauroids* transported it in their mouths and deposited
    it with care.

All forces have been steadily employ'd to complete and delight me,
Now on this spot I stand with my robust soul.

45

O span of youth ! ever-push'd elasticity !
O manhood, balanced, florid and full.

My lovers suffocate me,
Crowding my lips, thick in the pores of my skin,
Jostling me through streets and public halls, coming naked to me
    at night,
Crying by day *Ahoy!* from the rocks of the river, swinging and
    chirping over my head,
Calling my name from flower-beds, vines, tangled underbrush,
Lighting on every moment of my life,
Bussing my body with soft balsamic busses,
Noiselessly passing handfuls out of their hearts and giving them
    to be mine.

Old age superbly rising ! O welcome, ineffable grace of dying
    days !

Every condition promulges* not only itself, it promulges what grows
    after and out of itself,
And the dark hush promulges as much as any.

I open my scuttle at night and see the far-sprinkled systems,
And all I see multiplied as high as I can cipher edge but the rim
    of the farther systems.

Wider and wider they spread, expanding, always expanding,
Outward and outward and forever outward.

My sun has his sun and round him obediently wheels,
He joins with his partners a group of superior circuit,
And greater sets follow, making specks of the greatest inside them.

There is no stoppage and never can be stoppage,
If I, you, and the worlds, and all beneath or upon their surfaces,
        were this moment reduced back to a pallid float, it would
        not avail in the long run,
We should surely bring up again where we now stand,
And surely go as much farther, and then farther and farther.

A few quadrillions of eras, a few octillions of cubic leagues, do not
        hazard the span or make it impatient,
They are but parts, any thing is but a part.

See ever so far, there is limitless space outside of that,
Count ever so much, there is limitless time around that.

My rendezvous is appointed, it is certain,
The Lord will be there and wait till I come on perfect terms,
The great Camerado, the lover true for whom I pine will be there.

46

I know I have the best of time and space, and was never measured
        and never will be measured.

I tramp a perpetual journey, (come listen all !)
My signs are a rain-proof coat, good shoes, and a staff cut from
        the woods,
No friend of mine takes his ease in my chair,
I have no chair, no church, no philosophy,
I lead no man to a dinner-table, library, exchange,
But each man and each woman of you I lead upon a knoll,
My left hand hooking you round the waist,
My right hand pointing to landscapes of continents and the public
        road.

Not I, not any one else can travel that road for you,
You must travel it for yourself.

It is not far, it is within reach,
Perhaps you have been on it since you were born and did not
        know,
Perhaps it is everywhere on water and on land.

Shoulder your duds dear son, and I will mine, and let us hasten
      forth,
Wonderful cities and free nations we shall fetch as we go.

If you tire, give me both burdens, and rest the chuff*of your hand
      on my hip,
And in due time you shall repay the same service to me,
For after we start we never lie by again.

This day before dawn I ascended a hill and look'd at the crowded
      heaven,
And I said to my spirit *When we become the enfolders of those
      orbs, and the pleasure and knowledge of every thing in
      them, shall we be fill'd and satisfied then?*
And my spirit said *No, we but level that lift to pass and continue
      beyond.*

You are also asking me questions and I hear you,
I answer that I cannot answer, you must find out for yourself.

Sit a while dear son,
Here are biscuits to eat and here is milk to drink,
But as soon as you sleep and renew yourself in sweet clothes, I
      kiss you with a good-by kiss and open the gate for your
      egress hence.

Long enough have you dream'd contemptible dreams,
Now I wash the gum from your eyes,
You must habit yourself to the dazzle of the light and of every
      moment of your life.

Long have you timidly waded holding a plank by the shore,
Now I will you to be a bold swimmer,
To jump off in the midst of the sea, rise again, nod to me, shout,
      and laughingly dash with your hair.

47

I am the teacher of athletes,
He that by me spreads a wider breast than my own proves the
      width of my own,
He most honors my style who learns under it to destroy the
      teacher.

The boy I love, the same becomes a man not through derived
      power, but in his own right,

Wicked rather than virtuous out of conformity or fear,
Fond of his sweetheart, relishing well his steak,
Unrequited love or a slight cutting him worse than sharp steel
    cuts,
First-rate to ride, to fight, to hit the bull's eye, to sail a skiff, to
    sing a song or play on the banjo,
Preferring scars and the beard and faces pitted with small-pox
    over all latherers,
And those well-tann'd to those that keep out of the sun.

I teach straying from me, yet who can stray from me?
I follow you whoever you are from the present hour,
My words itch at your ears till you understand them.

I do not say these things for a dollar or to fill up the time while I
    wait for a boat,
(It is you talking just as much as myself, I act as the tongue of
    you,
Tied in your mouth, in mine it begins to be loosen'd.)

I swear I will never again mention love or death inside a house,
And I swear I will never translate myself at all, only to him or her
    who privately stays with me in the open air.

If you would understand me go to the heights or water-shore,
The nearest gnat is an explanation, and a drop or motion of waves
    a key,
The maul, the oar, the hand-saw, second my words.

No shutter'd room or school can commune with me,
But roughs and little children better than they.

The young mechanic is closest to me, he knows me well,
The woodman that takes his axe and jug with him shall take me
    with him all day,
The farm-boy ploughing in the field feels good at the sound of my
    voice,
In vessels that sail my words sail, I go with fishermen and seamen
    and love them.

The soldier camp'd or upon the march is mine,
On the night ere the pending battle many seek me, and I do not
    fail them,
On that solemn night (it may be their last) those that know me
    seek me.

My face rubs to the hunter's face when he lies down alone in his blanket,
The driver thinking of me does not mind the jolt of his wagon,
The young mother and old mother comprehend me,
The girl and the wife rest the needle a moment and forget where they are,
They and all would resume what I have told them.

48

I have said that the soul is not more than the body,
And I have said that the body is not more than the soul,
And nothing, not God, is greater to one than one's self is,
And whoever walks a furlong without sympathy walks to his own funeral drest in his shroud,
And I or you pocketless of a dime may purchase the pick of the earth,
And to glance with an eye or show a bean in its pod confounds the learning of all times,
And there is no trade or employment but the young man following it may become a hero,
And there is no object so soft but it makes a hub for the wheel'd universe,
And I say to any man or woman, Let your soul stand cool and composed before a million universes.

And I say to mankind, Be not curious about God,
For I who am curious about each am not curious about God,
(No array of terms can say how much I am at peace about God and about death.)

I hear and behold God in every object, yet understand God not in the least,
Nor do I understand who there can be more wonderful than myself.

Why should I wish to see God better than this day?
I see something of God each hour of the twenty-four, and each moment then,
In the faces of men and women I see God, and in my own face in the glass,
I find letters from God dropt in the street, and every one is sign'd by God's name,
And I leave them where they are, for I know that wheresoe'er I go.
Others will punctually come for ever and ever.

49

And as to you Death, and you bitter hug of mortality, it is idle to
    try to alarm me.

To his work without flinching the accoucheur comes,
I see the elder-hand pressing receiving supporting,
I recline by the sills of the exquisite flexible doors,
And mark the outlet, and mark the relief and escape.

And as to you Corpse I think you are good manure, but that does
    not offend me,
I smell the white roses sweet-scented and growing,
I reach to the leafy lips, I reach to the polish'd breasts of melons.

And as to you Life I reckon you are the leavings of many deaths,
(No doubt I have died myself ten thousand times before.)

I hear you whispering there O stars of heaven,
O suns — O grass of graves — O perpetual transfers and pro-
    motions,
If you do not say any thing how can I say any thing?

Of the turbid pool that lies in the autumn forest,
Of the moon that descends the steeps of the soughing twilight,
Toss, sparkles of day and dusk — toss on the black stems that
    decay in the muck,
Toss to the moaning gibberish of the dry limbs.

I ascend from the moon, I ascend from the night,
I perceive that the ghastly glimmer is noonday sunbeams reflected,
And debouch to the steady and central from the offspring great or
    small.

50

There is that in me — I do not know what it is — but I know it is
    in me.

Wrench'd and sweaty — calm and cool then my body becomes,
I sleep — I sleep long.

I do not know it — it is without name — it is a word unsaid,
It is not in any dictionary, utterance, symbol.

Something it swings on more than the earth I swing on,
To it the creation is the friend whose embracing awakes me.

Perhaps I might tell more. Outlines! I plead for my brothers and sisters.

Do you see O my brothers and sisters?
It is not chaos or death — it is form, union, plan — it is eternal life — it is Happiness.

51

The past and present wilt — I have fill'd them, emptied them.
And proceed to fill my next fold of the future.

Listener up there! what have you to confide to me?
Look in my face while I snuff the sidle of evening,
(Talk honestly, no one else hears you, and I stay only a minute longer.)

Do I contradict myself?
Very well then I contradict myself,
(I am large, I contain multitudes.)

I concentrate toward them that are nigh, I wait on the door-slab.

Who has done his day's work? who will soonest be through with his supper?
Who wishes to walk with me?

Will you speak before I am gone? will you prove already too late?

52

The spotted hawk swoops by and accuses me, he complains of my gab and my loitering.

I too am not a bit tamed, I too am untranslatable,
I sound my barbaric yawp over the roofs of the world.

The last scud of day holds back for me,
It flings my likeness after the rest and true as any on the shadow'd wilds,
It coaxes me to the vapor and the dusk.

I depart as air, I shake my white locks at the runaway sun,
I effuse my flesh in eddies, and drift it in lacy jags.

I bequeath myself to the dirt to grow from the grass I love,
If you want me again look for me under your boot-soles.

You will hardly know who I am or what I mean,
But I shall be good health to you nevertheless,
And filter and fibre your blood.

Failing to fetch me at first keep encouraged,
Missing me one place search another,
I stop somewhere waiting for you.

CHILDREN OF ADAM.

TO THE GARDEN THE WORLD

To the garden the world anew ascending,
Potent mates, daughters, sons, preluding,
The love, the life of their bodies, meaning and being,
Curious here behold my resurrection after slumber,
The revolving cycles in their wide sweep having brought me again,
Amorous, mature, all beautiful to me, all wondrous,
My limbs and the quivering fire that ever plays through them, for
    reasons, most wondrous,
Existing I peer and penetrate still,
Content with the present, content with the past,
By my side or back of me Eve following,
Or in front, and I following her just the same.

FROM PENT-UP ACHING RIVERS.

FROM pent-up aching rivers,
From that of myself without which I were nothing,
From what I am determin'd to make illustrious, even if I stand
    sole among men,
From my own voice resonant, singing the phallus,
Singing the song of procreation,
Singing the need of superb children and therein superb grown
    people,
Singing the muscular urge and the blending,
Singing the bedfellow's song, (O resistless yearning !
O for any and each the body correlative attracting !

O for you whoever you are your correlative body ! O it, more than
   all else, you delighting !)
From the hungry gnaw that eats me night and day,
From native moments, from bashful pains, singing them,
Seeking something yet unfound though I have diligently sought it
   many a long year,
Singing the true song of the soul fitful at random,
Renascent with grossest Nature or among animals,
Of that, of them and what goes with them my poems informing,
Of the smell of apples and lemons, of the pairing of birds,
Of the wet of woods, of the lapping of waves,
Of the mad pushes of waves upon the land, I them chanting,
The overture lightly sounding, the strain anticipating,
The welcome nearness, the sight of the perfect body,
The swimmer swimming naked in the bath, or motionless on his
   back lying and floating,
The female form approaching, I pensive, love-flesh tremulous
   aching,
The divine list for myself or you or for any one making,
The face, the limbs, the index from head to foot, and what it
   arouses,
The mystic deliria, the madness amorous, the utter abandonment,
(Hark close and still what I now whisper to you,
I love you, O you entirely possess me,
O that you and I escape from the rest and go utterly off, free and
   lawless,
Two hawks in the air, two fishes swimming in the sea not more
   lawless than we ;)
The furious storm through me careering, I passionately trembling.
The oath of the inseparableness of two together, of the woman
   that loves me and whom I love more than my life, that oath
   swearing,
(O I willingly stake all for you,
O let me be lost if it must be so !
O you and I ! what is it to us what the rest do or think?
What is all else to us? only that we enjoy each other and exhaust
   each other if it must be so ;)
From the master, the pilot I yield the vessel to,
The general commanding me, commanding all, from him permis-
   sion taking,
From time the programme hastening, (I have loiter'd too long as
   it is.)
From sex, from the warp and from the woof,
From privacy, from frequent repinings alone,
From plenty of persons near and yet the right person not near,

From the soft sliding of hands over me and thrusting of fingers
     through my hair and beard,
From the long sustain'd kiss upon the mouth or bosom,
From the close pressure that makes me or any man drunk, fainting
     with excess,
From what the divine husband knows, from the work of fatherhood,
From exultation, victory and relief, from the bedfellow's embrace
     in the night,
From the act-poems of eyes, hands, hips and bosoms,
From the cling of the trembling arm,
From the bending curve and the clinch,
From side by side the pliant coverlet off-throwing,
From the one so unwilling to have me leave, and me just as un-
     willing to leave,
(Yet a moment O tender waiter, and I return,)
From the hour of shining stars and dropping dews,
From the night a moment I emerging flitting out,
Celebrate you act divine and you children prepared for,
And you stalwart loins.

I SING THE BODY ELECTRIC.

1

I sing the body electric,
The armies of those I love engirth me and I engirth them,
They will not let me off till I go with them, respond to them,
And discorrupt them, and charge them full with the charge of the
     soul.

Was it doubted that those who corrupt their own bodies conceal
     themselves?
And if those who defile the living are as bad as they who defile
     the dead?
And if the body does not do fully as much as the soul?
And if the body were not the soul, what is the soul?

2

The love of the body of man or woman balks account, the body
     itself balks account,
That of the male is perfect, and that of the female is perfect.

The expression of the face balks account,
But the expression of a well-made man appears not only in his
     face,

It is in his limbs and joints also, it is curiously in the joints of his
    hips and wrists,
It is in his walk, the carriage of his neck, the flex of his waist and
    knees, dress does not hide him,
The strong sweet quality he has strikes through the cotton and
    broadcloth,
To see him pass conveys as much as the best poem, perhaps more,
You linger to see his back, and the back of his neck and shoul-
    der-side.

The sprawl and fulness of babes, the bosoms and heads of women,
    the folds of their dress, their style as we pass in the street,
    the contour of their shape downwards,
The swimmer naked in the swimming-bath, seen as he swims
    through the transparent green-shine, or lies with his face
    up and rolls silently to and fro in the heave of the water,
The bending forward and backward of rowers in row-boats, the
    horseman in his saddle,
Girls, mothers, house-keepers, in all their performances,
The group of laborers seated at noon-time with their open dinner-
    kettles, and their wives waiting,
The female soothing a child, the farmer's daughter in the garden
    or cow-yard,
The young fellow hoeing corn, the sleigh-driver driving his six
    horses through the crowd,
The wrestle of wrestlers, two apprentice-boys, quite grown, lusty,
    good-natured, native-born, out on the vacant lot at sun-
    down after work,
The coats and caps thrown down, the embrace of love and resistance,
The upper-hold and under-hold, the hair rumpled over and blind-
    ing the eyes ;
The march of firemen in their own costumes, the play of mascu-
    line muscle through clean-setting trowsers and waist-straps,
The slow return from the fire, the pause when the bell strikes
    suddenly again, and the listening on the alert,
The natural, perfect, varied attitudes, the bent head, the curv'd
    neck and the counting ;
Such-like I love — I loosen myself, pass freely, am at the mother's
    breast with the little child,
Swim with the swimmers, wrestle with wrestlers, march in line with
    the firemen, and pause, listen, count.

3

I knew a man, a common farmer, the father of five sons,
And in them the fathers of sons, and in them the fathers of sons.

This man was of wonderful vigor, calmness, beauty of person,

The shape of his head, the pale yellow and white of his hair and
          beard, the immeasurable meaning of his black eyes, the
          richness and breadth of his manners,

These I used to go and visit him to see, he was wise also,

He was six feet tall, he was over eighty years old, his sons were
          massive, clean, bearded, tan-faced, handsome,

They and his daughters loved him, all who saw him loved him,

They did not love him by allowance, they loved him with personal
          love,

He drank water only, the blood show'd like scarlet through the
          clear-brown skin of his face,

He was a frequent gunner and fisher, he sail'd his boat himself,
          he had a fine one presented to him by a ship-joiner, he
          had fowling-pieces presented to him by men that loved
          him,

When he went with his five sons and many grand-sons to hunt or
          fish, you would pick him out as the most beautiful and
          vigorous of the gang,

You would wish long and long to be with him, you would wish to
          sit by him in the boat that you and he might touch each
          other.

4

I have perceiv'd that to be with those I like is enough,

To stop in company with the rest at evening is enough,

To be surrounded by beautiful, curious, breathing, laughing flesh
          is enough,

To pass among them or touch any one, or rest my arm ever so
          lightly round his or her neck for a moment, what is this
          then?

I do not ask any more delight, I swim in it as in a sea.

There is something in staying close to men and women and look-
          ing on them, and in the contact and odor of them, that
          pleases the soul well,

All things please the soul, but these please the soul well.

5

This is the female form,

A divine nimbus exhales from it from head to foot,

It attracts with fierce undeniable attraction,

I am drawn by its breath as if I were no more than a helpless
          vapor, all falls aside but myself and it,

Books, art, religion, time, the visible and solid earth, and what was
          expected of heaven or fear'd of hell, are now consumed,

Mad filaments, ungovernable shoots play out of it, the response
    likewise ungovernable,
Hair, bosom, hips, bend of legs, negligent falling hands all dif
    fused, mine too diffused,
Ebb stung by the flow and flow stung by the ebb, love-flesh swell-
    ing and deliciously aching,
Limitless limpid jets of love hot and enormous, quivering jelly of
    love, white-blow and delirious juice,
Bridegroom night of love working surely and softly into the pros-
    trate dawn,
Undulating into the willing and yielding day,
Lost in the cleave of the clasping and sweet-flesh'd day.

This the nucleus — after the child is born of woman, man is born
    of woman,
This the bath of birth, this the merge of small and large, and the
    outlet again.

Be not ashamed women, your privilege encloses the rest, and is the
    exit of the rest,
You are the gates of the body, and you are the gates of the soul.

The female contains all qualities and tempers them,
She is in her place and moves with perfect balance,
She is all things duly veil'd, she is both passive and active,
She is to conceive daughters as well as sons, and sons as well as
    daughters.

As I see my soul reflected in Nature,
As I see through a mist, One with inexpressible completeness,
    sanity, beauty,
See the bent head and arms folded over the breast, the Female
    I see.

6

The male is not less the soul nor more, he too is in his place,
He too is all qualities, he is action and power,
The flush of the known universe is in him,
Scorn becomes him well, and appetite and defiance become him
    well,
The wildest largest passions, bliss that is utmost, sorrow that is
    utmost become him well, pride is for him,
The full-spread pride of man is calming and excellent to the soul,
Knowledge becomes him, he likes it always, he brings every thing
    to the test of himself,

Whatever the survey, whatever the sea and the sail he strikes
    soundings at last only here,
(Where else does he strike soundings except here?)

The man's body is sacred and the woman's body is sacred,
No matter who it is, it is sacred — is it the meanest one in the
    laborers' gang?
Is it one of the dull-faced immigrants just landed on the wharf?
Each belongs here or anywhere just as much as the well-off, just
    as much as you,
Each has his or her place in the procession.

(All is a procession,
The universe is a procession with measured and perfect motion.)

Do you know so much yourself that you call the meanest ignorant?
Do you suppose you have a right to a good sight, and he or she
    has no right to a sight?
Do you think matter has cohered together from its diffuse float,
    and the soil is on the surface, and water runs and vegeta-
    tion sprouts,
For you only, and not for him and her?

7

A man's body at auction,
(For before the war I often go to the slave-mart and watch the
    sale,)
I help the auctioneer, the sloven does not half know his business.

Gentlemen look on this wonder,
Whatever the bids of the bidders they cannot be high enough for it,
For it the globe lay preparing quintillions of years without one
    animal or plant,
For it the revolving cycles truly and steadily roll'd.

In this head the all-baffling brain,
In it and below it the makings of heroes.

Examine these limbs, red, black, or white, they are cunning in
    tendon and nerve,
They shall be stript that you may see them.

Exquisite senses, life-lit eyes, pluck, volition,
Flakes of breast-muscle, pliant backbone and neck, flesh not
    flabby, good-sized arms and legs,
And wonders within there yet.

Within there runs blood,
The same old blood! the same red-running blood!
There swells and jets a heart, there all passions, desires, reachings,
    aspirations,
(Do you think they are not there because they are not express'd in
    parlors and lecture-rooms?)

This is not only one man, this the father of those who shall be
    fathers in their turns,
In him the start of populous states and rich republics,
Of him countless immortal lives with countless embodiments and
    enjoyments.

How do you know who shall come from the offspring of his off-
    spring through the centuries?
(Who might you find you have come from yourself, if you could
    trace back through the centuries?)

8

A woman's body at auction,
She too is not only herself, she is the teeming mother of mothers,
She is the bearer of them that shall grow and be mates to the
    mothers.

Have you ever loved the body of a woman?
Have you ever loved the body of a man?
Do you not see that these are exactly the same to all in all nations
    and times all over the earth?

If any thing is sacred the human body is sacred,
And the glory and sweet of a man is the token of manhood
    untainted,
And in man or woman a clean, strong, firm-fibred body, is more
    beautiful than the most beautiful face.

Have you seen the fool that corrupted his own live body? or the
    fool that corrupted her own live body?
For they do not conceal themselves, and cannot conceal themselves.

9

O my body! I dare not desert the likes of you in other men and
    women, nor the likes of the parts of you,
I believe the likes of you are to stand or fall with the likes of the
    soul, (and that they are the soul,)

I believe the likes of you shall stand or fall with my poems, and
    that they are my poems,
Man's, woman's, child's, youth's, wife's, husband's, mother's, father's,
    young man's, young woman's poems,
Head, neck, hair, ears, drop and tympan of the ears,
Eyes, eye-fringes, iris of the eye, eyebrows, and the waking or
    sleeping of the lids,
Mouth, tongue, lips, teeth, roof of the mouth, jaws, and the jaw-
    hinges,
Nose, nostrils of the nose, and the partition,
Cheeks, temples, forehead, chin, throat, back of the neck, neck-
    slue,
Strong shoulders, manly beard, scapula, hind-shoulders, and the
    ample side-round of the chest,
Upper-arm, armpit, elbow-socket, lower-arm, arm-sinews, arm-
    bones,
Wrist and wrist-joints, hand, palm, knuckles, thumb, forefinger,
    finger-joints, finger-nails,
Broad breast-front, curling hair of the breast, breast-bone, breast-
    side,
Ribs, belly, backbone, joints of the backbone,
Hips, hip-sockets, hip-strength, inward and outward round, man-
    balls, man-root,
Strong set of thighs, well carrying the trunk above,
Leg-fibres, knee, knee-pan, upper-leg, under-leg,
Ankles, instep, foot-ball, toes, toe-joints, the heel ;
All attitudes, all the shapeliness, all the belongings of my or your
    body or of any one's body, male or female,
The lung-sponges, the stomach-sac, the bowels sweet and clean,
The brain in its folds inside the skull-frame,
Sympathies, heart-valves, palate-valves, sexuality, maternity,
Womanhood, and all that is a woman, and the man that comes
    from woman,
The womb, the teats, nipples, breast-milk, tears, laughter, weeping,
    love-looks, love-perturbations and risings,
The voice, articulation, language, whispering, shouting aloud,
Food, drink, pulse, digestion, sweat, sleep, walking, swimming,
Poise on the hips, leaping, reclining, embracing, arm-curving and
    tightening,
The continual changes of the flex of the mouth, and around the
    eyes,
The skin, the sunburnt shade, freckles, hair,
The curious sympathy one feels when feeling with the hand the
    naked meat of the body,
The circling rivers the breath, and breathing it in and out,

The beauty of the waist, and thence of the hips, and thence down-
ward toward the knees,
The thin red jellies within you or within me, the bones and the
marrow in the bones,
The exquisite realization of health;
O I say these are not the parts and poems of the body only, but
of the soul,
O I say now these are the soul!

A WOMAN WAITS FOR ME.

A WOMAN waits for me, she contains all, nothing is lacking,
Yet all were lacking if sex were lacking, or if the moisture of the
right man were lacking.

Sex contains all, bodies, souls,
Meanings, proofs, purities, delicacies, results, promulgations,
Songs, commands, health, pride, the maternal mystery, the seminal
milk,
All hopes, benefactions, bestowals, all the passions, loves, beauties,
delights of the earth,
All the governments, judges, gods, follow'd persons of the earth,
These are contain'd in sex as parts of itself and justifications of
itself.

Without shame the man I like knows and avows the deliciousness
of his sex,
Without shame the woman I like knows and avows hers.

Now I will dismiss myself from impassive women,
I will go stay with her who waits for me, and with those women
that are warm-blooded and sufficient for me,
I see that they understand me and do not deny me,
I see that they are worthy of me, I will be the robust husband
of those women.

They are not one jot less than I am,
They are tann'd in the face by shining suns and blowing winds,
Their flesh has the old divine suppleness and strength,
They know how to swim, row, ride, wrestle, shoot, run, strike,
retreat, advance, resist, defend themselves,
They are ultimate in their own right — they are calm, clear, well-
possess'd of themselves.

I draw you close to me, you women,
I cannot let you go, I would do you good,
I am for you, and you are for me, not only for our own sake, but
    for others' sakes,
Envelop'd in you sleep greater heroes and bards,
They refuse to awake at the touch of any man but me.

It is I, you women, I make my way,
I am stern, acrid, large, undissuadable, but I love you,
I do not hurt you any more than is necessary for you,
I pour the stuff to start sons and daughters fit for these States, I
    press with slow rude muscle,
I brace myself effectually, I listen to no entreaties,
I dare not withdraw till I deposit what has so long accumulated
    within me.

Through you I drain the pent-up rivers of myself,
In you I wrap a thousand onward years,
On you I graft the grafts of the best-beloved of me and America,
The drops I distil upon you shall grow fierce and athletic girls,
    new artists, musicians, and singers,
The babes I beget upon you are to beget babes in their turn,
I shall demand perfect men and women out of my love-spendings,
I shall expect them to interpenetrate with others, as I and you
    interpenetrate now,
I shall count on the fruits of the gushing showers of them, as I
    count on the fruits of the gushing showers I give now,
I shall look for loving crops from the birth, life, death, immortality,
    I plant so lovingly now.

SPONTANEOUS ME.

SPONTANEOUS me, Nature,
The loving day, the mounting sun, the friend I am happy with,
The arm of my friend hanging idly over my shoulder,
The hillside whiten'd with blossoms of the mountain ash,
The same late in autumn, the hues of red, yellow, drab, purple,
    and light and dark green,
The rich coverlet of the grass, animals and birds, the private
    untrimm'd bank, the primitive apples, the pebble-stones,
Beautiful dripping fragments, the negligent list of one after an-
    other as I happen to call them to me or think of them,
The real poems, (what we call poems being merely pictures,)
The poems of the privacy of the night, and of men like me,

This poem drooping shy and unseen that I always carry, and that
     all men carry,
(Know once for all, avow'd on purpose, wherever are men like
     me, are our lusty lurking masculine poems,)
Love-thoughts, love-juice, love-odor, love-yielding, love-climbers,
     and the climbing sap,
Arms and hands of love, lips of love, phallic thumb of love, breasts
     of love, bellies press'd and glued together with love,
Earth of chaste love, life that is only life after love,
The body of my love, the body of the woman I love, the body
     of the man, the body of the earth,
Soft forenoon airs that blow from the south-west,
The hairy wild-bee that murmurs and hankers up and down, that
     gripes the full-grown lady-flower, curves upon her with
     amorous firm legs, takes his will of her, and holds himself
     tremulous and tight till he is satisfied ;
The wet of woods through the early hours,
Two sleepers at night lying close together as they sleep, one with an
     arm slanting down across and below the waist of the other,
The smell of apples, aromas from crush'd sage-plant, mint, birch-
     bark,
The boy's longings, the glow and pressure as he confides to me
     what he was dreaming,
The dead leaf whirling its spiral whirl and falling still and content
     to the ground,
The no-form'd stings that sights, people, objects, sting me with,
The hubb'd sting of myself, stinging me as much as it ever can
     any one,
The sensitive, orbic, underlapp'd brothers, that only privileged
     feelers may be intimate where they are,
The curious roamer the hand roaming all over the body, the
     bashful withdrawing of flesh where the fingers soothingly
     pause and edge themselves,
The limpid liquid within the young man,
The vex'd corrosion so pensive and so painful,
The torment, the irritable tide that will not be at rest,
The like of the same I feel, the like of the same in others,
The young man that flushes and flushes, and the young woman
     that flushes and flushes,
The young man that wakes deep at night, the hot hand seeking to
     repress what would master him,
The mystic amorous night, the strange half-welcome pangs, visions,
     sweats,
The pulse pounding through palms and trembling encircling
     fingers, the young man all color'd, red, ashamed, angry ;

The souse upon me of my lover the sea, as I lie willing and naked,
The merriment of the twin babes that crawl over the grass in the
      sun, the mother never turning her vigilant eyes from them,
The walnut-trunk, the walnut-husks, and the ripening or ripen'd
      long-round walnuts,
The continence of vegetables, birds, animals,
The consequent meanness of me should I skulk or find myself
      indecent, while birds and animals never once skulk or
      find themselves indecent,
The great chastity of paternity, to match the great chastity of
      maternity,
The oath of procreation I have sworn, my Adamic and fresh
      daughters,
The greed that eats me day and night with hungry gnaw, till I
      saturate what shall produce boys to fill my place when I
      am through,
The wholesome relief, repose, content,
And this bunch pluck'd at random from myself,
It has done its work — I toss it carelessly to fall where it may.

ONE HOUR TO MADNESS AND JOY.

ONE hour to madness and joy! O furious! O confine me not!
(What is this that frees me so in storms?
What do my shouts amid lightnings and raging winds mean?)

O to drink the mystic deliria deeper than any other man!
O savage and tender achings! (I bequeath them to you my
      children,
I tell them to you, for reasons, O bridegroom and bride.)

O to be yielded to you whoever you are, and you to be yielded to
      me in defiance of the world!
O to return to Paradise! O bashful and feminine!
O to draw you to me, to plant on you for the first time the lips of
      a determin'd man.

O the puzzle, the thrice-tied knot, the deep and dark pool, all
      untied and illumin'd!
O to speed where there is space enough and air enough at last!
To be absolv'd from previous ties and conventions, I from mine
      and you from yours!
To find a new unthought-of nonchalance with the best of Nature!

To have the gag remov'd from one's mouth !
To have the feeling to-day or any day I am sufficient as I am.

O something unprov'd ! something in a trance !
To escape utterly from others' anchors and holds !
To drive free ! to love free ! to dash reckless and dangerous !
To court destruction with taunts, with invitations !
To ascend, to leap to the heavens of the love indicated to me !
To rise thither with my inebriate soul !
To be lost if it must be so !
To feed the remainder of life with one hour of fulness and freedom !
With one brief hour of madness and joy.

OUT OF THE ROLLING OCEAN THE CROWD.

OUT of the rolling ocean the crowd came a drop gently to me,
Whispering *I love you, before long I die,*
I have travel'd a long way merely to look on you to touch you,
For I could not die till I once look'd on you,
For I fear'd I might afterward lose you.

Now we have met, we have look'd, we are safe,
Return in peace to the ocean my love,
I too am part of that ocean my love, we are not so much separated,
Behold the great rondure, the cohesion of all, how perfect !
But as for me, for you, the irresistible sea is to separate us,
As for an hour carrying us diverse, yet cannot carry us diverse forever ;
Be not impatient — a little space — know you I salute the air, the ocean and the land,
Every day at sundown for your dear sake my love.

AGES AND AGES RETURNING AT INTERVALS.

AGES and ages returning at intervals,
Undestroy'd, wandering immortal,
Lusty, phallic, with the potent original loins, perfectly sweet,
I, chanter of Adamic songs,
Through the new garden the West, the great cities calling,
Deliriate, thus prelude what is generated, offering these, offering myself,
Bathing myself, bathing my songs in Sex,
Offspring of my loins.

WE TWO, HOW LONG WE WERE FOOL'D.

WE two, how long we were fool'd,*
Now transmuted, we swiftly escape as Nature escapes,
We are Nature, long have we been absent, but now we return,
We become plants, trunks, foliage, roots, bark,
We are bedded in the ground, we are rocks,
We are oaks, we grow in the openings side by side,
We browse, we are two among the wild herds spontaneous as
any,
We are two fishes swimming in the sea together,
We are what locust blossoms are, we drop scent around lanes
mornings and evenings,
We are also the coarse smut of beasts, vegetables, minerals,
We are two predatory hawks, we soar above and look down,
We are two resplendent suns, we it is who balance ourselves orbic
and stellar, we are as two comets,
We prowl fang'd and four-footed in the woods, we spring on
prey,
We are two clouds forenoons and afternoons driving overhead,
We are seas mingling, we are two of those cheerful waves rolling
over each other and interwetting each other,
We are what the atmosphere is, transparent, receptive, pervious,
impervious,
We are snow, rain, cold, darkness, we are each product and
influence of the globe,
We have circled and circled till we have arrived home again, we
two,
We have voided all but freedom and all but our own joy.

O HYMEN! O HYMENEE!

O HYMEN! O hymenee! why do you tantalize me thus?
O why sting me for a swift moment only?
Why can you not continue? O why do you now cease?
Is it because if you continued beyond the swift moment you
would soon certainly kill me?

I AM HE THAT ACHES WITH LOVE.

I AM he that aches with amorous love;
Does the earth gravitate? does not all matter, aching, attract all
matter?
So the body of me to all I meet or know.

NATIVE MOMENTS.

NATIVE moments — when you come upon me — ah you are here now,
Give me now libidinous joys only,
Give me the drench of my passions, give me life coarse and rank,
To-day I go consort with Nature's darlings, to-night too,
I am for those who believe in loose delights, I share the midnight orgies of young men,
I dance with the dancers and drink with the drinkers,
The echoes ring with our indecent calls, I pick out some low person for my dearest friend,
He shall be lawless, rude, illiterate, he shall be one condemn'd by others for deeds done,
I will play a part no longer, why should I exile myself from my companions?
O you shunn'd persons, I at least do not shun you,
I come forthwith in your midst, I will be your poet,
I will be more to you than to any of the rest.

ONCE I PASS'D THROUGH A POPULOUS CITY.

ONCE I pass'd through a populous city imprinting my brain for future use with its shows, architecture, customs, traditions,
Yet now of all that city I remember only a woman I casually met there who detain'd me for love of me,
Day by day and night by night we were together — all else has long been forgotten by me,
I remember I say only that woman who passionately clung to me,
Again we wander, we love, we separate again,
Again she holds me by the hand, I must not go,
I see her close beside me with silent lips sad and tremulous.

I HEARD YOU SOLEMN-SWEET PIPES OF THE ORGAN.

I HEARD you solemn-sweet pipes of the organ as last Sunday morn I pass'd the church,
Winds of autumn, as I walk'd the woods at dusk I heard your long-stretch'd sighs up above so mournful,
I heard the perfect Italian tenor singing at the opera, I heard the soprano in the midst of the quartet singing;
Heart of my love! you too I heard murmuring low through one of the wrists around my head,
Heard the pulse of you when all was still ringing little bells last night under my ear.

FACING WEST FROM CALIFORNIA'S SHORES.

FACING west from California's shores,
Inquiring, tireless, seeking what is yet unfound,
I, a child, very old, over waves, towards the house of maternity,
      the land of migrations, look afar,
Look off the shores of my Western sea, the circle almost circled ;
For starting westward from Hindustan, from the vales of Kash-
      mere,
From Asia, from the north, from the God, the sage, and the
      hero,
From the south, from the flowery peninsulas and the spice islands,
Long having wander'd since, round the earth having wander'd,
Now I face home again, very pleas'd and joyous,
(But where is what I started for so long ago?
And why is it yet unfound?)

AS ADAM EARLY IN THE MORNING.

As Adam early in the morning,
Walking forth from the bower refresh'd with sleep,
Behold me where I pass, hear my voice, approach,
Touch me, touch the palm of your hand to my body as I pass,
Be not afraid of my body.

CALAMUS.

IN PATHS UNTRODDEN.

IN paths untrodden,
In the growth by margins of pond-waters,
Escaped from the life that exhibits itself,
From all the standards hitherto publish'd, from the pleasures,
      profits, conformities,
Which too long I was offering to feed my soul,
Clear to me now standards not yet publish'd, clear to me that my
      soul,
That the soul of the man I speak for rejoices in comrades,
Here by myself away from the clank of the world,
Tallying and talk'd to here by tongues aromatic,

No longer abash'd, (for in this secluded spot I can respond as I
　　　would not dare elsewhere,)
Strong upon me the life that does not exhibit itself, yet contains
　　　all the rest,
Resolv'd to sing no songs to-day but those of manly attachment,
Projecting them along that substantial life,
Bequeathing hence types of athletic love,
Afternoon this delicious Ninth-month in my forty-first year,
I proceed for all who are or have been young men,
To tell the secret of my nights and days,
To celebrate the need of comrades.

SCENTED HERBAGE OF MY BREAST.

SCENTED herbage of my breast,
Leaves from you I glean, I write, to be perused best afterwards,
Tomb-leaves, body-leaves growing up above me above death,
Perennial roots, tall leaves, O the winter shall not freeze you
　　　delicate leaves,
Every year shall you bloom again, out from where you retired you
　　　shall emerge again ;
O I do not know whether many passing by will discover you or
　　　inhale your faint odor, but I believe a few will ;
O slender leaves ! O blossoms of my blood ! I permit you to tell
　　　in your own way of the heart that is under you,
O I do not know what you mean there underneath yourselves, you
　　　are not happiness,
You are often more bitter than I can bear, you burn and sting me,
Yet you are beautiful to me you faint tinged roots, you make me
　　　think of death,
Death is beautiful from you, (what indeed is finally beautiful except
　　　death and love ?)
O I think it is not for life I am chanting here my chant of lovers,
　　　I think it must be for death,
For how calm, how solemn it grows to ascend to the atmosphere
　　　of lovers,
Death or life I am then indifferent, my soul declines to prefer,
(I am not sure but the high soul of lovers welcomes death most,)
Indeed O death, I think now these leaves mean precisely the same
　　　as you mean,
Grow up taller sweet leaves that I may see ! grow up out of my
　　　breast !
Spring away from the conceal'd heart there !
Do not fold yourself so in your pink-tinged roots timid leaves !

Do not remain down there so ashamed, herbage of my breast!
Come I am determin'd to unbare this broad breast of mine, I
    have long enough stifled and choked;
Emblematic and capricious blades I leave you, now you serve me
    not,
I will say what I have to say by itself,
I will sound myself and comrades only, I will never again utter a
    call only their call,
I will raise with it immortal reverberations through the States,
I will give an example to lovers to take permanent shape and
    will through the States,
Through me shall the words be said to make death exhilarating,
Give me your tone therefore O death, that I may accord with it,
Give me yourself, for I see that you belong to me now above all,
    and are folded inseparably together, you love and death are,
Nor will I allow you to balk me any more with what I was calling life,
For now it is convey'd to me that you are the purports essential,
That you hide in these shifting forms of life, for reasons, and that
    they are mainly for you,
That you beyond them come forth to remain, the real reality,
That behind the mask of materials you patiently wait, no matter
    how long,
That you will one day perhaps take control of all,
That you will perhaps dissipate this entire show of appearance,
That may-be you are what it is all for, but it does not last so very
    long,
But you will last very long.

WHOEVER YOU ARE HOLDING ME NOW IN HAND.

WHOEVER you are holding me now in hand,
Without one thing all will be useless,
I give you fair warning before you attempt me further,
I am not what you supposed, but far different.

Who is he that would become my follower?
Who would sign himself a candidate for my affections?

The way is suspicious, the result uncertain, perhaps destructive,
You would have to give up all else, I alone would expect to be
    your sole and exclusive standard,
Your novitiate would even then be long and exhausting,
The whole past theory of your life and all conformity to the lives
    around you would have to be abandon'd,

Therefore release me now before troubling yourself any further, let
　　go your hand from my shoulders,
Put me down and depart on your way.

Or else by stealth in some wood for trial,
Or back of a rock in the open air,
(For in any roof'd room of a house I emerge not, nor in com-
　　pany,
And in libraries I lie as one dumb, a gawk, or unborn, or dead,)
But just possibly with you on a high hill, first watching lest any
　　person for miles around approach unawares,
Or possibly with you sailing at sea, or on the beach of the sea or
　　some quiet island,
Here to put your lips upon mine I permit you,
With the comrade's long-dwelling kiss or the new husband's kiss.
For I am the new husband and I am the comrade.

Or if you will, thrusting me beneath your clothing,
Where I may feel the throbs of your heart or rest upon your
　　hip,
Carry me when you go forth over land or sea ;
For thus merely touching you is enough, is best,
And thus touching you would I silently sleep and be carried
　　eternally.

But these leaves conning you con at peril,
For these leaves and me you will not understand,
They will elude you at first and still more afterward, I will
　　certainly elude you,
Even while you should think you had unquestionably caught me,
　　behold !
Already you see I have escaped from you.

For it is not for what I have put into it that I have written this
　　book,
Nor is it by reading it you will acquire it,
Nor do those know me best who admire me and vauntingly praise
　　me,
Nor will the candidates for my love (unless at most a very few)
　　prove victorious,
Nor will my poems do good only, they will do just as much evil,
　　perhaps more,
For all is useless without that which you may guess at many times
　　and not hit, that which I hinted at ;
Therefore release me and depart on your way.

FOR YOU O DEMOCRACY.

COME, I will make the continent indissoluble,
I will make the most splendid race the sun ever shone upon,
I will make divine magnetic lands,
   With the love of comrades,
   With the life-long love of comrades.

I will plant companionship thick as trees along all the rivers of
   America, and along the shores of the great lakes, and all
   over the prairies,
I will make inseparable cities with their arms about each other's
   necks,
   By the love of comrades,
   By the manly love of comrades.

For you these from me, O Democracy, to serve you ma femme!
For you, for you I am trilling these songs.

THESE I SINGING IN SPRING.

THESE I singing in spring collect for lovers,
(For who but I should understand lovers and all their sorrow and
   joy?
And who but I should be the poet of comrades?)
Collecting I traverse the garden the world, but soon I pass the
   gates,
Now along the pond-side, now wading in a little, fearing not the
   wet,
Now by the post-and-rail fences where the old stones thrown there,
   pick'd from the fields, have accumulated,
(Wild-flowers and vines and weeds come up through the stones
   and partly cover them, beyond these I pass,)
Far, far in the forest, or sauntering later in summer, before I think
   where I go,
Solitary, smelling the earthy smell, stopping now and then in the
   silence,
Alone I had thought, yet soon a troop gathers around me,
Some walk by my side and some behind, and some embrace my
   arms or neck,
They the spirits of dear friends dead or alive, thicker they come,
   a great crowd, and I in the middle,
Collecting, dispensing, singing, there I wander with them,
Plucking something for tokens, tossing toward whoever is near me,
Here, lilac, with a branch of pine,

Here, out of my pocket, some moss which I pull'd off a live-oak
      in Florida as it hung trailing down,
Here, some pinks and laurel leaves, and a handful of sage,
And here what I now draw from the water, wading in the pond-
      side,
(O here I last saw him that tenderly loves me, and returns again
      never to separate from me,
And this, O this shall henceforth be the token of comrades, this
      calamus-root shall,
Interchange it youths with each other! let none render it back!)
And twigs of maple and a bunch of wild orange and chestnut,
And stems of currants and plum-blows, and the aromatic cedar,
These I compass'd around by a thick cloud of spirits,
Wandering, point to or touch as I pass, or throw them loosely
      from me,
Indicating to each one what he shall have, giving something to
      each;
But what I drew from the water by the pond-side, that I reserve,
I will give of it, but only to them that love as I myself am capable
      of loving.

NOT HEAVING FROM MY RIBB'D BREAST ONLY.

NOT heaving from my ribb'd breast only,
Not in sighs at night in rage dissatisfied with myself,
Not in those long-drawn, ill-supprest sighs,
Not in many an oath and promise broken,
Not in my wilful and savage soul's volition,
Not in the subtle nourishment of the air,
Not in this beating and pounding at my temples and wrists,
Not in the curious systole and diastole within which will one day
      cease,
Not in many a hungry wish told to the skies only,
Not in cries, laughter, defiances, thrown from me when alone far
      in the wilds,
Not in husky pantings through clinch'd teeth,
Not in sounded and resounded words, chattering words, echoes,
      dead words,
Not in the murmurs of my dreams while I sleep,
Nor the other murmurs of these incredible dreams of every day,
Nor in the limbs and senses of my body that take you and dismiss
      you continually — not there,
Not in any or all of them O adhesiveness! O pulse of my life!
Need I that ·· ·xist and show yourself any more than in these
      song

OF THE TERRIBLE DOUBT OF APPEARANCES.

Of the terrible doubt of appearances,
Of the uncertainty after all, that we may be deluded,
That may-be reliance and hope are but speculations after all,
That may-be identity beyond the grave is a beautiful fable only,
May-be the things I perceive, the animals, plants, men, hills,
         shining and flowing waters,
The skies of day and night, colors, densities, forms, may-be these
         are (as doubtless they are) only apparitions, and the real
         something has yet to be known,
(How often they dart out of themselves as if to confound me and
         mock me !
How often I think neither I know, nor any man knows, aught of
         them,)
May-be seeming to me what they are (as doubtless they indeed
         but seem) as from my present point of view, and might
         prove (as of course they would) nought of what they
         appear, or nought anyhow, from entirely changed points
         of view ;
To me these and the like of these are curiously answer'd by my
         lovers, my dear friends,
When he whom I love travels with me or sits a long while holding
         me by the hand,
When the subtle air, the impalpable, the sense that words and
         reason hold not, surround us and pervade us,
Then I am charged with untold and untellable wisdom, I am
         silent, I require nothing further,
I cannot answer the question of appearances or that of identity
         beyond the grave,
But I walk or sit indifferent, I am satisfied,
He ahold of my hand has completely satisfied me.

THE BASE OF ALL METAPHYSICS.

And now gentlemen,
A word I give to remain in your memories and minds,
As base and finalè too for all metaphysics.

(So to the students the old professor,
At the close of his crowded course.)

Having studied the new and antique, the Greek and Germanic
         systems,
Kant having studied and stated, Fichte and Schelling and Hegel,

Stated the lore of Plato, and Socrates greater than Plato,
And greater than Socrates sought and stated, Christ divine having
    studied long,
I see reminiscent to-day those Greek and Germanic systems,
See the philosophies all, Christian churches and tenets see,
Yet underneath Socrates clearly see, and underneath Christ the
    divine I see,
The dear love of man for his comrade, the attraction of friend to
    friend,
Of the well-married husband and wife, of children and parents,
Of city for city and land for land.

RECORDERS AGES HENCE.

RECORDERS ages hence,
Come, I will take you down underneath this impassive exterior, I
    will tell you what to say of me,
Publish my name and hang up my picture as that of the tenderest
    lover,
The friend the lover's portrait, of whom his friend his lover was
    fondest,
Who was not proud of his songs, but of the measureless ocean of
    love within him, and freely pour'd it forth,
Who often walk'd lonesome walks thinking of his dear friends, his
    lovers,
Who pensive away from one he lov'd often lay sleepless and dissat-
    isfied at night,
Who knew too well the sick, sick dread lest the one he lov'd
    might secretly be indifferent to him,
Whose happiest days were far away through fields, in woods, on
    hills, he and another wandering hand in hand, they twain
    apart from other men,
Who oft as he saunter'd the streets curv'd with his arm the shoul-
    der of his friend, while the arm of his friend rested upon
    him also.

WHEN I HEARD AT THE CLOSE OF THE DAY.

WHEN I heard at the close of the day how my name had been
    receiv'd with plaudits in the capitol, still it was not a happy
    night for me that follow'd,
And else when I carous'd, or when my plans were accomplish'd,
    still I was not happy,

But the day when I rose at dawn from the bed of perfect health,
    refresh'd, singing, inhaling the ripe breath of autumn,
When I saw the full moon in the west grow pale and disappear in
    the morning light,
When I wander'd alone over the beach, and undressing bathed,
    laughing with the cool waters, and saw the sun rise,
And when I thought how my dear friend my lover was on his way
    coming, O then I was happy,
O then each breath tasted sweeter, and all that day my food
    nourish'd me more, and the beautiful day pass'd well,
And the next came with equal joy, and with the next at evening
    came my friend,
And that night while all was still I heard the waters roll slowly
    continually up the shores,
I heard the hissing rustle of the liquid and sands as directed to
    me whispering to congratulate me,
For the one I love most lay sleeping by me under the same cover
    in the cool night,
In the stillness in the autumn moonbeams his face was inclined
    toward me,
And his arm lay lightly around my breast—and that night I was
    happy.

ARE YOU THE NEW PERSON DRAWN TOWARD ME?

ARE you the new person drawn toward me?
To begin with take warning, I am surely far different from what
    you suppose;
Do you suppose you will find in me your ideal?
Do you think it so easy to have me become your lover?
Do you think the friendship of me would be unalloy'd satisfaction?
Do you think I am trusty and faithful?
Do you see no further than this façade, this smooth and tolerant
    manner of me?
Do you suppose yourself advancing on real ground toward a real
    heroic man?
Have you no thought O dreamer that it may be all maya, illusion?

ROOTS AND LEAVES THEMSELVES ALONE.

ROOTS and leaves themselves alone are these,
Scents brought to men and women from the wild woods and
    pond-side,

Breast-sorrel and pinks of love, fingers that wind around tighter
    than vines,
Gushes from the throats of birds hid in the foliage of trees as the
    sun is risen,
Breezes of land and love set from living shores to you on the living
    sea, to you O sailors !
Frost-mellow'd berries and Third-month twigs offer'd fresh to
    young persons wandering out in the fields when the winter
    breaks up,
Love-buds put before you and within you whoever you are,
Buds to be unfolded on the old terms,
If you bring the warmth of the sun to them they will open and
    bring form, color, perfume, to you,
If you become the aliment and the wet they will become flowers,
    fruits, tall branches and trees.

NOT HEAT FLAMES UP AND CONSUMES.

NOT heat flames up and consumes,
Not sea-waves hurry in and out,
Not the air delicious and dry, the air of ripe summer, bears lightly
    along white down-balls of myriads of seeds,
Wafted, sailing gracefully, to drop where they may ;
Not these, O none of these more than the flames of me, consum-
    ing, burning for his love whom I love,
O none more than I hurrying in and out ;
Does the tide hurry, seeking something, and never give up? O I
    the same,
O nor down-balls nor perfumes, nor the high rain-emitting clouds,
    are borne through the open air,
Any more than my soul is borne through the open air,
Wafted in all directions O love, for friendship, for you.

TRICKLE DROPS.

TRICKLE drops ! my blue veins leaving !
O drops of me ! trickle, slow drops,
Candid from me falling, drip, bleeding drops,
From wounds made to free you whence you were prison'd,
From my face, from my forehead and lips,
From my breast, from within where I was conceal'd, press forth
    red drops, confession drops,
Stain every page, stain every song I sing, every word I say, bloody
    drops,

Let them know your scarlet heat, let them glisten,
Saturate them with yourself all ashamed and wet,
Glow upon all I have written or shall write, bleeding drops,
Let it all be seen in your light, blushing drops.

CITY OF ORGIES.

CITY of orgies, walks and joys,
City whom that I have lived and sung in your midst will one day
    make you illustrious,
Not the pageants of you, not your shifting tableaus, your specta-
    cles, repay me,
Not the interminable rows of your houses, nor the ships at the
    wharves,
Nor the processions in the streets, nor the bright windows with
    goods in them,
Nor to converse with learn'd persons, or bear my share in the soiree
    or feast ;
Not those, but as I pass O Manhattan, your frequent and swift
    flash of eyes offering me love,
Offering response to my own — these repay me,
Lovers, continual lovers, only repay me.

BEHOLD THIS SWARTHY FACE.

BEHOLD this swarthy face, these gray eyes,
This beard, the white wool unclipt upon my neck,
My brown hands and the silent manner of me without charm ;
Yet comes one a Manhattanese and ever at parting kisses me
    lightly on the lips with robust love,
And I on the crossing of the street or on the ship's deck give a
    kiss in return,
We observe that salute of American comrades land and sea,
We are those two natural and nonchalant persons.

I SAW IN LOUISIANA A LIVE-OAK GROWING.

I SAW in Louisiana a live-oak growing,
All alone stood it and the moss hung down from the branches,
Without any companion it grew there uttering joyous leaves of
    dark green,
And its look, rude, unbending, lusty, made me think of myself,
But I wonder'd how it could utter joyous leaves standing alone
    there without its friend near, for I knew I could not,

And I broke off a twig with a certain number of leaves upon it,
    and twined around it a little moss,
And brought it away, and I have placed it in sight in my room,
It is not needed to remind me as of my own dear friends,
(For I believe lately I think of little else than of them,)
Yet it remains to me a curious token, it makes me think of manly
    love ;
For all that, and though the live-oak glistens there in Louisiana
    solitary in a wide flat space,
Uttering joyous leaves all its life without a friend a lover near,
I know very well I could not.

TO A STRANGER.

PASSING stranger ! you do not know how longingly I look upon
    you,
You must be he I was seeking, or she I was seeking, (it comes to
    me as of a dream,)
I have somewhere surely lived a life of joy with you,
All is recall'd as we flit by each other, fluid, affectionate, chaste,
    matured,
You grew up with me, were a boy with me or a girl with me,
I ate with you and slept with you, your body has become not yours
    only nor left my body mine only,
You give me the pleasure of your eyes, face, flesh, as we pass, you
    take of my beard, breast, hands, in return,
I am not to speak to you, I am to think of you when I sit alone
    or wake at night alone,
I am to wait, I do not doubt I am to meet you again,
I am to see to it that I do not lose you.

THIS MOMENT YEARNING AND THOUGHTFUL.

THIS moment yearning and thoughtful sitting alone,
It seems to me there are other men in other lands yearning and
    thoughtful,
It seems to me I can look over and behold them in Germany,
    Italy, France, Spain,
Or far, far away, in China, or in Russia or Japan, talking other
    dialects,
And it seems to me if I could know those men I should become
    attached to them as I do to men in my own lands,
O I know we should be brethren and lovers,
I know I should be happy with them.

I HEAR IT WAS CHARGED AGAINST ME.

I HEAR it was charged against me that I sought to destroy institutions,
But really I am neither for nor against institutions,
(What indeed have I in common with them? or what with the destruction of them?)
Only I will establish in the Mannahatta and in every city of these States inland and seaboard,
And in the fields and woods, and above every keel little or large that dents the water,
Without edifices or rules or trustees or any argument,
The institution of the dear love of comrades.

THE PRAIRIE-GRASS DIVIDING.

THE prairie-grass dividing, its special odor breathing,
I demand of it the spiritual corresponding,
Demand the most copious and close companionship of men,
Demand the blades to rise of words, acts, beings,
Those of the open atmosphere, coarse, sunlit, fresh, nutritious,
Those that go their own gait, erect, stepping with freedom and command, leading not following,
Those with a never-quell'd audacity, those with sweet and lusty flesh clear of taint,
Those that look carelessly in the faces of Presidents and governors, as to say *Who are you?*
Those of earth-born passion, simple, never constrain'd, never obedient,
Those of inland America.

WHEN I PERUSE THE CONQUER'D FAME.

WHEN I peruse the conquer'd fame of heroes and the victories of mighty generals, I do not envy the generals,
Nor the President in his Presidency, nor the rich in his great house,
But when I hear of the brotherhood of lovers, how it was with them,
How together through life, through dangers, odium, unchanging, long and long,
Through youth and through middle and old age, how unfaltering, how affectionate and faithful they were,
Then I am pensive — I hastily walk away fill'd with the bitterest envy.

WE TWO BOYS TOGETHER CLINGING.

WE two boys together clinging,
One the other never leaving,
Up and down the roads going, North and South excursions
    making,
Power enjoying, elbows stretching, fingers clutching,
Arm'd and fearless, eating, drinking, sleeping, loving,
No law less than ourselves owning, sailing, soldiering, thieving,
    threatening,
Misers, menials, priests alarming, air breathing, water drinking, on
    the turf or the sea-beach dancing,
Cities wrenching, ease scorning, statutes mocking, feebleness chas-
    ing,
Fulfilling our foray.

A PROMISE TO CALIFORNIA.

A ´PROMISE to California,
Or inland to the great pastoral Plains, and on to Puget sound and
    Oregon ;
Sojourning east a while longer, soon I travel toward you, to remain,
    to teach robust American love,
For I know very well that I and robust love belong among you,
    inland, and along the Western sea ;
For these States tend inland and toward the Western sea, and I
    will also.

HERE THE FRAILEST LEAVES OF ME.

HERE the frailest leaves of me and yet my strongest lasting,
Here I shade and hide my thoughts, I myself do not expose them,
And yet they expose me more than all my other poems.

NO LABOR-SAVING MACHINE.

No labor-saving machine,
Nor discovery have I made,
Nor will I be able to leave behind me any wealthy bequest to
    found a hospital or library,
Nor reminiscence of any deed of courage for America,
Nor literary success nor intellect, nor book for the book-shelf,
But a few carols vibrating through the air I leave,
For comrades and lovers.

A GLIMPSE.

A GLIMPSE through an interstice caught,
Of a crowd of workmen and drivers in a bar-room around the
      stove late of a winter night, and I unremark'd seated in a
      corner,
Of a youth who loves me and whom I love, silently approaching
      and seating himself near, that he may hold me by the hand,
A long while amid the noises of coming and going, of drinking
      and oath and smutty jest,
There we two, content, happy in being together, speaking little,
      perhaps not a word.

A LEAF FOR HAND IN HAND.

A LEAF for hand in hand;
You natural persons old and young!
You on the Mississippi and on all the branches and bayous of the
      Mississippi!
You friendly boatmen and mechanics! you roughs!
You twain! and all processions moving along the streets!
I wish to infuse myself among you till I see it common for you to
      walk hand in hand.

EARTH, MY LIKENESS.

EARTH, my likeness,
Though you look so impassive, ample and spheric there,
I now suspect that is not all;
I now suspect there is something fierce in you eligible to burst forth,
For an athlete is enamour'd of me, and I of him,
But toward him there is something fierce and terrible in me eligi-
      ble to burst forth,
I dare not tell it in words, not even in these songs.

I DREAM'D IN A DREAM.

I DREAM'D in a dream I saw a city invincible to the attacks of the
      whole of the rest of the earth,
I dream'd that was the new city of Friends,
Nothing was greater there than the quality of robust love, it led
      the rest,
It was seen every hour in the actions of the men of that city,
And in all their looks and words.

WHAT THINK YOU I TAKE MY PEN IN HAND?

WHAT think you I take my pen in hand to record?
The battle-ship, perfect-model'd, majestic, that I saw pass the
　　offing to-day under full sail?
The splendors of the past day? or the splendor of the night that
　　envelops me?
Or the vaunted glory and growth of the great city spread around
　　me?—no;
But merely of two simple men I saw to-day on the pier in the
　　midst of the crowd, parting the parting of dear friends,
The one to remain hung on the other's neck and passionately
　　kiss'd him,
While the one to depart tightly prest the one to remain in his
　　arms.

TO THE EAST AND TO THE WEST.

To the East and to the West,
To the man of the Seaside State and of Pennsylvania,
To the Kanadian of the north, to the Southerner I love,
These with perfect trust to depict you as myself, the germs are in
　　all men,
I believe the main purport of these States is to found a superb
　　friendship, exaltè, previously unknown,
Because I perceive it waits, and has been always waiting, latent in
　　all men.

SOMETIMES WITH ONE I LOVE.

SOMETIMES with one I love I fill myself with rage for fear I effuse
　　unreturn'd love,
But now I think there is no unreturn'd love, the pay is certain one
　　way or another,
(I loved a certain person ardently and my love was not return'd,
Yet out of that I have written these songs.)

TO A WESTERN BOY.

MANY things to absorb I teach to help you become eleve of mine;
Yet if blood like mine circle not in your veins,
If you be not silently selected by lovers and do not silently select
　　lovers,
Of what use is it that you seek to become eleve of mine?

FAST ANCHOR'D ETERNAL O LOVE!

FAST-ANCHOR'D eternal O love! O woman I love!
O bride! O wife! more resistless than I can tell, the thought of
    you!
Then separate, as disembodied or another born,
Ethereal, the last athletic reality, my consolation,
I ascend, I float in the regions of your love O man,
O sharer of my roving life.

AMONG THE MULTITUDE.

AMONG the men and women the multitude,
I perceive one picking me out by secret and divine signs,
Acknowledging none else, not parent, wife, husband, brother,
    child, any nearer than I am,
Some are baffled, but that one is not — that one knows me.

Ah lover and perfect equal,
I meant that you should discover me so by faint indirections,
And I when I meet you mean to discover you by the like in you.

O YOU WHOM I OFTEN AND SILENTLY COME.

O YOU whom I often and silently come where you are that I may
    be with you,
As I walk by your side or sit near, or remain in the same room
    with you,
Little you know the subtle electric fire that for your sake is play-
    ing within me.

THAT SHADOW MY LIKENESS.

THAT shadow my likeness that goes to and fro seeking a liveli-
    hood, chattering, chaffering,
How often I find myself standing and looking at it where it
    flits,
How often I question and doubt whether that is really me;
But among my lovers and caroling these songs,
O I never doubt whether that is really me.

FULL OF LIFE NOW.

FULL of life now, compact, visible,
I, forty years old the eighty-third year of the States,

To one a century hence or any number of centuries hence,
To you yet unborn these, seeking you.

When you read these I that was visible am become invisible,
Now it is you, compact, visible, realizing my poems, seeking me,
Fancying how happy you were if I could be with you and become
　　　your comrade ;
Be it as if I were with you.　(Be not too certain but I am now
　　　with you.)

SALUT AU MONDE!

1

O TAKE my hand Walt Whitman !
Such gliding wonders ! such sights and sounds !
Such join'd unended links, each hook'd to the next,
Each answering all, each sharing the earth with all.

What widens within you Walt Whitman?
What waves and soils exuding?
What climes? what persons and cities are here?
Who are the infants, some playing, some slumbering?
Who are the girls? who are the married women?
Who are the groups of old men going slowly with their arms about
　　　each other's necks?
What rivers are these? what forests and fruits are these?
What are the mountains call'd that rise so high in the mists?
What myriads of dwellings are they fill'd with dwellers?

2

Within me latitude widens, longitude lengthens,
Asia, Africa, Europe, are to the east — America is provided for in
　　　the west,
Banding the bulge of the earth winds the hot equator,
Curiously north and south turn the axis-ends,
Within me is the longest day, the sun wheels in slanting rings, it
　　　does not set for months,
Stretch'd in due time within me the midnight sun just rises above
　　　the horizon and sinks again,
Within me zones, seas, cataracts, forests, volcanoes, groups,
Malaysia, Polynesia, and the great West Indian islands.

3

What do you hear Walt Whitman?

I hear the workman singing and the farmer's wife singing,
I hear in the distance the sounds of children and of animals early
    in the day,
I hear emulous shouts of Australians pursuing the wild horse,
I hear the Spanish dance with castanets in the chestnut shade, to
    the rebeck and guitar,
I hear continual echoes from the Thames,
I hear fierce French liberty songs,
I hear of the Italian boat-sculler the musical recitative of old
    poems,
I hear the locusts in Syria as they strike the grain and grass with
    the showers of their terrible clouds,
I hear the Coptic refrain toward sundown, pensively falling on the
    breast of the black venerable vast mother the Nile,
I hear the chirp of the Mexican muleteer, and the bells of the
    mule,
I hear the Arab muezzin calling from the top of the mosque,
I hear the Christian priests at the altars of their churches, I hear
    the responsive base and soprano,
I hear the cry of the Cossack, and the sailor's voice putting to sea
    at Okotsk,
I hear the wheeze of the slave-coffle as the slaves march on, as
    the husky gangs pass on by twos and threes, fasten'd together
    with wrist-chains and ankle-chains,
I hear the Hebrew reading his records and psalms,
I hear the rhythmic myths of the Greeks, and the strong legends
    of the Romans,
I hear the tale of the divine life and bloody death of the beautiful
    God the Christ,
I hear the Hindoo teaching his favorite pupil the loves, wars,
    adages, transmitted safely to this day from poets who wrote
    three thousand years ago.

4

What do you see Walt Whitman?
Who are they you salute, and that one after another salute you?

I see a great round wonder rolling through space,
I see diminute farms, hamlets, ruins, graveyards, jails, factories,
    palaces, hovels, huts of barbarians, tents of nomads upon
    the surface,

I see the shaded part on one side where the sleepers are sleeping, and the sunlit part on the other side,
I see the curious rapid change of the light and shade,
I see distant lands, as real and near to the inhabitants of them as my land is to me.

I see plenteous waters,
I see mountain peaks, I see the sierras of Andes where they range,
I see plainly the Himalayas, Chian Shahs, Altays, Ghauts,
I see the giant pinnacles of Elbruz, Kazbek, Bazardjusi,*
I see the Styrian Alps, and the Karnac* Alps,
I see the Pyrenees, Balks, Carpathians, and to the north the Dofrafields, and off at sea mount Hecla,
I see Vesuvius and Etna, the mountains of the Moon, and the Red mountains of Madagascar,
I see the Lybian, Arabian, and Asiatic deserts,
I see huge dreadful Arctic and Antarctic icebergs,
I see the superior oceans and the inferior ones, the Atlantic and Pacific, the sea of Mexico, the Brazilian sea, and the sea of Peru,
The waters of Hindustan, the China sea, and the gulf of Guinea,
The Japan waters, the beautiful bay of Nagasaki land-lock'd in its mountains,
The spread of the Baltic, Caspian, Bothnia, the British shores, and the bay of Biscay,
The clear-sunn'd Mediterranean, and from one to another of its islands,
The White sea, and the sea around Greenland.

I behold the mariners of the world,
Some are in storms, some in the night with the watch on the look-out,
Some drifting helplessly, some with contagious diseases.

I behold the sail and steamships of the world, some in clusters in port, some on their voyages,
Some double the cape of Storms,* some cape Verde, others capes Guardafui, Bon, or Bajadore,
Others Dondra head, others pass the straits of Sunda, others cape Lopatka, others Behring's straits,
Others cape Horn, others sail the gulf of Mexico or along Cuba or Hayti, others Hudson's bay or Baffin's bay,
Others pass the straits of Dover, others enter the Wash, others the firth of Solway, others round cape Clear, others the Land's End,

Others traverse the Zuyder Zee or the Scheld,
Others as comers and goers at Gibraltar or the Dardanelles,
Others sternly push their way through the northern winter-packs,
Others descend or ascend the Obi or the Lena,
Others the Niger or the Congo, others the Indus, the Burampooter
    and Cambodia,
Others wait steam'd up ready to start in the ports of Australia,
Wait at Liverpool, Glasgow, Dublin, Marseilles, Lisbon, Naples,
       Hamburg, Bremen, Bordeaux, the Hague, Copenhagen,
Wait at Valparaiso, Rio Janeiro, Panama.

5

I see the tracks of the railroads of the earth,
I see them in Great Britain, I see them in Europe,
I see them in Asia and in Africa.

I see the electric telegraphs of the earth,
I see the filaments of the news of the wars, deaths, losses, gains,
      passions, of my race.

I see the long river-stripes of the earth,
I see the Amazon and the Paraguay,
I see the four great rivers of China, the Amour, the Yellow River,
      the Yiang-tse, and the Pearl,
I see where the Seine flows, and where the Danube, the Loire, the
      Rhone, and the Guadalquiver flow,
I see the windings of the Volga, the Dnieper, the Oder,
I see the Tuscan going down the Arno, and the Venetian along
      the Po,
I see the Greek seaman sailing out of Egina bay.

6

I see the site of the old empire of Assyria, and that of Persia, and
      that of India,
I see the falling of the Ganges over the high rim of Saukara.

I see the place of the idea of the Deity incarnated by avatars in
      human forms,
I see the spots of the successions of priests on the earth, oracles,
      sacrificers, brahmins, sabians, llamas, monks, muftis, ex-
      horters,
I see where druids walk'd the groves of Mona, I see the mistletoe
      and vervain,
I see the temples of the deaths of the bodies of Gods, I see the
      old signifiers.

I see Christ eating the bread of his last supper in the midst of youths and old persons,

I see where the strong divine young man the Hercules toil'd faithfully and long and then died,

I see the place of the innocent rich life and hapless fate of the beautiful nocturnal son, the full-limb'd Bacchus,

I see Kneph, blooming, drest in blue, with the crown of feathers on his head,

I see Hermes, unsuspected, dying, well-belov'd, saying to the people *Do not weep for me,*

This is not my true country, I have lived banish'd from my true country, I now go back there,

I return to the celestial sphere where every one goes in his turn.

7

I see the battle-fields of the earth, grass grows upon them and blossoms and corn,

I see the tracks of ancient and modern expeditions.

I see the nameless masonries, venerable messages of the unknown events, heroes, records of the earth.

I see the places of the sagas,

I see pine-trees and fir-trees torn by northern blasts,

I see granite bowlders and cliffs, I see green meadows and lakes,

I see the burial-cairns of Scandinavian warriors,

I see them raised high with stones by the marge of restless oceans, that the dead men's spirits when they wearied of their quiet graves might rise up through the mounds and gaze on the tossing billows, and be refresh'd by storms, immensity, liberty, action.

I see the steppes of Asia,

I see the tumuli of Mongolia, I see the tents of Kalmucks and Baskirs,

I see the nomadic tribes with herds of oxen and cows,

I see the table-lands notch'd with ravines, I see the jungles and deserts,

I see the camel, the wild steed, the bustard, the fat-tail'd sheep, the antelope, and the burrowing wolf.

I see the highlands of Abyssinia,

I see flocks of goats feeding, and see the fig-tree, tamarind, date, And see fields of teff-wheat and places of verdure and gold.

I see the Brazilian vaquero,
I see the Bolivian ascending mount Sorata,
I see the Wacho crossing the plains, I see the incomparable rider
    of horses with his lasso on his arm,
I see over the pampas the pursuit of wild cattle for their hides.

8

I see the regions of snow and ice,
I see the sharp-eyed Samoiede and the Finn,
I see the seal-seeker in his boat poising his lance,
I see the Siberian on his slight-built sledge drawn by dogs,
I see the porpoise-hunters, I see the whale-crews of the south Pa-
    cific and the north Atlantic,
I see the cliffs, glaciers, torrents, valleys, of Switzerland — I mark
    the long winters and the isolation.

I see the cities of the earth and make myself at random a part of
    them,
I am a real Parisian,
I am a habitan of Vienna, St. Petersburg, Berlin, Constantinople,
I am of Adelaide, Sidney, Melbourne,
I am of London, Manchester, Bristol, Edinburgh, Limerick,
I am of Madrid, Cadiz, Barcelona, Oporto, Lyons, Brussels, Berne,
    Frankfort, Stuttgart, Turin, Florence,
I belong in Moscow, Cracow, Warsaw, or northward in Christiania
    or Stockholm, or in Siberian Irkutsk, or in some street in
    Iceland,
I descend upon all those cities, and rise from them again.

10

I see vapors exhaling from unexplored countries,
I see the savage types, the bow and arrow, the poison'd splint, the
    fetich, and the obi.

I see African and Asiatic towns,
I see Algiers, Tripoli, Derne, Mogadore, Timbuctoo, Monrovia,
I see the swarms of Pekin, Canton, Benares, Delhi, Calcutta, Tokio,
I see the Kruman in his hut, and the Dahoman and Ashantee-man
    in their huts,
I see the Turk smoking opium in Aleppo,
I see the picturesque crowds at the fairs of Khiva and those of
    Herat,
I see Teheran, I see Muscat and Medina and the intervening sands,
    I see the caravans toiling onward,

I see Egypt and the Egyptians, I see the pyramids and obelisks,
I look on chisell'd histories, records of conquering kings, dynasties,
    cut in slabs of sand-stone, or on granite-blocks,
I see at Memphis mummy-pits containing mummies embalm'd,
    swathed in linen cloth, lying there many centuries,
I look on the fall'n Theban, the large-ball'd eyes, the side-drooping
    neck, the hands folded across the breast.

I see all the menials of the earth, laboring,
I see all the prisoners in the prisons,
I see the defective human bodies of the earth,
The blind, the deaf and dumb, idiots, hunchbacks, lunatics,
The pirates, thieves, betrayers, murderers, slave-makers of the earth,
The helpless infants, and the helpless old men and women.

I see male and female everywhere,
I see the serene brotherhood of philosophs,
I see the constructiveness of my race,
I see the results of the perseverance and industry of my race,
I see ranks, colors, barbarisms, civilizations, I go among them, I
    mix indiscriminately,
And I salute all the inhabitants of the earth.

11

You whoever you are !
You daughter or son of England !
You of the mighty Slavic tribes and empires ! you Russ in Russia !
You dim-descended, black, divine-soul'd African, large, fine-
    headed, nobly-form'd, superbly destin'd, on equal terms
    with me !
You Norwegian ! Swede ! Dane ! Icelander ! you Prussian !
You Spaniard of Spain ! you Portuguese !
You Frenchwoman and Frenchman of France !
You Belge ! you liberty-lover of the Netherlands ! (you stock
    whence I myself have descended ;)
You sturdy Austrian ! you Lombard ! Hun ! Bohemian ! farmer of
    Styria !
You neighbor of the Danube !
You working-man of the Rhine, the Elbe, or the Weser ! you,
    working-woman too !
You Sardinian ! you Bavarian ! Swabian ! Saxon ! Wallachian !
    Bulgarian !
You Roman ! Neapolitan ! you Greek !
You lithe matador in the arena at Seville !
You mountaineer living lawlessly on the Taurus or Caucasus !

You Bokh horse-herd watching your mares and stallions feeding!
You beautiful-bodied Persian at full speed in the saddle shooting
    arrows to the mark!
You Chinaman and Chinawoman of China! you Tartar of Tartary!
You women of the earth subordinated at your tasks!
You Jew journeying in your old age through every risk to stand
    once on Syrian ground!
You other Jews waiting in all lands for your Messiah!
You thoughtful Armenian pondering by some stream of the Eu-
    phrates! you peering amid the ruins of Nineveh! you
    ascending mount Ararat!
You foot-worn pilgrim welcoming the far-away sparkle of the
    minarets of Mecca!
You sheiks along the stretch from Suez to Bab-el-mandeb ruling
    your families and tribes!
You olive-grower tending your fruit on fields of Nazareth, Damas-
    cus, or lake Tiberias!
You Thibet trader on the wide inland or bargaining in the shops
    of Lassa!
You Japanese man or woman! you liver in Madagascar, Ceylon,
    Sumatra, Borneo!
All you continentals of Asia, Africa, Europe, Australia, indifferent
    of place!
All you on the numberless islands of the archipelagoes of the sea!
And you of centuries hence when you listen to me!
And you each and everywhere whom I specify not, but include
    just the same!
Health to you! good will to you all, from me and America sent!

Each of us inevitable,
Each of us limitless — each of us with his or her right upon the
    earth,
Each of us allow'd the eternal purports of the earth,
Each of us here as divinely as any is here.

12

You Hottentot with clicking palate! you woolly-hair'd hordes!
You own'd persons dropping sweat-drops or blood-drops!
You human forms with the fathomless ever-impressive counte-
    nances of brutes!
You poor koboo whom the meanest of the rest look down upon
    for all your glimmering language and spirituality!
You dwarf'd Kamtschatkan, Greenlander, Lapp!
You Austral negro, naked, red, sooty, with protrusive lip, groveling,
    seeking your food!

You Caffre, Berber, Soudanese !
You haggard, uncouth, untutor'd Bedowee !
You plague-swarms in Madras, Nankin, Kaubul, Cairo !
You benighted roamer of Amazonia ! you Patagonian ! you Feejee-
    man !
I do not prefer others so very much before you either,
I do not say one word against you, away back there where you
    stand,
(You will come forward in due time to my side.)

13

My spirit has pass'd in compassion and determination around the
    whole earth,
I have look'd for equals and lovers and found them ready for me
    in all lands,
I think some divine rapport has equalized me with them.

You vapors, I think I have risen with you, moved away to distant
    continents, and fallen down there, for reasons,
I think I have blown with you you winds ;
You waters I have finger'd every shore with you,
I have run through what any river or strait of the globe has run
    through,
I have taken my stand on the bases of peninsulas and on the high
    embedded rocks, to cry thence :

Salut au monde !
What cities the light or warmth penetrates I penetrate those cities
    myself,
All islands to which birds wing their way I wing my way myself.

Toward you all, in America's name,
I raise high the perpendicular hand, I make the signal,
To remain after me in sight forever,
For all the haunts and homes of men.

SONG OF THE OPEN ROAD.

1

AFOOT and light-hearted I take to the open road,
Healthy, free, the world before me,
The long brown path before me leading wherever I choose.

Henceforth I ask not good-fortune, I myself am good-fortune,
Henceforth I whimper no more, postpone no more, need nothing,
Done with indoor complaints, libraries, querulous criticisms,
Strong and content I travel the open road.

The earth, that is sufficient,
I do not want the constellations any nearer,
I know they are very well where they are,
I know they suffice for those who belong to them.

(Still here I carry my old delicious burdens,
I carry them, men and women, I carry them with me wherever I go,
I swear it is impossible for me to get rid of them,
I am fill'd with them, and I will fill them in return.)

2

You road I enter upon and look around, I believe you are not all
        that is here,
I believe that much unseen is also here.

Here the profound lesson of reception, nor preference nor denial,
The black with his woolly head, the felon, the diseas'd, the illiterate
        person, are not denied ;
The birth, the hasting after the physician, the beggar's tramp, the
        drunkard's stagger, the laughing party of mechanics,
The escaped youth, the rich person's carriage, the fop, the eloping
        couple,
The early market-man, the hearse, the moving of furniture into the
        town, the return back from the town,
They pass, I also pass, any thing passes, none can be interdicted,
None but are accepted, none but shall be dear to me.

3

You air that serves me with breath to speak !
You objects that call from diffusion my meanings and give them
        shape !
You light that wraps me and all things in delicate equable showers !
You paths worn in the irregular hollows by the roadsides !
I believe you are latent with unseen existences, you are so dear
        to me.

You flagg'd walks of the cities ! you strong curbs at the edges !
You ferries ! you planks and posts of wharves ! you timber-lined
        sides ! you distant ships !

You rows of houses! you window-pierc'd façades! you roofs!
You porches and entrances! you copings and iron guards!
You windows whose transparent shells might expose so much!
You doors and ascending steps! you arches!
You gray stones of interminable pavements! you trodden crossings!
From all that has touch'd you I believe you have imparted to
      yourselves, and now would impart the same secretly to me,
From the living and the dead you have peopled your impassive
      surfaces, and the spirits thereof would be evident and
      amicable with me.

4

The earth expanding right hand and left hand,
The picture alive, every part in its best light,
The music falling in where it is wanted, and stopping where it is
      not wanted,
The cheerful voice of the public road, the gay fresh sentiment of
      the road.

O highway I travel, do you say to me *Do not leave me?*
Do you say *Venture not — if you leave me you are lost?*
Do you say *I am already prepared, I am well-beaten and un-
      denied, adhere to me?*

O public road, I say back I am not afraid to leave you, yet I love
      you,
You express me better than I can express myself,
You shall be more to me than my poem.

I think heroic deeds were all conceiv'd in the open air, and all
      free poems also,
I think I could stop here myself and do miracles,
I think whatever I shall meet on the road I shall like, and who-
      ever beholds me shall like me,
I think whoever I see must be happy.

5

From this hour I ordain myself loos'd of limits and imaginary
      lines,
Going where I list, my own master total and absolute,
Listening to others, considering well what they say,
Pausing, searching, receiving, contemplating,
Gently, but with undeniable will, divesting myself of the holds
      that would hold me.

I inhale great draughts of space,
The east and the west are mine, and the north and the south are
    mine.

I am larger, better than I thought,
I did not know I held so much goodness.

All seems beautiful to me,
I can repeat over to men and women You have done such good
    to me I would do the same to you,
I will recruit for myself and you as I go,
I will scatter myself among men and women as I go,
I will toss a new gladness and roughness among them,
Whoever denies me it shall not trouble me,
Whoever accepts me he or she shall be blessed and shall bless me.

6

Now if a thousand perfect men were to appear it would not amaze
    me,
Now if a thousand beautiful forms of women appear'd it would
    not astonish me.

Now I see the secret of the making of the best persons,
It is to grow in the open air and to eat and sleep with the earth.

Here a great personal deed has room,
(Such a deed seizes upon the hearts of the whole race of men,
Its effusion of strength and will overwhelms law and mocks all
    authority and all argument against it.)

Here is the test of wisdom,
Wisdom is not finally tested in schools,
Wisdom cannot be pass'd from one having it to another not
    having it,
Wisdom is of the soul, is not susceptible of proof, is its own proof,
Applies to all stages and objects and qualities and is content,
Is the certainty of the reality and immortality of things, and the
    excellence of things ;
Something there is in the float of the sight of things that provokes
    it out of the soul.

Now I re-examine philosophies and religions,
They may prove well in lecture-rooms, yet not prove at all under
    the spacious clouds and along the landscape and flowing
    currents.

Here is realization,
Here is a man tallied — he realizes here what he has in him,
The past, the future, majesty, love — if they are vacant of you,
    you are vacant of them.

Only the kernel of every object nourishes ;
Where is he who tears off the husks for you and me ?
Where is he that undoes stratagems and envelopes for you and me ?

Here is adhesiveness, it is not previously fashion'd, it is apropos ;
Do you know what it is as you pass to be loved by strangers ?
Do you know the talk of those turning eye-balls ?

7

Here is the efflux of the soul,
The efflux of the soul comes from within through embower'd
    gates, ever provoking questions,
These yearnings why are they ? these thoughts in the darkness
    why are they ?
Why are there men and women that while they are nigh me the
    sunlight expands my blood ?
Why when they leave me do my pennants of joy sink flat and lank ?
Why are there trees I never walk under but large and melodious
    thoughts descend upon me ?
(I think they hang there winter and summer on those trees and
    always drop fruit as I pass ;)
What is it I interchange so suddenly with strangers ?
What with some driver as I ride on the seat by his side ?
What with some fisherman drawing his seine by the shore as I
    walk by and pause ?
What gives me to be free to a woman's and man's good-will ?
    what gives them to be free to mine ?

8

The efflux of the soul is happiness, here is happiness,
I think it pervades the open air, waiting at all times,
Now it flows unto us, we are rightly charged.

Here rises the fluid and attaching character,
The fluid and attaching character is the freshness and sweetness
    of man and woman,
(The herbs of the morning sprout no fresher and sweeter every
    day out of the roots of themselves, than it sprouts fresh
    and sweet continually out of itself.)

Toward the fluid and attaching character exudes the sweat of the
      love of young and old,
From it falls distill'd the charm that mocks beauty and attainments,
Toward it heaves the shuddering longing ache of contact.

9

Allons! whoever you are come travel with me!
Traveling with me you find what never tires.

The earth never tires,
The earth is rude, silent, incomprehensible at first, Nature is rude
      and incomprehensible at first,
Be not discouraged, keep on, there are divine things well envelop'd,
I swear to you there are divine things more beautiful than words
      can tell.

Allons! we must not stop here,
However sweet these laid-up stores, however convenient this dwell-
      ing we cannot remain here,
However shelter'd this port and however calm these waters we
      must not anchor here,
However welcome the hospitality that surrounds us we are per-
      mitted to receive it but a little while.

10

Allons! the inducements shall be greater,
We will sail pathless and wild seas,
We will go where winds blow, waves dash, and the Yankee clipper
      speeds by under full sail.

Allons! with power, liberty, the earth, the elements,
Health, defiance, gayety, self-esteem, curiosity;
Allons! from all formules!
From your formules, O bat-eyed and materialistic priests.

The stale cadaver blocks up the passage — the burial waits no
      longer.

Allons! yet take warning!
He traveling with me needs the best blood, thews, endurance,
None may come to the trial till he or she bring courage and health,
Come not here if you have already spent the best of yourself,
Only those may come who come in sweet and determin'd bodies,
No diseas'd person, no rum-drinker or venereal taint is permitted
      here.

(I and mine do not convince by arguments, similes, rhymes,
We convince by our presence.)

11

Listen ! I will be honest with you,
I do not offer the old smooth prizes, but offer rough new prizes,
These are the days that must happen to you :
You shall not heap up what is call'd riches,
You shall scatter with lavish hand all that you earn or achieve,
You but arrive at the city to which you were destin'd, you hardly
        settle yourself to satisfaction before you are call'd by an
        irresistible call to depart,
You shall be treated to the ironical smiles and mockings of those
        who remain behind you,
What beckonings of love you receive you shall only answer with
        passionate kisses of parting,
You shall not allow the hold of those who spread their reach'd
        hands toward you.

12

Allons ! after the great Companions, and to belong to them !
They too are on the road — they are the swift and majestic men —
        they are the greatest women,
Enjoyers of calms of seas and storms of seas,
Sailors of many a ship, walkers of many a mile of land,
Habituès of many distant countries, habituès of far-distant dwellings,
Trusters of men and women, observers of cities, solitary toilers,
Pausers and contemplators of tufts, blossoms, shells of the shore,
Dancers at wedding-dances, kissers of brides, tender helpers of
        children, bearers of children,
Soldiers of revolts, standers by gaping graves, lowerers-down of
        coffins,
Journeyers over consecutive seasons, over the years, the curious
        years each emerging from that which preceded it,
Journeyers as with companions, namely their own diverse phases,
Forth-steppers from the latent unrealized baby-days,
Journeyers gayly with their own youth, journeyers with their
        bearded and well-grain'd manhood,
Journeyers with their womanhood, ample, unsurpass'd, content,
Journeyers with their own sublime old age of manhood or woman-
        hood,
Old age, calm, expanded, broad with the haughty breadth of the
        universe,
Old age, flowing free with the delicious near-by freedom of death.

13

Allons ! to that which is endless as it was beginningless,

To undergo much, tramps of days, rests of nights,

To merge all in the travel they tend to, and the days and nights
    they tend to,

Again to merge them in the start of superior journeys,

To see nothing anywhere but what you may reach it and pass it,

To conceive no time, however distant, but what you may reach it
    and pass it,

To look up or down no road but it stretches and waits for you,
    however long but it stretches and waits for you,

To see no being, not God's or any, but you also go thither,

To see no possession but you may possess it, enjoying all without
    labor or purchase, abstracting the feast yet not abstracting
    one particle of it,

To take the best of the farmer's farm and the rich man's elegant
    villa, and the chaste blessings of the well-married couple,
    and the fruits of orchards and flowers of gardens,

To take to your use out of the compact cities as you pass through,

To carry buildings and streets with you afterward wherever you go,

To gather the minds of men out of their brains as you encounter
    them, to gather the love out of their hearts,

To take your lovers on the road with you, for all that you leave
    them behind you,

To know the universe itself as a road, as many roads, as roads for
    traveling souls.

All parts away for the progress of souls,

All religion, all solid things, arts, governments—all that was or is
    apparent upon this globe or any globe, falls into niches and
    corners before the procession of souls along the grand roads
    of the universe.

Of the progress of the souls of men and women along the grand
    roads of the universe, all other progress is the needed
    emblem and sustenance.

Forever alive, forever forward,

Stately, solemn, sad, withdrawn, baffled, mad, turbulent, feeble,
    dissatisfied,

Desperate, proud, fond, sick, accepted by men, rejected by men,

They go ! they go ! I know that they go, but I know not where
    they go,

But I know that they go toward the best — toward something
    great.

Whoever you are, come forth ! or man or woman come forth !
You must not stay sleeping and dallying there in the house,
    though you built it, or though it has been built for you.

Out of the dark confinement ! out from behind the screen !
It is useless to protest, I know all and expose it.

Behold through you as bad as the rest,
Through the laughter, dancing, dining, supping, of people,
Inside of dresses and ornaments, inside of those wash'd and
    trimm'd faces,
Behold a secret silent loathing and despair.

No husband, no wife, no friend, trusted to hear the confession,
Another self, a duplicate of every one, skulking and hiding it goes,
Formless and wordless through the streets of the cities, polite and
    bland in the parlors,
In the cars of railroads, in steamboats, in the public assembly,
Home to the houses of men and women, at the table, in the bed-
    room, everywhere,
Smartly attired, countenance smiling, form upright, death under
    the breast-bones, hell under the skull-bones,
Under the broadcloth and gloves, under the ribbons and artificial
    flowers,
Keeping fair with the customs, speaking not a syllable of itself,
Speaking of any thing else but never of itself.

14

Allons ! through struggles and wars !
The goal that was named cannot be countermanded.

Have the past struggles succeeded ?
What has succeeded ? yourself ? your nation ? Nature ?
Now understand me well — it is provided in the essence of things
    that from any fruition of success, no matter what, shall
    come forth something to make a greater struggle necessary.

My call is the call of battle, I nourish active rebellion,
He going with me must go well arm'd,
He going with me goes often with spare diet, poverty, angry
    enemies, desertions.

15

Allons ! the road is before us !
It is safe — I have tried it — my own feet have tried it well — be
    not detain'd !

Let the paper remain on the desk unwritten, and the book on the shelf unopen'd!
Let the tools remain in the workshop! let the money remain unearn'd!
Let the school stand! mind not the cry of the teacher!
Let the preacher preach in his pulpit! let the lawyer plead in the court, and the judge expound the law.

Camerado, I give you my hand!
I give you my love more precious than money,
I give you myself before preaching or law;
Will you give me yourself? will you come travel with me?
Shall we stick by each other as long as we live?

CROSSING BROOKLYN FERRY.

1

FLOOD-TIDE below me! I see you face to face!
Clouds of the west — sun there half an hour high — I see you also face to face.

Crowds of men and women attired in the usual costumes, how curious you are to me!
On the ferry-boats the hundreds and hundreds that cross, returning home, are more curious to me than you suppose,
And you that shall cross from shore to shore years hence are more to me, and more in my meditations, than you might suppose.

2

The impalpable sustenance of me from all things at all hours of the day,
The simple, compact, well-join'd scheme, myself disintegrated, every one disintegrated yet part of the scheme,
The similitudes of the past and those of the future,
The glories strung like beads on my smallest sights and hearings, on the walk in the street and the passage over the river,
The current rushing so swiftly and swimming with me far away,
The others that are to follow me, the ties between me and them,
The certainty of others, the life, love, sight, hearing of others.

Others will enter the gates of the ferry and cross from shore to shore,

Others will watch the run of the flood-tide,

Others will see the shipping of Manhattan north and west, and the heights of Brooklyn to the south and east,

Others will see the islands large and small;

Fifty years hence, others will see them as they cross, the sun half an hour high,

A hundred years hence, or ever so many hundred years hence, others will see them,

Will enjoy the sunset, the pouring-in of the flood-tide, the falling-back to the sea of the ebb-tide.

3

It avails not, time nor place — distance avails not,

I am with you, you men and women of a generation, or ever so many generations hence,

Just as you feel when you look on the river and sky, so I felt,

Just as any of you is one of a living crowd, I was one of a crowd,

Just as you are refresh'd by the gladness of the river and the bright flow, I was refresh'd,

Just as you stand and lean on the rail, yet hurry with the swift current, I stood yet was hurried,

Just as you look on the numberless masts of ships and the thick-stemm'd pipes of steamboats, I look'd.

I too many and many a time cross'd the river of old,

Watched the Twelfth-month sea-gulls, saw them high in the air floating with motionless wings, oscillating their bodies,

Saw how the glistening yellow lit up parts of their bodies and left the rest in strong shadow,

Saw the slow-wheeling circles and the gradual edging toward the south,

Saw the reflection of the summer sky in the water,

Had my eyes dazzled by the shimmering track of beams,

Look'd at the fine centrifugal spokes of light round the shape of my head in the sunlit water,

Look'd on the haze on the hills southward and south-westward,

Look'd on the vapor as it flew in fleeces tinged with violet,

Look'd toward the lower bay to notice the vessels arriving,

Saw their approach, saw aboard those that were near me,

Saw the white sails of schooners and sloops, saw the ships at anchor,

The sailors at work in the rigging or out astride the spars,

The round masts, the swinging motion of the hulls, the slender serpentine pennants,

The large and small steamers in motion, the pilots in their pilot-houses,

The white wake left by the passage, the quick tremulous whirl of
    the wheels,
The flags of all nations, the falling of them at sunset,
The scallop-edged waves in the twilight, the ladled cups, the
    frolicsome crests and glistening,
The stretch afar growing dimmer and dimmer, the gray walls of
    the granite storehouses by the docks,
On the river the shadowy group, the big steam-tug closely flank'd
    on each side by the barges, the hay-boat, the belated
    lighter,
On the neighboring shore the fires from the foundry chimneys
    burning high and glaringly into the night,
Casting their flicker of black contrasted with wild red and yellow
    light over the tops of houses, and down into the clefts of
    streets.

4

These and all else were to me the same as they are to you,
I loved well those cities, loved well the stately and rapid river,
The men and women I saw were all near to me,
Others the same — others who look back on me because I look'd
    forward to them,
(The time will come, though I stop here to-day and to-night.)

5

What is it then between us?
What is the count of the scores or hundreds of years between us?

Whatever it is, it avails not — distance avails not, and place avails
    not,
I too lived, Brooklyn of ample hills was mine,
I too walk'd the streets of Manhattan island, and bathed in the
    waters around it,
I too felt the curious abrupt questionings stir within me,
In the day among crowds of people sometimes they came upon me,
In my walks home late at night or as I lay in my bed they came
    upon me,
I too had been struck from the float forever held in solution,
I too had receiv'd identity by my body,
That I was I knew was of my body, and what I should be I knew
    I should be of my body.

6

It is not upon you alone the dark patches fall,
The dark threw its patches down upon me also,

The best I had done seem'd to me blank and suspicious,
My great thoughts as I supposed them, were they not in reality
          meagre?
Nor is it you alone who know what it is to be evil,
I am he who knew what it was to be evil,
I too knitted the old knot of contrariety,
Blabb'd, blush'd, resented, lied, stole, grudg'd,
Had guile, anger, lust, hot wishes I dared not speak,
Was wayward, vain, greedy, shallow, sly, cowardly, malignant,
The wolf, the snake, the hog, not wanting in me,
The cheating look, the frivolous word, the adulterous wish, not
          wanting,
Refusals, hates, postponements, meanness, laziness, none of these
          wanting,
Was one with the rest, the days and haps of the rest,
Was call'd by my nighest name by clear loud voices of young men
          as they saw me approaching or passing,
Felt their arms on my neck as I stood, or the negligent leaning of
          their flesh against me as I sat,
Saw many I loved in the street or ferry-boat or public assembly,
          yet never told them a word,
Lived the same life with the rest, the same old laughing, gnawing,
          sleeping,
Play'd the part that still looks back on the actor or actress,
The same old role, the role that is what we make it, as great as we
          like,
Or as small as we like, or both great and small.

7

Closer yet I approach you,
What thought you have of me now, I had as much of you — I laid
          in my stores in advance,
I consider'd long and seriously of you before you were born.

Who was to know what should come home to me?
Who knows but I am enjoying this?
Who knows, for all the distance, but I am as good as looking at
          you now, for all you cannot see me?

8

Ah, what can ever be more stately and admirable to me than mast-
          hemm'd Manhattan?
River and sunset and scallop-edg'd waves of flood-tide?
The sea-gulls oscillating their bodies, the hay-boat in the twilight,
          and the belated lighter?

What gods can exceed these that clasp me by the hand, and with
    voices I love call me promptly and loudly by my nighest
    name as I approach?
What is more subtle than this which ties me to the woman or man
    that looks in my face?
Which fuses me into you now, and pours my meaning into you?

We understand then do we not?
What I promis'd without mentioning it, have you not accepted?
What the study could not teach — what the preaching could not
    accomplish is accomplish'd, is it not?

9

Flow on, river! flow with the flood-tide, and ebb with the ebb-
    tide!
Frolic on, crested and scallop-edg'd waves!
Gorgeous clouds of the sunset! drench with your splendor me, or
    the men and women generations after me!
Cross from shore to shore, countless crowds of passengers!
Stand up, tall masts of Mannahatta! stand up, beautiful hills of
    Brooklyn!
Throb, baffled and curious brain! throw out questions and answers!
Suspend here and everywhere, eternal float of solution!
Gaze, loving and thirsting eyes, in the house or street or public
    assembly!
Sound out, voices of young men! loudly and musically call me by
    my nighest name!
Live, old life! play the part that looks back on the actor or actress!
Play the old role, the role that is great or small according as one
    makes it!
Consider, you who peruse me, whether I may not in unknown
    ways be looking upon you;
Be firm, rail over the river, to support those who lean idly, yet
    haste with the hasting current;
Fly on, sea-birds! fly sideways, or wheel in large circles high in
    the air;
Receive the summer sky, you water, and faithfully hold it till all
    downcast eyes have time to take it from you!
Diverge, fine spokes of light, from the shape of my head, or any
    one's head, in the sunlit water!
Come on, ships from the lower bay! pass up or down, white-sail'd
    schooners, sloops, lighters!
Flaunt away, flags of all nations! be duly lower'd at sunset!
Burn high your fires, foundry chimneys! cast black shadows at
    nightfall! cast red and yellow light over the tops of the
    houses!

Appearances, now or henceforth, indicate what you are,
You necessary film, continue to envelop the soul,
About my body for me, and your body for you, be hung out
    divinest aromas,
Thrive, cities — bring your freight, bring your shows, ample and
    sufficient rivers,
Expand, being than which none else is perhaps more spiritual,
Keep your places, objects than which none else is more lasting.

You have waited, you always wait, you dumb, beautiful ministers,
We receive you with free sense at last, and are insatiate hence-
    forward,
Not you any more shall be able to foil us, or withhold yourselves
    from us,
We use you, and do not cast you aside — we plant you perma-
    nently within us,
We fathom you not — we love you — there is perfection in you also,
You furnish your parts toward eternity,
Great or small, you furnish your parts toward the soul.

SONG OF THE ANSWERER.

I

Now list to my morning's romanza, I tell the signs of the Answerer,
To the cities and farms I sing as they spread in the sunshine
    before me.

A young man comes to me bearing a message from his brother,
How shall the young man know the whether and when of his
    brother?
Tell him to send me the signs.

And I stand before the young man face to face, and take his right
    hand in my left hand and his left hand in my right hand,
And I answer for his brother and for men, and I answer for him
    that answers for all, and send these signs.

Him all wait for, him all yield up to, his word is decisive and final,
Him they accept, in him lave, in him perceive themselves as amid
    light,
Him they immerse and he immerses them.

Beautiful women, the haughtiest nations, laws, the landscape,
    people, animals,
The profound earth and its attributes and the unquiet ocean, (so
    tell I my morning's romanza,)
All enjoyments and properties and money, and whatever money
    will buy,
The best farms, others toiling and planting and he unavoidably
    reaps,
The noblest and costliest cities, others grading and building and
    he domiciles there,
Nothing for any one but what is for him, near and far are for him,
    the ships in the offing,
The perpetual shows and marches on land are for him if they are
    for anybody.

He puts things in their attitudes,
He puts to-day out of himself with plasticity and love,
He places his own times, reminiscences, parents, brothers and
    sisters, associations, employment, politics, so that the rest
    never shame them afterward, nor assume to command
    them.

He is the Answerer,
What can be answer'd he answers, and what cannot be answer'd
    he shows how it cannot be answer'd.

A man is a summons and challenge,
(It is vain to skulk — do you hear that mocking and laughter? do
    you hear the ironical echoes?)

Books, friendships, philosophers, priests, action, pleasure, pride,
    beat up and down seeking to give satisfaction,
He indicates the satisfaction, and indicates them that beat up and
    down also.

Whichever the sex, whatever the season or place, he may go freshly
    and gently and safely by day or by night,
He has the pass-key of hearts, to him the response of the prying
    of hands on the knobs.

His welcome is universal, the flow of beauty is not more welcome
    or universal than he is,
The person he favors by day or sleeps with at night is blessed.

Every existence has its idiom, every thing has an idiom and tongue,

He resolves all tongues into his own and bestows it upon men, and
    any man translates, and any man translates himself also,
One part does not counteract another part, he is the joiner, he
    sees how they join.

He says indifferently and alike *How are you friend?* to the
    President at his levee,
And he says *Good-day my brother,* to Cudge* that hoes in the
    sugar-field,
And both understand him and know that his speech is right.

He walks with perfect ease in the capitol,
He walks among the Congress, and one Representative says to
    another, *Here is our equal appearing and new.*

Then the mechanics take him for a mechanic,
And the soldiers suppose him to be a soldier, and the sailors that
    he has follow'd the sea,
And the authors take him for an author, and the artists for an
    artist,
And the laborers perceive he could labor with them and love them,
No matter what the work is, that he is the one to follow it or has
    follow'd it,
No matter what the nation, that he might find his brothers and
    sisters there.

The English believe he comes of their English stock,
A Jew to the Jew he seems, a Russ to the Russ, usual and near,
    removed from none.

Whoever he looks at in the traveler's coffee-house claims him,
The Italian or Frenchman is sure, the German is sure, the Spaniard
    is sure, and the island Cuban is sure,
The engineer, the deck-hand on the great lakes, or on the Missis-
    sippi or St. Lawrence or Sacramento, or Hudson or Pau-
    manok sound, claims him.

The gentleman of perfect blood acknowledges his perfect blood,
The insulter, the prostitute, the angry person, the beggar, see
    themselves in the ways of him, he strangely transmutes them,
They are not vile any more, they hardly know themselves they are
    so grown.

2

The indications and tally of time,
Perfect sanity shows the master among philosophs,

Time, always without break, indicates itself in parts,
What always indicates the poet is the crowd of the pleasant company of singers, and their words,
The words of the singers are the hours or minutes of the light or dark, but the words of the maker of poems are the general light and dark,
The maker of poems settles justice, reality, immortality,
His insight and power encircle things and the human race,
He is the glory and extract thus far of things and of the human race.

The singers do not beget, only the Poet begets,
The singers are welcom'd, understood, appear often enough, but rare has the day been, likewise the spot, of the birth of the maker of poems, the Answerer,
(Not every century nor every five centuries has contain'd such a day, for all its names.)

The singers of successive hours of centuries may have ostensible names, but the name of each of them is one of the singers,
The name of each is, eye-singer, ear-singer, head-singer, sweet-singer, night-singer, parlor-singer, love-singer, weird-singer, or something else.

All this time and at all times wait the words of true poems,
The words of true poems do not merely please,
The true poets are not followers of beauty but the august masters of beauty ;
The greatness of sons is the exuding of the greatness of mothers and fathers,
The words of true poems are the tuft*and final applause of science.

Divine instinct, breadth of vision, the law of reason, health, rudeness of body, withdrawnness,
Gayety, sun-tan, air-sweetness, such are some of the words of poems.

The sailor and traveler underlie the maker of poems, the Answerer,
The builder, geometer, chemist, anatomist, phrenologist, artist, all these underlie the maker of poems, the Answerer.

The words of the true poems give you more than poems,
They give you to form for yourself poems, religions, politics, war, peace, behavior, histories, essays, daily life, and every thing else,
They balance ranks, colors, races, creeds, and the sexes,

They do not seek beauty, they are sought,
Forever touching them or close upon them follows beauty, longing,
　　fain, love-sick.

They prepare for death, yet are they not the finish, but rather the
　　outset,
They bring none to his or her terminus or to be content and full,
Whom they take they take into space to behold the birth of stars,
　　to learn one of the meanings,
To launch off with absolute faith, to sweep through the ceaseless
　　rings and never be quiet again.

OUR OLD FEUILLAGE.

ALWAYS our old feuillage !
Always Florida's green peninsula — always the priceless delta of
　　Louisiana — always the cotton-fields of Alabama and Texas,
Always California's golden hills and hollows, and the silver moun-
　　tains of New Mexico — always soft-breath'd Cuba,
Always the vast slope drain'd by the Southern sea, inseparable with
　　the slopes drain'd by the Eastern and Western seas,
The area the eighty-third year of these States, the three and a half
　　millions of square miles,
The eighteen thousand miles of sea-coast and bay-coast on the
　　main, the thirty thousand miles of river navigation,
The seven millions of distinct families and the same number of
　　dwellings — always these, and more, branching forth into
　　numberless branches,
Always the free range and diversity — always the continent of
　　Democracy ;
Always the prairies, pastures, forests, vast cities, travelers, Kanada,
　　the snows ;
Always these compact lands tied at the hips with the belt stringing
　　the huge· oval lakes ;
Always the West with strong native persons, the increasing density
　　there, the habitans, friendly, threatening, ironical, scorning
　　invaders ;
All sights, South, North, East — all deeds, promiscuously done at
　　all times,
All characters, movements, growths, a few noticed, myriads unno-
　　ticed,
Through Mannahatta's streets I walking, these things gathering,

On interior rivers by night in the glare of pine knots, steamboats
    wooding up,
Sunlight by day on the valley of the Susquehanna, and on the
    valleys of the Potomac and Rappahannock, and the valleys
    of the Roanoke and Delaware,
In their northerly wilds beasts of prey haunting the Adirondacks
    the hills, or lapping the Saginaw waters to drink,
In a lonesome inlet a sheldrake lost from the flock, sitting on the
    water rocking silently,
In farmers' barns oxen in the stable, their harvest labor done, they
    rest standing, they are too tired,
Afar on arctic ice the she-walrus lying drowsily while her cubs play
    around,
The hawk sailing where men have not yet sail'd, the farthest polar
    sea, ripply, crystalline, open, beyond the floes,
White drift spooning ahead where the ship in the tempest dashes,
On solid land what is done in cities as the bells strike midnight
    together,
In primitive woods the sounds there also sounding, the howl of the
    wolf, the scream of the panther, and the hoarse bellow of
    the elk,
In winter beneath the hard blue ice of Moosehead lake, in summer
    visible through the clear waters, the great trout swimming,
In lower latitudes in warmer air in the Carolinas the large black
    buzzard floating slowly high beyond the tree tops,
Below, the red cedar festoon'd with tylandria,* the pines and
    cypresses growing out of the white sand that spreads far
    and flat,
Rude boats descending the big Pedee, climbing plants, parasites
    with color'd flowers and berries enveloping huge trees,
The waving drapery on the live-oak trailing long and low, noise-
    lessly waved by the wind,
The camp of Georgia wagoners just after dark, the supper-fires
    and the cooking and eating by whites and negroes,
Thirty or forty great wagons, the mules, cattle, horses, feeding
    from troughs,
The shadows, gleams, up under the leaves of the old sycamore-
    trees, the flames with the black smoke from the pitch-pine
    curling and rising ;
Southern fishermen fishing, the sounds and inlets of North Caro-
    lina's coast, the shad-fishery and the herring-fishery, the
    large sweep-seines, the windlasses on shore work'd by
    horses, the clearing, curing, and packing-houses ;
Deep in the forest in piney woods turpentine dropping from the
    incisions in the trees, there are the turpentine works,

There are the negroes at work in good health, the ground in all
    directions is cover'd with pine straw ;
In Tennessee and Kentucky slaves busy in the coalings, at the
    forge, by the furnace-blaze, or at the corn-shucking,
In Virginia, the planter's son returning after a long absence, joy-
    fully welcom'd and kiss'd by the aged mulatto nurse,
On rivers boatmen safely moor'd at nightfall in their boats under
    shelter of high banks,
Some of the younger men dance to the sound of the banjo or
    fiddle, others sit on the gunwale smoking and talking ;
Late in the afternoon the mocking-bird, the American mimic,
    singing in the Great Dismal Swamp,
There are the greenish waters, the resinous odor, the plenteous
    moss, the cypress-tree, and the juniper-tree ;
Northward, young men of Mannahatta, the target company from
    an excursion returning home at evening, the musket-muz-
    zles all bear bunches of flowers presented by women ;
Children at play, or on his father's lap a young boy fallen asleep,
    (how his lips move ! how he smiles in his sleep !)
The scout riding on horseback over the plains west of the Missis-
    sippi, he ascends a knoll and sweeps his eyes around ;
California life, the miner, bearded, dress'd in his rude costume,
    the stanch California friendship, the sweet air, the graves
    one in passing meets solitary just aside the horse-path ;
Down in Texas the cotton-field, the negro-cabins, drivers driving
    mules or oxen before rude carts, cotton bales piled on
    banks and wharves ;
Encircling all, vast-darting up and wide, the American Soul, with
    equal hemispheres, one Love, one Dilation or Pride ;
In arriere the peace-talk with the Iroquois the aborigines, the
    calumet, the pipe of good-will, arbitration, and indorse-
    ment,
The sachem blowing the smoke first toward the sun and then
    toward the earth,
The drama of the scalp-dance enacted with painted faces and
    guttural exclamations,
The setting out of the war-party, the long and stealthy march,
The single file, the swinging hatchets, the surprise and slaughter
    of enemies ;
All the acts, scenes, ways, persons, attitudes of these States,
    reminiscences, institutions,
All these States compact, every square mile of these States without
    excepting a particle ;
Me pleas'd, rambling in lanes and country fields, Paumanok's
    fields,*

Observing the spiral flight of two little yellow butterflies shuffling
    between each other, ascending high in the air,
The darting swallow, the destroyer of insects, the fall traveler
    southward but returning northward early in the spring,
The country boy at the close of the day driving the herd of cows
    and shouting to them as they loiter to browse by the road-
    side,
The city wharf, Boston, Philadelphia, Baltimore, Charleston, New
    Orleans, San Francisco,
The departing ships when the sailors heave at the capstan ;
Evening — me in my room — the setting sun,
The setting summer sun shining in my open window, showing the
    swarm of flies, suspended, balancing in the air in the centre
    of the room, darting athwart, up and down, casting swift
    shadows in specks on the opposite wall where the shine is ;
The athletic American matron speaking in public to crowds of
    listeners,
Males, females, immigrants, combinations, the copiousness, the
    individuality of the States, each for itself — the money-
    makers,
Factories, machinery, the mechanical forces, the windlass, lever,
    pulley, all certainties,
The certainty of space, increase, freedom, futurity,
In space the sporades, the scatter'd islands, the stars — on the
    firm earth, the lands, my lands,
O lands ! all so dear to me — what you are, (whatever it is,) I
    putting it at random in these songs, become a part of that,
    whatever it is,
Southward there, I screaming, with wings slow flapping, with the
    myriads of gulls wintering along the coasts of Florida,
Otherways there atwixt the banks of the Arkansaw, the Rio
    Grande, the Nueces, the Brazos, the Tombigbee, the Red
    River, the Saskatchawan or the Osage, I with the spring
    waters laughing and skipping and running,
Northward, on the sands, on some shallow bay of Paumanok, I
    with parties of snowy herons wading in the wet to seek
    worms and aquatic plants,
Retreating, triumphantly twittering, the king-bird, from piercing
    the crow with its bill, for amusement — and I triumphantly
    twittering,
The migrating flock of wild geese alighting in autumn to refresh
    themselves, the body of the flock feed, the sentinels out-
    side move around with erect heads watching, and are from
    time to time reliev'd by other sentinels — and I feeding
    and taking turns with the rest,

In Kanadian forests the moose, large as an ox, corner'd by
    hunters, rising desperately on his hind-feet, and plunging
    with his fore-feet, the hoofs as sharp as knives — and I,
    plunging at the hunters, corner'd and desperate,
In the Mannahatta, streets, piers, shipping, store-houses, and the
    countless workmen working in the shops,
And I too of the Mannahatta, singing thereof — and no less in
    myself than the whole of the Mannahatta in itself,
Singing the song of These, my ever-united lands — my body no
    more inevitably united, part to part, and made out of a
    thousand diverse contributions one identity, any more than
    my lands are inevitably united and made ONE IDENTITY;
Nativities, climates, the grass of the great pastoral Plains,
Cities, labors, death, animals, products, war, good and evil —
    these me,
These affording, in all their particulars, the old feuillage to me
    and to America, how can I do less than pass the clew*of
    the union of them, to afford the like to you?
Whoever you are! how can I but offer you divine leaves, that you
    also be eligible as I am?
How can I but as here chanting, invite you for yourself to collect
    bouquets of the incomparable feuillage of these States?

A SONG OF JOYS.

O TO make the most jubilant song!
Full of music — full of manhood, womanhood, infancy!
Full of common employments — full of grain and trees.

O for the voices of animals — O for the swiftness and balance of
    fishes!
O for the dropping of raindrops in a song!
O for the sunshine and motion of waves in a song!

O the joy of my spirit — it is uncaged — it darts like lightning!
It is not enough to have this globe or a certain time,
I will have thousands of globes and all time.

O the engineer's joys! to go with a locomotive!
To hear the hiss of steam, the merry shriek, the steam-whistle, the
    laughing locomotive!
To push with resistless way and speed off in the distance.

O the gleesome saunter over fields and hillsides !
The leaves and flowers of the commonest weeds, the moist fresh
    stillness of the woods,
The exquisite smell of the earth at daybreak, and all through the
    forenoon.

O the horseman's and horsewoman's joys !
The saddle, the gallop, the pressure upon the seat, the cool gurgling
    by the ears and hair.

O the fireman's joys !
I hear the alarm at dead of night,
I hear bells, shouts ! I pass the crowd, I run !
The sight of the flames maddens me with pleasure.

O the joy of the strong-brawn'd fighter, towering in the arena in
    perfect condition, conscious of power, thirsting to meet his
    opponent.

O the joy of that vast elemental sympathy which only the human
    soul is capable of generating and emitting in steady and
    limitless floods.

O the mother's joys !
The watching, the endurance, the precious love, the anguish, the
    patiently yielded life.

O the joy of increase, growth, recuperation,
The joy of soothing and pacifying, the joy of concord and harmony.

O to go back to the place where I was born,
To hear the birds sing once more,
To ramble about the house and barn and over the fields once more,
And through the orchard and along the old lanes once more.

O to have been brought up on bays, lagoons, creeks, or along the
    coast,
To continue and be employ'd there all my life,
The briny and damp smell, the shore, the salt weeds exposed at
    low water,
The work of fishermen, the work of the eel-fisher and clam-fisher ;
I come with my clam-rake and spade, I come with my eel-spear,
Is the tide out? I join the group of clam-diggers on the flats,
I laugh and work with them, I joke at my work like a mettlesome
    young man ;

In winter I take my eel-basket and eel-spear and travel out on foot
  on the ice— I have a small axe to cut holes in the ice,
Behold me well-clothed going gayly or returning in the afternoon,
  my brood of tough boys accompanying me,
My brood of grown and part-grown boys, who love to be with no
  one else so well as they love to be with me,
By day to work with me, and by night to sleep with me.

Another time in warm weather out in a boat, to lift the lobster-pots
  where they are sunk with heavy stones, (I know the
  buoys,)
O the sweetness of the Fifth-month morning upon the water as I
  row just before sunrise toward the buoys,
I pull the wicker pots up slantingly, the dark green lobsters are
  desperate with their claws as I take them out, I insert
  wooden pegs in the joints of their pincers,
I go to all the places one after another, and then row back to the
  shore,
There in a huge kettle of boiling water the lobsters shall be boil'd
  till their color becomes scarlet.

Another time mackerel-taking,
Voracious, mad for the hook, near the surface, they seem to fill the
  water for miles ;
Another time fishing for rock-fish in Chesapeake bay, I one of the
  brown-faced crew ;
Another time trailing for blue-fish off Paumanok, I stand with
  braced body,
My left foot is on the gunwale, my right arm throws far out the
  coils of slender rope,
In sight around me the quick veering and darting of fifty skiffs,
  my companions.

O boating on the rivers,
The voyage down the St. Lawrence, the superb scenery, the
  steamers,
The ships sailing, the Thousand Islands, the occasional timber-raft
  and the raftsmen with long-reaching sweep-oars,
The little huts on the rafts, and the stream of smoke when they
  cook supper at evening.

(O something pernicious and dread !
Something far away from a puny and pious life !
Something unproved ! something in a trance !
Something escaped from the anchorage and driving free.)

O to work in mines, or forging iron,
Foundry casting, the foundry itself, the rude high roof, the ample
    and shadow'd space,
The furnace, the hot liquid pour'd out and running.

O to resume the joys of the soldier!
To feel the presence of a brave commanding officer — to feel his
    sympathy!
To behold his calmness — to be warm'd in the rays of his smile!
To go to battle — to hear the bugles play and the drums beat!
To hear the crash of artillery — to see the glittering of the bayonets
    and musket-barrels in the sun!
To see men fall and die and not complain!
To taste the savage taste of blood — to be so devilish!
To gloat so over the wounds and deaths of the enemy.

O the whaleman's joys! O I cruise my old cruise again!
I feel the ship's motion under me, I feel the Atlantic breezes fan-
    ning me,
I hear the cry again sent down from the mast-head, *There — she
    blows!*
Again I spring up the rigging to look with the rest — we descend,
    wild with excitement,
I leap in the lower'd boat, we row toward our prey where he lies,
We approach stealthy and silent, I see the mountainous mass,
    lethargic, basking,
I see the harpooneer standing up, I see the weapon dart from his
    vigorous arm;
O swift again far out in the ocean the wounded whale, settling,
    running to windward, tows me,
Again I see him rise to breathe, we row close again,
I see a lance driven through his side, press'd deep, turn'd in
    the wound,
Again we back off, I see him settle again, the life is leaving him
    fast,
As he rises he spouts blood, I see him swim in circles narrower
    and narrower, swiftly cutting the water — I see him die,
He gives one convulsive leap in the centre of the circle, and then
    falls flat and still in the bloody foam.

O the old manhood of me, my noblest joy of all!
My children and grand-children, my white hair and beard,
My largeness, calmness, majesty, out of the long stretch of my life.

O ripen'd joy of womanhood! O happiness at last!

I am more than eighty years of age, I am the most venerable
     mother,
How clear is my mind — how all people draw nigh to me!
What attractions are these beyond any before? what bloom more
     than the bloom of youth?
What beauty is this that descends upon me and rises out of me?

O the orator's joys!
To inflate the chest, to roll the thunder of the voice out from the
     ribs and throat,
To make the people rage, weep, hate, desire, with yourself,
To lead America — to quell America with a great tongue.

O the joy of my soul leaning pois'd on itself, receiving identity
     through materials and loving them, observing characters
     and absorbing them,
My soul vibrated back to me from them, from sight, hearing, touch,
     reason, articulation, comparison, memory, and the like,
The real life of my senses and flesh transcending my senses and flesh,
My body done with materials, my sight done with my material eyes,
Proved to me this day beyond cavil that it is not my material eyes
     which finally see,
Nor my material body which finally loves, walks, laughs, shouts,
     embraces, procreates.

O the farmer's joys!
Ohioan's, Illinoisian's, Wisconsinese', Kanadian's, Iowan's, Kan-
     sian's, Missourian's, Oregonese' joys!
To rise at peep of day and pass forth nimbly to work,
To plough land in the fall for winter-sown crops,
To plough land in the spring for maize,
To train orchards, to graft the trees, to gather apples in the fall.

O to bathe in the swimming-bath, or in a good place along shore,
To splash the water! to walk ankle-deep, or race naked along the
     shore.

O to realize space!
The plenteousness of all, that there are no bounds,
To emerge and be of the sky, of the sun and moon and flying
     clouds, as one with them.

O the joy of a manly self-hood!
To be servile to none, to defer to none, not to any tyrant known
     or unknown,

To walk with erect carriage, a step springy and elastic,
To look with calm gaze or with a flashing eye,
To speak with a full and sonorous voice out of a broad chest,
To confront with your personality all the other personalities of the
      earth.

Know'st thou the excellent joys of youth?
Joys of the dear companions and of the merry word and laughing
      face?
Joy of the glad light-beaming day, joy of the wide-breath'd games?
Joy of sweet music, joy of the lighted ball-room and the dancers?
Joy of the plenteous dinner, strong carouse and drinking?

Yet O my soul supreme!
Know'st thou the joys of pensive thought?
Joys of the free and lonesome heart, the tender, gloomy heart?
Joys of the solitary walk, the spirit bow'd yet proud, the suffering
      and the struggle?
The agonistic throes, the ecstasies, joys of the solemn musings day
      or night?
Joys of the thought of Death, the great spheres Time and Space?
Prophetic joys of better, loftier love's ideals, the divine wife, the
      sweet, eternal, perfect comrade?
Joys all thine own undying one, joys worthy thee O soul.

O while I live to be the ruler of life, not a slave,
To meet life as a powerful conqueror,
No fumes, no ennui, no more complaints or scornful criticisms,
To these proud laws of the air, the water and the ground, proving
      my interior soul impregnable,
And nothing exterior shall ever take command of me.

For not life's joys alone I sing, repeating — the joy of death!
The beautiful touch of Death, soothing and benumbing a few
      moments, for reasons,
Myself discharging my excrementitious body to be burn'd, or
      render'd to powder, or buried,
My real body doubtless left to me for other spheres,
My voided body nothing more to me, returning to the purifications,
      further offices, eternal uses of the earth.

O to attract by more than attraction!
How it is I know not — yet behold! the something which obeys
      none of the rest,
It is offensive, never defensive — yet how magnetic it draws.

O to struggle against great odds, to meet enemies undaunted !
To be entirely alone with them, to find how much one can stand !
To look strife, torture, prison, popular odium, face to face !
To mount the scaffold, to advance to the muzzles of guns with
      perfect nonchalance !
To be indeed a God !

O to sail to sea in a ship !
To leave this steady unendurable land,
To leave the tiresome sameness of the streets, the sidewalks and
      the houses,
To leave you O you solid motionless land, and entering a ship,
To sail and sail and sail !

O to have life henceforth a poem of new joys !
To dance, clap hands, exult, shout, skip, leap, roll on, float on !
To be a sailor of the world bound for all ports,
A ship itself, (see indeed these sails I spread to the sun and air,)
A swift and swelling ship full of rich words, full of joys.

SONG OF THE BROAD-AXE.

1

WEAPON shapely, naked, wan,
Head from the mother's bowels drawn,
Wooded flesh and metal bone, limb only one and lip only one,
Gray-blue leaf by red-heat grown, helve produced from a little
      seed sown,
Resting the grass amid and upon,
To be lean'd and to lean on.

Strong shapes and attributes of strong shapes, masculine trades,
      sights and sounds,
Long varied train of an emblem, dabs of music,
Fingers of the organist skipping staccato over the keys of the
      great organ.

2

Welcome are all earth's lands, each for its kind,
Welcome are lands of pine and oak,
Welcome are lands of the lemon and fig,
Welcome are lands of gold,

Welcome are lands of wheat and maize, welcome those of the
    grape,
Welcome are lands of sugar and rice,
Welcome the cotton-lands, welcome those of the white potato
    and sweet potato,
Welcome are mountains, flats, sands, forests, prairies,
Welcome the rich borders of rivers, table-lands, openings,
Welcome the measureless grazing-lands, welcome the teeming soil
    of orchards, flax, honey, hemp ;
Welcome just as much the other more hard-faced lands,
Lands rich as lands of gold or wheat and fruit lands,
Lands of mines, lands of the manly and rugged ores,
Lands of coal, copper, lead, tin, zinc,
Lands of iron — lands of the make of the axe.

3

The log at the wood-pile, the axe supported by it,
The sylvan hut, the vine over the doorway, the space clear'd for a
    garden,
The irregular tapping of rain down on the leaves after the storm
    is lull'd,
The wailing and moaning at intervals, the thought of the sea,
The thought of ships struck in the storm and put on their beam
    ends, and the cutting away of masts,
The sentiment of the huge timbers of old-fashion'd houses and
    barns,
The remember'd print or narrative, the voyage at a venture of
    men, families, goods,
The disembarkation, the founding of a new city,
The voyage of those who sought a New England and found it, the
    outset anywhere,
The settlements of the Arkansas, Colorado, Ottawa, Willamette,
The slow progress, the scant fare, the axe, rifle, saddle-bags ;
The beauty of all adventurous and daring persons,
The beauty of wood-boys and wood-men with their clear un-
    trimm'd faces,
The beauty of independence, departure, actions that rely on
    themselves,
The American contempt for statutes and ceremonies, the bound-
    less impatience of restraint,
The loose drift of character, the inkling through random types,
    the solidification ;
The butcher in the slaughter-house, the hands aboard schooners
    and sloops, the raftsman, the pioneer,

Lumbermen in their winter camp, daybreak in the woods, stripes
  of snow on the limbs of trees, the occasional snapping,
The glad clear sound of one's own voice, the merry song, the
  natural life of the woods, the strong day's work,
The blazing fire at night, the sweet taste of supper, the talk, the
  bed of hemlock-boughs and the bear-skin ;
The house-builder at work in cities or anywhere,
The preparatory jointing, squaring, sawing, mortising,
The hoist-up of beams, the push of them in their places, laying
  them regular,
Setting the studs by their tenons in the mortises according as they
  were prepared,
The blows of mallets and hammers, the attitudes of the men,
  their curv'd limbs,
Bending, standing, astride the beams, driving in pins, holding on
  by posts and braces,
The hook'd arm over the plate, the other arm wielding the axe,
The floor-men forcing the planks close to be nail'd,
Their postures bringing their weapons downward on the bearers,
The echoes resounding through the vacant building ;
The huge storehouse carried up in the city well under way,
The six framing-men, two in the middle and two at each end,
  carefully bearing on their shoulders a heavy stick for a
  cross-beam,
The crowded line of masons with trowels in their right hands
  rapidly laying the long side-wall, two hundred feet from
  front to rear,
The flexible rise and fall of backs, the continual click of the
  trowels striking the bricks,
The bricks one after another each laid so workmanlike in its
  place, and set with a knock of the trowel-handle,
The piles of materials, the mortar on the mortar-boards, and the
  steady replenishing by the hod-men ;
Spar-makers in the spar-yard, the swarming row of well-grown
  apprentices,
The swing of their axes on the square-hew'd log shaping it towa:.i
  the shape of a mast,
The brisk short crackle of the steel driven slantingly into the pine,
The butter-color'd chips flying off in great flakes and slivers,
The limber motion of brawny young arms and hips in easy cos-
  tumes,
The constructor of wharves, bridges, piers, bulk-heads, floats,
  stays against the sea ;
The city fireman, the fire that suddenly bursts forth in the close-
  pack'd square,

The arriving engines, the hoarse shouts, the nimble stepping and daring,
The strong command through the fire-trumpets, the falling in line, the rise and fall of the arms forcing the water,
The slender, spasmic, blue-white jets, the bringing to bear of the hooks and ladders and their execution,
The crash and cut away of connecting wood-work, or through floors if the fire smoulders under them,
The crowd with their lit faces watching, the glare and dense shadows ;
The forger at his forge-furnace and the user of iron after him,
The maker of the axe large and small, and the welder and temperer,
The chooser breathing his breath on the cold steel and trying the edge with his thumb,
The one who clean-shapes the handle and sets it firmly in the socket ;
The shadowy processions of the portraits of the past users also,
The primal patient mechanics, the architects and engineers,
The far-off Assyrian edifice and Mizra' edifice,
The Roman lictors*preceding the consuls,
The antique European warrior with his axe in combat,
The uplifted arm, the clatter of blows on the helmeted head,
The death-howl, the limpsy tumbling body, the rush of friend and foe thither,
The siege of revolted lieges determin'd for liberty,
The summons to surrender, the battering at castle gates, the truce and parley,
The sack of an old city in its time,
The bursting in of mercenaries and bigots tumultuously and disorderly,
Roar, flames, blood, drunkenness, madness,
Goods freely rifled from houses and temples, screams of women in the gripe of brigands,
Craft and thievery of camp-followers, men running, old persons despairing,
The hell of war, the cruelties of creeds,
The list of all executive deeds and words just or unjust,
The power of personality just or unjust.

4

Muscle and pluck forever !
What invigorates life invigorates death,
And the dead advance as much as the living advance,
And the future is no more uncertain than the present,

For the roughness of the earth and of man encloses as much as
    the delicatesse of the earth and of man,
And nothing endures but personal qualities.

What do you think endures?
Do you think a great city endures?
Or a teeming manufacturing state? or a prepared constitution? or
    the best built steamships?
Or hotels of granite and iron? or any chef-d'œuvres of engineering,
    forts, armaments?

Away! these are not to be cherish'd for themselves,
They fill their hour, the dancers dance, the musicians play for
    them,
The show passes, all does well enough of course,
All does very well till one flash of defiance.

A great city is that which has the greatest men and women,
If it be a few ragged huts it is still the greatest city in the whole
    world.

5

The place where a great city stands is not the place of stretch'd
    wharves, docks, manufactures, deposits of produce merely,
Nor the place of ceaseless salutes of new-comers or the anchor-
    lifters of the departing,
Nor the place of the tallest and costliest buildings or shops selling
    goods from the rest of the earth,
Nor the place of the best libraries and schools, nor the place where
    money is plentiest,
Nor the place of the most numerous population.

Where the city stands with the brawniest breed of orators and
    bards,
Where the city stands that is belov'd by these, and loves them in
    return and understands them,
Where no monuments exist to heroes but in the common words
    and deeds,
Where thrift is in its place, and prudence is in its place,
Where the men and women think lightly of the laws,
Where the slave ceases, and the master of slaves ceases,
Where the populace rise at once against the never-ending audacity
    of elected persons,
Where fierce men and women pour forth as the sea to the whistle
    of death pours its sweeping and unript waves,

Where outside authority enters always after the precedence of
    inside authority,
Where the citizen is always the head and ideal, and President,
    Mayor, Governor and what not, are agents for pay,
Where children are taught to be laws to themselves, and to depend
    on themselves,
Where equanimity is illustrated in affairs,
Where speculations on the soul are encouraged,
Where women walk in public processions in the streets the same
    as the men,
Where they enter the public assembly and take places the same as
    the men ;
Where the city of the faithfulest friends stands,
Where the city of the cleanliness of the sexes stands,
Where the city of the healthiest fathers stands,
Where the city of the best-bodied mothers stands,
There the great city stands.

6

How beggarly appear arguments before a defiant deed !
How the floridness of the materials of cities shrivels before a man's
    or woman's look !

All waits or goes by default till a strong being appears ;
A strong being is the proof of the race and of the ability of the
    universe,
When he or she appears materials are overaw'd,
The dispute on the soul stops,
The old customs and phrases are confronted, turn'd back, or laid
    away.

What is your money-making now? what can it do now?
What is your respectability now?
What are your theology, tuition, society, traditions, statute-books,
    now?
Where are your jibes of being now?
Where are your cavils about the soul now?

7

A sterile landscape covers the ore, there is as good as the best for
    all the forbidding appearance,
There is the mine, there are the miners,
The forge-furnace is there, the melt is accomplish'd, the hammers-
    men are at hand with their tongs and hammers,
What always served and always serves is at hand.

Than this nothing has better served, it has served all,
Served the fluent-tongued and subtle-sensed Greek, and long ere
the Greek,
Served in building the buildings that last longer than any,
Served the Hebrew, the Persian, the most ancient Hindustanee,
Served the mound-raiser on the Mississippi, served those whose
relics remain in Central America,
Served Albic temples in woods or on plains, with unhewn pillars
and the druids,
Served the artificial clefts, vast, high, silent, on the snow-cover'd
hills of Scandinavia,
Served those who time out of mind made on the granite walls
rough sketches of the sun, moon, stars, ships, ocean waves,
Served the paths of the irruptions of the Goths, served the pas-
toral tribes and nomads,
Served the long distant Kelt, served the hardy pirates of the Baltic,
Served before any of those the venerable and harmless men of
Ethiopia,
Served the making of helms for the galleys of pleasure and the
making of those for war,
Served all great works on land and all great works on the sea,
For the mediæval ages and before the mediæval ages,
Served not the living only then as now, but served the dead.

8

I see the European headsman,
He stands mask'd, clothed in red, with huge legs and strong naked
arms,
And leans on a ponderous axe:

(Whom have you slaughter'd lately European headsman?
Whose is that blood upon you so wet and sticky?)

I see the clear sunsets of the martyrs,
I see from the scaffolds the descending ghosts,
Ghosts of dead lords, uncrown'd ladies, impeach'd ministers,
rejected kings,
Rivals, traitors, poisoners, disgraced chieftains and the rest.

I see those who in any land have died for the good cause,
The seed is spare, nevertheless the crop shall never run out,
(Mind you O foreign kings, O priests, the crop shall never run out.)

I see the blood wash'd entirely away from the axe,
Both blade and helve are clean,

They spirt no more the blood of European nobles, they clasp no
more the necks of queens.

I see the headsman withdraw and become useless,
I see the scaffold untrodden and mouldy, I see no longer any axe
upon it,
I see the mighty and friendly emblem of the power of my own
race, the newest, largest race.

9

(America! I do not vaunt my love for you,
I have what I have.)

The axe leaps!
The solid forest gives fluid utterances,
They tumble forth, they rise and form,
Hut, tent, landing, survey,
Flail, plough, pick, crowbar, spade,
Shingle, rail, prop, wainscot, jamb, lath, panel, gable,
Citadel, ceiling, saloon, academy, organ, exhibition-house, li-
brary,
Cornice, trellis, pilaster, balcony, window, turret, porch,
Hoe, rake, pitchfork, pencil, wagon, staff, saw, jack-plane, mallet,
wedge, rounce,
Chair, tub, hoop, table, wicket, vane, sash, floor,
Work-box, chest, string'd instrument, boat, frame, and what not,
Capitols of States, and capitol of the nation of States,
Long stately rows in avenues, hospitals for orphans or for the poor
or sick,
Manhattan steamboats and clippers taking the measure of all seas.

The shapes arise!
Shapes of the using of axes anyhow, and the users and all that
neighbors them,
Cutters down of wood and haulers of it to the Penobscot or Ken-
nebec,
Dwellers in cabins among the Californian mountains or by the little
lakes, or on the Columbia,
Dwellers south on the banks of the Gila or Rio Grande, friendly
gatherings, the characters and fun,
Dwellers along the St. Lawrence, or north in Kanada, or down by
the Yellowstone, dwellers on coasts and off coasts,
Seal-fishers, whalers, arctic seamen breaking passages through the
ice.

The shapes arise !
Shapes of factories, arsenals, foundries, markets,
Shapes of the two-threaded tracks of railroads,
Shapes of the sleepers of bridges, vast frameworks, girders, arches,
Shapes of the fleets of barges, tows, lake and canal craft, river craft,
Ship-yards and dry-docks along the Eastern and Western seas, and
    in many a bay and by-place,
The live-oak kelsons, the pine planks, the spars, the hackmatack-
    roots for knees,
The ships themselves on their ways, the tiers of scaffolds, the
    workmen busy outside and inside,
The tools lying around, the great auger and little auger, the adze,
    bolt, line, square, gouge, and bead-plane.

10

The shapes arise !
The shape measur'd, saw'd, jack'd, join'd, stain'd,
The coffin-shape for the dead to lie within in his shroud,
The shape got out in posts, in the bedstead posts, in the posts of
    the bride's bed,
The shape of the little trough, the shape of the rockers beneath,
    the shape of the babe's cradle,
The shape of the floor-planks, the floor-planks for dancers' feet,
The shape of the planks of the family home, the home of the
    friendly parents and children,
The shape of the roof of the home of the happy young man and
    woman, the roof over the well-married young man and
    woman,
The roof over the supper joyously cook'd by the chaste wife, and
    joyously eaten by the chaste husband, content after his
    day's work.

The shapes arise !
The shape of the prisoner's place in the court-room, and of him
    or her seated in the place,
The shape of the liquor-bar lean'd against by the young rum-
    drinker and the old rum-drinker,
The shape of the shamed and angry stairs trod by sneaking foot-
    steps,
The shape of the sly settee, and the adulterous unwholesome
    couple,
The shape of the gambling-board with its devilish winnings and
    losings,
The shape of the step-ladder for the convicted and sentenced
    murderer, the murderer with haggard face and pinion'd arms,

The sheriff at hand with his deputies, the silent and white-lipp'd
　　crowd, the dangling of the rope.

The shapes arise !
Shapes of doors giving many exits and entrances,
The door passing the dissever'd friend flush'd and in haste,
The door that admits good news and bad news,
The door whence the son left home confident and puff'd up,
The door he enter'd again from a long and scandalous absence,
　　diseas'd, broken down, without innocence, without means.

11

Her shape arises,
She less guarded than ever, yet more guarded than ever,
The gross and soil'd she moves among do not make her gross and
　　soil'd,
She knows the thoughts as she passes, nothing is conceal'd from her,
She is none the less considerate or friendly therefor,
She is the best belov'd, it is without exception, she has no reason
　　to fear and she does not fear,
Oaths, quarrels, hiccupp'd songs, smutty expressions, are idle to
　　her as she passes,
She is silent, she is possess'd of herself, they do not offend her,
She receives them as the laws of Nature receive them, she is strong,
She too is a law of Nature — there is no law stronger than she is.

12

The main shapes arise !
Shapes of Democracy total, result of centuries,
Shapes ever projecting other shapes,
Shapes of turbulent manly cities,
Shapes of the friends and home-givers of the whole earth,
Shapes bracing the earth and braced with the whole earth.

SONG OF THE EXPOSITION.

1

(Ah little recks the laborer,
How near his work is holding him to God,
The loving Laborer through space and time.)

After all not to create only, or found only,

But to bring perhaps from afar what is already founded,
To give it our own identity, average, limitless, free,
To fill the gross the torpid bulk with vital religious fire,
Not to repel or destroy so much as accept, fuse, rehabilitate,
To obey as well as command, to follow more than to lead,
These also are the lessons of our New World ;
While how little the New after all, how much the Old, Old World !

Long and long has the grass been growing,
Long and long has the rain been falling,
Long has the globe been rolling round.

2

Come Muse migrate from Greece and Ionia,
Cross out please those immensely overpaid accounts,
That matter of Troy and Achilles' wrath, and Æneas', Odysseus'
    wanderings,
Placard "Removed" and "To Let" on the rocks of your snowy
    Parnassus,
Repeat at Jerusalem, place the notice high on Jaffa's gate and on
    Mount Moriah,
The same on the walls of your German, French and Spanish
    castles, and Italian collections,
For know a better, fresher, busier sphere, a wide, untried domain
    awaits, demands you.

3

Responsive to our summons,
Or rather to her long-nurs'd inclination,
Join'd with an irresistible, natural gravitation,
She comes ! I hear the rustling of her gown,
I scent the odor of her breath's delicious fragrance,
I mark her step divine, her curious eyes a-turning, rolling,
Upon this very scene.

The dame of dames ! can I believe then,
Those ancient temples, sculptures classic, could none of them
    retain her ?
Nor shades of Virgil and Dante, nor myriad memories, poems,
    old associations, magnetize and hold on to her ?
But that she's left them all — and here ?

Yes, if you will allow me to say so,
I, my friends, if you do not, can plainly see her,

The same undying soul of earth's, activity's, beauty's, heroism's
      expression,
Out from her evolutions hither come, ended the strata of her
      former themes,
Hidden and cover'd by to-day's, foundation of to-day's,
Ended, deceas'd through time, her voice by Castaly's fountain,
Silent the broken-lipp'd Sphynx in Egypt, silent all those century-
      baffling tombs,
Ended for aye the epics of Asia's, Europe's helmeted warriors,
      ended the primitive call of the muses,
Calliope's call forever closed, Clio, Melpomene, Thalia dead,
Ended the stately rhythmus of Una and Oriana, ended the quest
      of the holy Graal,
Jerusalem a handful of ashes blown by the wind, extinct,
The Crusaders' streams of shadowy midnight troops sped with the
      sunrise,
Amadis, Tancred, utterly gone, Charlemagne, Roland, Oliver gone,
Palmerin, ogre, departed, vanish'd the turrets that Usk from its
      waters reflected,
Arthur vanish'd with all his knights, Merlin and Lancelot and
      Galahad, all gone, dissolv'd utterly like an exhalation;
Pass'd! pass'd! for us, forever pass'd, that once so mighty world,
      now void, inanimate, phantom world,
Embroider'd, dazzling, foreign world, with all its gorgeous legends,
      myths,
Its kings and castles proud, its priests and warlike lords and
      courtly dames,
Pass'd to its charnel vault, coffin'd with crown and armor on,
Blazon'd with Shakspere's purple page,
And dirged by Tennyson's sweet sad rhyme.

I say I see, my friends, if you do not, the illustrious emigré,
      (having it is true in her day, although the same, changed,
      journey'd considerable,)
Making directly for this rendezvous, vigorously clearing a path for
      herself, striding through the confusion,
By thud of machinery and shrill steam-whistle undismay'd,
Bluff'd not a bit by drain-pipe, gasometers, artificial fertilizers,
Smiling and pleas'd with palpable intent to stay,
She's here, install'd amid the kitchen ware!

4

But hold — don't I forget my manners?
To introduce the stranger, (what else indeed do I live to chant
      for?) to thee Columbia;

In liberty's name welcome immortal ! clasp hands,
And ever henceforth sisters dear be both.

Fear not O Muse ! truly new ways and days receive, surround you,
I candidly confess a queer, queer race, of novel fashion,
And yet the same old human race, the same within, without,
Faces and hearts the same, feelings the same, yearnings the same,
The same old love, beauty and use the same.

5

We do not blame thee elder World, nor really separate ourselves
    from thee,
(Would the son separate himself from the father?)
Looking back on thee, seeing thee to thy duties, grandeurs,
    through past ages bending, building,
We build to ours to-day.

Mightier than Egypt's tombs,
Fairer than Grecia's, Roma's temples,
Prouder than Milan's statued, spired cathedral,
More picturesque than Rhenish castle-keeps,
We plan even now to raise, beyond them all,
Thy great cathedral sacred industry, no tomb,
A keep for life for practical invention.

As in a waking vision,
E'en while I chant I see it rise, I scan and prophesy outside
    and in,
Its manifold ensemble.

Around a palace, loftier, fairer, ampler than any yet,
Earth's modern wonder, history's seven outstripping,
High rising tier on tier with glass and iron façades,
Gladdening the sun and sky, enhued in cheerfulest hues,
Bronze, lilac, robin's-egg, marine and crimson,
Over whose golden roof shall flaunt, beneath thy banner Freedom,
The banners of the States and flags of every land,
A brood of lofty, fair, but lesser palaces shall cluster.

Somewhere within their walls shall all that forwards perfect human
    life be started,
Tried, taught, advanced, visibly exhibited.

Not only all the world of works, trade, products,
But all the workmen of the world here to be represented.

Here shall you trace in flowing operation,
In every state of practical, busy movement, the rills of civilization,
Materials here under your eye shall change their shape as if by
    magic,
The cotton shall be pick'd almost in the very field,
Shall be dried, clean'd, ginn'd, baled, spun into thread and cloth
    before you,
You shall see hands at work at all the old processes and all the
    new ones,
You shall see the various grains and how flour is made and then
    bread baked by the bakers,
You shall see the crude ores of California and Nevada passing on
    and on till they become bullion,
You shall watch how the printer sets type, and learn what a com-
    posing-stick is,
You shall mark in amazement the Hoe press*whirling its cylinders,
    shedding the printed leaves steady and fast,
The photograph, model, watch, pin, nail, shall be created before
    you.

In large calm halls, a stately museum shall teach you the infinite
    lessons of minerals,
In another, woods, plants, vegetation shall be illustrated — in
    another animals, animal life and development.

One stately house shall be the music house,
Others for other arts — learning, the sciences, shall all be here,
None shall be slighted, none but shall here be honor'd, help'd,
    exampled.

6

(This, this and these, America, shall be *your* pyramids and
    obelisks,
Your Alexandrian Pharos, gardens of Babylon,
Your temple at Olympia.)

The male and female many laboring not,
Shall ever here confront the laboring many,
With precious benefits to both, glory to all,
To thee America, and thee eternal Muse.

And here shall ye inhabit powerful Matrons !
In your vast state vaster than all the old,
Echoed through long, long centuries to come,
To sound of different, prouder songs, with stronger themes,

Practical, peaceful life, the people's life, the People themselves,
Lifted, illumin'd, bathed in peace — elate, secure in peace.

7

Away with themes of war ! away with war itself !
Hence from my shuddering sight to never more return that show
     of blacken'd, mutilated corpses !
That hell unpent and raid of blood, fit for wild tigers or for lop-
     tongued wolves, not reasoning men,
And in its stead speed industry's campaigns,
With thy undaunted armies, engineering,
Thy pennants labor, loosen'd to the breeze,
Thy bugles sounding loud and clear.

Away with old romance !
Away with novels, plots and plays of foreign courts,
Away with love-verses sugar'd in rhyme, the intrigues, amours of
     idlers,
Fitted for only banquets of the night where dancers to late music
     slide,
The unhealthy pleasures, extravagant dissipations of the few,
With perfumes, heat and wine, beneath the dazzling chandeliers.

To you ye reverent sane sisters,
I raise a voice for far superber themes for poets and for art,
To exalt the present and the real,
To teach the average man the glory of his daily walk and trade,
To sing in songs how exercise and chemical life are never to be
     baffled,
To manual work for each and all, to plough, hoe, dig,
To plant and tend the tree, the berry, vegetables, flowers,
For every man to see to it that he really do something, for every
     woman too ;
To use the hammer and the saw, (rip, or cross-cut,)
To cultivate a turn for carpentering, plastering, painting,
To work as tailor, tailoress, nurse, hostler, porter,
To invent a little, something ingenious, to aid the washing, cook-
     ing, cleaning,
And hold it no disgrace to take a hand at them themselves.

I say I bring thee Muse to-day and here,
All occupations, duties broad and close,
Toil, healthy toil and sweat, endless, without cessation,
The old, old practical burdens, interests, joys,

The family, parentage, childhood, husband and wife,
The house-comforts, the house itself and all its belongings,
Food and its preservation, chemistry applied to it,
Whatever forms the average, strong, complete, sweet-blooded man
        or woman, the perfect longeve*personality,
And helps its present life to health and happiness, and shapes its soul,
For the eternal real life to come.

With latest connections, works, the inter-transportation of the world,
Steam-power, the great express lines, gas, petroleum,
These triumphs of our time, the Atlantic's delicate cable,
The Pacific railroad, the Suez canal, the Mont Cenis and Gothard
        and Hoosac tunnels, the Brooklyn bridge,
This earth all spann'd with iron rails, with lines of steamships
        threading every sea,
Our own rondure, the current globe I bring.

8

And thou America,
Thy offspring towering e'er so high, yet higher Thee above all
        towering,
With Victory on thy left, and at thy right hand Law;
Thou Union holding all, fusing, absorbing, tolerating all,
Thee, ever thee, I sing.

Thou, also thou, a World,
With all thy wide geographies, manifold, different, distant,
Rounded by thee in one — one common orbic language,
One common indivisible destiny for All.

And by the spells which ye vouchsafe to those your ministers in
        earnest,
I here personify and call my themes, to make them pass before ye.

Behold, America ! (and thou, ineffable guest and sister !)
For thee come trooping up thy waters and thy lands ;
Behold ! thy fields and farms, thy far-off woods and mountains,
As in procession coming.

Behold, the sea itself,
And on its limitless, heaving breast, the ships ;
See, where their white sails, bellying in the wind, speckle the green
        and blue,
See, the steamers coming and going, steaming in or out of port,
See, dusky and undulating, the long pennants of smoke.

Behold, in Oregon, far in the north and west,
Or in Maine, far in the north and east, thy cheerful axemen,
Wielding all day their axes.

Behold, on the lakes, thy pilots at their wheels, thy oarsmen,
How the ash writhes under those muscular arms !

There by the furnace, and there by the anvil,
Behold thy sturdy blacksmiths swinging their sledges,
Overhand so steady, overhand they turn and fall with joyous clank,
Like a tumult of laughter.

Mark the spirit of invention everywhere, thy rapid patents,
Thy continual workshops, foundries, risen or rising,
See, from their chimneys how the tall flame-fires stream.

Mark, thy interminable farms, North, South,
Thy wealthy daughter-states, Eastern and Western,
The varied products of Ohio, Pennsylvania, Missouri, Georgia,
　　　　Texas, and the rest,
Thy limitless crops, grass, wheat, sugar, oil, corn, rice, hemp, hops,
Thy barns all fill'd, the endless freight-train and the bulging
　　　　storehouse,
The grapes that ripen on thy vines, the apples in thy orchards,
Thy incalculable lumber, beef, pork, potatoes, thy coal, thy gold
　　　　and silver,
The inexhaustible iron in thy mines.

All thine O sacred Union !
Ships, farms, shops, barns, factories, mines,
City and State, North, South, item and aggregate,
We dedicate, dread Mother, all to thee !

Protectress absolute, thou ! bulwark of all !
For well we know that while thou givest each and all, (generous
　　　　as God,)
Without thee neither all nor each, nor land, home,
Nor ship, nor mine, nor any here this day secure,
Nor aught, nor any day secure.

9

And thou, the Emblem waving over all !
Delicate beauty, a word to thee, (it may be salutary,)
Remember thou hast not always been as here to-day so comfortably
　　　　ensovereign'd,

In other scenes than these have I observ'd thee flag,
Not quite so trim and whole and freshly blooming in folds of stain-
    less silk,
But I have seen thee bunting, to tatters torn upon thy splinter'd staff,
Or clutch'd to some young color-bearer's breast with desperate hands,
Savagely struggled for, for life or death, fought over long,
'Mid cannons' thunder-crash and many a curse and groan and yell,
    and rifle-volleys cracking sharp,
And moving masses as wild demons surging, and lives as nothing
    risk'd,
For thy mere remnant grimed with dirt and smoke and sopp'd in
    blood,
For sake of that, my beauty, and that thou might'st dally as now
    secure up there,
Many a good man have I seen go under.

Now here and these and hence in peace, all thine O Flag!
And here and hence for thee, O universal Muse! and thou for them!
And here and hence O Union, all the work and workmen thine!
None separate from thee — henceforth One only, we and thou,
(For the blood of the children, what is it, only the blood
    maternal?
And lives and works, what are they all at last, except the roads to
    faith and death?)

While we rehearse our measureless wealth, it is for thee, dear
    Mother,
We own it all and several to-day indissoluble in thee;
Think not our chant, our show, merely for products gross or lucre
    — it is for thee, the soul in thee, electric, spiritual!
Our farms, inventions, crops, we own in thee! cities and States in
    thee!
Our freedom all in thee! our very lives in thee!

SONG OF THE REDWOOD-TREE.

I

A CALIFORNIA song,
A prophecy and indirection, a thought impalpable to breathe as air,
A chorus of dryads, fading, departing, or hamadryads departing,
A murmuring, fateful, giant voice, out of the earth and sky,
Voice of a mighty dying tree in the redwood forest dense.

Farewell my brethren,
Farewell O earth and sky, farewell ye neighboring waters,
My time has ended, my term has come.

Along the northern coast,
Just back from the rock-bound shore and the caves,
In the saline air from the sea in the Mendocino* country,
With the surge for base and accompaniment low and hoarse,
With crackling blows of axes sounding musically driven by strong
　　　　arms,
Riven deep by the sharp tongues of the axes, there in the redwood
　　　　forest dense,
I heard the mighty tree its death-chant chanting.

The choppers heard not, the camp shanties echoed not,
The quick-ear'd teamsters and chain and jack-screw men heard
　　　　not,
As the wood-spirits came from their haunts of a thousand years to
　　　　join the refrain,
But in my soul I plainly heard.

Murmuring out of its myriad leaves,
Down from its lofty top rising two hundred feet high,
Out of its stalwart trunk and limbs, out of its foot-thick bark,
That chant of the seasons and time, chant not of the past only
　　　　but the future.

You untold life of me,
And all you venerable and innocent joys,
Perennial hardy life of me with joys 'mid rain and many a
　　　　summer sun,
And the white snows and night and the wild winds;
O the great patient rugged joys, my soul's strong joys unreck'd by
　　　　man,
(For know I bear the soul befitting me, I too have consciousness,
　　　　identity,
And all the rocks and mountains have, and all the earth,)
Joys of the life befitting me and brothers mine,
Our time, our term has come.

Nor yield we mournfully majestic brothers,
We who have grandly fill'd our time;
With Nature's calm content, with tacit huge delight,
We welcome what we wrought for through the past,
And leave the field for them.

For them predicted long,
For a superber race, they too to grandly fill their time,
For them we abdicate, in them ourselves ye forest kings!
In them these skies and airs, these mountain peaks, Shasta,
          Nevadas,
These huge precipitous cliffs, this amplitude, these valleys, far
          Yosemite,
To be in them absorb'd, assimilated.

Then to a loftier strain,
Still prouder, more ecstatic rose the chant,
As if the heirs, the deities of the West,
Joining with master-tongue bore part.

Not wan from Asia's fetiches,
Nor red from Europe's old dynastic slaughter-house,
(Area of murder-plots of thrones, with scent left yet of wars and
          scaffolds everywhere,)
But come from Nature's long and harmless throes, peacefully
          builded thence,
These virgin lands, lands of the Western shore,
To the new culminating man, to you, the empire new,
You promis'd long, we pledge, we dedicate.

You occult deep volitions,
You average spiritual manhood, purpose of all, pois'd on yourself,
          giving not taking law,
You womanhood divine, mistress and source of all, whence life
          and love and aught that comes from life and love,
You unseen moral essence of all the vast materials of America,
          (age upon age working in death the same as life,)
You that, sometimes known, oftener unknown, really shape and
          mould the New World, adjusting it to Time and Space,
You hidden national will lying in your abysms, conceal'd but ever
          alert,
You past and present purposes tenaciously pursued, may-be uncon-
          scious of yourselves,
Unswerv'd by all the passing errors, perturbations of the surface;
You vital, universal, deathless germs, beneath all creeds, arts,
          statutes, literatures,
Here build your homes for good, establish here, these areas entire,
          lands of the Western shore,
We pledge, we dedicate to you.

For man of you, your characteristic race,

Here may he hardy, sweet, gigantic grow, here tower proportion-
*   ate to Nature,*
Here climb the vast pure spaces unconfined, uncheck'd by wall or
*   roof,*
Here laugh with storm or sun, here joy, here patiently inure,
Here heed himself, unfold himself, (not others' formulas heed,)
*   here fill his time,*
To duly fall, to aid, unreck'd at last,
To disappear, to serve.

Thus on the northern coast,
In the echo of teamsters' calls and the clinking chains, and the
    music of choppers' axes,
The falling trunk and limbs, the crash, the muffled shriek, the
    groan,
Such words combined from the redwood-tree, as of voices ecstatic,
    ancient and rustling,
The century-lasting, unseen dryads, singing, withdrawing,
All their recesses of forests and mountains leaving,
From the Cascade range to the Wahsatch, or Idaho far, or Utah,
To the deities of the modern henceforth yielding,
The chorus and indications, the vistas of coming humanity, the
    settlements, features all,
In the Mendocino woods I caught.

2

The flashing and golden pageant of California,
The sudden and gorgeous drama, the sunny and ample lands,
The long and varied stretch from Puget sound to Colorado south,
Lands bathed in sweeter, rarer, healthier air, valleys and mountain
    cliffs,
The fields of Nature long prepared and fallow, the silent, cyclic
    chemistry,
The slow and steady ages plodding, the unoccupied surface ripen-
    ing, the rich ores forming beneath ;
At last the New arriving, assuming, taking possession,
A swarming and busy race settling and organizing everywhere,
Ships coming in from the whole round world, and going out to
    the whole world,
To India and China and Australia and the thousand island para-
    dises of the Pacific,
Populous cities, the latest inventions, the steamers on the rivers,
    the railroads, with many a thrifty farm, with machinery,
And wool and wheat and the grape, and diggings of yellow gold.

3

But more in you than these, lands of the Western shore,
(These but the means, the implements, the standing-ground,)
I see in you, certain to come, the promise of thousands of years,
    till now deferr'd,
Promis'd to be fulfill'd, our common kind, the race.

The new society at last, proportionate to Nature,
In man of you, more than your mountain peaks or stalwart trees
    imperial,
In woman more, far more, than all your gold or vines, or even
    vital air.

Fresh come, to a new world indeed, yet long prepared,
I see the genius of the modern, child of the real and ideal,
Clearing the ground for broad humanity, the true America, heir
    of the past so grand,
To build a grander future.

A SONG FOR OCCUPATIONS.

1

A song for occupations!
In the labor of engines and trades and the labor of fields I find
    the developments,
And find the eternal meanings.

Workmen and Workwomen!
Were all educations practical and ornamental well display'd out
    of me, what would it amount to?
Were I as the head teacher, charitable proprietor, wise statesman,
    what would it amount to?
Were I to you as the boss employing and paying you, would that
    satisfy you?

The learn'd, virtuous, benevolent, and the usual terms,
A man like me and never the usual terms.

Neither a servant nor a master I,
I take no sooner a large price than a small price, I will have my
    own whoever enjoys me,
I will be even with you and you shall be even with me.

If you stand at work in a shop I stand as nigh as the nighest in
    the same shop,
If you bestow gifts on your brother or dearest friend I demand as
    good as your brother or dearest friend,
If your lover, husband, wife, is welcome by day or night, I must
    be personally as welcome,
If you become degraded, criminal, ill, then I become so for your
    sake,
If you remember your foolish and outlaw'd deeds, do you think
    I cannot remember my own foolish and outlaw'd deeds?
If you carouse at the table I carouse at the opposite side of the
    table,
If you meet some stranger in the streets and love him or her, why
    I often meet strangers in the street and love them.

Why what have you thought of yourself?
Is it you then that thought yourself less?
Is it you that thought the President greater than you?
Or the rich better off than you? or the educated wiser than you?

(Because you are greasy or pimpled, or were once drunk, or a
    thief,
Or that you are diseas'd, or rheumatic, or a prostitute,
Or from frivolity or impotence, or that you are no scholar and
    never saw your name in print,
Do you give in that you are any less immortal?)

2

Souls of men and women! it is not you I call unseen, unheard,
    untouchable and untouching,
It is not you I go argue pro and con about, and to settle whether
    you are alive or no,
I own publicly who you are, if nobody else owns.

Grown, half-grown and babe, of this country and every country, in-
    doors and out-doors, one just as much as the other, I see,
And all else behind or through them.

The wife, and she is not one jot less than the husband,
The daughter, and she is just as good as the son,
The mother, and she is every bit as much as the father.

Offspring of ignorant and poor, boys apprenticed to trades,
Young fellows working on farms and old fellows working on farms,
Sailor-men, merchant-men, coasters, immigrants,

All these I see, but nigher and farther the same I see,
None shall escape me and none shall wish to escape me.

I bring what you much need yet always have,
Not money, amours, dress, eating, erudition, but as good,
I send no agent or medium, offer no representative of value, but
    offer the value itself.

There is something that comes to one now and perpetually,
It is not what is printed, preach'd, discussed, it eludes discussion
        and print,
It is not to be put in a book, it is not in this book,
It is for you whoever you are, it is no farther from you than your
        hearing and sight are from you,
It is hinted by nearest, commonest, readiest, it is ever provoked
    by them.

You may read in many languages, yet read nothing about it,
You may read the President's message and read nothing about it
        there,
Nothing in the reports from the State department or Treasury
        department, or in the daily papers or weekly papers,
Or in the census or revenue returns, prices current, or any
        accounts of stock.

3

The sun and stars that float in the open air,
The apple-shaped earth and we upon it, surely the drift of them
        is something grand,
I do not know what it is except that it is grand, and that it is
        happiness,
And that the enclosing purport of us here is not a speculation or
        bon-mot or reconnoissance,
And that it is not something which by luck may turn out well for
        us, and without luck must be a failure for us,
And not something which may yet be retracted in a certain
        contingency.

The light and shade, the curious sense of body and identity, the
        greed that with perfect complaisance devours all things,
The endless pride and outstretching of man, unspeakable joys
        and sorrows,
The wonder every one sees in every one else he sees, and the
        wonders that fill each minute of time forever,
What have you reckon'd them for, camerado?

Have you reckon'd them for your trade or farm-work? or for the
       profits of your store?
Or to achieve yourself a position? or to fill a gentleman's leisure,
       or a lady's leisure?

Have you reckon'd that the landscape took substance and form
       that it might be painted in a picture?
Or men and women that they might be written of, and songs sung?
Or the attraction of gravity, and the great laws and harmonious
       combinations and the fluids of the air, as subjects for the
       savans?
Or the brown land and the blue sea for maps and charts?
Or the stars to be put in constellations and named fancy names?
Or that the growth of seeds is for agricultural tables, or agricul-
       ture itself?

Old institutions, these arts, libraries, legends, collections, and the
       practice handed along in manufactures, will we rate them
       so high?
Will we rate our cash and business high? I have no objection,
I rate them as high as the highest — then a child born of a
       woman and man I rate beyond all rate.

We thought our Union grand, and our Constitution grand,
I do not say they are not grand and good, for they are,
I am this day just as much in love with them as you,
Then I am in love with You, and with all my fellows upon the
       earth.

We consider bibles and religions divine — I do not say they are
       not divine,
I say they have all grown out of you, and may grow out of you
       still,
It is not they who give the life, it is you who give the life,
Leaves are not more shed from the trees, or trees from the earth,
       than they are shed out of you.

4

The sum of all known reverence I add up in you whoever you are,
The President is there in the White House for you, it is not you
       who are here for him,
The Secretaries act in their bureaus for you, not you here for them,
The Congress convenes every Twelfth-month for you,
Laws, courts, the forming of States, the charters of cities, the
       going and coming of commerce and mails, are all for you.

List close my scholars dear,
Doctrines, politics and civilization exurge from you,
Sculpture and monuments and any thing inscribed anywhere are
    tallied in you,
The gist of histories and statistics as far back as the records reach
    is in you this hour, and myths and tales the same,
If you were not breathing and walking here, where would they
    all be?
The most renown'd poems would be ashes, orations and plays
    would be vacuums.

All architecture is what you do to it when you look upon it,
(Did you think it was in the white or gray stone? or the lines of
    the arches and cornices?)

All music is what awakes from you when you are reminded by the
    instruments,
It is not the violins and the cornets, it is not the oboe nor the
    beating drums, nor the score of the baritone singer singing
    his sweet romanza, nor that of the men's chorus, nor that
    of the women's chorus,
It is nearer and farther than they.

5

Will the whole come back then?
Can each see signs of the best by a look in the looking-glass? is
    there nothing greater or more?
Does all sit there with you, with the mystic unseen soul?

Strange and hard that paradox true I give,
Objects gross and the unseen soul are one.

House-building, measuring, sawing the boards,
Blacksmithing, glass-blowing, nail-making, coopering, tin-roofing,
    shingle-dressing,
Ship-joining, dock-building, fish-curing, flagging of sidewalks by
    flaggers,
The pump, the pile-driver, the great derrick, the coal-kiln and
    brick-kiln,
Coal-mines and all that is down there, the lamps in the darkness,
    echoes, songs, what meditations, what vast native thoughts
    looking through smutch'd faces,
Iron-works, forge-fires in the mountains or by river-banks, men
    around feeling the melt with huge crowbars, lumps of ore,
    the due combining of ore, limestone, coal,

The blast-furnace and the puddling-furnace, the loup-lump at the
    bottom of the melt at last, the rolling-mill, the stumpy
    bars of pig-iron, the strong clean-shaped T-rail for rail-
    roads,
Oil-works, silk-works, white-lead-works, the sugar-house, steam-
    saws, the great mills and factories,
Stone-cutting, shapely trimmings for façades or window or door-
    lintels, the mallet, the tooth-chisel, the jib to protect the
    thumb,
The calking-iron, the kettle of boiling vault-cement, and the fire
    under the kettle,
The cotton-bale, the stevedore's hook, the saw and buck of the
    sawyer, the mould of the moulder, the working-knife of
    the butcher, the ice-saw, and all the work with ice,
The work and tools of the rigger, grappler, sail-maker, block-
    maker,
Goods of gutta-percha, papier-maché, colors, brushes, brush-
    making, glazier's implements,
The veneer and glue-pot, the confectioner's ornaments, the
    decanter and glasses, the shears and flat-iron,
The awl and knee-strap, the pint measure and quart measure, the
    counter and stool, the writing-pen of quill or metal, the
    making of all sorts of edged tools,
The brewery, brewing, the malt, the vats, every thing that is done
    by brewers, wine-makers, vinegar-makers,
Leather-dressing, coach-making, boiler-making, rope-twisting, dis-
    tilling, sign-painting, lime-burning, cotton-picking, electro-
    plating, electrotyping, stereotyping,
Stave-machines, planing-machines, reaping-machines, ploughing-
    machines, thrashing-machines, steam wagons,
The cart of the carman, the omnibus, the ponderous dray,
Pyrotechny, letting off color'd fireworks at night, fancy figures and
    jets ;
Beef on the butcher's stall, the slaughter-house of the butcher, the
    butcher in his killing-clothes,
The pens of live pork, the killing-hammer, the hog-hook, the
    scalder's tub, gutting, the cutter's cleaver, the packer's maul,
    and the plenteous winterwork of pork-packing,
Flour-works, grinding of wheat, rye, maize, rice, the barrels and
    the half and quarter barrels, the loaded barges, the high
    piles on wharves and levees,
The men and the work of the men on ferries, railroads, coasters,
    fish-boats, canals ;
The hourly routine of your own or any man's life, the shop, yard,
    store, or factory,

These shows all near you by day and night — workman ! whoever
    you are, your daily life !
In that and them the heft of the heaviest — in that and them far
    more than you estimated, (and far less also,)
In them realities for you and me, in them poems for you and me,
In them, not yourself — you and your soul enclose all things, re-
    gardless of estimation,
In them the development good — in them all themes, hints, possi-
    bilities.

I do not affirm that what you see beyond is futile, I do not advise
    you to stop,
I do not say leadings you thought great are not great,
But I say that none lead to greater than these lead to.

6

Will you seek afar off ? you surely come back at last,
In things best known to you finding the best, or as good as the
    best,
In folks nearest to you finding the sweetest, strongest, lovingest,
Happiness, knowledge, not in another place but this place, not for
    another hour but this hour,
Man in the first you see or touch, always in friend, brother,
    nighest neighbor — woman in mother, sister, wife,
The popular tastes and employments taking precedence in poems
    or anywhere,
You workwomen and workmen of these States having your own
    divine and strong life,
And all else giving place to men and women like you.

When the psalm sings instead of the singer,
When the script preaches instead of the preacher,
When the pulpit descends and goes instead of the carver that
    carved the supporting desk,
When I can touch the body of books by night or by day, and
    when they touch my body back again,
When a university course convinces like a slumbering woman and
    child convince,
When the minted gold in the vault smiles like the night-watchman's
    daughter,
When warrantee deeds loafe in chairs opposite and are my friendly
    companions,
I intend to reach them my hand, and make as much of them as
    I do of men and women like you.

A SONG OF THE ROLLING EARTH.

1

A SONG of the rolling earth, and of words according,
Were you thinking that those were the words, those upright lines?
    those curves, angles, dots?
No, those are not the words, the substantial words are in the
    ground and sea,
They are in the air, they are in you.

Were you thinking that those were the words, those delicious sounds
    out of your friends' mouths?
No, the real words are more delicious than they.

Human bodies are words, myriads of words,
(In the best poems re-appears the body, man's or woman's, well-
    shaped, natural, gay,
Every part able, active, receptive, without shame or the need of
    shame.)

Air, soil, water, fire — those are words,
I myself am a word with them — my qualities interpenetrate with
    theirs — my name is nothing to them,
Though it were told in the three thousand languages, what would
    air, soil, water, fire, know of my name?

A healthy presence, a friendly or commanding gesture, are words,
    sayings, meanings,
The charms that go with the mere looks of some men and women,
    are sayings and meanings also.

The workmanship of souls is by those inaudible words of the earth,
The masters know the earth's words and use them more than
    audible words.

Amelioration is one of the earth's words,
The earth neither lags nor hastens,
It has all attributes, growths, effects, latent in itself from the jump,
It is not half beautiful only, defects and excrescences show just as
    much as perfections show.

The earth does not withhold, it is generous enough,
The truths of the earth continually wait, they are not so conceal'd
    either,

They are calm, subtle, untransmissible by print,
They are imbued through all things conveying themselves willingly,
Conveying a sentiment and invitation, I utter and utter,
I speak not, yet if you hear me not of what avail am I to you?
To bear, to better, lacking these of what avail am I?

(Accouche! accouchez!
Will you rot your own fruit in yourself there?
Will you squat and stifle there?)

The earth does not argue,
Is not pathetic, has no arrangements,
Does not scream, haste, persuade, threaten, promise,
Makes no discriminations, has no conceivable failures,
Closes nothing, refuses nothing, shuts none out,
Of all the powers, objects, states, it notifies, shuts none out.

The earth does not exhibit itself nor refuse to exhibit itself, pos-
      sesses still underneath,
Underneath the ostensible sounds, the august chorus of heroes, the
      wail of slaves,
Persuasions of lovers, curses, gasps of the dying, laughter of young
      people, accents of bargainers,
Underneath these possessing words that never fail.

To her children the words of the eloquent dumb great mother
      never fail,
The true words do not fail, for motion does not fail and reflection
      does not fail,
Also the day and night do not fail, and the voyage we pursue does
      not fail.

Of the interminable sisters,
Of the ceaseless cotillons of sisters,
Of the centripetal and centrifugal sisters, the elder and younger
      sisters,
The beautiful sister we know dances on with the rest.

With her ample back towards every beholder,
With the fascinations of youth and the equal fascinations of age,
Sits she whom I too love like the rest, sits undisturb'd,
Holding up in her hand what has the character of a mirror, while
      her eyes glance back from it,
Glance as she sits, inviting none, denying none,
Holding a mirror day and night tirelessly before her own face.

Seen at hand or seen at a distance,
Duly the twenty-four appear in public every day,
Duly approach and pass with their companions or a companion,
Looking from no countenances of their own, but from the counte-
          nances of those who are with them,
From the countenances of children or women or the manly coun-
          tenance,
From the open countenances of animals or from inanimate things,
From the landscape or waters or from the exquisite apparition of
          the sky,
From our countenances, mine and yours, faithfully returning them,
Every day in public appearing without fail, but never twice with
          the same companions.

Embracing man, embracing all, proceed the three hundred and
          sixty-five resistlessly round the sun ;
Embracing all, soothing, supporting, follow close three hundred
          and sixty-five offsets of the first, sure and necessary as they.

Tumbling on steadily, nothing dreading,
Sunshine, storm, cold, heat, forever withstanding, passing, carrying,
The soul's realization and determination still inheriting,
The fluid vacuum around and ahead still entering and dividing,
No balk retarding, no anchor anchoring, on no rock striking,
Swift, glad, content, unbereav'd, nothing losing,
Of all able and ready at any time to give strict account,
The divine ship sails the divine sea.

2

Whoever you are ! motion and reflection are especially for you,
The divine ship sails the divine sea for you.

Whoever you are ! you are he or she for whom the earth is solid
          and liquid,
You are he or she for whom the sun and moon hang in the sky,
For none more than you are the present and the past,
For none more than you is immortality.

Each man to himself and each woman to herself, is the word of
          the past and present, and the true word of immortality ;
No one can acquire for another — not one,
Not one can grow for another — not one.

The song is to the singer, and comes back most to him,
The teaching is to the teacher, and comes back most to him,

The murder is to the murderer, and comes back most to him,
The theft is to the thief, and comes back most to him,
The love is to the lover, and comes back most to him,
The gift is to the giver, and comes back most to him — it cannot
     fail,
The oration is to the orator, the acting is to the actor and actress
     not to the audience,
And no man understands any greatness or goodness but his own,
     or the indication of his own.

3

I swear the earth shall surely be complete to him or her who shall
     be complete,
The earth remains jagged and broken only to him or her who
     remains jagged and broken.

I swear there is no greatness or power that does not emulate
     those of the earth,
There can be no theory of any account unless it corroborate the
     theory of the earth,
No politics, song, religion, behavior, or what not, is of account,
     unless it compare with the amplitude of the earth,
Unless it face the exactness, vitality, impartiality, rectitude of the
     earth.

I swear I begin to see love with sweeter spasms than that which
     responds love,
It is that which contains itself, which never invites and never
     refuses.

I swear I begin to see little or nothing in audible words,
All merges toward the presentation of the unspoken meanings
     of the earth,
Toward him who sings the songs of the body and of the truths
     of the earth,
Toward him who makes the dictionaries of words that print can-
     not touch.

I swear I see what is better than to tell the best,
It is always to leave the best untold.

When I undertake to tell the best I find I cannot,
My tongue is ineffectual on its pivots,
My breath will not be obedient to its organs,
I become a dumb man.

The best of the earth cannot be told anyhow, all or any is best,
It is not what you anticipated, it is cheaper, easier, nearer,
Things are not dismiss'd from the places they held before,
The earth is just as positive and direct as it was before,
Facts, religions, improvements, politics, trades, are as real as before,
But the soul is also real, it too is positive and direct,
No reasoning, no proof has establish'd it,
Undeniable growth has establish'd it.

4

These to echo the tones of souls and the phrases of souls,
(If they did not echo the phrases of souls what were they then?
If they had not reference to you in especial what were they then?)

I swear I will never henceforth have to do with the faith that tells
the best,
I will have to do only with that faith that leaves the best untold.

Say on, sayers! sing on, singers!
Delve! mould! pile the words of the earth!
Work on, age after age, nothing is to be lost,
It may have to wait long, but it will certainly come in use,
When the materials are all prepared and ready, the architects shall
appear.

I swear to you the architects shall appear without fail,
I swear to you they will understand you and justify you,
The greatest among them shall be he who best knows you, and
encloses all and is faithful to all,
He and the rest shall not forget you, they shall perceive that you
are not an iota less than they,
You shall be fully glorified in them.

YOUTH, DAY, OLD AGE AND NIGHT.

YOUTH, large, lusty, loving—youth full of grace, force, fascination,
Do you know that Old Age may come after you with equal grace,
force, fascination?

Day full-blown and splendid — day of the immense sun, action,
ambition, laughter,
The Night follows close with millions of suns, and sleep and
restoring darkness.

BIRDS OF PASSAGE.

SONG OF THE UNIVERSAL.

1

COME said the Muse,
Sing me a song no poet yet has chanted,
Sing me the universal.

In this broad earth of ours,
Amid the measureless grossness and the slag,
Enclosed and safe within its central heart,
Nestles the seed perfection.

By every life a share or more or less,
None born but it is born, conceal'd or unconceal'd the seed is
        waiting.

2

Lo! keen-eyed towering science,
As from tall peaks the modern overlooking,
Successive absolute fiats issuing.

Yet again, lo! the soul, above all science,
For it has history gather'd like husks around the globe,
For it the entire star-myriads roll through the sky.

In spiral routes by long detours,
(As a much-tacking ship upon the sea,)
For it the partial to the permanent flowing,
For it the real to the ideal tends.

For it the mystic evolution,
Not the right only justified, what we call evil also justified.

Forth from their masks, no matter what,
From the huge festering trunk, from craft and guile and tears,
Health to emerge and joy, joy universal.

Out of the bulk, the morbid and the shallow,
Out of the bad majority, the varied countless frauds of men and
        states,
Electric, antiseptic yet, cleaving, suffusing all,
Only the good is universal.

3

Over the mountain-growths disease and sorrow,
An uncaught bird is ever hovering, hovering,
High in the purer, happier air:

From imperfection's murkiest cloud,
Darts always forth one ray of perfect light,
One flash of heaven's glory.

To fashion's, custom's discord,
To the mad Babel-din, the deafening orgies,
Soothing each lull a strain is heard, just heard,
From some far shore the final chorus sounding.

O the blest eyes, the happy hearts,
That see, that know the guiding thread so fine,
Along the mighty labyrinth.

4

And thou America,
For the scheme's culmination, its thought and its reality,
For these (not for thyself) thou hast arrived.

Thou too surroundest all,
Embracing carrying welcoming all, thou too by pathways broad
          and new,
To the ideal tendest.

The measur'd faiths of other lands, the grandeurs of the past,
Are not for thee, but grandeurs of thine own,
Deific faiths and amplitudes, absorbing, comprehending all,
All eligible to all.

All, all for immortality,
Love like the light silently wrapping all,
Nature's amelioration blessing all,
The blossoms, fruits of ages, orchards divine and certain,
Forms, objects, growths, humanities, to spiritual images ripening.

Give me O God to sing that thought,
Give me, give him or her I love this quenchless faith,
In Thy ensemble, whatever else withheld withhold not from us,
Belief in plan of Thee enclosed in Time and Space,
Health, peace, salvation universal.

Is it a dream?
Nay but the lack of it the dream,
And failing it life's lore and wealth a dream,
And all the world a dream.

PIONEERS! O PIONEERS!

COME my tan-faced children,
Follow well in order, get your weapons ready,
Have you your pistols? have you your sharp-edged axes?
　　　Pioneers! O pioneers!

For we cannot tarry here,
We must march my darlings, we must bear the brunt of danger,
We the youthful sinewy races, all the rest on us depend,
　　　Pioneers! O pioneers!

O you youths, Western youths,
So impatient, full of action, full of manly pride and friendship,
Plain I see you Western youths, see you tramping with the fore-
　　　most,
　　　Pioneers! O pioneers!

Have the elder races halted?
Do they droop and end their lesson, wearied over there beyond
　　　the seas?
We take up the task eternal, and the burden and the lesson,
　　　Pioneers! O pioneers!

All the past we leave behind,
We debouch upon a newer mightier world, varied world,
Fresh and strong the world we seize, world of labor and the march,
　　　Pioneers! O pioneers!

We detachments steady throwing,
Down the edges, through the passes, up the mountains steep,
Conquering, holding, daring, venturing as we go the unknown ways,
　　　Pioneers! O pioneers!

We primeval forests felling,
We the rivers stemming, vexing we and piercing deep the mines
　　　within,
We the surface broad surveying, we the virgin soil upheaving,
　　　Pioneers! O pioneers!

Colorado men are we,
From the peaks gigantic, from the great sierras and the high
plateaus,
From the mine and from the gully, from the hunting trail we come,
Pioneers! O pioneers!

From Nebraska, from Arkansas,
Central inland race are we, from Missouri, with the continental
blood intervein'd,
All the hands of comrades clasping, all the Southern, all the
Northern,
Pioneers! O pioneers!

O resistless restless race!
O beloved race in all! O my breast aches with tender love for all!
O I mourn and yet exult, I am rapt with love for all,
Pioneers! O pioneers!

Raise the mighty mother mistress,
Waving high the delicate mistress, over all the starry mistress,
(bend your heads all,)
Raise the fang'd and warlike mistress, stern, impassive, weapon'd
mistress,
Pioneers! O pioneers!

See my children, resolute children,
By those swarms upon our rear we must never yield or falter,
Ages back in ghostly millions frowning there behind us urging,
Pioneers! O pioneers!

On and on the compact ranks,
With accessions ever waiting, with the places of the dead quickly
fill'd,
Through the battle, through defeat, moving yet and never stopping,
Pioneers! O pioneers!

O to die advancing on!
Are there some of us to droop and die? has the hour come?
Then upon the march we fittest die, soon and sure the gap is fill'd.
Pioneers! O pioneers!

All the pulses of the world,
Falling in they beat for us, with the Western movement beat,
Holding single or together, steady moving to the front, all for us,
Pioneers! O pioneers!

Life's involv'd and varied pageants,
All the forms and shows, all the workmen at their work,
All the seamen and the landsmen, all the masters with their slaves,
     Pioneers ! O pioneers !

All the hapless silent lovers,
All the prisoners in the prisons, all the righteous and the wicked,
All the joyous, all the sorrowing, all the living, all the dying,
     Pioneers ! O pioneers !

I too with my soul and body,
We, a curious trio, picking, wandering on our way,
Through these shores amid the shadows, with the apparitions
     pressing,
     Pioneers ! O pioneers !

Lo, the darting bowling orb !
Lo, the brother orbs around, all the clustering suns and planets,
All the dazzling days, all the mystic nights with dreams,
     Pioneers ! O pioneers !

These are of us, they are with us,
All for primal needed work, while the followers there in embryo
     wait behind,
We to-day's procession heading, we the route for travel clearing,
     Pioneers ! O pioneers !

O you daughters of the West !
O you young and elder daughters ! O you mothers and you wives !
Never must you be divided, in our ranks you move united,
     Pioneers ! O pioneers !

Minstrels latent on the prairies !
(Shrouded bards of other lands, you may rest, you have done
     your work,)
Soon I hear you coming warbling, soon you rise and tramp amid us,
     Pioneers ! O pioneers !

Not for delectations sweet,
Not the cushion and the slipper, not the peaceful and the studious,
Not the riches safe and palling, not for us the tame enjoyment,
     Pioneers ! O pioneers !

Do the feasters gluttonous feast?
Do the corpulent sleepers sleep? have they lock'd and bolted doors?
Still be ours the diet hard, and the blanket on the ground,
     Pioneers ! O pioneers !

Has the night descended?
Was the road of late so toilsome? did we stop discouraged nodding
    on our way?
Yet a passing hour I yield you in your tracks to pause oblivious,
    Pioneers! O pioneers!

Till with sound of trumpet,
Far, far off the daybreak call — hark! how loud and clear I hear
    it wind,
Swift! to the head of the army! — swift! spring to your places,
    Pioneers! O pioneers!

TO YOU.

WHOEVER you are, I fear you are walking the walks of dreams,
I fear these supposed realities are to melt from under your feet
    and hands,
Even now your features, joys, speech, house, trade, manners,
    troubles, follies, costume, crimes, dissipate away from you,
Your true soul and body appear before me,
They stand forth out of affairs, out of commerce, shops, work,
    farms, clothes, the house, buying, selling, eating, drinking,
    suffering, dying.

Whoever you are, now I place my hand upon you, that you be my
    poem,
I whisper with my lips close to your ear,
I have loved many women and men, but I love none better than
    you.

O I have been dilatory and dumb,
I should have made my way straight to you long ago,
I should have blabb'd nothing but you, I should have chanted
    nothing but you.

I will leave all and come and make the hymns of you,
None has understood you, but I understand you,
None has done justice to you, you have not done justice to your-
    self,
None but has found you imperfect, I only find no imperfection in
    you,
None but would subordinate you, I only am he who will never
    consent to subordinate you,
I only am he who places over you no master, owner, better, God,
    beyond what waits intrinsically in yourself.

Painters have painted their swarming groups and the centre-figure
    of all,
From the head of the centre-figure spreading a nimbus of gold-
    color'd light,
But I paint myriads of heads, but paint no head without its nim-
    bus of gold-color'd light,
From my hand from the brain of every man and woman it streams,
    effulgently flowing forever.

O I could sing such grandeurs and glories about you!
You have not known what you are, you have slumber'd upon
    yourself all your life,
Your eyelids have been the same as closed most of the time,
What you have done returns already in mockeries,
(Your thrift, knowledge, prayers, if they do not return in mock-
    eries, what is their return?)

The mockeries are not you,
Underneath them and within them I see you lurk,
I pursue you where none else has pursued you,
Silence, the desk, the flippant expression, the night, the accustom'd
    routine, if these conceal you from others or from yourself,
    they do not conceal you from me,
The shaved face, the unsteady eye, the impure complexion, if these
    balk others they do not balk me,
The pert apparel, the deform'd attitude, drunkenness, greed, pre-
    mature death, all these I part aside.

There is no endowment in man or woman that is not tallied in
    you,
There is no virtue, no beauty in man or woman, but as good is in
    you,
No pluck, no endurance in others, but as good is in you,
No pleasure waiting for others, but an equal pleasure waits for you.

As for me, I give nothing to any one except I give the like care-
    fully to you,
I sing the songs of the glory of none, not God, sooner than I
    sing the songs of the glory of you.

Whoever you are! claim your own at any hazard!
These shows of the East and West are tame compared to you,
These immense meadows, these interminable rivers, you are
    immense and interminable as they,

These furies, elements, storms, motions of Nature, throes of apparent dissolution, you are he or she who is master or mistress over them,
Master or mistress in your own right over Nature, elements, pain, passion, dissolution.

The hopples fall from your ankles, you find an unfailing sufficiency,
Old or young, male or female, rude, low, rejected by the rest, whatever you are promulges itself,
Through birth, life, death, burial, the means are provided, nothing is scanted,
Through angers, losses, ambition, ignorance, ennui, what you are picks its way.

FRANCE,

*The 18th Year of these States.**

A GREAT year and place.
A harsh discordant natal scream out-sounding, to touch the mother's heart closer than any yet.

I walk'd the shores of my Eastern sea,
Heard over the waves the little voice,
Saw the divine infant where she woke mournfully wailing, amid the roar of cannon, curses, shouts, crash of falling buildings,
Was not so sick from the blood in the gutters running, nor from the single corpses, nor those in heaps, nor those borne away in the tumbrils,
Was not so desperate at the battues of death — was not so shock'd at the repeated fusillades of the guns.

Pale, silent, stern, what could I say to that long-accrued retribution?
Could I wish humanity different?
Could I wish the people made of wood and stone?
Or that there be no justice in destiny or time?

O Liberty! O mate for me!
Here too the blaze, the grape-shot and the axe, in reserve, to fetch them out in case of need,
Here too, though long represt, can never be destroy'd,
Here too could rise at last murdering and ecstatic,
Here too demanding full arrears of vengeance.

Hence I sign this salute over the sea,
And I do not deny that terrible red birth and baptism,

But remember the little voice that I heard wailing, and wait with
      perfect trust, no matter how long,
And from to-day sad and cogent I maintain the bequeath'd cause,
      as for all lands,
And I send these words to Paris with my love,
And I guess some chansonniers there will understand them,
For I guess there is latent music yet in France, floods of it,
O I hear already the bustle of instruments, they will soon be
      drowning all that would interrupt them,
O I think the east wind brings a triumphal and free march,
It reaches hither, it swells me to joyful madness,
I will run transpose it in words, to justify it,
I will yet sing a song for you ma femme.*

MYSELF AND MINE.

MYSELF and mine gymnastic ever,
To stand the cold or heat, to take good aim with a gun, to sail a
      boat, to manage horses, to beget superb children,
To speak readily and clearly, to feel at home among common
      people,
And to hold our own in terrible positions on land and sea.

Not for an embroiderer,
(There will always be plenty of embroiderers, I welcome them also,)
But for the fibre of things and for inherent men and women.

Not to chisel ornaments,
But to chisel with free stroke the heads and limbs of plenteous
      supreme Gods, that the States may realize them walking
      and talking.

Let me have my own way,
Let others promulge the laws, I will make no account of the laws,
Let others praise eminent men and hold up peace, I hold up
      agitation and conflict,
I praise no eminent man, I rebuke to his face the one that was
      thought most worthy.

(Who are you? and what are you secretly guilty of all your life?
Will you turn aside all your life? will you grub and chatter all
      your life?
And who are you, blabbing by rote, years, pages, languages,
      reminiscences,

Unwitting to-day that you do not know how to speak properly a
　　single word?)

Let others finish specimens, I never finish specimens,
I start them by exhaustless laws as Nature does, fresh and modern
　　continually.

I give nothing as duties,
What others give as duties I give as living impulses,
(Shall I give the heart's action as a duty?)

Let others dispose of questions, I dispose of nothing, I arouse
　　unanswerable questions,
Who are they I see and touch, and what about them?
What about these likes of myself that draw me so close by tender
　　directions and indirections?

I call to the world to distrust the accounts of my friends, but
　　listen to my enemies, as I myself do,
I charge you forever reject those who would expound me, for I
　　cannot expound myself,
I charge that there be no theory or school founded out of me,
I charge you to leave all free, as I have left all free.

After me, vista!
O I see life is not short, but immeasurably long,
I henceforth tread the world chaste, temperate, an early riser, a
　　steady grower,
Every hour the semen of centuries, and still of centuries.

I must follow up these continual lessons of the air, water, earth,
I perceive I have no time to lose.

YEAR OF METEORS.

(1859-60.)

YEAR of meteors! brooding year!
I would bind in words retrospective some of your deeds and signs,
I would sing your contest for the 19th Presidentiad,*
I would sing how an old man, tall, with white hair, mounted the
　　scaffold*in Virginia,
(I was at hand, silent I stood with teeth shut close, I watch'd,
I stood very near you old man when cool and indifferent, but
　　trembling with age and your unheal'd wounds you mounted
　　the scaffold;)

I would sing in my copious song your census returns of the States,
The tables of population and products, I would sing of your ships
    and their cargoes,
The proud black ships of Manhattan arriving, some fill'd with
    immigrants, some from the isthmus with cargoes of gold,
Songs thereof would I sing, to all that hitherward comes would I
    welcome give,
And you would I sing, fair stripling! welcome to you from me,
    young prince of England!*
(Remember you surging Manhattan's crowds as you pass'd with
    your cortege of nobles?
There in the crowds stood I, and singled you out with attachment;)
Nor forget I to sing of the wonder, the ship as she swam up my
    bay,
Well-shaped and stately the Great Eastern* swam up my bay, she
    was 600 feet long,
Her moving swiftly surrounded by myriads of small craft I forget
    not to sing;
Nor the comet that came unannounced out of the north flaring in
    heaven,
Nor the strange huge meteor-procession dazzling and clear shoot-
    ing over our heads,
(A moment, a moment long it sail'd its balls of unearthly light
    over our heads,
Then departed, dropt in the night, and was gone;)
Of such, and fitful as they, I sing — with gleams from them would
    I gleam and patch these chants,
Your chants, O year all mottled with evil and good — year of
    forebodings!
Year of comets and meteors transient and strange — lo! even here
    one equally transient and strange!
As I flit through you hastily, soon to fall and be gone, what is this
    chant,
What am I myself but one of your meteors?

WITH ANTECEDENTS.

1

WITH antecedents,
With my fathers and mothers and the accumulations of past
    ages,
With all which, had it not been, I would not now be here, as I
    am,
With Egypt, India, Phenicia, Greece and Rome,
With the Kelt, the Scandinavian, the Alb* and the Saxon,

With antique maritime ventures, laws, artisanship, wars and jour-
neys,
With the poet, the skald, the saga, the myth, and the oracle,
With the sale of slaves, with enthusiasts, with the troubadour, the
crusader, and the monk,
With those old continents whence we have come to this new
continent,
With the fading kingdoms and kings over there,
With the fading religions and priests,
With the small shores we look back to from our own large and
present shores,
With countless years drawing themselves onward and arrived at
these years,
You and me arrived — America arrived and making this year,
This year ! sending itself ahead countless years to come.

2

O but it is not the years — it is I, it is You,
We touch all laws and tally all antecedents,
We are the skald, the oracle, the monk and the knight, we easily
include them and more,
We stand amid time beginningless and endless, we stand amid evil
and good,
All swings around us, there is as much darkness as light,
The very sun swings itself and its system of planets around us,
Its sun, and its again, all swing around us.

As for me, (torn, stormy, amid these vehement days,)
I have the idea of all, and am all and believe in all,
I believe materialism is true and spiritualism is true, I reject no
part.

(Have I forgotten any part? any thing in the past?
Come to me whoever and whatever, till I give you recogni-
tion.)

I respect Assyria, China, Teutonia, and the Hebrews,
I adopt each theory, myth, god, and demi-god,
I see that the old accounts, bibles, genealogies, are true, without
exception,
I assert that all past days were what they must have been,
And that they could no-how have been better than they were,
And that to-day is what it must be, and that America is,
And that to-day and America could no-how be better than they
are.

3

In the name of these States and in your and my name, the Past,
And in the name of these States and in your and my name, the Present time.

I know that the past was great and the future will be great,
And I know that both curiously conjoint in the present time,
(For the sake of him I typify, for the common average man's sake, your sake if you are he,)
And that where I am or you are this present day, there is the centre of all days, all races,
And there is the meaning to us of all that has ever come of races and days, or ever will come.

A BROADWAY PAGEANT.

I

Over the Western sea hither from Niphon*come,
Courteous, the swart-cheek'd two-sworded envoys,
Leaning back in their open barouches, bare-headed, impassive,
Ride to-day through Manhattan.

Libertad! I do not know whether others behold what I behold,
In the procession along with the nobles of Niphon, the errand-bearers,
Bringing up the rear, hovering above, around, or in the ranks marching,
But I will sing you a song of what I behold Libertad.

When million-footed Manhattan unpent descends to her pavements,
When the thunder-cracking guns arouse me with the proud roar I love,
When the round-mouth'd guns out of the smoke and smell I love spit their salutes,
When the fire-flashing guns have fully alerted me, and heaven-clouds canopy my city with a delicate thin haze,
When gorgeous the countless straight stems, the forests at the wharves, thicken with colors,
When every ship richly drest carries her flag at the peak,
When pennants trail and street-festoons hang from the windows,

When Broadway is entirely given up to foot-passengers and foot-
    standers, when the mass is densest,
When the façades of the houses are alive with people, when eyes
    gaze riveted tens of thousands at a time,
When the guests from the islands advance, when the pageant
    moves forward visible,
When the summons is made, when the answer that waited thou-
    sands of years answers,
I too arising, answering, descend to the pavements, merge with
    the crowd, and gaze with them.

2

Superb-faced Manhattan !
Comrade Americanos ! to us, then at last the Orient comes.

To us, my city,
Where our tall-topt marble and iron beauties range on opposite
    sides, to walk in the space between,
To-day our Antipodes comes.

The Originatress comes,
The nest of languages, the bequeather of poems, the race of eld,
Florid with blood, pensive, rapt with musings, hot with passion,
Sultry with perfume, with ample and flowing garments,
With sunburnt visage, with intense soul and glittering eyes,
The race of Brahma comes.

See my cantabile ! these and more are flashing to us from the
    procession,
As it moves changing, a kaleidoscope divine it moves changing
    before us.

For not the envoys nor the tann'd Japanee from his island only,
Lithe and silent the Hindoo appears, the Asiatic continent itself
    appears, the past, the dead,
The murky night-morning of wonder and fable inscrutable,
The envelop'd mysteries, the old and unknown hive-bees,
The north, the sweltering south, eastern Assyria, the Hebrews, the
    ancient of ancients,
Vast desolated cities, the gliding present, all of these and more are
    in the pageant-procession.

Geography, the world, is in it,
The Great Sea, the brood of islands, Polynesia, the coast beyond,
The coast you henceforth are facing — you Libertad ! from your
    Western golden shores,

The countries there with their populations, the millions en-masse
    are curiously here,
The swarming market-places, the temples with idols ranged along
    the sides or at the end, bonze, brahmin, and llama,
Mandarin, farmer, merchant, mechanic, and fisherman,
The singing-girl and the dancing-girl, the ecstatic persons, the
    secluded emperors,
Confucius himself, the great poets and heroes, the warriors, the
    castes, all,
Trooping up, crowding from all directions, from the Altay moun-
    tains,
From Thibet, from the four winding and far-flowing rivers of
    China,
From the southern peninsulas and the demi-continental islands,
    from Malaysia,
These and whatever belongs to them palpable show forth to me,
    and are seiz'd by me,
And I am seiz'd by them, and friendlily held by them,
Till as here them all I chant, Libertad! for themselves and for
    you.

For I too raising my voice join the ranks of this pageant,
I am the chanter, I chant aloud over the pageant,
I chant the world on my Western sea,
I chant copious the islands beyond, thick as stars in the sky,
I chant the new empire grander than any before, as in a vision it
    comes to me,
I chant America the mistress, I chant a greater supremacy,
I chant projected a thousand blooming cities yet in time on those
    groups of sea-islands,
My sail-ships and steam-ships threading the archipelagoes,
My stars and stripes fluttering in the wind,
Commerce opening, the sleep of ages having done its work, races
    reborn, refresh'd,
Lives, works resumed — the object I know not — but the old, the
    Asiatic renew'd as it must be,
Commencing from this day surrounded by the world.

3

And you Libertad of the world!
You shall sit in the middle well-pois'd thousands and thousands of
    years,
As to-day from one side the nobles of Asia come to you,
As to-morrow from the other side the queen of England sends her
    eldest son* to you.

The sign is reversing, the orb is enclosed,
The ring is circled, the journey is done,
The box-lid is but perceptibly open'd, nevertheless the perfume
　　pours copiously out of the whole box.

Young Libertad! with the venerable Asia, the all-mother,
Be considerate with her now and ever hot Libertad, for you are all,
Bend your proud neck to the long-off mother now sending mes-
　　sages over the archipelagoes to you,
Bend your proud neck low for once, young Libertad.

Were the children straying westward so long? so wide the tramping?
Were the precedent dim ages debouching westward from Paradise
　　so long?
Were the centuries steadily footing it that way, all the while
　　unknown, for you, for reasons?

They are justified, they are accomplish'd, they shall now be turn'd
　　the other way also, to travel toward you thence,
They shall now also march obediently eastward for your sake
　　Libertad.

SEA-DRIFT.

OUT OF THE CRADLE ENDLESSLY ROCKING.

OUT of the cradle endlessly rocking,
Out of the mocking-bird's throat, the musical shuttle,
Out of the Ninth-month* midnight,
Over the sterile sands and the fields beyond, where the child
　　leaving his bed wander'd alone, bareheaded, barefoot,
Down from the shower'd halo,
Up from the mystic play of shadows twining and twisting as if
　　they were alive,
Out from the patches of briers and blackberries,
From the memories of the bird that chanted to me,
From your memories sad brother, from the fitful risings and fall-
　　ings I heard,
From under that yellow half-moon late-risen and swollen as if with
　　tears,

From those beginning notes of yearning and love there in the mist,
From the thousand responses of my heart never to cease,
From the myriad thence-arous'd words,
From the word stronger and more delicious than any,
From such as now they start the scene revisiting,
As a flock, twittering, rising, or overhead passing,
Borne hither, ere all eludes me, hurriedly,
A man, yet by these tears a little boy again,
Throwing myself on the sand, confronting the waves,
I, chanter of pains and joys, uniter of here and hereafter,
Taking all hints to use them, but swiftly leaping beyond them,
A reminiscence sing.

Once Paumanok,*
When the lilac-scent was in the air and Fifth-month grass was
          growing,
Up this seashore in some briers,
Two feather'd guests from Alabama, two together,
And their nest, and four light-green eggs spotted with brown,
And every day the he-bird to and fro near at hand,
And every day the she-bird crouch'd on her nest, silent, with
          bright eyes,
And every day I, a curious boy, never too close, never disturbing
          them,
Cautiously peering, absorbing, translating.

Shine! shine! shine!
Pour down your warmth, great sun!
While we bask, we two together.

Two together!
Winds blow south, or winds blow north,
Day come white, or night come black,
Home, or rivers and mountains from home,
Singing all time, minding no time,
While we two keep together.

Till of a sudden,
May-be kill'd, unknown to her mate,
One forenoon the she-bird crouch'd not on the nest,
Nor return'd that afternoon, nor the next,
Nor ever appear'd again.

And thenceforward all summer in the sound of the sea,
And at night under the full of the moon in calmer weather,

Over the hoarse surging of the sea,
Or flitting from brier to brier by day,
I saw, I heard at intervals the remaining one, the he-bird,
The solitary guest from Alabama.

Blow! blow! blow!
Blow up sea-winds along Paumanok's shore;
I wait and I wait till you blow my mate to me.

Yes, when the stars glisten'd,
All night long on the prong of a moss-scallop'd stake,
Down almost amid the slapping waves,
Sat the lone singer wonderful causing tears.

He call'd on his mate,
He pour'd forth the meanings which I of all men know.

Yes my brother I know,
The rest might not, but I have treasur'd every note,
For more than once dimly down to the beach gliding,
Silent, avoiding the moonbeams, blending myself with the shadows,
Recalling now the obscure shapes, the echoes, the sounds and
          sights after their sorts,
The white arms out in the breakers tirelessly tossing,
I, with bare feet, a child, the wind wafting my hair,
Listen'd long and long.

Listen'd to keep, to sing, now translating the notes,
Following you my brother.

Soothe! soothe! soothe!
Close on its wave soothes the wave behind,
And again another behind embracing and lapping, every one close,
But my love soothes not me, not me.

Low hangs the moon, it rose late,
It is lagging — O I think it is heavy with love, with love.

O madly the sea pushes upon the land,
With love, with love.

O night! do I not see my love fluttering out among the breakers?
What is that little black thing I see there in the white?

Loud! loud! loud!
Loud I call to you, my love!

High and clear I shoot my voice over the waves,
Surely you must know who is here, is here,
You must know who I am, my love.

Low-hanging moon!
What is that dusky spot in your brown yellow?
O it is the shape, the shape of my mate!
O moon do not keep her from me any longer.

Land! land! O land!
Whichever way I turn, O I think you could give me my mate
      back again if you only would,
For I am almost sure I see her dimly whichever way I look.

O rising stars!
Perhaps the one I want so much will rise, will rise with some
      of you.

O throat! O trembling throat!
Sound clearer through the atmosphere!
Pierce the woods, the earth,
Somewhere listening to catch you must be the one I want.

Shake out carols!
Solitary here, the night's carols!
Carols of lonesome love! death's carols!
Carols under that lagging, yellow, waning moon!
O under that moon where she droops almost down into the sea!
O reckless despairing carols.

But soft! sink low!
Soft! let me just murmur,
And do you wait a moment you husky-nois'd sea,
For somewhere I believe I heard my mate responding to me,
So faint, I must be still, be still to listen,
But not altogether still, for then she might not come immediately
      to me.

Hither my love!
Here I am! here!
With this just-sustain'd note I announce myself to you,
This gentle call is for you my love, for you.

Do not be decoy'd elsewhere,
That is the whistle of the wind, it is not my voice,

That is the fluttering, the fluttering of the spray,
Those are the shadows of leaves.

O darkness! O in vain!
O I am very sick and sorrowful.

O brown halo in the sky near the moon, drooping upon the sea!
O troubled reflection in the sea!
O throat! O throbbing heart!
And I singing uselessly, uselessly all the night.

O past! O happy life! O songs of joy!
In the air, in the woods, over fields,
Loved! loved! loved! loved! loved!
But my mate no more, no more with me!
We two together no more.

The aria sinking,
All else continuing, the stars shining,
The winds blowing, the notes of the bird continuous echoing,
With angry moans the fierce old mother incessantly moaning,
On the sands of Paumanok's shore gray and rustling,
The yellow half-moon enlarged, sagging down, drooping, the face
　　of the sea almost touching,
The boy ecstatic, with his bare feet the waves, with his hair the
　　atmosphere dallying,
The love in the heart long pent, now loose, now at last tumultu-
　　ously bursting,
The aria's meaning, the ears, the soul, swiftly depositing,
The strange tears down the cheeks coursing,
The colloquy there, the trio, each uttering,
The undertone, the savage old mother incessantly crying,
To the boy's soul's questions sullenly timing, some drown'd secret
　　hissing,
To the outsetting bard.

Demon or bird! (said the boy's soul,)
Is it indeed toward your mate you sing? or is it really to me?
For I, that was a child, my tongue's use sleeping, now I have
　　heard you,
Now in a moment I know what I am for, I awake,
And already a thousand singers, a thousand songs, clearer, louder
　　and more sorrowful than yours,
A thousand warbling echoes have started to life within me, never
　　to die.

O you singer solitary, singing by yourself, projecting me,
O solitary me listening, never more shall I cease perpetuating
    you,
Never more shall I escape, never more the reverberations,
Never more the cries of unsatisfied love be absent from me,
Never again leave me to be the peaceful child I was before what
    there in the night,
By the sea under the yellow and sagging moon,
The messenger there arous'd, the fire, the sweet hell within,
The unknown want, the destiny of me.

O give me the clew! (it lurks in the night here somewhere,)
O if I am to have so much, let me have more!

A word then, (for I will conquer it,)
The word final, superior to all,
Subtle, sent up — what is it? — I listen;
Are you whispering it, and have been all the time, you sea-
    waves?
Is that it from your liquid rims and wet sands?

Whereto answering, the sea,
Delaying not, hurrying not,
Whisper'd me through the night, and very plainly before day-
    break,
Lisp'd to me the low and delicious word death,
And again death, death, death, death,
Hissing melodious, neither like the bird nor like my arous'd child's
    heart,
But edging near as privately for me rustling at my feet,
Creeping thence steadily up to my ears and laving me softly all
    over,
Death, death, death, death, death.

Which I do not forget,
But fuse the song of my dusky demon and brother,
That he sang to me in the moonlight on Paumanok's gray beach,
With the thousand responsive songs at random,
My own songs awaked from that hour,
And with them the key, the word up from the waves,
The word of the sweetest song and all songs,
That strong and delicious word which, creeping to my feet,
(Or like some old crone rocking the cradle, swathed in sweet
    garments, bending aside,)
The sea whisper'd me.

AS I EBB'D WITH THE OCEAN OF LIFE.

1

As I ebb'd with the ocean of life,
As I wended the shores I know,
As I walk'd where the ripples continually wash you Paumanok,*
Where they rustle up hoarse and sibilant,
Where the fierce old mother endlessly cries for her castaways,
I musing late in the autumn day, gazing off southward,
Held by this electric self out of the pride of which I utter poems,
Was seiz'd by the spirit that trails in the lines underfoot,
The rim, the sediment that stands for all the water and all the
　　　land of the globe.

Fascinated, my eyes reverting from the south, dropt, to follow
　　　those slender windrows,
Chaff, straw, splinters of wood, weeds, and the sea-gluten,
Scum, scales from shining rocks, leaves of salt-lettuce, left by the
　　　tide,
Miles walking, the sound of breaking waves the other side of me,
Paumanok there and then as I thought the old thought of likenesses,
These you presented to me you fish-shaped island,
As I wended the shores I know,
As I walk'd with that electric self seeking types.

2

As I wend to the shores I know not,
As I list to the dirge, the voices of men and women wreck'd,
As I inhale the impalpable breezes that set in upon me,
As the ocean so mysterious rolls toward me closer and closer,
I too but signify at the utmost a little wash'd-up drift,
A few sands and dead leaves to gather,
Gather, and merge myself as part of the sands and drift.

O baffled, balk'd, bent to the very earth,
Oppress'd with myself that I have dared to open my mouth,
Aware now that amid all that blab whose echoes recoil upon me I
　　　have not once had the least idea who or what I am,
But that before all my arrogant poems the real Me stands yet
　　　untouch'd, untold, altogether unreach'd,
Withdrawn far, mocking me with mock-congratulatory signs and
　　　bows,
With peals of distant ironical laughter at every word I have written,
Pointing in silence to these songs, and then to the sand beneath.

I perceive I have not really understood any thing, not a single
      object, and that no man ever can,
Nature here in sight of the sea taking advantage of me to dart
      upon me and sting me,
Because I have dared to open my mouth to sing at all.

3

You oceans both, I close with you,
We murmur alike reproachfully rolling sands and drift, knowing
      not why,
These little shreds indeed standing for you and me and all.

You friable shore with trails of debris,
You fish-shaped island, I take what is underfoot,
What is yours is mine my father.

I too Paumanok,
I too have bubbled up, floated the measureless float, and been
      wash'd on your shores,
I too am but a trail of drift and debris,
I too leave little wrecks upon you, you fish-shaped island.

I throw myself upon your breast my father,
I cling to you so that you cannot unloose me,
I hold you so firm till you answer me something.

Kiss me my father,
Touch me with your lips as I touch those I love,
Breathe to me while I hold you close the secret of the murmuring
      I envy.

4

Ebb, ocean of life, (the flow will return,)
Cease not your moaning you fierce old mother,
Endlessly cry for your castaways, but fear not, deny not me,
Rustle not up so hoarse and angry against my feet as I touch you
      or gather from you.

I mean tenderly by you and all,
I gather for myself and for this phantom looking down where we
      lead, and following me and mine.

Me and mine, loose windrows, little corpses,
Froth, snowy white, and bubbles,
(See, from my dead lips the ooze exuding at last,

See, the prismatic colors glistening and rolling,)
Tufts of straw, sands, fragments,
Buoy'd hither from many moods, one contradicting another,
From the storm, the long calm, the darkness, the swell,
Musing, pondering, a breath, a briny tear, a dab of liquid or soil,
Up just as much out of fathomless workings fermented and thrown,
A limp blossom or two, torn, just as much over waves floating,
        drifted at random,
Just as much for us that sobbing dirge of Nature,
Just as much whence we come that blare of the cloud-trumpets,
We, capricious, brought hither we know not whence, spread out
        before you,
You up there walking or sitting,
Whoever you are, we too lie in drifts at your feet.

TEARS.

TEARS! tears! tears!
In the night, in solitude, tears,
On the white shore dripping, dripping, suck'd in by the sand,
Tears, not a star shining, all dark and desolate,
Moist tears from the eyes of a muffled head;
O who is that ghost? that form in the dark, with tears?
What shapeless lump is that, bent, crouch'd there on the sand?
Streaming tears, sobbing tears, throes, choked with wild cries;
O storm, embodied, rising, careering with swift steps along the
        beach!
O wild and dismal night storm, with wind — O belching and des-
        perate!
O shade so sedate and decorous by day, with calm countenance
        and regulated pace,
But away at night as you fly, none looking — O then the unloosen'd
        ocean,
Of tears! tears! tears!

TO THE MAN-OF-WAR-BIRD.

THOU who hast slept all night upon the storm,
Waking renew'd on thy prodigious pinions,
(Burst the wild storm? above it thou ascended'st,
And rested on the sky, thy slave that cradled thee,)
Now a blue point, far, far in heaven floating,
As to the light emerging here on deck I watch thee,
(Myself a speck, a point on the world's floating vast.)

Far, far at sea,
After the night's fierce drifts have strewn the shore with wrecks,
With re-appearing day as now so happy and serene,
The rosy and elastic dawn, the flashing sun,
The limpid spread of air cerulean,
Thou also re-appearest.

Thou born to match the gale, (thou art all wings,)
To cope with heaven and earth and sea and hurricane,
Thou ship of air that never furl'st thy sails,
Days, even weeks untired and onward, through spaces, realms
    gyrating,
At dusk that look'st on Senegal, at morn America,
That sport'st amid the lightning-flash and thunder-cloud,
In them, in thy experiences, had'st thou my soul,
What joys! what joys were thine!

ABOARD AT A SHIP'S HELM.

ABOARD at a ship's helm,
A young steersman steering with care.

Through fog on a sea-coast dolefully ringing,
An ocean-bell — O a warning bell, rock'd by the waves.

O you give good notice indeed, you bell by the sea-reefs ringing,
Ringing, ringing, to warn the ship from its wreck-place.

For as on the alert O steersman, you mind the loud admonition,
The bows turn, the freighted ship tacking speeds away under her
    gray sails,
The beautiful and noble ship with all her precious wealth speeds
    away gayly and safe.

But O the ship, the immortal ship! O ship aboard the ship!
Ship of the body, ship of the soul, voyaging, voyaging, voyaging.

ON THE BEACH AT NIGHT.

ON the beach at night,
Stands a child with her father,
Watching the east, the autumn sky.

Up through the darkness,

While ravening clouds, the burial clouds, in black masses spreading,
Lower sullen and fast athwart and down the sky,
Amid a transparent clear belt of ether yet left in the east,
Ascends large and calm the lord-star Jupiter,
And nigh at hand, only a very little above,
Swim the delicate sisters the Pleiades.

From the beach the child holding the hand of her father,
Those burial-clouds that lower victorious soon to devour all,
Watching, silently weeps.

Weep not, child,
Weep not, my darling,
With these kisses let me remove your tears,
The ravening clouds shall not long be victorious,
They shall not long possess the sky, they devour the stars only in
    apparition,
Jupiter shall emerge, be patient, watch again another night, the
    Pleiades shall emerge,
They are immortal, all those stars both silvery and golden shall
    shine out again,
The great stars and the little ones shall shine out again, they
    endure,
The vast immortal suns and the long-enduring pensive moons
    shall again shine.

Then dearest child mournest thou only for Jupiter?
Considerest thou alone the burial of the stars?

Something there is,
(With my lips soothing thee, adding I whisper,
I give thee the first suggestion, the problem and indirection,)
Something there is more immortal even than the stars,
(Many the burials, many the days and nights, passing away,)
Something that shall endure longer even than lustrous Jupiter,
Longer than sun or any revolving satellite,
Or the radiant sisters the Pleiades.

THE WORLD BELOW THE BRINE.

THE world below the brine,
Forests at the bottom of the sea, the branches and leaves,
Sea-lettuce, vast lichens, strange flowers and seeds, the thick tangle,
    openings, and pink turf,

Different colors, pale gray and green, purple, white, and gold, the
  play of light through the water,
Dumb swimmers there among the rocks, coral, gluten, grass, rushes,
  and the aliment of the swimmers,
Sluggish existences grazing there suspended, or slowly crawling
  close to the bottom,
The sperm-whale at the surface blowing air and spray, or disporting
  with his flukes,
The leaden-eyed shark, the walrus, the turtle, the hairy sea-leopard,
  and the sting-ray,
Passions there, wars, pursuits, tribes, sight in those ocean-depths,
  breathing that thick-breathing air, as so many do,
The change thence to the sight here, and to the subtle air breathed
  by beings like us who walk this sphere,
The change onward from ours to that of beings who walk other
  spheres.

ON THE BEACH AT NIGHT ALONE.

On the beach at night alone,
As the old mother sways her to and fro singing her husky song,
As I watch the bright stars shining, I think a thought of the clef
  of the universes and of the future.

A vast similitude interlocks all,
All spheres, grown, ungrown, small, large, suns, moons, planets,
All distances of place however wide,
All distances of time, all inanimate forms,
All souls, all living bodies though they be ever so different, or in
  different worlds,
All gaseous, watery, vegetable, mineral processes, the fishes, the
  brutes,
All nations, colors, barbarisms, civilizations, languages,
All identities that have existed or may exist on this globe, or any
  globe,
All lives and deaths, all of the past, present, future,
This vast similitude spans them, and always has spann'd,
And shall forever span them and compactly hold and enclose them.

SONG FOR ALL SEAS, ALL SHIPS.

I

To-day a rude brief recitative,
Of ships sailing the seas, each with its special flag or ship-signal,

Of unnamed heroes in the ships — of waves spreading and spread-
ing far as the eye can reach,
Of dashing spray, and the winds piping and blowing,
And out of these a chant for the sailors of all nations,
Fitful, like a surge.

Of sea-captains young or old, and the mates, and of all intrepid
sailors,
Of the few, very choice, taciturn, whom fate can never surprise
nor death dismay,
Pick'd sparingly without noise by thee old ocean, chosen by thee,
Thou sea that pickest and cullest the race in time, and unitest
nations,
Suckled by thee, old husky nurse, embodying thee,
Indomitable, untamed as thee.

(Ever the heroes on water or on land, by ones or twos appearing,
Ever the stock preserv'd and never lost, though rare, enough for
seed preserv'd.)

2

Flaunt out O sea your separate flags of nations !
Flaunt out visible as ever the various ship-signals !
But do you reserve especially for yourself and for the soul of man
one flag above all the rest,
A spiritual woven signal for all nations, emblem of man elate above
death,
Token of all brave captains and all intrepid sailors and mates,
And all that went down doing their duty,
Reminiscent of them, twined from all intrepid captains young or old,
A pennant universal, subtly waving all time, o'er all brave sailors,
All seas, all ships.

PATROLING BARNEGAT.

WILD, wild the storm, and the sea high running,
Steady the roar of the gale, with incessant undertone muttering,
Shouts of demoniac laughter fitfully piercing and pealing,
Waves, air, midnight, their savagest trinity lashing,
Out in the shadows there milk-white combs careering,
On beachy slush and sand spirts of snow fierce slanting,
Where through the murk the easterly death-wind breasting,
Through cutting swirl and spray watchful and firm advancing,
(That in the distance ! is that a wreck ? is the red signal flaring ?)

Slush and sand of the beach tireless till daylight wending,
Steadily, slowly, through hoarse roar never remitting,
Along the midnight edge by those milk-white combs careering,
A group of dim, weird forms, struggling, the night confronting,
That savage trinity warily watching.

AFTER THE SEA-SHIP.

AFTER the sea-ship, after the whistling winds,
After the white-gray sails taut to their spars and ropes,
Below, a myriad myriad waves hastening, lifting up their necks,
Tending in ceaseless flow toward the track of the ship,
Waves of the ocean bubbling and gurgling, blithely prying,
Waves, undulating waves, liquid, uneven, emulous waves,
Toward that whirling current, laughing and buoyant, with curves,
Where the great vessel sailing and tacking displaced the surface,
Larger and smaller waves in the spread of the ocean yearnfully
    flowing,
The wake of the sea-ship after she passes, flashing and frolicsome
    under the sun,
A motley procession with many a fleck of foam and many fragments,
Following the stately and rapid ship, in the wake following.

BY THE ROADSIDE.

A BOSTON BALLAD.

(1854.)

To get betimes in Boston town I rose this morning early,
Here's a good place at the corner, I must stand and see the show.*

Clear the way there Jonathan !*
Way for the President's marshal — way for the government cannon !
Way for the Federal foot and dragoons, (and the apparitions
    copiously tumbling.)

I love to look on the Stars and Stripes, I hope the fifes will play
    Yankee Doodle.

How bright shine the cutlasses of the foremost troops !
Every man holds his revolver, marching stiff through Boston town.

A fog follows, antiques of the same come limping,
Some appear wooden-legged, and some appear bandaged and
    bloodless.

Why this is indeed a show — it has called the dead out of the
    earth !
The old graveyards of the hills have hurried to see !
Phantoms ! phantoms countless by flank and rear !
Cock'd hats of mothy mould — crutches made of mist !
Arms in slings — old men leaning on young men's shoulders.

What troubles you Yankee phantoms ? what is all this chattering
    of bare gums ?
Does the ague convulse your limbs ? do you mistake your crutches
    for firelocks and level them ?

If you blind your eyes with tears you will not see the President's
    marshal,
If you groan such groans you might balk the government cannon.

For shame old maniacs — bring down those toss'd arms, and let
    your white hair be,
Here gape your great grandsons, their wives gaze at them from
    the windows,
See how well dress'd, see how orderly they conduct themselves.

Worse and worse — can't you stand it ? are you retreating ?
Is this hour with the living too dead for you ?

Retreat then — pell-mell !
To your graves — back — back to the hills old limpers !
I do not think you belong here anyhow.

But there is one thing that belongs here — shall I tell you what it
    is, gentlemen of Boston ?

I will whisper it to the Mayor, he shall send a committee to
    England,
They shall get a grant from the Parliament, go with a cart to the
    royal vault,
Dig out King George's coffin, unwrap him quick from the grave-
    clothes, box up his bones for a journey,

Find a swift Yankee clipper — here is freight for you, black-bellied
    clipper,
Up with your anchor — shake out your sails — steer straight toward
    Boston bay.

Now call for the President's marshal again, bring out the govern-
    ment cannon,
Fetch home the roarers from Congress, make another procession,
    guard it with foot and dragoons.

This centre-piece for them ;
Look, all orderly citizens — look from the windows, women !

The committee open the box, set up the regal ribs, glue those that
    will not stay,
Clap the skull on top of the ribs, and clap a crown on top of the
    skull.

You have got your revenge, old buster — the crown is come to its
    own, and more than its own.

Stick your hands in your pockets, Jonathan — you are a made
    man from this day,
You are mighty cute*— and here is one of your bargains.

EUROPE,

*The 72d and 73d Years of These States.**

SUDDENLY out of its stale and drowsy lair, the lair of slaves,
Like lightning it le'pt forth half startled at itself,
Its feet upon the ashes and the rags, its hands tight to the throats
    of kings.

O hope and faith !
O aching close of exiled patriots' lives !
O many a sicken'd heart !
Turn back unto this day and make yourselves afresh.

And you, paid to defile the People — you liars, mark !
Not for numberless agonies, murders, lusts,
For court thieving in its manifold mean forms, worming from his
    simplicity the poor man's wages,
For many a promise sworn by royal lips and broken and laugh'd
    at in the breaking,

Then in their power not for all these did the blows strike revenge,
　　or the heads of the nobles fall ;
The People scorn'd the ferocity of kings.

But the sweetness of mercy brew'd bitter destruction, and the
　　frighten'd monarchs come back,
Each comes in state with his train, hangman, priest, tax-gatherer,
Soldier, lawyer, lord, jailer, and sycophant.

Yet behind all lowering stealing, lo, a shape,
Vague as the night, draped interminably, head, front and form, in
　　scarlet folds,
Whose face and eyes none may see,
Out of its robes only this, the red robes lifted by the arm,
One finger crook'd pointed high over the top, like the head of a
　　snake appears.

Meanwhile corpses lie in new-made graves, bloody corpses of
　　young men,
The rope of the gibbet hangs heavily, the bullets of princes are
　　flying, the creatures of power laugh aloud,
And all these things bear fruits, and they are good.

Those corpses of young men,
Those martyrs that hang from the gibbets, those hearts pierc'd by
　　the gray lead,
Cold and motionless as they seem live elsewhere with unslaugh-
　　ter'd vitality.

They live in other young men O kings !
They live in brothers again ready to defy you,
They were purified by death, they were taught and exalted.

Not a grave of the murder'd for freedom but grows seed for free-
　　dom, in its turn to bear seed,
Which the winds carry afar and re-sow, and the rains and the
　　snows nourish.

Not a disembodied spirit can the weapons of tyrants let loose,
But it stalks invisibly over the earth, whispering, counseling,
　　cautioning.

Liberty, let others despair of you — I never despair of you.

Is the house shut? is the master away?
Nevertheless, be ready, be not weary of watching,
He will soon return, his messengers come anon.

A HAND-MIRROR.

Hold it up sternly — see this it sends back, (who is it? is it
     you?)
Outside fair costume, within ashes and filth,
No more a flashing eye, no more a sonorous voice or springy
     step,
Now some slave's eye, voice, hands, step,
A drunkard's breath, unwholesome eater's face, venerealee's flesh,
Lungs rotting away piecemeal, stomach sour and cankerous,
Joints rheumatic, bowels clogged with abomination,
Blood circulating dark and poisonous streams,
Words babble, hearing and touch callous,
No brain, no heart left, no magnetism of sex;
Such from one look in this looking-glass ere you go hence,
Such a result so soon — and from such a beginning!

GODS.

Lover divine and perfect Comrade,
Waiting content, invisible yet, but certain,
Be thou my God.

Thou, thou, the Ideal Man,
Fair, able, beautiful, content, and loving,
Complete in body and dilate in spirit,
Be thou my God.

O Death, (for Life has served its turn,)
Opener and usher to the heavenly mansion,
Be thou my God.

Aught, aught of mightiest, best I see, conceive, or know,
(To break the stagnant tie — thee, thee to free, O soul,)
Be thou my God.

All great ideas, the races' aspirations,
All heroisms, deeds of rapt enthusiasts,
Be ye my Gods.

Or Time and Space,
Or shape of Earth divine and wondrous,
Or some fair shape I viewing, worship,
Or lustrous orb of sun or star by night,
Be ye my Gods.

GERMS.

Forms, qualities, lives, humanity, language, thoughts,
The ones known, and the ones unknown, the ones on the stars,
The stars themselves, some shaped, others unshaped,
Wonders as of those countries, the soil, trees, cities, inhabitants,
whatever they may be,
Splendid suns, the moons and rings, the countless combinations
and effects,
Such-like, and as good as such-like, visible here or anywhere,
stand provided for in a handful of space, which I extend
my arm and half enclose with my hand,
That containing the start of each and all, the virtue, the germs
of all.

THOUGHTS.

Of ownership — as if one fit to own things could not at pleasure
enter upon all, and incorporate them into himself or herself ;
Of vista — suppose some sight in arriere through the formative
chaos, presuming the growth, fulness, life, now attain'd on
the journey,
(But I see the road continued, and the journey ever continued ;)
Of what was once lacking on earth, and in due time has become
supplied — and of what will yet be supplied,
Because all I see and know I believe to have its main purport in
what will yet be supplied.

WHEN I HEARD THE LEARN'D ASTRONOMER.

When I heard the learn'd astronomer,
When the proofs, the figures, were ranged in columns before me,
When I was shown the charts and diagrams, to add, divide, and
measure them,
When I sitting heard the astronomer where he lectured with much
applause in the lecture-room,
How soon unaccountable I became tired and sick,
Till rising and gliding out I wander'd off by myself,
In the mystical moist night-air, and from time to time,
Look'd up in perfect silence at the stars.

PERFECTIONS.

Only themselves understand themselves and the like of themselves,
As souls only understand souls.

O ME! O LIFE!

O ME ! O life ! of the questions of these recurring,
Of the endless trains of the faithless, of cities fill'd with the
    foolish,
Of myself forever reproaching myself, (for who more foolish than
    I, and who more faithless?)
Of eyes that vainly crave the light, of the objects mean, of the
    struggle ever renew'd,
Of the poor results of all, of the plodding and sordid crowds I
    see around me,
Of the empty and useless years of the rest, with the rest me inter-
    twined,
The question, O me ! so sad, recurring — What good amid these,
    O me, O life?

Answer.

That you are here — that life exists and identity,
That the powerful play goes on, and you may contribute a verse.

TO A PRESIDENT.*

ALL you are doing and saying is to America dangled mirages,
You have not learn'd of Nature — of the politics of Nature you
    have not learn'd the great amplitude, rectitude, impartiality,
You have not seen that only such as they are for these States,
And that what is less than they must sooner or later lift off from
    these States.

I SIT AND LOOK OUT.

I SIT and look out upon all the sorrows of the world, and upon all
    oppression and shame,
I hear secret convulsive sobs from young men at anguish with
    themselves, remorseful after deeds done,
I see in low life the mother misused by her children, dying,
    neglected, gaunt, desperate,
I see the wife misused by her husband, I see the treacherous
    seducer of young women,
I mark the ranklings of jealousy and unrequited love attempted to
    be hid, I see these sights on the earth,
I see the workings of battle, pestilence, tyranny, I see martyrs and
    prisoners,
I observe a famine at sea, I observe the sailors casting lots who
    shall be kill'd to preserve the lives of the rest,

I observe the slights and degradations cast by arrogant persons
      upon laborers, the poor, and upon negroes, and the like ;
All these — all the meanness and agony without end I sitting look
      out upon,
See, hear, and am silent.

TO RICH GIVERS.

WHAT you give me I cheerfully accept,
A little sustenance, a hut and garden, a little money, as I rendez-
      vous with my poems,
A traveler's lodging and breakfast as I journey through the States,
      — why should I be ashamed to own such gifts? why to
      advertise for them?
For I myself am not one who bestows nothing upon man and woman,
For I bestow upon any man or woman the entrance to all the gifts
      of the universe.

THE DALLIANCE OF THE EAGLES.

SKIRTING the river road, (my forenoon walk, my rest,)
Skyward in air a sudden muffled sound, the dalliance of the eagles,
The rushing amorous contact high in space together,
The clinching interlocking claws, a living, fierce, gyrating wheel,
Four beating wings, two beaks, a swirling mass tight grappling,
In tumbling turning clustering loops, straight downward falling,
Till o'er the river pois'd, the twain yet one, a moment's lull,
A motionless still balance in the air, then parting, talons loosing,
Upward again on slow-firm pinions slanting, their separate diverse
      flight,
She hers, he his, pursuing.

ROAMING IN THOUGHT.

(*After reading* HEGEL.)

Roaming in thought over the Universe, I saw the little that is
      Good steadily hastening towards immortality,
And the vast all that is call'd Evil I saw hastening to merge itself
      and become lost and dead.

A FARM PICTURE.

THROUGH the ample open door of the peaceful country barn,
A sunlit pasture field with cattle and horses feeding,
And haze and vista, and the far horizon fading away.

A CHILD'S AMAZE.

Silent and amazed even when a little boy,
I remember I heard the preacher every Sunday put God in his
    statements,
As contending against some being or influence.

THE RUNNER.

On a flat road runs the well-train'd runner,
He is lean and sinewy with muscular legs,
He is thinly clothed, he leans forward as he runs,
With lightly closed fists and arms partially rais'd.

BEAUTIFUL WOMEN.

Women sit or move to and fro, some old, some young,
The young are beautiful — but the old are more beautiful than the
    young.

MOTHER AND BABE.

I see the sleeping babe nestling the breast of its mother,
The sleeping mother and babe — hush'd, I study them long and
    long.

THOUGHT.

Of obedience, faith, adhesiveness ;*
As I stand aloof and look there is to me something profoundly
    affecting in large masses of men following the lead of those
    who do not believe in men.

VISOR'D.

A mask, a perpetual natural disguiser of herself,
Concealing her face, concealing her form,
Changes and transformations every hour, every moment,
Falling upon her even when she sleeps.

THOUGHT.

Of Justice — as if Justice could be any thing but the same ample
    law, expounded by natural judges and saviors,
As if it might be this thing or that thing, according to decisions.

GLIDING O'ER ALL.

GLIDING o'er all, through all,
Through Nature, Time, and Space,
As a ship on the waters advancing,
The voyage of the soul — not life alone,
Death, many deaths I'll sing.

HAST NEVER COME TO THEE AN HOUR.

HAST never come to thee an hour,
A sudden gleam divine, precipitating, bursting all these bubbles,
fashions, wealth?
These eager business aims — books, politics, art, amours,
To utter nothingness?

THOUGHT.

OF Equality — as if it harm'd me, giving others the same chances
and rights as myself — as if it were not indispensable to
my own rights that others possess the same.

TO OLD AGE.

I SEE in you the estuary that enlarges and spreads itself grandly as
it pours in the great sea.

LOCATIONS AND TIMES.

LOCATIONS and times — what is it in me that meets them all, when-
ever and wherever, and makes me at home?
Forms, colors, densities, odors — what is it in me that corresponds
with them?

OFFERINGS.

A THOUSAND perfect men and women appear,
Around each gathers a cluster of friends, and gay children and
youths, with offerings.

TO THE STATES,

To Identify the 16th, 17th, or 18th Presidentiad.

WHY reclining, interrogating? why myself and all drowsing?
What deepening twilight — scum floating atop of the waters,

Who are they as bats and night-dogs askant in the capitol?
What a filthy Presidentiad! (O South, your torrid suns! O North,
    your arctic freezings!)
Are those really Congressmen? are those the great Judges? is that
    the President?
Then I will sleep awhile yet, for I see that these States sleep, for
    reasons;
(With gathering murk, with muttering thunder and lambent shoots
    we all duly awake,
South, North, East, West, inland and seaboard, we will surely
    awake.)

DRUM-TAPS.

FIRST O SONGS FOR A PRELUDE.

FIRST O songs for a prelude,
Lightly strike on the stretch'd tympanum pride and joy in my city,
How she led the rest to arms, how she gave the cue,
How at once with lithe limbs unwaiting a moment she sprang,
(O superb! O Manhattan, my own, my peerless!
O strongest you in the hour of danger, in crisis! O truer than steel!)
How you sprang — how you threw off the costumes of peace with
    indifferent hand,
How your soft opera-music changed, and the drum and fife were
    heard in their stead,
How you led to the war, (that shall serve for our prelude, songs
    of soldiers,)
How Manhattan drum-taps led.

Forty years had I in my city seen soldiers parading,
Forty years as a pageant, till unawares the lady of this teeming
    and turbulent city,
Sleepless amid her ships, her houses, her incalculable wealth,
With her million children around her, suddenly,
At dead of night, at news from the south,
Incens'd struck with clinch'd hand the pavement.

A shock electric, the night sustain'd it,
Till with ominous hum our hive at daybreak pour'd out its myriads.

From the houses then and the workshops, and through all the
    doorways,
Leapt they tumultuous, and lo ! Manhattan arming.

To the drum-taps prompt,
The young men falling in and arming,
The mechanics arming, (the trowel, the jack-plane, the black-
    smith's hammer, tost aside with precipitation,)
The lawyer leaving his office and arming, the judge leaving the
    court,
The driver deserting his wagon in the street, jumping down,
    throwing the reins abruptly down on the horses' backs,
The salesman leaving the store, the boss, book-keeper, porter, all
    leaving ;
Squads gather everywhere by common consent and arm,
The new recruits, even boys, the old men show them how to wear
    their accoutrements, they buckle the straps carefully,
Outdoors arming, indoors arming, the flash of the musket-barrels,
The white tents cluster in camps, the arm'd sentries around, the
    sunrise cannon and again at sunset,
Arm'd regiments arrive every day, pass through the city, and
    embark from the wharves,
(How good they look as they tramp down to the river, sweaty,
    with their guns on their shoulders !
How I love them ! how I could hug them, with their brown faces
    and their clothes and knapsacks cover'd with dust !)
The blood of the city up — arm'd ! arm'd ! the cry everywhere,
The flags flung out from the steeples of churches and from all the
    public buildings and stores,
The tearful parting, the mother kisses her son, the son kisses his
    mother,
(Loth is the mother to part, yet not a word does she speak to
    detain him,)
The tumultuous escort, the ranks of policemen preceding, clearing
    the way,
The unpent enthusiasm, the wild cheers of the crowd for their
    favorites,
The artillery, the silent cannons bright as gold, drawn along,
    rumble lightly over the stones,
(Silent cannons, soon to cease your silence,
Soon unlimber'd to begin the red business ;)
All the mutter of preparation, all the determin'd arming,
The hospital service, the lint, bandages and medicines,
The women volunteering for nurses, the work begun for in earnest,
    no mere parade now ;

War! an arm'd race is advancing! the welcome for battle, no
  turning away;
War! be it weeks, months, or years, an arm'd race is advancing
  to welcome it.

Mannahatta a-march — and it's O to sing it well!
It's O for a manly life in the camp.

And the sturdy artillery,
The guns bright as gold, the work for giants, to serve well the guns,
Unlimber them! (no more as the past forty years for salutes for
  courtesies merely,
Put in something now besides powder and wadding.)

And you lady of ships, you Mannahatta,
Old matron of this proud, friendly, turbulent city,
Often in peace and wealth you were pensive or covertly frown'd
  amid all your children,
But now you smile with joy exulting old Mannahatta.

EIGHTEEN SIXTY-ONE.

ARM'D year — year of the struggle,
No dainty rhymes or sentimental love verses for you terrible year,
Not you as some pale poetling seated at a desk lisping cadenzas
  piano,
But as a strong man erect, clothed in blue clothes, advancing,
  carrying a rifle on your shoulder,
With well-gristled body and sunburnt face and hands, with a knife
  in the belt at your side,
As I heard you shouting loud, your sonorous voice ringing across
  the continent,
Your masculine voice O year, as rising amid the great cities,
Amid the men of Manhattan I saw you as one of the workmen,
  the dwellers in Manhattan,
Or with large steps crossing the prairies out of Illinois and
  Indiana,
Rapidly crossing the West with springy gait and descending the
  Alleghanics,
Or down from the great lakes or in Pennsylvania, or on deck
  along the Ohio river,
Or southward along the Tennessee or Cumberland rivers, or at
  Chattanooga on the mountain top,
Saw I your gait and saw I your sinewy limbs clothed in blue,
  bearing weapons, robust year,

Heard your determin'd voice launch'd forth again and again,
Year that suddenly sang by the mouths of the round-lipp'd cannon,
I repeat you, hurrying, crashing, sad, distracted year.

BEAT! BEAT! DRUMS!

BEAT! beat! drums! — blow! bugles! blow!
Through the windows — through doors — burst like a ruthless
    force,
Into the solemn church, and scatter the congregation,
Into the school where the scholar is studying;
Leave not the bridegroom quiet — no happiness must he have
    now with his bride,
Nor the peaceful farmer any peace, ploughing his field or gathering
    his grain,
So fierce you whirr and pound you drums — so shrill you bugles
    blow.

Beat! beat! drums! — blow! bugles! blow!
Over the traffic of cities — over the rumble of wheels in the
    streets;
Are beds prepared for sleepers at night in the houses? no sleepers
    must sleep in those beds,
No bargainers' bargains by day — no brokers or speculators —
    would they continue?
Would the talkers be talking? would the singer attempt to sing?
Would the lawyer rise in the court to state his case before the
    judge?
Then rattle quicker, heavier drums — you bugles wilder blow.

Beat! beat! drums! — blow! bugles! blow!
Make no parley — stop for no expostulation,
Mind not the timid — mind not the weeper or prayer,
Mind not the old man beseeching the young man,
Let not the child's voice be heard, nor the mother's entreaties,
Make even the trestles to shake the dead where they lie awaiting
    the hearses,
So strong you thump O terrible drums — so loud you bugles blow.

FROM PAUMANOK STARTING I FLY LIKE A BIRD.

FROM Paumanok* starting I fly like a bird,
Around and around to soar to sing the idea of all,
To the north betaking myself to sing there arctic songs,

To Kanada till I absorb Kanada in myself, to Michigan then,
To Wisconsin, Iowa, Minnesota, to sing their songs, (they are
    inimitable ;)
Then to Ohio and Indiana to sing theirs, to Missouri and Kansas
    and Arkansas to sing theirs,
To Tennessee and Kentucky, to the Carolinas and Georgia to sing
    theirs,
To Texas and so along up toward California, to roam accepted
    everywhere ;
To sing first, (to the tap of the war-drum if need be,)
The idea of all, of the Western world one and inseparable,
And then the song of each member of these States.

SONG OF THE BANNER AT DAYBREAK.

Poet.

O A new song, a free song,
Flapping, flapping, flapping, flapping, by sounds, by voices clearer,
By the wind's voice and that of the drum,
By the banner's voice and child's voice and sea's voice and father's
    voice,
Low on the ground and high in the air,
On the ground where father and child stand,
In the upward air where their eyes turn,
Where the banner at daybreak is flapping.

Words ! book-words ! what are you?
Words no more, for hearken and see,
My song is there in the open air, and I must sing,
With the banner and pennant a-flapping.

I'll weave the chord and twine in,
Man's desire and babe's desire, I'll twine them in, I'll put in life,
I'll put the bayonet's flashing point, I'll let bullets and slugs whizz,
(As one carrying a symbol and menace far into the future,
Crying with trumpet voice, *Arouse and beware ! Beware and
    arouse !*)
I'll pour the verse with streams of blood, full of volition, full of joy,
Then loosen, launch forth, to go and compete,
With the banner and pennant a-flapping.

Pennant.

Come up here, bard, bard,
Come up here, soul, soul,

Come up here, dear little child,
To fly in the clouds and winds with me, and play with the measure-
    less light.

Child.

Father what is that in the sky beckoning to me with long finger?
And what does it say to me all the while?

Father.

Nothing my babe you see in the sky,
And nothing at all to you it says — but look you my babe,
Look at these dazzling things in the houses, and see you the
    money-shops opening,
And see you the vehicles preparing to crawl along the streets with
    goods;
These, ah these, how valued and toil'd for these!
How envied by all the earth.

Poet.

Fresh and rosy red the sun is mounting high,
On floats the sea in distant blue careering through its channels,
On floats the wind over the breast of the sea setting in toward
    land,
The great steady wind from west or west-by-south,
Floating so buoyant with milk-white foam on the waters.

But I am not the sea nor the red sun,
I am not the wind with girlish laughter,
Not the immense wind which strengthens, not the wind which
    lashes,
Not the spirit that ever lashes its own body to terror and death,
But I am that which unseen comes and sings, sings, sings,
Which babbles in brooks and scoots in showers on the land,
Which the birds know in the woods mornings and evenings,
And the shore-sands know and the hissing wave, and that banner
    and pennant,
Aloft there flapping and flapping.

Child.

O father it is alive — it is full of people — it has children,
O now it seems to me it is talking to its children,
I hear it — it talks to me — O it is wonderful!
O it stretches — it spreads and runs so fast — O my father,
It is so broad it covers the whole sky.

Father.

Cease, cease, my foolish babe,
What you are saying is sorrowful to me, much it displeases me ;
Behold with the rest again I say, behold not banners and pennants
 aloft,
But the well-prepared pavements behold, and mark the solid-wall'd
 houses.

Banner and Pennant.

Speak to the child O bard out of Manhattan,
To our children all, or north or south of Manhattan,
Point this day, leaving all the rest, to us over all — and yet we
 know not why,
For what are we, mere strips of cloth profiting nothing,
Only flapping in the wind?

Poet.

I hear and see not strips of cloth alone,
I hear the tramp of armies, I hear the challenging sentry,
I hear the jubilant shouts of millions of men, I hear Liberty !
I hear the drums beat and the trumpets blowing,
I myself move abroad swift-rising flying then,
I use the wings of the land-bird and use the wings of the sea-bird,
 and look down as from a height,
I do not deny the precious results of peace, I see populous cities
 with wealth incalculable,
I see numberless farms, I see the farmers working in their fields
 or barns,
I see mechanics working, I see buildings everywhere founded,
 going up, or finish'd,
I see trains of cars swiftly speeding along railroad tracks drawn
 by the locomotives,
I see the stores, depots, of Boston, Baltimore, Charleston, New
 Orleans,
I see far in the West the immense area of grain, I dwell awhile
 hovering,
I pass to the lumber forests of the North, and again to the South-
 ern plantation, and again to California ;
Sweeping the whole I see the countless profit, the busy gatherings,
 earn'd wages,
See the Identity formed out of thirty-eight spacious and haughty
 States, (and many more to come,)
See forts on the shores of harbors, see ships sailing in and out ;
Then over all, (aye ! aye !) my little and lengthen'd pennant
 shaped like a sword,

Runs swiftly up indicating war and defiance — and now the hal-
        yards have rais'd it,
Side of my banner broad and blue, side of my starry banner,
Discarding peace over all the sea and land.

Banner and Pennant.

Yet louder, higher, stronger, bard ! yet farther, wider cleave !
No longer let our children deem us riches and peace alone,
We may be terror and carnage, and are so now,
Not now are we any one of these spacious and haughty States.
        (nor any five, nor ten,)
Nor market nor depot we, nor money-bank in the city,
But these and all, and the brown and spreading land, and the
        mines below, are ours,
And the shores of the sea are ours, and the rivers great and small,
And the fields they moisten, and the crops and the fruits are ours,
Bays and channels and ships sailing in and out are ours — while
        we over all,
Over the area spread below, the three or four millions of square
        miles, the capitals,
The forty millions of people, — O bard ! in life and death supreme,
We, even we, henceforth flaunt out masterful, high up above,
Not for the present alone, for a thousand years chanting through
        you,
This song to the soul of one poor little child.

Child.

O my father I like not the houses,
They will never to me be any thing, nor do I like money,
But to mount up there I would like, O father dear, that banner I
        like,
That pennant I would be and must be.

Father.

Child of mine you fill me with anguish,
To be that pennant would be too fearful,
Little you know what it is this day, and after this day, forever,
It is to gain nothing, but risk and defy every thing,
Forward to stand in front of wars — and O, such wars ! — what
        have you to do with them ?
With passions of demons, slaughter, premature death ?

Banner.

Demons and death then I sing,
Put in all, aye all will I, sword-shaped pennant for war,

And a pleasure new and ecstatic, and the prattled yearning of
  children,
Blent with the sounds of the peaceful land and the liquid wash
  of the sea,
And the black ships fighting on the sea envelop'd in smoke,
And the icy cool of the far, far north, with rustling cedars and
  pines,
And the whirr of drums and the sound of soldiers marching, and
  the hot sun shining south,
And the beach-waves combing over the beach on my Eastern
  shore, and my Western shore the same,
And all between those shores, and my ever running Mississippi
  with bends and chutes,
And my Illinois fields, and my Kansas fields, and my fields of
  Missouri,
The Continent, devoting the whole identity without reserving an
  atom,
Pour in ! whelm that which asks, which sings, with all and the
  yield of all,
Fusing and holding, claiming, devouring the whole,
No more with tender lip, nor musical labial sound,
But out of the night emerging for good, our voice persuasive no
  more,
Croaking like crows here in the wind.

Poet.

My limbs, my veins dilate, my theme is clear at last,
Banner so broad advancing out of the night, I sing you haughty
  and resolute,
I burst through where I waited long, too long, deafen'd and
  blinded,
My hearing and tongue are come to me, (a little child taught me,)
I hear from above O pennant of war your ironical call and demand,
Insensate ! insensate ! (yet I at any rate chant you,) O banner !
Not houses of peace indeed are you, nor any nor all their pros-
  perity, (if need be, you shall again have every one of those
  houses to destroy them,
You thought not to destroy those valuable houses, standing fast,
  full of comfort, built with money,
May they stand fast, then ? not an hour except you above them
  and all stand fast ;)
O banner, not money so precious are you, not farm produce you,
  nor the material good nutriment,
Nor excellent stores, nor landed on wharves from the ships,

Not the superb ships with sail-power or steam-power, fetching and
    carrying cargoes,
Nor machinery, vehicles, trade, nor revenues — but you as hence-
    forth I see you,
Running up out of the night, bringing your cluster of stars, (ever-
    enlarging stars,)
Divider of daybreak you, cutting the air, touch'd by the sun,
    measuring the sky,
(Passionately seen and yearn'd for by one poor little child,
While others remain busy or smartly talking, forever teaching
    thrift, thrift;)
O you up there! O pennant! where you undulate like a snake
    hissing so curious,
Out of reach, an idea only, yet furiously fought for, risking bloody
    death, loved by me,
So loved — O you banner leading the day with stars brought from
    the night!
Valueless, object of eyes, over all and demanding all — (absolute
    owner of all) — O banner and pennant!
I too leave the rest — great as it is, it is nothing — houses,
    machines are nothing — I see them not,
I see but you, O warlike pennant! O banner so broad, with stripes,
    I sing you only,
Flapping up there in the wind.

RISE O DAYS FROM YOUR FATHOMLESS DEEPS.

I

Rise O days from your fathomless deeps, till you loftier, fiercer
    sweep,
Long for my soul hungering gymnastic I devour'd what the earth
    gave me,
Long I roam'd the woods of the north, long I watch'd Niagara
    pouring,
I travel'd the prairies over and slept on their breast, I cross'd the
    Nevadas, I cross'd the plateaus,
I ascended the towering rocks along the Pacific, I sail'd out to
    sea,
I sail'd through the storm, I was refresh'd by the storm,
I watch'd with joy the threatening maws of the waves,
I mark'd the white combs where they career'd so high, curling
    over,
I heard the wind piping, I saw the black clouds,

Saw from below what arose and mounted, (O superb! O wild as
    my heart, and powerful!)
Heard the continuous thunder as it bellow'd after the lightning,
Noted the slender and jagged threads of lightning as sudden and
    fast amid the din they chased each other across the sky;
These, and such as these, I, elate, saw — saw with wonder, yet
    pensive and masterful,
All the menacing might of the globe uprisen around me,
Yet there with my soul I fed, I fed content, supercilious.

2

'Twas well, O soul — 'twas a good preparation you gave me,
Now we advance our latent and ampler hunger to fill,
Now we go forth to receive what the earth and the sea never
    gave us,
Not through the mighty woods we go, but through the mightier
    cities,
Something for us is pouring now more than Niagara pouring,
Torrents of men, (sources and rills of the Northwest are you
    indeed inexhaustible?)
What, to pavements and homesteads here, what were those storms
    of the mountains and sea?
What, to passions I witness around me to-day? was the sea risen?
Was the wind piping the pipe of death under the black clouds?
Lo! from deeps more unfathomable, something more deadly and
    savage,
Manhattan rising, advancing with menacing front — Cincinnati,
    Chicago, unchain'd;
What was that swell I saw on the ocean? behold what comes here,
How it climbs with daring feet and hands — how it dashes!
How the true thunder bellows after the lightning — how bright
    the flashes of lightning!
How Democracy with desperate vengeful port strides on, shown
    through the dark by those flashes of lightning!
(Yet a mournful wail and low sob I fancied I heard through the
    dark,
In a lull of the deafening confusion.)

3

Thunder on! stride on, Democracy! strike with vengeful stroke!
And do you rise higher than ever yet O days, O cities!
Crash heavier, heavier yet O storms! you have done me good,
My soul prepared in the mountains absorbs your immortal strong
    nutriment,

Long had I walk'd my cities, my country roads through farms,
    only half satisfied,
One doubt nauseous undulating like a snake, crawl'd on the
    ground before me,
Continually preceding my steps, turning upon me oft, ironically
    hissing low ;
The cities I loved so well I abandon'd and left, I sped to the
    certainties suitable to me,
Hungering, hungering, hungering, for primal energies and Nature's
    dauntlessness,
I refresh'd myself with it only, I could relish it only,
I waited the bursting forth of the pent fire — on the water and air
    I waited long ;
But now I no longer wait, I am fully satisfied, I am glutted,
I have witness'd the true lightning, I have witness'd my cities
    electric,
I have lived to behold man burst forth and warlike America rise,
Hence I will seek no more the food of the northern solitary wilds,
No more the mountains roam or sail the stormy sea.

VIRGINIA—THE WEST.

THE noble sire*fallen on evil days,
I saw with hand uplifted, menacing, brandishing,
(Memories of old in abeyance, love and faith in abeyance,)
The insane knife toward the Mother of All.

The noble son on sinewy feet advancing,
I saw, out of the land of prairies, land of Ohio's waters and of
    Indiana,
To the rescue the stalwart giant hurry his plenteous offspring,
Drest in blue, bearing their trusty rifles on their shoulders.

Then the Mother of All with calm voice speaking,
As to you Rebellious, (I seemed to hear her say,) why strive
    against me, and why seek my life?
When you yourself forever provide to defend me?
For you provided me Washington — and now these also.

CITY OF SHIPS.

CITY of ships !
(O the black ships ! O the fierce ships !
O the beautiful sharp-bow'd steam-ships and sail-ships !)

City of the world ! (for all races are here,
All the lands of the earth make contributions here ;)
City of the sea ! city of hurried and glittering tides !
City whose gleeful tides continually rush or recede, whirling in
and out with eddies and foam !
City of wharves and stores — city of tall façades of marble and
iron !
Proud and passionate city — mettlesome, mad, extravagant city !
Spring up O city — not for peace alone, but be indeed yourself,
warlike !
Fear not — submit to no models but your own O city !
Behold me — incarnate me as I have incarnated you !
I have rejected nothing you offer'd me — whom you adopted I
have adopted,
Good or bad I never question you — I love all — I do not con-
demn any thing,
I chant and celebrate all that is yours — yet peace no more,
In peace I chanted peace, but now the drum of war is mine,
War, red war is my song through your streets, O city !

THE CENTENARIAN'S STORY.

Volunteer of 1861-2, (at Washington Park, Brooklyn, assisting the Centenarian.)

GIVE me your hand old Revolutionary,
The hill-top is nigh, but a few steps, (make room gentlemen,)
Up the path you have follow'd me well, spite of your hundred and
extra years,
You can walk old man, though your eyes are almost done,
Your faculties serve you, and presently I must have them serve me.

Rest, while I tell what the crowd around us means,
On the plain below recruits are drilling and exercising,
There is the camp, one regiment departs to-morrow,
Do you hear the officers giving their orders?
Do you hear the clank of the muskets?

Why what comes over you now old man?
Why do you tremble and clutch my hand so convulsively?
The troops are but drilling, they are yet surrounded with smiles,
Around them at hand the well-drest friends and the women,
While splendid and warm the afternoon sun shines down,
Green the midsummer verdure and fresh blows the dallying
breeze,
O'er proud and peaceful cities and arm of the sea between.

But drill and parade are over, they march back to quarters,
Only hear that approval of hands ! hear what a clapping !

As wending the crowds now part and disperse — but we old man,
Not for nothing have I brought you hither — we must remain,
You to speak in your turn, and I to listen and tell.

The Centenarian.

When I clutch'd your hand it was not with terror,
But suddenly pouring about me here on every side,
And below there where the boys were drilling, and up the slopes
            they ran,
And where tents are pitch'd, and wherever you see south and
            south-east and south-west,
Over hills, across lowlands, and in the skirts of woods,
And along the shores, in mire (now fill'd over) came again and
            suddenly raged,
As eighty-five years a-gone no mere parade receiv'd with applause
            of friends,
But a battle which I took part in myself — aye, long ago as it is,
            I took part in it,
Walking then this hilltop, this same ground.

Aye, this is the ground,
My blind eyes even as I speak behold it re-peopled from graves,
The years recede, pavements and stately houses disappear,
Rude forts appear again, the old hoop'd guns are mounted,
I see the lines of rais'd earth stretching from river to bay,
I mark the vista of waters, I mark the uplands and slopes ;
Here we lay encamp'd, it was this time in summer also.

As I talk I remember all, I remember the Declaration,*
It was read here, the whole army paraded, it was read to us here,
By his staff surrounded the General*stood in the middle, he held
            up his unsheath'd sword,
It glitter'd in the sun in full sight of the army.

'Twas a bold act then — the English war-ships had just arrived,
We could watch down the lower bay where they lay at anchor,
And the transports swarming with soldiers.

A few days more and they landed, and then the battle.

Twenty thousand were brought against us,
A veteran force furnish'd with good artillery.

I tell not now the whole of the battle,
But one brigade early in the forenoon order'd forward to engage
the red-coats,
Of that brigade I tell, and how steadily it march'd,
And how long and well it stood confronting death.

Who do you think that was marching steadily sternly confronting
death?
It was the brigade of the youngest men, two thousand strong,
Rais'd in Virginia and Maryland, and most of them known per-
sonally to the General.

Jauntily forward they went with quick step toward Gowanus' waters,
Till of a sudden unlook'd for by defiles through the woods, gain'd
at night,
The British advancing, rounding in from the east, fiercely playing
their guns,
That brigade of the youngest was cut off and at the enemy's mercy.

The General watch'd them from this hill,
They made repeated desperate attempts to burst their environment,
Then drew close together, very compact, their flag flying in the
middle,
But O from the hills how the cannon were thinning and thinning
them!

It sickens me yet, that slaughter!
I saw the moisture gather in drops on the face of the General.
I saw how he wrung his hands in anguish.

Meanwhile the British manœuvr'd to draw us out for a pitch'd
battle,
But we dared not trust the chances of a pitch'd battle.

We fought the fight in detachments,
Sallying forth we fought at several points, but in each the luck was
against us,
Our foe advancing, steadily getting the best of it, push'd us back
to the works on this hill,
Till we turn'd menacing here, and then he left us.

That was the going out of the brigade of the youngest men, two
thousand strong,
Few return'd, nearly all remain in Brooklyn.

That and here my General's first battle,
No women looking on nor sunshine to bask in, it did not conclude
    with applause,
Nobody clapp'd hands here then.

But in darkness in mist on the ground under a chill rain,
Wearied that night we lay foil'd and sullen,
While scornfully laugh'd many an arrogant lord off against us
    encamp'd,
Quite within hearing, feasting, clinking wineglasses together over
    their victory.

So dull and damp and another day,
But the night of that, mist lifting, rain ceasing,
Silent as a ghost while they thought they were sure of him, my
    General retreated.

I saw him at the river-side,
Down by the ferry lit by torches, hastening the embarcation ;
My General waited till the soldiers and wounded were all pass'd
    over,
And then, (it was just ere sunrise,) these eyes rested on him for
    the last time.

Every one else seem'd fill'd with gloom,
Many no doubt thought of capitulation.

But when my General pass'd me,
As he stood in his boat and look'd toward the coming sun,
I saw something different from capitulation.

Terminus.

Enough, the Centenarian's story ends,
The two, the past and present, have interchanged,
I myself as connecter, as chansonnier of a great future, am now
    speaking.

And is this the ground Washington trod ?
And these waters I listlessly daily cross, are these the waters he
    cross'd,
As resolute in defeat as other generals in their proudest triumphs ?

I must copy the story, and send it eastward and westward,
I must preserve that look as it beam'd on you rivers of Brooklyn.

See — as the annual round returns the phantoms return,
It is the 27th of August*and the British have landed,

The battle begins and goes against us, behold through the smoke
    Washington's face,
The brigade of Virginia and Maryland have march'd forth to inter-
    cept the enemy,
They are cut off, murderous artillery from the hills plays upon
    them,
Rank after rank falls, while over them silently droops the flag,
Baptized that day in many a young man's bloody wounds,
In death, defeat, and sisters', mothers' tears.

Ah, hills and slopes of Brooklyn! I perceive you are more valuable
    than your owners supposed;
In the midst of you stands an encampment very old,
Stands forever the camp of that dead brigade.

CAVALRY CROSSING A FORD.

A LINE in long array where they wind betwixt green islands,
They take a serpentine course, their arms flash in the sun — hark
    to the musical clank,
Behold the silvery river, in it the splashing horses loitering stop to
    drink,
Behold the brown-faced men, each group, each person a picture,
    the negligent rest on the saddles,
Some emerge on the opposite bank, others are just entering the
    ford — while,
Scarlet and blue and snowy white,
The guidon flags flutter gayly in the wind.

BIVOUAC ON A MOUNTAIN SIDE.

I SEE before me now a traveling army halting,
Below a fertile valley spread, with barns and the orchards of
    summer,
Behind, the terraced sides of a mountain, abrupt, in places rising
    high,
Broken, with rocks, with clinging cedars, with tall shapes dingily
    seen,
The numerous camp-fires scatter'd near and far, some away up on
    the mountain,
The shadowy forms of men and horses, looming, large-sized,
    flickering,
And over all the sky — the sky! far, far out of reach, studded,
    breaking out, the eternal stars.

AN ARMY CORPS ON THE MARCH.

WITH its cloud of skirmishers in advance,
With now the sound of a single shot snapping like a whip, and
      now an irregular volley,
The swarming ranks press on and on, the dense brigades press
      on,
Glittering dimly, toiling under the sun — the dust-cover'd men,
In columns rise and fall to the undulations of the ground,
With artillery interspers'd — the wheels rumble, the horses sweat,
As the army corps advances.

BY THE BIVOUAC'S FITFUL FLAME.

By the bivouac's fitful flame,
A procession winding around me, solemn and sweet and slow — but
      first I note,
The tents of the sleeping army, the fields' and woods' dim
      outline,
The darkness lit by spots of kindled fire, the silence,
Like a phantom far or near an occasional figure moving,
The shrubs and trees, (as I lift my eyes they seem to be stealthily
      watching me,)
While wind in procession thoughts, O tender and wondrous
      thoughts,
Of life and death, of home and the past and loved, and of those
      that are far away ;
A solemn and slow procession there as I sit on the ground,
By the bivouac's fitful flame.

COME UP FROM THE FIELDS FATHER.

COME up from the fields father, here's a letter from our Pete,
And come to the front door mother, here's a letter from thy dear
      son.

Lo, 'tis autumn,
Lo, where the trees, deeper green, yellower and redder,
Cool and sweeten Ohio's villages with leaves fluttering in the
      moderate wind,
Where apples ripe in the orchards hang and grapes on the trellis'd
      vines,
(Smell you the smell of the grapes on the vines?
Smell you the buckwheat where the bees were lately buzzing?)

Above all, lo, the sky so calm, so transparent after the rain, and
  with wondrous clouds,
Below too, all calm, all vital and beautiful, and the farm prospers
  well.

Down in the fields all prospers well,
But now from the fields come father, come at the daughter's call,
And come to the entry mother, to the front door come right away.

Fast as she can she hurries, something ominous, her steps
  trembling,
She does not tarry to smooth her hair nor adjust her cap.

Open the envelope quickly,
O this is not our son's writing, yet his name is sign'd,
O a strange hand writes for our dear son, O stricken mother's soul!
All swims before her eyes, flashes with black, she catches the main
  words only,
Sentences broken, *gunshot wound in the breast, cavalry skirmish,
  taken to hospital,*
At present low, but will soon be better.

Ah now the single figure to me,
Amid all teeming and wealthy Ohio with all its cities and farms,
Sickly white in the face and dull in the head, very faint,
By the jamb of a door leans.

Grieve not so, dear mother, (the just-grown daughter speaks
  through her sobs,
The little sisters huddle around speechless and dismay'd,)
See, dearest mother, the letter says Pete will soon be better.

Alas poor boy, he will never be better, (nor may-be needs to be
  better, that brave and simple soul,)
While they stand at home at the door he is dead already,
The only son is dead.

But the mother needs to be better,
She with thin form presently drest in black,
By day her meals untouch'd, then at night fitfully sleeping, often
  waking,
In the midnight waking, weeping, longing with one deep longing,
O that she might withdraw unnoticed, silent from life escape and
  withdraw,
To follow, to seek, to be with her dear dead son.

VIGIL STRANGE I KEPT ON THE FIELD ONE NIGHT.

VIGIL strange I kept on the field one night;

When you my son and my comrade dropt at my side that day,

One look I but gave which your dear eyes return'd with a look I shall never forget,

One touch of your hand to mine O boy, reach'd up as you lay on the ground,

Then onward I sped in the battle, the even-contested battle,

Till late in the night reliev'd to the place at last again I made my way,

Found you in death so cold dear comrade, found your body son of responding kisses, (never again on earth responding,)

Bared your face in the starlight, curious the scene, cool blew the moderate night-wind,

Long there and then in vigil I stood, dimly around me the battle-field spreading,

Vigil wondrous and vigil sweet there in the fragrant silent night,

But not a tear fell, not even a long-drawn sigh, long, long I gazed,

Then on the earth partially reclining sat by your side leaning my chin in my hands,

Passing sweet hours, immortal and mystic hours with you dearest comrade — not a tear, not a word,

Vigil of silence, love and death, vigil for you my son and my soldier,

As onward silently stars aloft, eastward new ones upward stole,

Vigil final for you brave boy, (I could not save you, swift was your death,

I faithfully loved you and cared for you living, I think we shall surely meet again,)

Till at latest lingering of the night, indeed just as the dawn appear'd,

My comrade I wrapt in his blanket, envelop'd well his form,

Folded the blanket well, tucking it carefully over head and carefully under feet,

And there and then and bathed by the rising sun, my son in his grave, in his rude-dug grave I deposited,

Ending my vigil strange with that, vigil of night and battle-field dim,

Vigil for boy of responding kisses, (never again on earth responding,)

Vigil for comrade swiftly slain, vigil I never forget, how as day brighten'd,

I rose from the chill ground and folded my soldier well in his blanket,

And buried him where he fell.

A MARCH IN THE RANKS HARD-PREST, AND THE ROAD UNKNOWN.

A MARCH in the ranks hard-prest, and the road unknown,
A route through a heavy wood with muffled steps in the darkness,
Our army foil'd with loss severe, and the sullen remnant retreating,
Till after midnight glimmer upon us the lights of a dim-lighted
    building,
We come to an open space in the woods, and halt by the dim-
    lighted building,
'Tis a large old church at the crossing roads, now an impromptu
    hospital,
Entering but for a minute I see a sight beyond all the pictures and
    poems ever made,
Shadows of deepest, deepest black, just lit by moving candles and
    lamps,
And by one great pitchy torch stationary with wild red flame and
    clouds of smoke, .
By these, crowds, groups of forms vaguely I see on the floor, some
    in the pews laid down,
At my feet more distinctly a soldier, a mere lad, in danger of
    bleeding to death, (he is shot in the abdomen,)
I stanch the blood temporarily, (the youngster's face is white as
    a lily,)
Then before I depart I sweep my eyes o'er the scene fain to
    absorb it all,
Faces, varieties, postures beyond description, most in obscurity,
    some of them dead,
Surgeons operating, attendants holding lights, the smell of ether,
    the odor of blood,
The crowd, O the crowd of the bloody forms, the yard outside
    also fill'd,
Some on the bare ground, some on planks or stretchers, some in
    the death-spasm sweating,
An occasional scream or cry, the doctor's shouted orders or calls,
The glisten of the little steel instruments catching the glint of the
    torches,
These I resume as I chant, I see again the forms, I smell the odor,
Then hear outside the orders given, *Fall in, my men, fall in;*
But first I bend to the dying lad, his eyes open, a half-smile gives
    he me,
Then the eyes close, calmly close, and I speed forth to the
    darkness,
Resuming, marching, ever in darkness marching, on in the ranks,
The unknown road still marching.

A SIGHT IN CAMP IN THE DAYBREAK GRAY AND DIM.

A SIGHT in camp in the daybreak gray and dim,
As from my tent I emerge so early sleepless,
As slow I walk in the cool fresh air the path near by the hospital
  tent,
Three forms I see on stretchers lying, brought out there untended
  lying,
Over each the blanket spread, ample brownish woolen blanket,
Gray and heavy blanket, folding, covering all.

Curious I halt and silent stand,
Then with light fingers I from the face of the nearest the first just
  lift the blanket;
Who are you elderly man so gaunt and grim, with well-gray'd
  hair, and flesh all sunken about the eyes?
Who are you my dear comrade?

Then to the second I step — and who are you my child and
  darling?
Who are you sweet boy with cheeks yet blooming?

Then to the third — a face nor child nor old, very calm, as of
  beautiful yellow-white ivory;
Young man I think I know you — I think this face is the face
  of the Christ himself,
Dead and divine and brother of all, and here again he lies.

AS TOILSOME I WANDER'D VIRGINIA'S WOODS.

As toilsome I wander'd Virginia's woods,
To the music of rustling leaves kick'd by my feet, (for 'twas
  autumn,)
I mark'd at the foot of a tree the grave of a soldier;
Mortally wounded he and buried on the retreat, (easily all could
  I understand,)
The halt of a mid-day hour, when up! no time to lose — yet this
  sign left,
On a tablet scrawl'd and nail'd on the tree by the grave,
Bold, cautious, true, and my loving comrade.

Long, long I muse, then on my way go wandering,
Many a changeful season to follow, and many a scene of life,

Yet at times through changeful season and scene, abrupt, alone,
  or in the crowded street,
Comes before me the unknown soldier's grave, comes the inscrip-
  tion rude in Virginia's woods,
Bold, cautious, true, and my loving comrade.

NOT THE PILOT.

NOT the pilot has charged himself to bring his ship into port,
  though beaten back and many times baffled;
Not the pathfinder penetrating inland weary and long,
By deserts parch'd, snows chill'd, rivers wet, perseveres till he
  reaches his destination,
More than I have charged myself, heeded or unheeded, to com-
  pose a march for these States,
For a battle-call, rousing to arms if need be, years, centuries
  hence.

YEAR THAT TREMBLED AND REEL'D BENEATH ME.

YEAR that trembled and reel'd beneath me!
Your summer wind was warm enough, yet the air I breathed
  froze me,
A thick gloom fell through the sunshine and darken'd me,
Must I change my triumphant songs? said I to myself,
Must I indeed learn to chant the cold dirges of the baffled?
And sullen hymns of defeat?

THE WOUND-DRESSER.*

1

AN old man bending I come among new faces,
Years looking backward resuming in answer to children,
Come tell us old man, as from young men and maidens that love
  me,
(Arous'd and angry, I'd thought to beat the alarm, and urge
  relentless war,
But soon my fingers fail'd me, my face droop'd and I resign'd
  myself,
To sit by the wounded and soothe them, or silently watch the
  dead ;)
Years hence of these scenes, of these furious passions, these
  chances,

Of unsurpass'd heroes, (was one side so brave? the other was
    equally brave ;)
Now be witness again, paint the mightiest armies of earth,
Of those armies so rapid so wondrous what saw you to tell us ?
What stays with you latest and deepest? of curious panics,
Of hard-fought engagements or sieges tremendous what deepest
    remains ?

2

O maidens and young men I love and that love me,
What you ask of my days those the strangest and sudden your
    talking recalls,
Soldier alert I arrive after a long march cover'd with sweat and
    dust,
In the nick of time I come, plunge in the fight, loudly shout in
    the rush of successful charge,
Enter the captur'd works — yet lo, like a swift-running river they
    fade,
Pass and are gone they fade — I dwell not on soldiers' perils or
    soldiers' joys,
(Both I remember well — many the hardships, few the joys, yet I
    was content.)

But in silence, in dreams' projections,
While the world of gain and appearance and mirth goes on,
So soon what is over forgotten, and waves wash the imprints off
    the sand,
With hinged knees returning I enter the doors, (while for you up
    there,
Whoever you are, follow without noise and be of strong heart.)

Bearing the bandages, water and sponge,
Straight and swift to my wounded I go,
Where they lie on the ground after the battle brought in,
Where their priceless blood reddens the grass the ground,
Or to the rows of the hospital tent, or under the roof'd hospital,
To the long rows of cots up and down each side I return,
To each and all one after another I draw near, not one do I miss,
An attendant follows holding a tray, he carries a refuse pail,
Soon to be fill'd with clotted rags and blood, emptied, and fill'd
    again.

I onward go, I stop,
With hinged knees and steady hand to dress wounds,
I am firm with each, the pangs are sharp yet unavoidable,

One turns to me his appealing eyes — poor boy! I never knew
   you,
Yet I think I could not refuse this moment to die for you, if that
   would save you.

3

On, on I go, (open doors of time! open hospital doors!)
The crush'd head I dress, (poor crazed hand tear not the bandage
   away,)
The neck of the cavalry-man with the bullet through and through
   I examine,
Hard the breathing rattles, quite glazed already the eye, yet life
   struggles hard,
(Come sweet death! be persuaded O beautiful death!
In mercy come quickly.)

From the stump of the arm, the amputated hand,
I undo the clotted lint, remove the slough, wash off the matter
   and blood,
Back on his pillow the soldier bends with curv'd neck and side-
   falling head,
His eyes are closed, his face is pale, he dares not look on the
   bloody stump,
And has not yet look'd on it.

I dress a wound in the side, deep, deep,
But a day or two more, for see the frame all wasted and sinking,
And the yellow-blue countenance see.

I dress the perforated shoulder, the foot with the bullet-wound,
Cleanse the one with a gnawing and putrid gangrene, so sicken-
   ing, so offensive,
While the attendant stands behind aside me holding the tray and
   pail.

I am faithful, I do not give out,
The fractur'd thigh, the knee, the wound in the abdomen,
These and more I dress with impassive hand, (yet deep in my
   breast a fire, a burning flame.)

4

Thus in silence in dreams' projections,
Returning, resuming, I thread my way through the hospitals,
The hurt and wounded I pacify with soothing hand,
I sit by the restless all the dark night, some are so young,

Some suffer so much, I recall the experience sweet and sad,
(Many a soldier's loving arms about this neck have cross'd and rested,
Many a soldier's kiss dwells on these bearded lips.)

LONG, TOO LONG AMERICA.

LONG, too long America,
Traveling roads all even and peaceful you learn'd from joys and prosperity only,
But now, ah now, to learn from crises of anguish, advancing, grappling with direst fate and recoiling not,
And now to conceive and show to the world what your children en-masse really are,
(For who except myself has yet conceiv'd what your children en-masse really are?)

GIVE ME THE SPLENDID SILENT SUN.

1

GIVE me the splendid silent sun with all his beams full-dazzling,
Give me juicy autumnal fruit ripe and red from the orchard,
Give me a field where the unmow'd grass grows,
Give me an arbor, give me the trellis'd grape,
Give me fresh corn and wheat, give me serene-moving animals teaching content,
Give me nights perfectly quiet as on high plateaus west of the Mississippi, and I looking up at the stars,
Give me odorous at sunrise a garden of beautiful flowers where I can walk undisturb'd,
Give me for marriage a sweet-breath'd woman of whom I should never tire,
Give me a perfect child, give me away aside from the noise of the world a rural domestic life,
Give me to warble spontaneous songs recluse by myself, for my own ears only,
Give me solitude, give me Nature, give me again O Nature your primal sanities !

These demanding to have them, (tired with ceaseless excitement, and rack'd by the war-strife,)
These to procure incessantly asking, rising in cries from my heart,
While yet incessantly asking still I adhere to my city,

Day upon day and year upon year O city, walking your streets,
Where you hold me enchain'd a certain time refusing to give me
    up,
Yet giving to make me glutted, enrich'd of soul, you give me
    forever faces;
(O I see what I sought to escape, confronting, reversing my cries,
I see my own soul trampling down what it ask'd for.)

2

Keep your splendid silent sun,
Keep your woods O Nature, and the quiet places by the
    woods,
Keep your fields of clover and timothy, and your corn-fields and
    orchards,
Keep the blossoming buckwheat fields where the Ninth-month
    bees hum;
Give me faces and streets — give me these phantoms incessant
    and endless along the trottoirs!
Give me interminable eyes — give me women — give me comrades
    and lovers by the thousand!
Let me see new ones every day — let me hold new ones by the
    hand every day!
Give me such shows — give me the streets of Manhattan!
Give me Broadway, with the soldiers marching — give me the
    sound of the trumpets and drums!
(The soldiers in companies or regiments — some starting away,
    flush'd and reckless,
Some, their time up, returning with thinn'd ranks, young, yet very
    old, worn, marching, noticing nothing;)
Give me the shores and wharves heavy-fringed with black
    ships!
O such for me! O an intense life, full to repletion and varied!
The life of the theatre, bar-room, huge hotel, for me!
The saloon of the steamer! the crowded excursion for me! the
    torchlight procession!
The dense brigade bound for the war, with high piled military
    wagons following;
People, endless, streaming, with strong voices, passions, pageants,
Manhattan streets with their powerful throbs, with beating drums
    as now,
The endless and noisy chorus, the rustle and clank of muskets,
    (even the sight of the wounded,)
Manhattan crowds, with their turbulent musical chorus!
Manhattan faces and eyes forever for me.

DIRGE FOR TWO VETERANS.

THE last sunbeam
Lightly falls from the finish'd Sabbath,
On the pavement here, and there beyond it is looking,
    Down a new-made double grave.

Lo, the moon ascending,
Up from the east the silvery round moon,
Beautiful over the house-tops, ghastly, phantom moon,
    Immense and silent moon.

I see a sad procession,
And I hear the sound of coming full-key'd bugles,
All the channels of the city streets they're flooding,
    As with voices and with tears.

I hear the great drums pounding,
And the small drums steady whirring,
And every blow of the great convulsive drums,
    Strikes me through and through.

For the son is brought with the father,
(In the foremost ranks of the fierce assault they fell,
Two veterans son and father dropt together,
    And the double grave awaits them.)

Now nearer blow the bugles,
And the drums strike more convulsive,
And the daylight o'er the pavement quite has faded,
    And the strong dead-march enwraps me.

In the eastern sky up-buoying,
The sorrowful vast phantom moves illumin'd,
('Tis some mother's large transparent face,
    In heaven brighter growing.)

O strong dead-march you please me!
O moon immense with your silvery face you soothe me!
O my soldiers twain! O my veterans passing to burial!
    What I have I also give you.

The moon gives you light,
And the bugles and the drums give you music,
And my heart, O my soldiers, my veterans,
    My heart gives you love.

OVER THE CARNAGE ROSE PROPHETIC A VOICE.

Over the carnage rose prophetic a voice,
Be not dishearten'd, affection shall solve the problems of freedom
    yet,
Those who love each other shall become invincible,
They shall yet make Columbia victorious.

Sons of the Mother of All, you shall yet be victorious,
You shall yet laugh to scorn the attacks of all the remainder of
    the earth.

No danger shall balk Columbia's lovers,
If need be a thousand shall sternly immolate themselves for one.

One from Massachusetts shall be a Missourian's comrade,
From Maine and from hot Carolina, and another an Oregonese,
    shall be friends triune,
More precious to each other than all the riches of the earth.

To Michigan, Florida perfumes shall tenderly come,
Not the perfumes of flowers, but sweeter, and wafted beyond death.

It shall be customary in the houses and streets to see manly
    affection,
The most dauntless and rude shall touch face to face lightly,
The dependence of Liberty shall be lovers,
The continuance of Equality shall be comrades.

These shall tie you and band you stronger than hoops of iron,
I, ecstatic, O partners! O lands! with the love of lovers tie you.

(Were you looking to be held together by lawyers?
Or by an agreement on a paper? or by arms?
Nay, nor the world, nor any living thing, will so cohere.)

I SAW OLD GENERAL AT BAY.

I saw old General at bay,
(Old as he was, his gray eyes yet shone out in battle like stars,)
His small force was now completely hemm'd in, in his works,
He call'd for volunteers to run the enemy's lines, a desperate
    emergency,
I saw a hundred and more step forth from the ranks, but two or
    three were selected,

I saw them receive their orders aside, they listen'd with care, the adjutant was very grave,
I saw them depart with cheerfulness, freely risking their lives.

THE ARTILLERYMAN'S VISION.

WHILE my wife at my side lies slumbering, and the wars are over long,
And my head on the pillow rests at home, and the vacant midnight passes,
And through the stillness, through the dark, I hear, just hear, the breath of my infant,
There in the room as I wake from sleep this vision presses upon me ;
The engagement opens there and then in fantasy unreal,
The skirmishers begin, they crawl cautiously ahead, I hear the irregular snap ! snap !
I hear the sounds of the different missiles, the short *t-h-t! t-h-t!* of the rifle-balls,
I see the shells exploding leaving small white clouds, I hear the great shells shrieking as they pass,
The grape like the hum and whirr of wind through the trees, (tumultuous now the contest rages,)
All the scenes at the batteries rise in detail before me again,
The crashing and smoking, the pride of the men in their pieces,
The chief-gunner ranges and sights his piece and selects a fuse of the right time,
After firing I see him lean aside and look eagerly off to note the effect ;
Elsewhere I hear the cry of a regiment charging, (the young colonel leads himself this time with brandish'd sword,)
I see the gaps cut by the enemy's volleys, (quickly fill'd up, no delay,)
I breathe the suffocating smoke, then the flat clouds hover low concealing all ;
Now a strange lull for a few seconds, not a shot fired on either side,
Then resumed the chaos louder than ever, with eager calls and orders of officers,
While from some distant part of the field the wind wafts to my ears a shout of applause, (some special success,)
And ever the sound of the cannon far or near, (rousing even in dreams a devilish exultation and all the old mad joy in the depths of my soul,)
And ever the hastening of infantry shifting positions, batteries, cavalry, moving hither and thither,

(The falling, dying, I heed not, the wounded dripping and red I
    heed not, some to the rear are hobbling,)
Grime, heat, rush, aide-de-camps galloping by or on a full run,
With the patter of small arms, the warning *s-s-t* of the rifles, (these
    in my vision I hear or see,)
And bombs bursting in air, and at night the vari-color'd rockets.

ETHIOPIA SALUTING THE COLORS.

WHO are you dusky woman, so ancient hardly human,
With your woolly-white and turban'd head, and bare bony feet?
Why rising by the roadside here, do you the colors greet?

('Tis while our army lines Carolina's sands and pines,
Forth from thy hovel door thou Ethiopia com'st to me,
As under doughty Sherman I march toward the sea.)

Me master years a hundred since from my parents sunder'd,
A little child, they caught me as the savage beast is caught,
Then hither me across the sea the cruel slaver brought.

No further does she say, but lingering all the day,
Her high-borne turban'd head she wags, and rolls her darkling
    eye,
And courtesies to the regiments, the guidons moving by.

What is it fateful woman, so blear, hardly human?
Why wag your head with turban bound, yellow, red and green?
Are the things so strange and marvelous you see or have seen?

NOT YOUTH PERTAINS TO ME.

NOT youth pertains to me,
Nor delicatesse, I cannot beguile the time with talk,
Awkward in the parlor, neither a dancer nor elegant,
In the learn'd coterie sitting constrain'd and still, for learning
    inures not to me,
Beauty, knowledge, inure not to me — yet there are two or three
    things inure to me,
I have nourish'd the wounded and sooth'd many a dying soldier,
And at intervals waiting or in the midst of camp,
Composed these songs.

RACE OF VETERANS.

RACE of veterans — race of victors !
Race of the soil, ready for conflict — race of the conquering march !
(No more credulity's race, abiding-temper'd race,)
Race henceforth owning no law but the law of itself,
Race of passion and the storm.

WORLD TAKE GOOD NOTICE.

WORLD take good notice, silver stars fading,
Milky hue ript, weft of white detaching,
Coals thirty-eight,* baleful and burning,
Scarlet, significant, hands off warning,
Now and henceforth flaunt from these shores.

O TAN-FACED PRAIRIE-BOY.

O TAN-FACED prairie-boy,
Before you came to camp came many a welcome gift,
Praises and presents came and nourishing food, till at last among
    the recruits,
You came, taciturn, with nothing to give — we but look'd on each
    other,
When lo ! more than all the gifts of the world you gave me.

LOOK DOWN FAIR MOON.

LOOK down fair moon and bathe this scene,
Pour softly down night's nimbus floods on faces ghastly, swollen,
    purple,
On the dead on their backs with arms toss'd wide,
Pour down your unstinted nimbus sacred moon.

RECONCILIATION.

WORD over all, beautiful as the sky,
Beautiful that war and all its deeds of carnage must in time be
    utterly lost,
That the hands of the sisters Death and Night incessantly softly
    wash again, and ever again, this soil'd world ;

For my enemy is dead, a man divine as myself is dead,
I look where he lies white-faced and still in the coffin — I draw
    near,
Bend down and touch lightly with my lips the white face in the
    coffin.

HOW SOLEMN AS ONE BY ONE.

(*Washington City*, 1865.)

How solemn as one by one,
As the ranks returning worn and sweaty, as the men file by where
    I stand,
As the faces the masks appear, as I glance at the faces studying the
    masks,
(As I glance upward out of this page studying you, dear friend,
    whoever you are,)
How solemn the thought of my whispering soul to each in the
    ranks, and to you,
I see behind each mask that wonder a kindred soul,
O the bullet could never kill what you really are, dear friend,
Nor the bayonet stab what you really are ;
The soul ! yourself I see, great as any, good as the best,
Waiting secure and content, which the bullet could never kill,
Nor the bayonet stab O friend.

AS I LAY WITH MY HEAD IN YOUR LAP CAMERADO.

As I lay with my head in your lap camerado,
The confession I made I resume, what I said to you and the open
    air I resume,
I know I am restless and make others so,
I know my words are weapons full of danger, full of death,
For I confront peace, security, and all the settled laws, to unsettle
    them,
I am more resolute because all have denied me than I could ever
    have been had all accepted me,
I heed not and have never heeded either experience, cautions,
    majorities, nor ridicule,
And the threat of what is call'd hell is little or nothing to me,
And the lure of what is call'd heaven is little or nothing to me ;
Dear camerado ! I confess I have urged you onward with me, and
    still urge you, without the least idea what is our destination,
Or whether we shall be victorious, or utterly quell'd and defeated.

DELICATE CLUSTER.

DELICATE cluster ! flag of teeming life !
Covering all my lands — all my seashores lining !
Flag of death ! (how I watch'd you through the smoke of battle
    pressing !
How I heard you flap and rustle, cloth defiant !)
Flag cerulean — sunny flag, with the orbs of night dappled !
Ah my silvery beauty — ah my woolly white and crimson !
Ah to sing the song of you, my matron mighty !
My sacred one, my mother.

TO A CERTAIN CIVILIAN.

DID you ask dulcet rhymes from me ?
Did you seek the civilian's peaceful and languishing rhymes ?
Did you find what I sang erewhile so hard to follow ?
Why I was not singing erewhile for you to follow, to understand —
    nor am I now ;
(I have been born of the same as the war was born,
The drum-corps' rattle is ever to me sweet music, I love well the
    martial dirge,
With slow wail and convulsive throb leading the officer's funeral ;)
What to such as you anyhow such a poet as I ? therefore leave my
    works,
And go lull yourself with what you can understand, and with piano-
    tunes,
For I lull nobody, and you will never understand me.

LO, VICTRESS ON THE PEAKS.

Lo, Victress on the peaks,
Where thou with mighty brow regarding the world,
(The world O Libertad, that vainly conspired against thee,)
Out of its countless beleaguering toils, after thwarting them all,
Dominant, with the dazzling sun around thee,
Flauntest now unharm'd in immortal soundness and bloom — lo, in
    these hours supreme,
No poem proud, I chanting bring to thee, nor mastery's rapturous
    verse,
But a cluster containing night's darkness and blood-dripping
    wounds,
And psalms of the dead.

SPIRIT WHOSE WORK IS DONE.

(Washington City, 1865.)

SPIRIT whose work is done — spirit of dreadful hours !
Ere departing fade from my eyes your forests of bayonets ;
Spirit of gloomiest fears and doubts, (yet onward ever unfaltering
      pressing,)
Spirit of many a solemn day and many a savage scene — electric
      spirit,
That with muttering voice through the war now closed, like a tire-
      less phantom flitted,
Rousing the land with breath of flame, while you beat and beat
      the drum,
Now as the sound of the drum, hollow and harsh to the last,
      reverberates round me,
As your ranks, your immortal ranks, return, return from the battles,
As the muskets of the young men yet lean over their shoulders,
As I look on the bayonets bristling over their shoulders,
As those slanted bayonets, whole forests of them appearing in the
      distance, approach and pass on, returning homeward,
Moving with steady motion, swaying to and fro to the right and
      left,
Evenly lightly rising and falling while the steps keep time ;
Spirit of hours I knew, all hectic red one day, but pale as death
      next day,
Touch my mouth ere you depart, press my lips close,
Leave me your pulses of rage — bequeath them to me — fill me
      with currents convulsive,
Let them scorch and blister out of my chants when you are gone,
Let them identify you to the future in these songs.

ADIEU TO A SOLDIER.

ADIEU O soldier,
You of the rude campaigning, (which we shared,)
The rapid march, the life of the camp,
The hot contention of opposing fronts, the long manœuvre,
Red battles with their slaughter, the stimulus, the strong terrific
      game,
Spell of all brave and manly hearts, the trains of time through you
      and like of you all fill'd,
With war and war's expression.

Adieu dear comrade,
Your mission is fulfill'd — but I, more warlike,

Myself and this contentious soul of mine,
Still on our own campaigning bound,
Through untried roads with ambushes opponents lined,
Through many a sharp defeat and many a crisis, often baffled,
Here marching, ever marching on, a war fight out — aye here,
To fiercer, weightier battles give expression.

TURN O LIBERTAD.

Turn O Libertad, for the war is over,
From it and all henceforth expanding, doubting no more, resolute,
    sweeping the world,
Turn from lands retrospective recording proofs of the past,
From the singers that sing the trailing glories of the past,
From the chants of the feudal world, the triumphs of kings, slavery,
    caste,
Turn to the world, the triumphs reserv'd and to come — give up
    that backward world,
Leave to the singers of hitherto, give them the trailing past,
But what remains remains for singers for you — wars to come are
    for you,
(Lo, how the wars of the past have duly inured to you, and the
    wars of the present also inure ;)
Then turn, and be not alarm'd O Libertad — turn your undying
    face,
To where the future, greater than all the past,
Is swiftly, surely preparing for you.

TO THE LEAVEN'D SOIL THEY TROD.

To the leaven'd soil they trod calling I sing for the last,
(Forth from my tent emerging for good, loosing, untying the tent-
    ropes,)
In the freshness the forenoon air, in the far-stretching circuits and
    vistas again to peace restored,
To the fiery fields emanative and the endless vistas beyond, to the
    South and the North,
To the leaven'd soil of the general Western world to attest my
    songs,
To the Alleghanian hills and the tireless Mississippi,
To the rocks I calling sing, and all the trees in the woods,
To the plains of the poems of heroes, to the prairies spreading
    wide,

To the far-off sea and the unseen winds, and the sane impalpable
    air;
And responding they answer all, (but not in words,)
The average earth, the witness of war and peace, acknowledges
    mutely,
The prairie draws me close, as the father to bosom broad the son,
The Northern ice and rain that began me nourish me to the end,
But the hot sun of the South is to fully ripen my songs.

MEMORIES OF PRESIDENT LINCOLN.

WHEN LILACS LAST IN THE DOORYARD BLOOM'D.

1

WHEN lilacs last in the dooryard bloom'd,
And the great star early droop'd in the western sky in the night,
I mourn'd, and yet shall mourn with ever-returning spring.

Ever-returning spring, trinity sure to me you bring,
Lilac blooming perennial and drooping star in the west,
And thought of him I love.

2

O powerful western fallen star!
O shades of night — O moody, tearful night!
O great star disappear'd — O the black murk that hides the star!
O cruel hands that hold me powerless — O helpless soul of me!
O harsh surrounding cloud that will not free my soul.

3

In the dooryard fronting an old farm-house near the white-wash'd
    palings,
Stands the lilac-bush tall-growing with heart-shaped leaves of rich
    green,
With many a pointed blossom rising delicate, with the perfume
    strong I love,

With every leaf a miracle — and from this bush in the dooryard,
With delicate-color'd blossoms and heart-shaped leaves of rich
    green,
A sprig with its flower I break.

4

In the swamp in secluded recesses,
A shy and hidden bird is warbling a song.

Solitary the thrush,
The hermit withdrawn to himself, avoiding the settlements,
Sings by himself a song.

Song of the bleeding throat,
Death's outlet song of life, (for well dear brother I know,
If thou wast not granted to sing thou would'st surely die.)

5

Over the breast of the spring, the land, amid cities,
Amid lanes and through old woods, where lately the violets peep'd
    from the ground, spotting the gray debris,
Amid the grass in the fields each side of the lanes, passing the
    endless grass,
Passing the yellow-spear'd wheat, every grain from its shroud in
    the dark-brown fields uprisen,
Passing the apple-tree blows of white and pink in the orchards,
Carrying a corpse to where it shall rest in the grave,
Night and day journeys a coffin.

6

Coffin that passes through lanes and streets,
Through day and night with the great cloud darkening the land,
With the pomp of the inloop'd flags with the cities draped in black,
With the show of the States themselves as of crape-veil'd women
    standing,
With processions long and winding and the flambeaus of the night,
With the countless torches lit, with the silent sea of faces and the
    unbared heads,
With the waiting depot, the arriving coffin, and the sombre faces,
With dirges through the night, with the thousand voices rising
    strong and solemn,
With all the mournful voices of the dirges pour'd around the coffin,
The dim-lit churches and the shuddering organs — where amid
    these you journey,

With the tolling tolling bells' perpetual clang,
Here, coffin that slowly passes,
I give you my sprig of lilac.

7

(Nor for you, for one alone,
Blossoms and branches green to coffins all I bring,
For fresh as the morning, thus would I chant a song for you O
    sane and sacred death.

All over bouquets of roses,
O death, I cover you over with roses and early lilies,
But mostly and now the lilac that blooms the first,
Copious I break, I break the sprigs from the bushes,
With loaded arms I come, pouring for you,
For you and the coffins all of you O death.)

8

O western orb sailing the heaven,
Now I know what you must have meant as a month since I
    walk'd,
As I walk'd in silence the transparent shadowy night,
As I saw you had something to tell as you bent to me night after
    night,
As you droop'd from the sky low down as if to my side, (while
    the other stars all look'd on,)
As we wander'd together the solemn night, (for something I know
    not what kept me from sleep,)
As the night advanced, and I saw on the rim of the west how full
    you were of woe,
As I stood on the rising ground in the breeze in the cool trans-
    parent night,
As I watch'd where you pass'd and was lost in the netherward
    black of the night,
As my soul in its trouble dissatisfied sank, as where you sad orb,
Concluded, dropt in the night, and was gone.

9

Sing on there in the swamp,
O singer bashful and tender, I hear your notes, I hear your call,
I hear, I come presently, I understand you,
But a moment I linger, for the lustrous star has detain'd me,
The star my departing comrade holds and detains me.

10

O how shall I warble myself for the dead one there I loved?
And how shall I deck my song for the large sweet soul that has
gone?
And what shall my perfume be for the grave of him I love?

Sea-winds blown from east and west,
Blown from the Eastern sea and blown from the Western sea, till
there on the prairies meeting,
These and with these and the breath of my chant,
I'll perfume the grave of him I love.

11

O what shall I hang on the chamber walls?
And what shall the pictures be that I hang on the walls,
To adorn the burial-house of him I love?

Pictures of growing spring and farms and homes,
With the Fourth-month eve at sundown, and the gray smoke lucid
and bright,
With floods of the yellow gold of the gorgeous, indolent, sinking
sun, burning, expanding the air,
With the fresh sweet herbage under foot, and the pale green leaves
of the trees prolific,
In the distance the flowing glaze, the breast of the river, with a
wind-dapple here and there,
With ranging hills on the banks, with many a line against the sky,
and shadows,
And the city at hand with dwellings so dense, and stacks of chim-
neys,
And all the scenes of life and the workshops, and the workmen
homeward returning.

12

Lo, body and soul — this land,
My own Manhattan with spires, and the sparkling and hurrying
tides, and the ships,
The varied and ample land, the South and the North in the light,
Ohio's shores and flashing Missouri,
And ever the far-spreading prairies cover'd with grass and corn.

Lo, the most excellent sun so calm and haughty,
The violet and purple morn with just-felt breezes,
The gentle soft-born measureless light,

The miracle spreading bathing all, the fulfill'd noon,
The coming eve delicious, the welcome night and the stars,
Over my cities shining all, enveloping man and land.

13

Sing on, sing on you gray-brown bird,
Sing from the swamps, the recesses, pour your chant from the
    bushes,
Limitless out of the dusk, out of the cedars and pines.

Sing on dearest brother, warble your reedy song,
Loud human song, with voice of uttermost woe.

O liquid and free and tender !
O wild and loose to my soul — O wondrous singer !
You only I hear — yet the star holds me, (but will soon depart,)
Yet the lilac with mastering odor holds me.

14

Now while I sat in the day and look'd forth,
In the close of the day with its light and the fields of spring, and
    the farmers preparing their crops,
In the large unconscious scenery of my land with its lakes and
    forests,
In the heavenly aerial beauty, (after the perturb'd winds and the
    storms,)
Under the arching heavens of the afternoon swift passing, and the
    voices of children and women,
The many-moving sea-tides, and I saw the ships how they
    sail'd,
And the summer approaching with richness, and the fields all busy
    with labor,
And the infinite separate houses, how they all went on, each with
    its meals and minutia of daily usages,
And the streets how their throbbings throbb'd, and the cities pent
    — lo, then and there,
Falling upon them all and among them all, enveloping me with the
    rest,
Appear'd the cloud, appear'd the long black trail,
And I knew death, its thought, and the sacred knowledge of
    death.

Then with the knowledge of death as walking one side of me,
And the thought of death close-walking the other side of me,

And I in the middle as with companions, and as holding the
        hands of companions,
I fled forth to the hiding receiving night that talks not,
Down to the shores of the water, the path by the swamp in the
        dimness,
To the solemn shadowy cedars and ghostly pines so still.

And the singer so shy to the rest receiv'd me,
The gray-brown bird I know receiv'd us comrades three,
And he sang the carol of death, and a verse for him I love.

From deep secluded recesses,
From the fragrant cedars and the ghostly pines so still,
Came the carol of the bird.

And the charm of the carol rapt me,
As I held as if by their hands my comrades in the night,
And the voice of my spirit tallied the song of the bird.

Come lovely and soothing death,
Undulate round the world, serenely arriving, arriving,
In the day, in the night, to all, to each,
Sooner or later delicate death.

Prais'd be the fathomless universe,
For life and joy, and for objects and knowledge curious,
And for love, sweet love — but praise! praise! praise!
For the sure-enwinding arms of cool-enfolding death.

Dark mother always gliding near with soft feet,
Have none chanted for thee a chant of fullest welcome?
Then I chant it for thee, I glorify thee above all,
I bring thee a song that when thou must indeed come, come unfal-
teringly.

Approach strong deliveress,
When it is so, when thou hast taken them I joyously sing the dead,
Lost in the loving floating ocean of thee,
Laved in the flood of thy bliss O death.

From me to thee glad serenades,
Dances for thee I propose saluting thee, adornments and feast-
ings for thee,
And the sights of the open landscape and the high-spread sky are
fitting,
And life and the fields, and the huge and thoughtful night.

The night in silence under many a star,
The ocean shore and the husky whispering wave whose voice I
*   know,*
And the soul turning to thee O vast and well-veil'd death,
And the body gratefully nestling close to thee.

Over the tree-tops I float thee a song,
Over the rising and sinking waves, over the myriad fields and the
*   prairies wide,*
Over the dense-pack'd cities all and the teeming wharves and ways,
I float this carol with joy, with joy to thee O death.

15

To the tally of my soul,
Loud and strong kept up the gray-brown bird,
With pure deliberate notes spreading filling the night.

Loud in the pines and cedars dim,
Clear in the freshness moist and the swamp-perfume,
And I with my comrades there in the night.

While my sight that was bound in my eyes unclosed,
As to long panoramas of visions.

And I saw askant the armies,
I saw as in noiseless dreams hundreds of battle-flags,
Borne through the smoke of the battles and pierc'd with missiles
      I saw them,
And carried hither and yon through the smoke, and torn and
      bloody,
And at last but a few shreds left on the staffs, (and all in silence,)
And the staffs all splinter'd and broken.

I saw battle-corpses, myriads of them,
And the white skeletons of young men, I saw them,
I saw the debris and debris of all the slain soldiers of the war,
But I saw they were not as was thought,
They themselves were fully at rest, they suffer'd not,
The living remain'd and suffer'd, the mother suffer'd,
And the wife and the child and the musing comrade suffer'd,
And the armies that remain'd suffer'd.

16

Passing the visions, passing the night,
Passing, unloosing the hold of my comrades' hands,

Passing the song of the hermit bird and the tallying song of my
        soul,
Victorious song, death's outlet song, yet varying ever-altering song,
As low and wailing, yet clear the notes, rising and falling, flooding
        the night,
Sadly sinking and fainting, as warning and warning, and yet again
        bursting with joy,
Covering the earth and filling the spread of the heaven,
As that powerful psalm in the night I heard from recesses,
Passing, I leave thee lilac with heart-shaped leaves,
I leave thee there in the door-yard, blooming, returning with
        spring.

I cease from my song for thee,
From my gaze on thee in the west, fronting the west, communing
        with thee,
O comrade lustrous with silver face in the night.

Yet each to keep and all, retrievements out of the night,
The song, the wondrous chant of the gray-brown bird,
And the tallying chant, the echo arous'd in my soul,
With the lustrous and drooping star with the countenance full
        of woe,
With the holders holding my hand nearing the call of the bird,
Comrades mine and I in the midst, and their memory ever to
        keep, for the dead I loved so well,
For the sweetest, wisest soul of all my days and lands — and this
        for his dear sake,
Lilac and star and bird twined with the chant of my soul,
There in the fragrant pines and the cedars dusk and dim.

O CAPTAIN! MY CAPTAIN!

O Captain! my Captain! our fearful trip is done,
The ship has weather'd every rack, the prize we sought is won,
The port is near, the bells I hear, the people all exulting,
While follow eyes the steady keel, the vessel grim and daring;
            But O heart! heart! heart!
                O the bleeding drops of red,
                    Where on the deck my Captain lies,
                        Fallen cold and dead.

O Captain! my Captain! rise up and hear the bells;
Rise up — for you the flag is flung — for you the bugle trills,

For you bouquets and ribbon'd wreaths — for you the shores
    a-crowding,
For you they call, the swaying mass, their eager faces turning;
      Here Captain! dear father!
        This arm beneath your head!
          It is some dream that on the deck,
            You've fallen cold and dead.

My Captain does not answer, his lips are pale and still,
My father does not feel my arm, he has no pulse nor will,
The ship is anchor'd safe and sound, its voyage closed and done,
From fearful trip the victor ship comes in with object won;
      Exult O shores, and ring O bells!
        But I with mournful tread,
          Walk the deck my Captain lies,
            Fallen cold and dead.

HUSH'D BE THE CAMPS TO-DAY.

(*May 4, 1865.*)

HUSH'D be the camps to-day,
And soldiers let us drape our war-worn weapons,
And each with musing soul retire to celebrate,
    Our dear commander's death.

No more for him life's stormy conflicts,
Nor victory, nor defeat — no more time's dark events,
Charging like ceaseless clouds across the sky.

But sing poet in our name,
Sing of the love we bore him — because you, dweller in camps,
    know it truly.

As they invault the coffin there,
Sing — as they close the doors of earth upon him — one verse,
For the heavy hearts of soldiers.

THIS DUST WAS ONCE THE MAN.

THIS dust was once the man,
Gentle, plain, just and resolute, under whose cautious hand,
Against the foulest crime in history known in any land or age,
Was saved the Union of these States.

BY BLUE ONTARIO'S SHORE.

1

By blue Ontario's shore,
As I mused of these warlike days and of peace return'd, and the
    dead that return no more,
A Phantom gigantic superb, with stern visage accosted me,
Chant me the poem, it said, *that comes from the soul of America,
    chant me the carol of victory,
And strike up the marches of Libertad, marches more powerful yet,
And sing me before you go the song of the throes of Democracy.*

(Democracy, the destin'd conqueror, yet treacherous lip-smiles
    everywhere,
And death and infidelity at every step.)

2

A Nation announcing itself,
I myself make the only growth by which I can be appreciated,
I reject none, accept all, then reproduce all in my own forms.

A breed whose proof is in time and deeds,
What we are we are, nativity is answer enough to objections,
We wield ourselves as a weapon is wielded,
We are powerful and tremendous in ourselves,
We are executive in ourselves, we are sufficient in the variety of
    ourselves,
We are the most beautiful to ourselves and in ourselves,
We stand self-pois'd in the middle, branching thence over the
    world,
From Missouri, Nebraska, or Kansas, laughing attacks to scorn.

Nothing is sinful to us outside of ourselves,
Whatever appears, whatever does not appear, we are beautiful or
    sinful in ourselves only.

(O Mother — O Sisters dear !
If we are lost, no victor else has destroy'd us,
It is by ourselves we go down to eternal night.)

3

Have you thought there could be but a single supreme?
There can be any number of supremes — one does not counter-
    vail another any more than one eyesight countervails
    another, or one life countervails another.

All is eligible to all,
All is for individuals, all is for you,
No condition is prohibited, not God's or any.

All comes by the body, only health puts you rapport with the
    universe.

Produce great Persons, the rest follows.

4

Piety and conformity to them that like,
Peace, obesity, allegiance, to them that like,
I am he who tauntingly compels men, women, nations,
Crying, Leap from your seats and contend for your lives!

I am he who walks the States with a barb'd tongue, questioning
    every one I meet,
Who are you that wanted only to be told what you knew before?
Who are you that wanted only a book to join you in your nonsense?

(With pangs and cries as thine own O bearer of many children,
These clamors wild to a race of pride I give.)

O lands, would you be freer than all that has ever been before?
If you would be freer than all that has been before, come listen
    to me.

Fear grace, elegance, civilization, delicatesse,
Fear the mellow sweet, the sucking of honey-juice,
Beware the advancing mortal ripening of Nature,
Beware what precedes the decay of the ruggedness of states and
    men.

5

Ages, precedents, have long been accumulating undirected
    materials,
America brings builders, and brings its own styles.

The immortal poets of Asia and Europe have done their work
    and pass'd to other spheres,
A work remains, the work of surpassing all they have done.

America, curious toward foreign characters, stands by its own at
    all hazards,

Stands removed, spacious, composite, sound, initiates the true
 use of precedents,
Does not repel them or the past or what they have produced
 under their forms,
Takes the lesson with calmness, perceives the corpse slowly borne
 from the house,
Perceives that it waits a little while in the door, that it was fittest
 for its days,
That its life has descended to the stalwart and well-shaped heir
 who approaches,
And that he shall be fittest for his days.

Any period one nation must lead,
One land must be the promise and reliance of the future.

These States are the amplest poem,
Here is not merely a nation but a teeming Nation of nations,
Here the doings of men correspond with the broadcast doings of
 the day and night,
Here is what moves in magnificent masses careless of particulars,
Here are the roughs, beards, friendliness, combativeness, the soul
 loves,
Here the flowing trains, here the crowds, equality, diversity, the
 soul loves.

6

Land of lands and bards to corroborate !
Of them standing among them, one lifts to the light a west-bred
 face,
To him the hereditary countenance bequeath'd both mother's and
 father's,
His first parts substances, earth, water, animals, trees,
Built of the common stock, having room for far and near,
Used to dispense with other lands, incarnating this land,
Attracting it body and soul to himself, hanging on its neck with
 incomparable love,
Plunging his seminal muscle into its merits and demerits,
Making its cities, beginnings, events, diversities, wars, vocal in him,
Making its rivers, lakes, bays, embouchure in him,
Mississippi with yearly freshets and changing chutes, Columbia,
 Niagara, Hudson, spending themselves lovingly in him,
If the Atlantic coast stretch or the Pacific coast stretch, he stretch-
 ing with them North or South,
Spanning between them East and West, and touching whatever is
 between them,

Growths growing from him to offset the growths of pine, cedar, hemlock, live-oak, locust, chestnut, hickory, cottonwood, orange, magnolia,

Tangles as tangled in him as any canebrake or swamp,

He likening sides and peaks of mountains, forests coated with northern transparent ice,

Off him pasturage sweet and natural as savanna, upland, prairie,

Through him flights, whirls, screams, answering those of the fish-hawk, mocking-bird, night-heron, and eagle,

His spirit surrounding his country's spirit, unclosed to good and evil,

Surrounding the essences of real things, old times and present times,

Surrounding just found shores, islands, tribes of red aborigines,

Weather-beaten vessels, landings, settlements, embryo stature and muscle,

The haughty defiance of the Year One, war, peace, the formation of the Constitution,

The separate States, the simple elastic scheme, the immigrants,

The Union always swarming with blatherers and always sure and impregnable,

The unsurvey'd interior, log-houses, clearings, wild animals, hunters, trappers,

Surrounding the multiform agriculture, mines, temperature, the gestation of new States,

Congress convening every Twelfth-month, the members duly coming up from the uttermost parts,

Surrounding the noble character of mechanics and farmers, especially the young men,

Responding their manners, speech, dress, friendships, the gait they have of persons who never knew how it felt to stand in the presence of superiors,

The freshness and candor of their physiognomy, the copiousness and decision of their phrenology,

The picturesque looseness of their carriage, their fierceness when wrong'd,

The fluency of their speech, their delight in music, their curiosity, good temper and open-handedness, the whole composite make,

The prevailing ardor and enterprise, the large amativeness,

The perfect equality of the female with the male, the fluid movement of the population,

The superior marine, free commerce, fisheries, whaling, gold-digging,

Wharf-hemm'd cities, railroad and steamboat lines intersecting all points,

Factories, mercantile life, labor-saving machinery, the Northeast, Northwest, Southwest,
Manhattan firemen, the Yankee swap, southern plantation life,
Slavery — the murderous, treacherous conspiracy to raise it upon the ruins of all the rest,
On and on to the grapple with it — Assassin! then your life or ours be the stake, and respite no more.

7

(Lo, high toward heaven, this day,
Libertad, from the conqueress' field return'd,
I mark the new aureola around your head,
No more of soft astral, but dazzling and fierce,
With war's flames and the lambent lightnings playing,
And your port immovable where you stand,
With still the inextinguishable glance and the clinch'd and lifted fist,
And your foot on the neck of the menacing one, the scorner utterly crush'd beneath you,
The menacing arrogant one that strode and advanced with his senseless scorn, bearing the murderous knife,
The wide-swelling one, the braggart that would yesterday do so much,
To-day a carrion dead and damn'd, the despised of all the earth,
An offal rank, to the dunghill maggots spurn'd.)

8

Others take finish, but the Republic is ever constructive and ever keeps vista,
Others adorn the past, but you O days of the present, I adorn you,
O days of the future I believe in you — I isolate myself for your sake,
O America because you build for mankind I build for you,
O well-beloved stone-cutters, I lead them who plan with decision and science,
Lead the present with friendly hand toward the future.

(Bravas to all impulses sending sane children to the next age!
But damn that which spends itself with no thought of the stain, pains, dismay, feebleness, it is bequeathing.)

9

I listened to the Phantom* by Ontario's shore,
I heard the voice arising demanding bards,

By them all native and grand, by them alone can these States be
    fused into the compact organism of a Nation.

To hold men together by paper and seal or by compulsion is no
    account,
That only holds men together which aggregates all in a living
    principle, as the hold of the limbs of the body or the fibres
    of plants.

Of all races and eras these States with veins full of poetical stuff
    most need poets, and are to have the greatest, and use
    them the greatest,
Their Presidents shall not be their common referee so much as
    their poets shall.

(Soul of love and tongue of fire!
Eye to pierce the deepest deeps and sweep the world!
Ah Mother, prolific and full in all besides, yet how long barren,
    barren?)

10

Of these States the poet is the equable man,
Not in him but off from him things are grotesque, eccentric, fail
    of their full returns,
Nothing out of its place is good, nothing in its place is bad,
He bestows on every object or quality its fit proportion, neither
    more nor less,
He is the arbiter of the diverse, he is the key,
He is the equalizer of his age and land,
He supplies what wants supplying, he checks what wants checking,
In peace out of him speaks the spirit of peace, large, rich, thrifty,
    building populous towns, encouraging agriculture, arts,
    commerce, lighting the study of man, the soul, health,
    immortality, government,
In war he is the best backer of the war, he fetches artillery as good
    as the engineer's, he can make every word he speaks draw
    blood,
The years straying toward infidelity he withholds by his steady
    faith,
He is no arguer, he is judgment, (Nature accepts him absolutely,)
He judges not as the judge judges but as the sun falling round a
    helpless thing,
As he sees the farthest he has the most faith,
His thoughts are the hymns of the praise of things,
In the dispute on God and eternity he is silent,

He sees eternity less like a play with a prologue and denouement,
He sees eternity in men and women, he does not see men and
　　women as dreams or dots.

For the great Idea, the idea of perfect and free individuals,
For that, the bard walks in advance, leader of leaders,
The attitude of him cheers up slaves and horrifies foreign despots.

Without extinction is Liberty, without retrograde is Equality,
They live in the feelings of young men and the best women,
(Not for nothing have the indomitable heads of the earth been
　　always ready to fall for Liberty.)

11

For the great Idea,*
That, O my brethren, that is the mission of poets.

Songs of stern defiance ever ready,
Songs of the rapid arming and the march,
The flag of peace quick-folded, and instead the flag we know,
Warlike flag of the great Idea.

(Angry cloth I saw there leaping !
I stand again in leaden rain your flapping folds saluting,
I sing you over all, flying beckoning through the fight — O the
　　hard-contested fight !
The cannons ope their rosy-flashing muzzles — the hurtled balls
　　scream,
The battle-front forms amid the smoke — the volleys pour incessant
　　from the line,
Hark, the ringing word *Charge !* — now the tussle and the furious
　　maddening yells,
Now the corpses tumble curl'd upon the ground,
Cold, cold in death, for precious life of you,
Angry cloth I saw there leaping.)

12

Are you he who would assume a place to teach or be a poet here
　　in the States?
The place is august, the terms obdurate.

Who would assume to teach here may well prepare himself body
　　and mind,
He may well survey, ponder, arm, fortify, harden, make lithe him-
　　self,
He shall surely be question'd beforehand by me with many and
　　stern questions.

Who are you indeed who would talk or sing to America?
Have you studied out the land, its idioms and men?
Have you learn'd the physiology, phrenology, politics, geography,
    pride, freedom, friendship of the land? its substratums and
    objects?
Have you consider'd the organic compact of the first day of the
    first year of Independence, sign'd by the Commissioners,
    ratified by the States, and read by Washington at the head
    of the army?
Have you possess'd yourself of the Federal Constitution?
Do you see who have left all feudal processes and poems behind
    them, and assumed the poems and processes of Democracy?
Are you faithful to things? do you teach what the land and sea,
    the bodies of men, womanhood, amativeness, heroic angers,
    teach?
Have you sped through fleeting customs, popularities?
Can you hold your hand against all seductions, follies, whirls, fierce
    contentions? are you very strong? are you really of the
    whole People?
Are you not of some coterie? some school or mere religion?
Are you done with reviews and criticisms of life? animating now
    to life itself?
Have you vivified yourself from the maternity of these States?
Have you too the old ever-fresh forbearance and impartiality?
Do you hold the like love for those hardening to maturity? for the
    last-born? little and big? and for the errant?

What is this you bring my America?
Is it uniform with my country?
Is it not something that has been better told or done before?
Have you not imported this or the spirit of it in some ship?
Is it not a mere tale? a rhyme? a prettiness?—is the good old
    cause in it?
Has it not dangled long at the heels of the poets, politicians,
    literats, of enemies' lands?
Does it not assume that what is notoriously gone is still here?
Does it answer universal needs? will it improve manners?
Does it sound with trumpet-voice the proud victory of the Union
    in that secession war?
Can your performance face the open fields and the seaside?
Will it absorb into me as I absorb food, air, to appear again in my
    strength, gait, face?
Have real employments contributed to it? original makers, not
    mere amanuenses?
Does it meet modern discoveries, calibres, facts, face to face?

What does it mean to American persons, progresses, cities? Chi-
cago, Kanada, Arkansas?
Does it see behind the apparent custodians the real custodians
standing, menacing, silent, the mechanics, Manhattanese,
Western men, Southerners, significant alike in their apathy,
and in the promptness of their love?
Does it see what finally befalls, and has always finally befallen, each
temporizer, patcher, outsider, partialist, alarmist, infidel,
who has ever ask'd any thing of America?
What mocking and scornful negligence?
The track strew'd with the dust of skeletons,
By the roadside others disdainfully toss'd.

13

Rhymes and rhymers pass away, poems distill'd from poems pass
away,
The swarms of reflectors and the polite pass, and leave ashes,
Admirers, importers, obedient persons, make but the soil of litera-
ture,
America justifies itself, give it time, no disguise can deceive it or
conceal from it, it is impassive enough,
Only toward the likes of itself will it advance to meet them,
If its poets appear it will in due time advance to meet them,
there is no fear of mistake,
(The proof of a poet shall be sternly deferr'd till his country
absorbs him as affectionately as he has absorb'd it.)

He masters whose spirit masters, he tastes sweetest who results
sweetest in the long run,
The blood of the brawn beloved of time is unconstraint;
In the need of songs, philosophy, an appropriate native grand-
opera, shipcraft, any craft,
He or she is greatest who contributes the greatest original prac-
tical example.

Already a nonchalant breed, silently emerging, appears on the
streets,
People's lips salute only doers, lovers, satisfiers, positive knowers,
There will shortly be no more priests, I say their work is done,
Death is without emergencies here, but life is perpetual emer-
gencies here,
Are your body, days, manners, superb? after death you shall be
superb,
Justice, health, self-esteem, clear the way with irresistible power;
How dare you place any thing before a man?

14

Fall behind me States!
A man before all — myself, typical, before all.

Give me the pay I have served for,
Give me to sing the songs of the great Idea, take all the rest,
I have loved the earth, sun, animals, I have despised riches,
I have given alms to every one that ask'd, stood up for the stupid
    and crazy, devoted my income and labor to others,
Hated tyrants, argued not concerning God, had patience and
    indulgence toward the people, taken off my hat to nothing
    known or unknown,
Gone freely with powerful uneducated persons and with the young,
    and with the mothers of families,
Read these leaves to myself in the open air, tried them by trees,
    stars, rivers,
Dismiss'd whatever insulted my own soul or defiled my body,
Claim'd nothing to myself which I have not carefully claim'd for
    others on the same terms,
Sped to the camps, and comrades found and accepted from every
    State,
(Upon this breast has many a dying soldier lean'd to breathe his
    last,
This arm, this hand, this voice, have nourish'd, rais'd, restored,
To life recalling many a prostrate form;)
I am willing to wait to be understood by the growth of the taste
    of myself,
Rejecting none, permitting all.

(Say O Mother, have I not to your thought been faithful?
Have I not through life kept you and yours before me?)

15

I swear I begin to see the meaning of these things,
It is not the earth, it is not America who is so great,
It is I who am great or to be great, it is You up there, or any one,
It is to walk rapidly through civilizations, governments, theories,
Through poems, pageants, shows, to form individuals.

Underneath all, individuals,
I swear nothing is good to me now that ignores individuals,
The American compact is altogether with individuals,
The only government is that which makes minute of individuals,
The whole theory of the universe is directed unerringly to one
    single individual — namely to You.

(Mother ! with subtle sense severe, with the naked sword in your
      hand,
I saw you at last refuse to treat but directly with individuals.)

16

Underneath all, Nativity,
I swear I will stand by my own nativity, pious or impious so be it ;
I swear I am charm'd with nothing except nativity,
Men, women, cities, nations, are only beautiful from nativity.

Underneath all is the Expression of love for men and women,
(I swear I have seen enough of mean and impotent modes of
      expressing love for men and women,
After this day I take my own modes of expressing love for men
      and women.)

I swear I will have each quality of my race in myself,
(Talk as you like, he only suits these States whose manners favor
      the audacity and sublime turbulence of the States.)

Underneath the lessons of things, spirits, Nature, governments,
      ownerships, I swear I perceive other lessons,
Underneath all to me is myself, to you yourself, (the same monoto-
      nous old song.)

17

O I see flashing that this America is only you and me,
Its power, weapons, testimony, are you and me,
Its crimes, lies, thefts, defections, are you and me,
Its Congress is you and me, the officers, capitols, armies, ships, are
      you and me,
Its endless gestations of new States are you and me,
The war, (that war so bloody and grim, the war I will henceforth
      forget), was you and me,
Natural and artificial are you and me,
Freedom, language, poems, employments, are you and me,
Past, present, future, are you and me.

I dare not shirk any part of myself,
Not any part of America good or bad,
Not to build for that which builds for mankind,
Not to balance ranks, complexions, creeds, and the sexes,
Not to justify science nor the march of equality,
Nor to feed the arrogant blood of the brawn belov'd of time.

I am for those that have never been master'd,
For men and women whose tempers have never been master'd,
For those whom laws, theories, conventions, can never master.

I am for those who walk abreast with the whole earth,
Who inaugurate one to inaugurate all.

I will not be outfaced by irrational things,
I will penetrate what it is in them that is sarcastic upon me,
I will make cities and civilizations defer to me,
This is what I have learnt from America — it is the amount, and it
    I teach again.

(Democracy, while weapons were everywhere aim'd at your breast,
I saw you serenely give birth to immortal children, saw in dreams
    your dilating form,
Saw you with spreading mantle covering the world.)

18

I will confront these shows of the day and night,
I will know if I am to be less than they,
I will see if I am not as majestic as they,
I will see if I am not as subtle and real as they,
I will see if I am to be less generous than they,
I will see if I have no meaning, while the houses and ships have
    meaning,
I will see if the fishes and birds are to be enough for themselves,
    and I am not to be enough for myself.

I match my spirit against yours you orbs, growths, mountains,
    brutes,
Copious as you are I absorb you all in myself, and become the
    master myself,
America isolated yet embodying all, what is it finally except
    myself?
These States, what are they except myself?

I know now why the earth is gross, tantalizing, wicked, it is for my
    sake,
I take you specially to be mine, you terrible, rude forms.

(Mother, bend down, bend close to me your face,
I know not what these plots and wars and deferments are for,
I know not fruition's success, but I know that through war and
    crime your work goes on, and must yet go on.)

19

Thus by blue Ontario's shore,
While the winds fann'd me and the waves came trooping toward me,
I thrill'd with the power's pulsations, and the charm of my theme was upon me,
Till the tissues that held me parted their ties upon me.

And I saw the free souls of poets,
The loftiest bards of past ages strode before me,
Strange large men, long unwaked, undisclosed, were disclosed to me.

20

O my rapt verse, my call, mock me not!
Not for the bards of the past, not to invoke them have I launch'd you forth,
Not to call even those lofty bards here by Ontario's shores,
Have I sung so capricious and loud my savage song.

Bards for my own land only I invoke,
(For the war the war is over, the field is clear'd,)
Till they strike up marches henceforth triumphant and onward,
To cheer O Mother your boundless expectant soul.

Bards of the great Idea! bards of the peaceful inventions! (for the war, the war is over!)
Yet bards of latent armies, a million soldiers waiting ever-ready,
Bards with songs as from burning coals or the lightning's fork'd stripes!
Ample Ohio's, Kanada's bards — bards of California! inland bards — bards of the war!
You by my charm I invoke.

REVERSALS.

LET that which stood in front go behind,
Let that which was behind advance to the front,
Let bigots, fools, unclean persons, offer new propositions,
Let the old propositions be postponed,
Let a man seek pleasure everywhere except in himself,
Let a woman seek happiness everywhere except in herself.

AUTUMN RIVULETS.

AS CONSEQUENT, *Etc.*

As consequent from store of summer rains,
Or wayward rivulets in autumn flowing,
Or many a herb-lined brook's reticulations,
Or subterranean sea-rills making for the sea,
Songs of continued years I sing.

Life's ever-modern rapids first, (soon, soon to blend,
With the old streams of death.)

Some threading Ohio's farm-fields or the woods,
Some down Colorado's cañons from sources of perpetual snow,
Some half-hid in Oregon, or away southward in Texas,
Some in the north finding their way to Erie, Niagara, Ottawa,
Some to Atlantica's bays, and so to the great salt brine.

In you whoe'er you are my book perusing,
In I myself, in all the world, these currents flowing,
All, all toward the mystic ocean tending.

Currents for starting a continent new,
Overtures sent to the solid out of the liquid,
Fusion of ocean and land, tender and pensive waves,
(Not safe and peaceful only, waves rous'd and ominous too,
Out of the depths the storm's abysmic waves, who knows whence?
Raging over the vast, with many a broken spar and tatter'd sail.)

Or from the sea of Time, collecting vasting all, I bring,
A windrow-drift of weeds and shells.

O little shells, so curious-convolute, so limpid-cold and voiceless,
Will you not little shells to the tympans of temples held,
Murmurs and echoes still call up, eternity's music faint and far,
Wafted inland, sent from Atlantica's rim, strains for the soul of the
    prairies,
Whisper'd reverberations, chords for the ear of the West joyously
    sounding,
Your tidings old, yet ever new and untranslatable,
Infinitesimals out of my life, and many a life,

(For not my life and years alone I give — all, all I give,)
These waifs from the deep, cast high and dry,
Wash'd on America's shores?

THE RETURN OF THE HEROES.

1

For the lands and for these passionate days and for myself,
Now I awhile retire to thee O soil of autumn fields,
Reclining on thy breast, giving myself to thee,
Answering the pulses of thy sane and equable heart,
Tuning a verse for thee.

O earth that hast no voice, confide to me a voice,
O harvest of my lands — O boundless summer growths,
O lavish brown parturient earth — O infinite teeming womb,
A song to narrate thee.

2

Ever upon this stage,
Is acted God's calm annual drama,
Gorgeous processions, songs of birds,
Sunrise that fullest feeds and freshens most the soul,
The heaving sea, the waves upon the shore, the musical, strong
    waves,
The woods, the stalwart trees, the slender, tapering trees,
The liliput countless armies of the grass,
The heat, the showers, the measureless pasturages,
The scenery of the snows, the winds' free orchestra,
The stretching light-hung roof of clouds, the clear cerulean and
    the silvery fringes,
The high dilating stars, the placid beckoning stars,
The moving flocks and herds, the plains and emerald meadows,
The shows of all the varied lands and all the growths and products.

3

Fecund America — to-day,
Thou art all over set in births and joys!
Thou groan'st with riches, thy wealth clothes thee as a swathing-
    garment,
Thou laughest loud with ache of great possessions,
A myriad-twining life like interlacing vines binds all thy vast
    demesne,

As some huge ship freighted to water's edge thou ridest into
    port,
As rain falls from the heaven and vapors rise from earth, so have
    the precious values fallen upon thee and risen out of thee;
Thou envy of the globe! thou miracle!
Thou, bathed, choked, swimming in plenty,
Thou lucky Mistress of the tranquil barns,
Thou Prairie Dame that sittest in the middle and lookest out upon
    thy world, and lookest East and lookest West,
Dispensatress, that by a word givest a thousand miles, a million
    farms, and missest nothing,
Thou all-acceptress — thou hospitable, (thou only art hospitable as ·
    God is hospitable.)

4

When late I sang sad was my voice,
Sad were the shows around me with deafening noises of hatred
    and smoke of war;
In the midst of the conflict, the heroes, I stood,
Or pass'd with slow step through the wounded and dying.

But now I sing not war,
Nor the measur'd march of soldiers, nor the tents of camps,
Nor the regiments hastily coming up deploying in line of battle;
No more the sad, unnatural shows of war.

Ask'd room those flush'd immortal ranks, the first forth-stepping
    armies?
Ask room alas the ghastly ranks, the armies dread that follow'd.

(Pass, pass, ye proud brigades, with your tramping sinewy legs,
With your shoulders young and strong, with your knapsacks and
    your muskets;
How elate I stood and watch'd you, where starting off you
    march'd.

Pass — then rattle drums again,
For an army heaves in sight, O another gathering army,
Swarming, trailing on the rear, O you dread accruing army,
O you regiments so piteous, with your mortal diarrhœa, with your
    fever,
O my land's maim'd darlings, with the plenteous bloody bandage
    and the crutch,
Lo, your pallid army follows.)

5

But on these days of brightness,
On the far-stretching beauteous landscape, the roads and lanes
    the high-piled farm-wagons, and the fruits and barns,
Should the dead intrude?

Ah the dead to me mar not, they fit well in Nature,
They fit very well in the landscape under the trees and grass,
And along the edge of the sky in the horizon's far margin.

Nor do I forget you Departed,
Nor in winter or summer my lost ones,
But most in the open air as now when my soul is rapt and at
    peace, like pleasing phantoms,
Your memories rising glide silently by me.

6

I saw the day the return of the heroes,
(Yet the heroes never surpass'd shall never return,
Them that day I saw not.)

I saw the interminable corps, I saw the processions of armies,
I saw them approaching, defiling by with divisions,
Streaming northward, their work done, camping awhile in clusters
    of mighty camps.

No holiday soldiers — youthful, yet veterans,
Worn, swart, handsome, strong, of the stock of homestead and
    workshop,
Harden'd of many a long campaign and sweaty march,
Inured on many a hard-fought bloody field.

A pause — the armies wait,
A million flush'd embattled conquerors wait,
The world too waits, then soft as breaking night and sure as dawn,
They melt, they disappear.

Exult O lands! victorious lands!
Not there your victory on those red shuddering fields,
But here and hence your victory.

Melt, melt away ye armies — disperse ye blue-clad soldiers,
Resolve ye back again, give up for good your deadly arms,
Other the arms the fields henceforth for you, or South or North,
With saner wars, sweet wars, life-giving wars.

7

Loud O my throat, and clear O soul!
The season of thanks and the voice of full-yielding,
The chant of joy and power for boundless fertility.

All till'd and untill'd fields expand before me,
I see the true arenas of my race, or first or last,
Man's innocent and strong arenas.

I see the heroes at other toils,
I see well-wielded in their hands the better weapons.

I see where the Mother of All,
With full-spanning eye gazes forth, dwells long,
And counts the varied gathering of the products.

Busy the far, the sunlit panorama,
Prairie, orchard, and yellow grain of the North,
Cotton and rice of the South and Louisianian cane,
Open unseeded fallows, rich fields of clover and timothy,
Kine and horses feeding, and droves of sheep and swine,
And many a stately river flowing and many a jocund brook,
And healthy uplands with herby-perfumed breezes,
And the good green grass, that delicate miracle the ever-recurring
        grass.

8

Toil on heroes! harvest the products!
Not alone on those warlike fields the Mother of All,
With dilated form and lambent eyes watch'd you.

Toil on heroes! toil well! handle the weapons well!
The Mother of All, yet here as ever she watches you.

Well-pleased America thou beholdest,
Over the fields of the West those crawling monsters,
The human-divine inventions, the labor-saving implements;
Beholdest moving in every direction imbued as with life the
        revolving hay-rakes,
The steam-power reaping-machines and the horse-power machines,
The engines, thrashers of grain and cleaners of grain, well sepa-
        rating the straw, the nimble work of the patent pitchfork,
Beholdest the newer saw-mill, the southern cotton-gin, and the
        rice-cleanser.

Beneath thy look O Maternal,
With these and else and with their own strong hands the heroes
    harvest.

All gather and all harvest,
Yet but for thee O Powerful, not a scythe might swing as now in
    security,
Not a maize-stalk dangle as now its silken tassels in peace.

Under thee only they harvest, even but a wisp of hay under thy
    great face only,
Harvest the wheat of Ohio, Illinois, Wisconsin, every barbed spear
    under thee,
Harvest the maize of Missouri, Kentucky, Tennessee, each ear in
    its light-green sheath,
Gather the hay to its myriad mows in the odorous tranquil barns,
Oats to their bins, the white potato, the buckwheat of Michigan,
    to theirs ;
Gather the cotton in Mississippi or Alabama, dig and hoard the
    golden the sweet potato of Georgia and the Carolinas,
Clip the wool of California or Pennsylvania,
Cut the flax in the Middle States, or hemp or tobacco in the
    Borders,
Pick the pea and the bean, or pull apples from the trees or bunches
    of grapes from the vines,
Or aught that ripens in all these States or North or South,
Under the beaming sun and under thee.

THERE WAS A CHILD WENT FORTH.

THERE was a child went forth every day,
And the first object he look'd upon, that object he became,
And that object became part of him for the day or a certain part
    of the day,
Or for many years or stretching cycles of years.

The early lilacs became part of this child,
And grass and white and red morning-glories, and white and red
    clover, and the song of the phœbe-bird,
And the Third-month* lambs and the sow's pink-faint litter, and
    the mare's foal and the cow's calf,
And the noisy brood of the barnyard or by the mire of the pond-
    side,

And the fish suspending themselves so curiously below there, and the beautiful curious liquid,
And the water-plants with their graceful flat heads, all became part of him.

The field-sprouts of Fourth-month and Fifth-month became part of him,
Winter-grain sprouts and those of the light-yellow corn, and the esculent roots of the garden,
And the apple-trees cover'd with blossoms and the fruit afterward, and wood-berries, and the commonest weeds by the road,
And the old drunkard staggering home from the outhouse of the tavern whence he had lately risen,
And the schoolmistress that pass'd on her way to the school,
And the friendly boys that pass'd, and the quarrelsome boys,
And the tidy and fresh-cheek'd girls, and the barefoot negro boy and girl,
And all the changes of city and country wherever he went.

His own parents, he that had father'd him and she that had conceiv'd him in her womb and birth'd him,
They gave this child more of themselves than that,
They gave him afterward every day, they became part of him.

The mother at home quietly placing the dishes on the supper-table,
The mother with mild words, clean her cap and gown, a wholesome odor falling off her person and clothes as she walks by,
The father, strong, self-sufficient, manly, mean, anger'd, unjust,
The blow, the quick loud word, the tight bargain, the crafty lure,
The family usages, the language, the company, the furniture, the yearning and swelling heart,
Affection that will not be gainsay'd, the sense of what is real, the thought if after all it should prove unreal,
The doubts of day-time and the doubts of night-time, the curious whether and how,
Whether that which appears so is so, or is it all flashes and specks?
Men and women crowding fast in the streets, if they are not flashes and specks what are they?
The streets themselves and the façades of houses, and goods in the windows,
Vehicles, teams, the heavy-plank'd wharves, the huge crossing at the ferries,
The village on the highland seen from afar at sunset, the river between,

Shadows, aureola and mist, the light falling on roofs and gables of
    white or brown two miles off,
The schooner near by sleepily dropping down the tide, the little
    boat slack-tow'd astern,
The hurrying tumbling waves, quick-broken crests, slapping,
The strata of color'd clouds, the long bar of maroon-tint away
    solitary by itself, the spread of purity it lies motionless in,
The horizon's edge, the flying sea-crow, the fragrance of salt
    marsh and shore mud,
These became part of that child who went forth every day, and
    who now goes, and will always go forth every day.

OLD IRELAND.

FAR hence amid an isle of wondrous beauty,
Crouching over a grave an ancient sorrowful mother,
Once a queen, now lean and tatter'd seated on the ground,
Her old white hair drooping dishevel'd round her shoulders,
At her feet fallen an unused royal harp,
Long silent, she too long silent, mourning her shrouded hope and
    heir,
Of all the earth her heart most full of sorrow because most full of
    love.

Yet a word ancient mother,
You need crouch there no longer on the cold ground with fore-
    head between your knees,
O you need not sit there veil'd in your old white hair so dishevel'd,
For know you the one you mourn is not in that grave,
It was an illusion, the son you love was not really dead,
The Lord is not dead, he is risen again young and strong in
    another country,
Even while you wept there by your fallen harp by the grave,
What you wept for was translated, pass'd from the grave,
The winds favor'd and the sea sail'd it,
And now with rosy and new blood,
Moves to-day in a new country.

THE CITY DEAD-HOUSE.

BY the city dead-house by the gate,
As idly sauntering wending my way from the clangor,
I curious pause, for lo, an outcast form, a poor dead prostitute
    brought,

Her corpse they deposit unclaim'd, it lies on the damp brick
    pavement,
The divine woman, her body, I see the body, I look on it alone,
That house once full of passion and beauty, all else I notice not,
Nor stillness so cold, nor running water from faucet, nor odors
    morbific impress me,
But the house alone — that wondrous house — that delicate fair
    house — that ruin !
That immortal house more than all the rows of dwellings ever
    built !
Or white-domed capitol with majestic figure surmounted, or all
    the old high-spired cathedrals,
That little house alone more than them all — poor, desperate
    house !
Fair, fearful wreck — tenement of a soul — itself a soul,
Unclaim'd, avoided house — take one breath from my tremulous
    lips,
Take one tear dropt aside as I go for thought of you,
Dead house of love — house of madness and sin, crumbled,
    crush'd,
House of life, erewhile talking and laughing — but ah, poor house,
    dead even then,
Months, years, an echoing, garnish'd house — but dead, dead,
    dead.

THIS COMPOST.

1

Something startles me where I thought I was safest,
I withdraw from the still woods I loved,
I will not go now on the pastures to walk,
I will not strip the clothes from my body to meet my lover the sea,
I will not touch my flesh to the earth as to other flesh to renew me.

O how can it be that the ground itself does not sicken?
How can you be alive you growths of spring?
How can you furnish health you blood of herbs, roots, orchards,
    grain?
Are they not continually putting distemper'd corpses within you?
Is not every continent work'd over and over with sour dead?

Where have you disposed of their carcasses?
Those drunkards and gluttons of so many generations?

Where have you drawn off all the foul liquid and meat?
I do not see any of it upon you to-day, or perhaps I am deceiv'd,
I will run a furrow with my plough, I will press my spade through
    the sod and turn it up underneath,
I am sure I shall expose some of the foul meat.

2

Behold this compost! behold it well!
Perhaps every mite has once form'd part of a sick person — yet
    behold!
The grass of spring covers the prairies,
The bean bursts noiselessly through the mould in the garden,
The delicate spear of the onion pierces upward,
The apple-buds cluster together on the apple-branches,
The resurrection of the wheat appears with pale visage out of its
    graves,
The tinge awakes over the willow-tree and the mulberry-tree,
The he-birds carol mornings and evenings while the she-birds sit
    on their nests,
The young of poultry break through the hatch'd eggs,
The new-born of animals appear, the calf is dropt from the cow,
    the colt from the mare,
Out of its little hill faithfully rise the potato's dark green leaves,
Out of its hill rises the yellow maize-stalk, the lilacs bloom in the
    dooryards,
The summer growth is innocent and disdainful above all those
    strata of sour dead.

What chemistry!
That the winds are really not infectious,
That this is no cheat, this transparent green-wash of the sea
    which is so amorous after me,
That it is safe to allow it to lick my naked body all over with its
    tongues,
That it will not endanger me with the fevers that have deposited
    themselves in it,
That all is clean forever and forever,
That the cool drink from the well tastes so good,
That blackberries are so flavorous and juicy,
That the fruits of the apple-orchard and the orange-orchard, that
    melons, grapes, peaches, plums, will none of them poison me,
That when I recline on the grass I do not catch any disease,
Though probably every spear of grass rises out of what was once
    a catching disease.

Now I am terrified at the Earth, it is that calm and patient,
It grows such sweet things out of such corruptions,
It turns harmless and stainless on its axis, with such endless
      successions of diseas'd corpses,
It distills such exquisite winds out of such infused fetor,
It renews with such unwitting looks its prodigal, annual, sumptu-
      ous crops,
It gives such divine materials to men, and accepts such leavings
      from them at last.

TO A FOIL'D EUROPEAN REVOLUTIONAIRE.

Courage yet, my brother or my sister!
Keep on — Liberty is to be subserv'd whatever occurs;
That is nothing that is quell'd by one or two failures, or any num-
      ber of failures,
Or by the indifference or ingratitude of the people, or by any
      unfaithfulness,
Or the show of the tushes of power, soldiers, cannon, penal statutes.

What we believe in waits latent forever through all the continents,
Invites no one, promises nothing, sits in calmness and light, is
      positive and composed, knows no discouragement,
Waiting patiently, waiting its time.

(Not songs of loyalty alone are these,
But songs of insurrection also,
For I am the sworn poet of every dauntless rebel the world over,
And he going with me leaves peace and routine behind him,
And stakes his life to be lost at any moment.)

The battle rages with many a loud alarm and frequent advance
      and retreat,
The infidel triumphs, or supposes he triumphs,
The prison, scaffold, garroté, handcuffs, iron necklace and lead-
      balls do their work,
The named and unnamed heroes pass to other spheres,
The great speakers and writers are exiled, they lie sick in distant
      lands,
The cause is asleep, the strongest throats are choked with their
      own blood,
The young men droop their eyelashes toward the ground when
      they meet;
But for all this Liberty has not gone out of the place, nor the
      infidel enter'd into full possession.

When liberty goes out of a place it is not the first to go, nor the
    second or third to go,
It waits for all the rest to go, it is the last.

When there are no more memories of heroes and martyrs,
And when all life and all the souls of men and women are dis-
    charged from any part of the earth,
Then only shall liberty or the idea of liberty be discharged from
    that part of the earth,
And the infidel come into full possession.

Then courage European revolter, revoltress !
For till all ceases neither must you cease.

I do not know what you are for, (I do not know what I am for
    myself, nor what any thing is for,)
But I will search carefully for it even in being foil'd,
In defeat, poverty, misconception, imprisonment — for they too
    are great.

Did we think victory great?
So it is — but now it seems to me, when it cannot be help'd, that
    defeat is great,
And that death and dismay are great.

UNNAMED LANDS.

NATIONS ten thousand years before these States, and many times
    ten thousand years before these States,
Garner'd clusters of ages that men and women like us grew up and
    travel'd their course and pass'd on,
What vast-built cities, what orderly republics, what pastoral tribes
    and nomads,
What histories, rulers, heroes, perhaps transcending all others,
What laws, customs, wealth, arts, traditions,
What sort of marriage, what costumes, what physiology and
    phrenology,
What of liberty and slavery among them, what they thought of
    death and the soul,
Who were witty and wise, who beautiful and poetic, who brutish
    and undevelop'd,
Not a mark, not a record remains — and yet all remains.

O I know that those men and women were not for nothing, any
    more than we are for nothing,

I know that they belong to the scheme of the world every bit as
    much as we now belong to it.

Afar they stand, yet near to me they stand,
Some with oval countenances learn'd and calm,
Some naked and savage, some like huge collections of insects,
Some in tents, herdsmen, patriarchs, tribes, horsemen,
Some prowling through woods, some living peaceably on farms,
    laboring, reaping, filling barns,
Some traversing paved avenues, amid temples, palaces, factories,
    libraries, shows, courts, theatres, wonderful monuments,

Are those billions of men really gone?
Are those women of the old experience of the earth gone?
Do their lives, cities, arts, rest only with us?
Did they achieve nothing for good for themselves?

I believe of all those men and women that fill'd the unnamed
    lands, every one exists this hour here or elsewhere, invisible
    to us,
In exact proportion to what he or she grew from in life, and out
    of what he or she did, felt, became, loved, sinn'd, in life.

I believe that was not the end of those nations or any person of
    them, any more than this shall be the end of my nation, or
    of me ;
Of their languages, governments, marriage, literature, products,
    games, wars, manners, crimes, prisons, slaves, heroes, poets,
I suspect their results curiously await in the yet unseen world,
    counterparts of what accrued to them in the seen world,
I suspect I shall meet them there,
I suspect I shall there find each old particular of those unnamed
    lands.

SONG OF PRUDENCE.

Manhattan's streets I saunter'd pondering,
On Time, Space, Reality — on such as these, and abreast with
    them Prudence.

The last explanation always remains to be made about prudence,
Little and large alike drop quietly aside from the prudence that
    suits immortality.

The soul is of itself,
All verges to it, all has reference to what ensues,

All that a person does, says, thinks, is of consequence,
Not a move can a man or woman make, that affects him or her in
    a day, month, any part of the direct lifetime, or the hour
    of death,
But the same affects him or her onward afterward through the
    indirect lifetime.

The indirect is just as much as the direct,
The spirit receives from the body just as much as it gives to the
    body, if not more.

Not one word or deed, not venereal sore, discoloration, privacy
    of the onanist,
Putridity of gluttons or rum-drinkers, peculation, cunning, betrayal,
    murder, seduction, prostitution,
But has results beyond death as really as before death.

Charity and personal force are the only investments worth any
    thing.

No specification is necessary, all that a male or female does, that is
    vigorous, benevolent, clean, is so much profit to him or her,
In the unshakable order of the universe and through the whole
    scope of it forever.

Who has been wise receives interest,
Savage, felon, President, judge, farmer, sailor, mechanic, literat,
    young, old, it is the same,
The interest will come round—all will come round.

Singly, wholly, to affect now, affected their time, will forever affect,
    all of the past and all of the present and all of the future,
All the brave actions of war and peace,
All help given to relatives, strangers, the poor, old, sorrowful, young
    children, widows, the sick, and to shunn'd persons,
All self-denial that stood steady and aloof on wrecks, and saw
    others fill the seats of the boats,
All offering of substance or life for the good old cause,* or for a
    friend's sake, or opinion's sake,
All pains of enthusiasts scoff'd at by their neighbors,
All the limitless sweet love and precious suffering of mothers,
All honest men baffled in strifes recorded or unrecorded,
All the grandeur and good of ancient nations whose fragments we
    inherit,
All the good of the dozens of ancient nations unknown to us by
    name, date, location,

All that was ever manfully begun, whether it succeeded or no,
All suggestions of the divine mind of man or the divinity of his
    mouth, or the shaping of his great hands,
All that is well thought or said this day on any part of the globe,
    or on any of the wandering stars, or on any of the fix'd
    stars, by those there as we are here,
All that is henceforth to be thought or done by you whoever you
    are, or by any one,
These inure, have inured, shall inure, to the identities from which
    they sprang, or shall spring.

Did you guess any thing lived only its moment?
The world does not so exist, no parts palpable or impalpable so
    exist,
No consummation exists without being from some long previous
    consummation, and that from some other,
Without the farthest conceivable one coming a bit nearer the
    beginning than any.

Whatever satisfies souls is true ;
Prudence entirely satisfies the craving and glut of souls,
Itself only finally satisfies the soul,
The soul has that measureless pride which revolts from every lesson
    but its own.

Now I breathe the word of the prudence that walks abreast with
    time, space, reality,
That answers the pride which refuses every lesson but its own.

What is prudence is indivisible,
Declines to separate one part of life from every part,
Divides not the righteous from the unrighteous or the living from
    the dead,
Matches every thought or act by its correlative,
Knows no possible forgiveness or deputed atonement,
Knows that the young man who composedly peril'd his life and
    lost it has done exceedingly well for himself without doubt,
That he who never peril'd his life, but retains it to old age in
    riches and ease, has probably achiev'd nothing for himself
    worth mentioning,
Knows that only that person has really learn'd who has learn'd to
    prefer results,
Who favors body and soul the same,
Who perceives the indirect assuredly following the direct,
Who in his spirit in any emergency whatever neither hurries nor
    avoids death.

THE SINGER IN THE PRISON.

I

O sight of pity, shame and dole !
O fearful thought — a convict soul.

RANG the refrain along the hall, the prison,
Rose to the roof, the vaults of heaven above,
Pouring in floods of melody in tones so pensive sweet and strong
    the like whereof was never heard,
Reaching the far-off sentry and the armed guards, who ceas'd their
    pacing,
Making the hearer's pulses stop for ecstasy and awe.

2

The sun was low in the west one winter day,
When down a narrow aisle amid the thieves and outlaws of the
    land,
(There by the hundreds seated, sear-faced murderers, wily counter-
    feiters,
Gather'd to Sunday church in prison walls, the keepers round,
Plenteous, well-armed, watching with vigilant eyes,)
Calmly a lady walk'd holding a little innocent child by either
    hand,
Whom seating on their stools beside her on the platform,
She, first preluding with the instrument a low and musical prelude,
In voice surpassing all, sang forth a quaint old hymn.

    A soul confined by bars and bands,
    Cries, help ! O help ! and wrings her hands,
    Blinded her eyes, bleeding her breast,
    Nor pardon finds, nor balm of rest.

    Ceaseless she paces to and fro,
    O heart-sick days ! O nights of woe !
    Nor hand of friend, nor loving face,
    Nor favor comes, nor word of grace.

    It was not I that sinn'd the sin,
    The ruthless body dragg'd me in ;
    Though long I strove courageously,
    The body was too much for me.

    Dear prison'd soul bear up a space,
    For soon or late the certain grace ;

To set thee free and bear thee home,
The heavenly pardoner death shall come.

> *Convict no more, nor shame, nor dole!*
> *Depart — a God-enfranchis'd soul!*

3

The singer ceas'd,
One glance swept from her clear calm eyes o'er all those upturn'd
  faces,
Strange sea of prison faces, a thousand varied, crafty, brutal,
  seam'd and beauteous faces,
Then rising, passing back along the narrow aisle between them,
While her gown touch'd them rustling in the silence,
She vanish'd with her children in the dusk.

While upon all, convicts and armed keepers ere they stirr'd,
(Convict forgetting prison, keeper his loaded pistol,)
A hush and pause fell down a wondrous minute,
With deep half-stifled sobs and sound of bad men bow'd and
  moved to weeping,
And youth's convulsive breathings, memories of home,
The mother's voice in lullaby, the sister's care, the happy childhood,
The long-pent spirit rous'd to reminiscence;
A wondrous minute then — but after in the solitary night, to many,
  many there,
Years after, even in the hour of death, the sad refrain, the tune,
  the voice, the words,
Resumed, the large calm lady walks the narrow aisle,
The wailing melody again, the singer in the prison sings,

> *O sight of pity, shame and dole!*
> *O fearful thought — a convict soul.*

WARBLE FOR LILAC-TIME.

WARBLE me now for joy of lilac-time, (returning in reminiscence,)
Sort me O tongue and lips for Nature's sake, souvenirs of earliest
  summer,
Gather the welcome signs, (as children with pebbles or stringing
  shells,)
Put in April and May, the hylas croaking in the ponds, the elastic
  air,
Bees, butterflies, the sparrow with its simple notes,

Blue-bird and darting swallow, nor forget the high-hole* flashing
   his golden wings,
The tranquil sunny haze, the clinging smoke, the vapor,
Shimmer of waters with fish in them, the cerulean above,
All that is jocund and sparkling, the brooks running,
The maple woods, the crisp February days and the sugar-making,
The robin where he hops, bright-eyed, brown-breasted,
With musical clear call at sunrise, and again at sunset,
Or flitting among the trees of the apple-orchard, building the nest
   of his mate,
The melted snow of March, the willow sending forth its yellow-
   green sprouts,
For spring-time is here! the summer is here! and what is this
   in it and from it?
Thou, soul, unloosen'd — the restlessness after I know not what;
Come, let us lag here no longer, let us be up and away!
O if one could but fly like a bird!
O to escape, to sail forth as in a ship!
To glide with thee O soul, o'er all, in all, as a ship o'er the waters;
Gathering these hints, the preludes, the blue sky, the grass, the
   morning drops of dew,
The lilac-scent, the bushes with dark green heart-shaped leaves,
Wood-violets, the little delicate pale blossoms called innocence,
Samples and sorts not for themselves alone, but for their atmos-
   phere,
To grace the bush I love — to sing with the birds,
A warble for joy of lilac-time, returning in reminiscence.

OUTLINES FOR A TOMB.

(G. P.,* Buried 1870.)

1

WHAT may we chant, O thou within this tomb?
What tablets, outlines, hang for thee, O millionnaire?
The life thou lived'st we know not,
But that thou walk'dst thy years in barter, 'mid the haunts of
   brokers,
Nor heroism thine, nor war, nor glory.

2

Silent, my soul,
With drooping lids, as waiting, ponder'd,
Turning from all the samples, monuments of heroes.

While through the interior vistas,
Noiseless uprose, phantasmic, (as by night Auroras of the north,)
Lambent tableaus, prophetic, bodiless scenes,
Spiritual projections.

In one, among the city streets a laborer's home appear'd,
After his day's work done, cleanly, sweet-air'd, the gaslight burning,
The carpet swept and a fire in the cheerful stove.

In one, the sacred parturition scene,
A happy painless mother birth'd a perfect child.

In one, at a bounteous morning meal,
Sat peaceful parents with contented sons.

In one, by twos and threes, young people,
Hundreds concentring, walk'd the paths and streets and roads,
Toward a tall-domed school.

In one a trio beautiful,
Grandmother, loving daughter, loving daughter's daughter, sat,
Chatting and sewing.

In one, along a suite of noble rooms,
'Mid plenteous books and journals, paintings on the walls, fine
    statuettes,
Were groups of friendly journeymen, mechanics young and old,
Reading, conversing.

All, all the shows of laboring life,
City and country, women's, men's and children's,
Their wants provided for, hued in the sun and tinged for once
    with joy,
Marriage, the street, the factory, farm, the house-room, lodging-
    room,
Labor and toil, the bath, gymnasium, playground, library, college,
The student, boy or girl, led forward to be taught,
The sick cared for, the shoeless shod, the orphan father'd and
    mother'd,
The hungry fed, the houseless housed;
(The intentions perfect and divine,
The workings, details, haply human.)

3

O thou within this tomb,
From thee such scenes, thou stintless, lavish giver,

Tallying the gifts of earth, large as the earth,
Thy name an earth, with mountains, fields and tides.

Nor by your streams alone, you rivers,
By you, your banks Connecticut,
By you and all your teeming life old Thames,
By you Potomac laving the ground Washington trod, by you
      Patapsco,
You Hudson, you endless Mississippi — nor you alone,
But to the high seas launch, my thought, his memory.

OUT FROM BEHIND THIS MASK.

(To Confront a Portrait.)

1

OUT from behind this bending rough-cut mask,
These lights and shades, this drama of the whole,
This common curtain of the face contain'd in me for me, in you
      for you, in each for each,
(Tragedies, sorrows, laughter, tears — O heaven !
The passionate teeming plays this curtain hid !)
This glaze of God's serenest purest sky,
This film of Satan's seething pit,
This heart's geography's map, this limitless small continent, this
      soundless sea ;
Out from the convolutions of this globe,
This subtler astronomic orb than sun or moon, than Jupiter, Venus,
      Mars,
This condensation of the universe, (nay here the only universe,
Here the idea, all in this mystic handful wrapt ;)
These burin'd eyes, flashing to you to pass to future time,
To launch and spin through space revolving sideling, from these
      to emanate,
To you whoe'er you are — a look.

2

A traveler of thoughts and years, of peace and war,
Of youth long sped and middle age declining,
(As the first volume of a tale perused and laid away, and this the
      second,
Songs, ventures, speculations, presently to close,)
Lingering a moment here and now, to you I opposite turn,

As on the road or at some crevice door by chance, or open'd win-
     dow,
Pausing, inclining, baring my head, you specially I greet,
To draw and clinch your soul for once inseparably with mine,
Then travel travel on.

VOCALISM.

1

VOCALISM, measure, concentration, determination, and the divine
     power to speak words;
Are you full-lung'd and limber-lipp'd from long trial? from vigor-
     ous practice? from physique?
Do you move in these broad lands as broad as they?
Come duly to the divine power to speak words?
For only at last after many years, after chastity, friendship, procrea-
     tion, prudence, and nakedness,
After treading ground and breasting river and lake,
After a loosen'd throat, after absorbing eras, temperaments, races,
     after knowledge, freedom, crimes,
After complete faith, after clarifyings, elevations, and removing
     obstructions,
After these and more, it is just possible there comes to a man, a
     woman, the divine power to speak words;
Then toward that man or that woman swiftly hasten all — none
     refuse, all attend,
Armies, ships, antiquities, libraries, paintings, machines, cities,
     hate, despair, amity, pain, theft, murder, aspiration, form in
     close ranks,
They debouch as they are wanted to march obediently through
     the mouth of that man or that woman.

2

O what is it in me that makes me tremble so at voices?
Surely whoever speaks to me in the right voice, him or her I shall
     follow,
As the water follows the moon, silently, with fluid steps, anywhere
     around the globe.

All waits for the right voices;
Where is the practis'd and perfect organ? where is the develop'd
     soul?
For I see every word utter'd thence has deeper, sweeter, new
     sounds, impossible on less terms.

I see brains and lips closed, tympans and temples unstruck,
Until that comes which has the quality to strike and to unclose,
Until that comes which has the quality to bring forth what lies
    slumbering forever ready in all words.

TO HIM THAT WAS CRUCIFIED.

My spirit to yours dear brother,
Do not mind because many sounding your name do not under-
    stand you,
I do not sound your name, but I understand you,
I specify you with joy O my comrade to salute you, and to salute
    those who are with you, before and since, and those to
    come also,
That we all labor together transmitting the same charge and suc-
    cession,
We few equals indifferent of lands, indifferent of times,
We, enclosers of all continents, all castes, allowers of all theologies,
Compassionaters, perceivers, rapport of men,
We walk silent among disputes and assertions, but reject not the
    disputers nor any thing that is asserted,
We hear the bawling and din, we are reach'd at by divisions, jeal-
    ousies, recriminations on every side,
They close peremptorily upon us to surround us, my comrade,
Yet we walk unheld, free, the whole earth over, journeying up and
    down till we make our ineffaceable mark upon time and the
    diverse eras,
Till we saturate time and eras, that the men and women of races,
    ages to come, may prove brethren and lovers as we are.

YOU FELONS ON TRIAL IN COURTS.

You felons on trial in courts,
You convicts in prison-cells, you sentenced assassins chain'd and
    handcuff'd with iron,
Who am I too that I am not on trial or in prison?
Me ruthless and devilish as any, that my wrists are not chain'd
    with iron, or my ankles with iron?

You prostitutes flaunting over the trottoirs or obscene in your
    rooms,
Who am I that I should call you more obscene than myself?

O culpable ! I acknowledge — I exposé !
(O admirers, praise not me — compliment not me — you make
me wince,
I see what you do not — I know what you do not.)

Inside these breast-bones I lie smutch'd and choked,
Beneath this face that appears so impassive hell's tides continually
run,
Lusts and wickedness are acceptable to me,
I walk with delinquents with passionate love,
I feel I am of them — I belong to those convicts and prostitutes
myself,
And henceforth I will not deny them — for how can I deny myself ?

LAWS FOR CREATIONS.

Laws for creations,
For strong artists and leaders, for fresh broods of teachers and
perfect literats for America,
For noble savans and coming musicians.

All must have reference to the ensemble of the world, and the
compact truth of the world,
There shall be no subject too pronounced — all works shall illus-
trate the divine law of indirections.

What do you suppose creation is?
What do you suppose will satisfy the soul, except to walk free and
own no superior?
What do you suppose I would intimate to you in a hundred ways,
but that man or woman is as good as God?
And that there is no God any more divine than Yourself ?
And that that is what the oldest and newest myths finally mean?
And that you or any one must approach creations through such
laws?

TO A COMMON PROSTITUTE.

Be composed — be at ease with me — I am Walt Whitman, liberal
and lusty as Nature,
Not till the sun excludes you do I exclude you,
Not till the waters refuse to glisten for you and the leaves to rustle
for you, do my words refuse to glisten and rustle for you.

My girl I appoint with you an appointment, and I charge you that
    you make preparation to be worthy to meet me,
And I charge you that you be patient and perfect till I come.

Till then I salute you·with a significant look that you do not forget
    me.

I WAS LOOKING A LONG WHILE.

I was looking a long while for Intentions,
For a clew to the history of the past for myself, and for these
    chants — and now I have found it,
It is not in those paged fables in the libraries, (them I neither
    accept nor reject,)
It is no more in the legends than in all else,
It is in the present — it is this earth to-day,
It is in Democracy — (the purport and aim of all the past,)
It is the life of one man or one woman to-day — the average man
    of to-day,
It is in languages, social customs, literatures, arts,
It is in the broad show of artificial things, ships, machinery, poli-
    tics, creeds, modern improvements, and the interchange of
    nations,
All for the modern — all for the average man of to-day.

THOUGHT.

Of persons arrived at high positions, ceremonies, wealth, scholar-
    ships, and the like ;
(To me all that those persons have arrived at sinks away from
    them, except as it results to their bodies and souls,
So that often to me they appear gaunt and naked,
And often to me each one mocks the others, and mocks himself or
    herself,
And of each one the core of life, namely happiness, is full of the
    rotten excrement of maggots,
And often to me those men and women pass unwittingly the true
    realities of life, and go toward false realities,
And often to me they are alive after what custom has served them,
    but nothing more;
And often to me they are sad, hasty, unwaked sonnambules walk-
    ing the dusk.)

MIRACLES.

WHY, who makes much of a miracle?
As to me I know of nothing else but miracles,
Whether I walk the streets of Manhattan,
Or dart my sight over the roofs of houses toward the sky,
Or wade with naked feet along the beach just in the edge of the
  water,
Or stand under trees in the woods,
Or talk by day with any one I love, or sleep in the bed at night
  with any one I love,
Or sit at table at dinner with the rest,
Or look at strangers opposite me riding in the car,
Or watch honey-bees busy around the hive of a summer forenoon,
Or animals feeding in the fields,
Or birds, or the wonderfulness of insects in the air,
Or the wonderfulness of the sundown, or of stars shining so quiet
  and bright,
Or the exquisite delicate thin curve of the new moon in spring;
These with the rest, one and all, are to me miracles,
The whole referring, yet each distinct and in its place.

To me every hour of the light and dark is a miracle,
Every cubic inch of space is a miracle,
Every square yard of the surface of the earth is spread with the
  same,
Every foot of the interior swarms with the same.

To me the sea is a continual miracle,
The fishes that swim — the rocks — the motion of the waves —
  the ships with men in them,
What stranger miracles are there?

SPARKLES FROM THE WHEEL.

WHERE the city's ceaseless crowd moves on the livelong day,
Withdrawn I join a group of children watching, I pause aside with
  them.

By the curb toward the edge of the flagging,
A knife-grinder works at his wheel sharpening a great knife,
Bending over he carefully holds it to the stone, by foot and knee,
With measur'd tread he turns rapidly, as he presses with light but
  firm hand,

Forth issue then in copious golden jets,
Sparkles from the wheel.

The scene and all its belongings, how they seize and affect me,
The sad sharp-chinn'd old man with worn clothes and broad
    shoulder-band of leather,
Myself effusing and fluid, a phantom curiously floating, now here
    absorb'd and arrested,
The group, (an unminded point set in a vast surrounding,)
The attentive, quiet children, the loud, proud, restive base of the
    streets,
The low hoarse purr of the whirling stone, the light-press'd blade,
Diffusing, dropping, sideways-darting, in tiny showers of gold,
Sparkles from the wheel.

TO A PUPIL.

Is reform needed? is it through you?
The greater the reform needed, the greater the Personality you
    need to accomplish it.

You! do you not see how it would serve to have eyes, blood,
    complexion, clean and sweet?
Do you not see how it would serve to have such a body and soul
    that when you enter the crowd an atmosphere of desire
    and command enters with you, and every one is impress'd
    with your Personality?

O the magnet! the flesh over and over!
Go, dear friend, if need be give up all else, and commence to-day
    to inure yourself to pluck, reality, self-esteem, definiteness,
    elevatedness,
Rest not till you rivet and publish yourself of your own Personality.

UNFOLDED OUT OF THE FOLDS.

Unfolded out of the folds of the woman man comes unfolded,
    and is always to come unfolded,
Unfolded only out of the superbest woman of the earth is to come
    the superbest man of the earth,
Unfolded out of the friendliest woman is to come the friendliest
    man,
Unfolded only out of the perfect body of a woman can a man be
    form'd of perfect body,

Unfolded only out of the inimitable poems of woman can come
    the poems of man, (only thence have my poems come;)
Unfolded out of the strong and arrogant woman I love, only
    thence can appear the strong and arrogant man I love,
Unfolded by brawny embraces from the well-muscled woman I
    love, only thence come the brawny embraces of the man,
Unfolded out of the folds of the woman's brain come all the folds
    of the man's brain, duly obedient,
Unfolded out of the justice of the woman all justice is unfolded,
Unfolded out of the sympathy of the woman is all sympathy;
A man is a great thing upon the earth and through eternity, but
    every jot of the greatness of man is unfolded out of
    woman;
First the man is shaped in the woman, he can then be shaped in
    himself.

WHAT AM I AFTER ALL.

WHAT am I after all but a child, pleas'd with the sound of my own
    name? repeating it over and over;
I stand apart to hear— it never tires me.

To you your name also;
Did you think there was nothing but two or three pronunciations
    in the sound of your name?

KOSMOS.

WHO includes diversity and is Nature,
Who is the amplitude of the earth, and the coarseness and sex-
    uality of the earth, and the great charity of the earth, and
    the equilibrium also,
Who has not look'd forth from the windows the eyes for nothing,
    or whose brain held audience with messengers for nothing,
Who contains believers and disbelievers, who is the most majestic
    lover,
Who holds duly his or her triune proportion of realism, spiritualism,
    and of the æsthetic or intellectual,
Who having consider'd the body finds all its organs and parts
    good,
Who, out of the theory of the earth and of his or her body under-
    stands by subtle analogies all other theories,
The theory of a city, a poem, and of the large politics of these
    States;

Who believes not only in our globe with its sun and moon, but in other globes with their suns and moons,
Who, constructing the house of himself or herself, not for a day but for all time, sees races, eras, dates, generations,
The past, the future, dwelling there, like space, inseparable together.

OTHERS MAY PRAISE WHAT THEY LIKE.

OTHERS may praise what they like ;
But I, from the banks of the running Missouri, praise nothing in art or aught else,
Till it has well inhaled the atmosphere of this river, also the western prairie-scent,
And exudes it all again.

WHO LEARNS MY LESSON COMPLETE?

WHO learns my lesson complete?
Boss, journeyman, apprentice, churchman and atheist,
The stupid and the wise thinker, parents and offspring, merchant, clerk, porter and customer,
Editor, author, artist, and schoolboy — draw nigh and commence ;
It is no lesson — it lets down the bars to a good lesson,
And that to another, and every one to another still.

The great laws take and effuse without argument,
I am of the same style, for I am their friend,
I love them quits and quits,* I do not halt and make salaams.

I lie abstracted and hear beautiful tales of things and the reasons of things,
They are so beautiful I nudge myself to listen.

I cannot say to any person what I hear — I cannot say it to myself — it is very wonderful.

It is no small matter, this round and delicious globe moving so exactly in its orbit for ever and ever, without one jolt or the untruth of a single second,
I do not think it was made in six days, nor in ten thousand years, nor ten billions of years,
Nor plann'd and built one thing after another as an architect plans and builds a house.

I do not think seventy years is the time of a man or woman,
Nor that seventy millions of years is the time of a man or woman,
Nor that years will ever stop the existence of me, or any one else.

Is it wonderful that I should be immortal? as every one is immortal;
I know it is wonderful, but my eyesight is equally wonderful, and
    how I was conceived in my mother's womb is equally
    wonderful,
And pass'd from a babe in the creeping trance of a couple of
    summers and winters to articulate and walk — all this is
    equally wonderful.

And that my soul embraces you this hour, and we affect each
    other without ever seeing each other, and never perhaps to
    see each other, is every bit as wonderful.

And that I can think such thoughts as these is just as wonderful,
And that I can remind you, and you think them and know them
    to be true, is just as wonderful.

And that the moon spins round the earth and on with the earth, is
    equally wonderful,
And that they balance themselves with the sun and stars is equally
    wonderful.

TESTS.

ALL submit to them where they sit, inner, secure, unapproachable
    to analysis in the soul,
Not traditions, not the outer authorities are the judges,
They are the judges of outer authorities and of all traditions,
They corroborate as they go only whatever corroborates themselves, and touches themselves;
For all that, they have it forever in themselves to corroborate far
    and near without one exception.

THE TORCH.

ON my Northwest coast in the midst of the night a fishermen's
    group stands watching,
Out on the lake that expands before them, others are spearing
    salmon,
The canoe, a dim shadowy thing, moves across the black water,
Bearing a torch ablaze at the prow.

O STAR OF FRANCE.

1870-71.*

O STAR of France,
The brightness of thy hope and strength and fame,
Like some proud ship that led the fleet so long,
Beseems to-day a wreck driven by the gale, a mastless hulk,
And 'mid its teeming madden'd half-drown'd crowds,
Nor helm nor helmsman.

Dim smitten star,
Orb not of France alone, pale symbol of my soul, its dearest
    hopes,
The struggle and the daring, rage divine for liberty,
Of aspirations toward the far ideal, enthusiast's dreams of brother-
    hood,
Of terror to the tyrant and the priest.

Star crucified — by traitors sold,
Star panting o'er a land of death, heroic land,
Strange, passionate, mocking, frivolous land.

Miserable ! yet for thy errors, vanities, sins, I will not now rebuke
    thee,
Thy unexampled woes and pangs have quell'd them all,
And left thee sacred.

In that amid thy many faults thou ever aimedst highly,
In that thou wouldst not really sell thyself however great the price,
In that thou surely wakedst weeping from thy drugg'd sleep,
In that alone among thy sisters thou, giantess, didst rend the ones
    that shamed thee,
In that thou couldst not, wouldst not, wear the usual chains,
This cross, thy livid face, thy pierced hands and feet,
The spear thrust in thy side.

O star ! O ship of France, beat back and baffled long !
Bear up O smitten orb ! O ship continue on !

Sure as the ship of all, the Earth itself,
Product of deathly fire and turbulent chaos,
Forth from its spasms of fury and its poisons,
Issuing at last in perfect power and beauty,
Onward beneath the sun following its course,
So thee O ship of France !

Finish'd the days, the clouds dispel'd,
The travail o'er, the long-sought extrication,
When lo ! reborn, high o'er the European world,
(In gladness answering thence, as face afar to face, reflecting ours
    Columbia,)
Again thy star O France, fair lustrous star,
In heavenly peace, clearer, more bright than ever,
Shall beam immortal.

THE OX-TAMER.

In a far-away northern county in the placid pastoral region,
Lives my farmer friend, the theme of my recitative, a famous
    tamer of oxen,
There they bring him the three-year-olds and the four-year-olds to
    break them,
He will take the wildest steer in the world and break him and
    tame him,
He will go fearless without any whip where the young bullock
    chafes up and down the yard,
The bullock's head tosses restless high in the air with raging eyes,
Yet see you ! how soon his rage subsides — how soon this tamer
    tames him ;
See you ! on the farms hereabout a hundred oxen young and old,
    and he is the man who has tamed them,
They all know him, all are affectionate to him ;
See you ! some are such beautiful animals, so lofty looking ;
Some are buff-color'd, some mottled, one has a white line running
    along his back, some are brindled,
Some have wide flaring horns (a good sign) — see you ! the
    bright hides,
See, the two with stars on their foreheads — see, the round bodies
    and broad backs,
How straight and square they stand on their legs — what fine
    sagacious eyes !
How they watch their tamer — they wish him near them — how
    they turn to look after him !
What yearning expression ! how uneasy they are when he moves
    away from them ;
Now I marvel what it can be he appears to them, (books, politics,
    poems, depart — all else departs,)
I confess I envy only his fascination — my silent, illiterate friend,
Whom a hundred oxen love there in his life on farms,
In the northern county far, in the placid pastoral region.

AN OLD MAN'S THOUGHT OF SCHOOL.

For the Inauguration of a Public School, Camden, New Jersey, 1874.

An old man's thought of school;
An old man gathering youthful memories and blooms that youth
    itself cannot.

Now only do I know you,
O fair auroral skies — O morning dew upon the grass !

And these I see, these sparkling eyes,
These stores of mystic meaning, these young lives,
Building, equipping like a fleet of ships, immortal ships,
Soon to sail out over the measureless seas,
On the soul's voyage.

Only a lot of boys and girls?
Only the tiresome spelling, writing, ciphering classes?
Only a public school?

Ah more, infinitely more ;
(As George Fox* rais'd his warning cry, "Is it this pile of brick
    and mortar, these dead floors, windows, rails, you call the
    church?
Why this is not the church at all — the church is living, ever living
    souls.")

And you America,
Cast you the real reckoning for your present?
The lights and shadows of your future, good or evil?
To girlhood, boyhood look, the teacher and the school.

WANDERING AT MORN.

Wandering at morn,
Emerging from the night from gloomy thoughts, thee in my
    thoughts,
Yearning for thee harmonious Union ! thee, singing bird divine !
Thee coil'd in evil times* my country, with craft and black dismay,
    with every meanness, treason thrust upon thee,
This common marvel I beheld — the parent thrush I watch'd feed-
    ing its young,
The singing thrush whose tones of joy and faith ecstatic,
Fail not to certify and cheer my soul.

There ponder'd, felt I,
If worms, snakes, loathsome grubs, may to sweet spiritual songs
    be turn'd,
If vermin so transposed, so used and bless'd may be,
Then may I trust in you, your fortunes, days, my country;
Who knows but these may be the lessons fit for you?
From these your future song may rise with joyous trills,
Destin'd to fill the world.

ITALIAN MUSIC IN DAKOTA.

[" *The Seventeenth — the finest Regimental Band I ever heard.*"]

THROUGH the soft evening air enwinding all,
Rocks, woods, fort, cannon, pacing sentries, endless wilds,
In dulcet streams, in flutes' and cornets' notes,
Electric, pensive, turbulent, artificial,
(Yet strangely fitting even here, meanings unknown before,
Subtler than ever, more harmony, as if born here, related here,
Not to the city's fresco'd rooms, not to the audience of the opera
    house,
Sounds, echoes, wandering strains, as really here at home,
Sonnambula's innocent love, trios with *Norma's* anguish,
And thy ecstatic chorus *Poliuto;*)
Ray'd in the limpid yellow slanting sundown,
Music, Italian music in Dakota.

While Nature, sovereign of this gnarl'd realm,
Lurking in hidden barbaric grim recesses,
Acknowledging rapport however far remov'd,
(As some old root or soil of earth its last-born flower or fruit,)
Listens well pleas'd.

WITH ALL THY GIFTS.

WITH all thy gifts America,
Standing secure, rapidly tending, overlooking the world,
Power, wealth, extent, vouchsafed to thee — with these and like
    of these vouchsafed to thee,
What if one gift thou lackest? (the ultimate human problem never
    solving,)
The gift of perfect women fit for thee — what if that gift of gifts
    thou lackest?
The towering feminine of thee? the beauty, health, completion,
    fit for thee?
The mothers fit for thee?

MY PICTURE-GALLERY.

IN a little house*keep I pictures suspended, it is not a fix'd house,
It is round, it is only a few inches from one side to the other;
Yet behold, it has room for all the shows of the world, all memories!
Here the tableaus of life, and here the groupings of death;
Here, do you know this? this is cicerone himself,
With finger rais'd he points to the prodigal pictures.

THE PRAIRIE STATES.

A NEWER garden of creation, no primal solitude,
Dense, joyous, modern, populous millions, cities and farms,
With iron interlaced, composite, tied, many in one,
By all the world contributed — freedom's and law's and thrift's society,
The crown and teeming paradise, so far, of time's accumulations,
To justify the past.

PROUD MUSIC OF THE STORM.

1

PROUD music of the storm,
Blast that careers so free, whistling across the prairies,
Strong hum of forest tree-tops — wind of the mountains,
Personified dim shapes — you hidden orchestras,
You serenades of phantoms with instruments alert,
Blending with Nature's rhythmus all the tongues of nations;
You chords left as by vast composers — you choruses,
You formless, free, religious dances — you from the Orient,
You undertone of rivers, roar of pouring cataracts,
You sounds from distant guns with galloping cavalry,
Echoes of camps with all the different bugle-calls,
Trooping tumultuous, filling the midnight late, bending me powerless,
Entering my lonesome slumber-chamber, why have you seiz'd me?

2

Come forward O my soul, and let the rest retire,
Listen, lose not, it is toward thee they tend,
Parting the midnight, entering my slumber-chamber,
For thee they sing and dance O soul.

A festival song,
The duet of the bridegroom and the bride, a marriage-march,
With lips of love, and hearts of lovers fill'd to the brim with love,
The red-flush'd cheeks and perfumes, the cortege swarming full of
      friendly faces young and old,
To flutes' clear notes and sounding harps' cantabile.*

Now loud approaching drums,
Victoria! see'st thou in powder-smoke the banners torn but flying?
      the rout of the baffled?
Hearest those shouts of a conquering army?

(Ah soul, the sobs of women, the wounded groaning in agony,
The hiss and crackle of flames, the blacken'd ruins, the embers
      of cities,
The dirge and desolation of mankind.)

Now airs antique and mediæval fill me,
I see and hear old harpers with their harps at Welsh festivals,
I hear the minnesingers singing their lays of love,
I hear the minstrels, gleemen, troubadours, of the middle ages.

Now the great organ sounds,
Tremulous, while underneath, (as the hid footholds of the earth,
On which arising rest, and leaping forth depend,
All shapes of beauty, grace and strength, all hues we know,
Green blades of grass and warbling birds, children that gambol
      and play, the clouds of heaven above,)
The strong base stands, and its pulsations intermits not,
Bathing, supporting, merging all the rest, maternity of all the
      rest,
And with it every instrument in multitudes,
The players playing, all the world's musicians,
The solemn hymns and masses rousing adoration,
All passionate heart-chants, sorrowful appeals,
The measureless sweet vocalists of ages,
And for their solvent setting earth's own diapason,*
Of winds and woods and mighty ocean waves,
A new composite orchestra, binder of years and climes, ten-fold
      renewer,
As of the far-back days the poets tell, the Paradiso,
The straying thence, the separation long, but now the wandering
      done,
The journey done, the journeyman come home,
And man and art with Nature fused again.

Tutti ! for earth and heaven ;
(The Almighty leader now for once has signal'd with his wand.)

The manly strophe of the husbands of the world,
And all the wives responding.

The tongues of violins,
(I think O tongues ye tell this heart, that cannot tell itself,
This brooding yearning heart, that cannot tell itself.)

3

Ah from a little child,
Thou knowest soul how to me all sounds became music,
My mother's voice in lullaby or hymn,
(The voice, O tender voices, memory's loving voices,
Last miracle of all, O dearest mother's, sister's, voices ;)
The rain, the growing corn, the breeze among the long-leav'd corn,
The measur'd sea-surf beating on the sand,
The twittering bird, the hawk's sharp scream,
The wild-fowl's notes at night as flying low migrating north or
    south,
The psalm in the country church or mid the clustering trees, the
    open air camp-meeting,
The fiddler in the tavern, the glee, the long-strung sailor-song,
The lowing cattle, bleating sheep, the crowing cock at dawn.

All songs of current lands come sounding round me,
The German airs of friendship, wine and love,
Irish ballads, merry jigs and dances, English warbles,
Chansons of France, Scotch tunes, and o'er the rest,
Italia's peerless compositions.

Across the stage with pallor on her face, yet lurid passion,
Stalks Norma*brandishing the dagger in her hand.

I see poor crazed Lucia's eyes'*unnatural gleam,
Her hair down her back falls loose and dishevel'd.

I see where Ernani*walking the bridal garden,
Amid the scent of night-roses, radiant, holding his bride by the
    hand,
Hears the infernal call, the death-pledge of the horn.

To crossing swords and gray hairs bared to heaven,
The clear electric base and baritone of the world,
The trombone duo, Libertad forever !

From Spanish chestnut trees' dense shade,
By old and heavy convent walls a wailing song,
Song of lost love, the torch of youth and life quench'd in despair,
Song of the dying swan, Fernando's heart is breaking.

Awaking from her woes at last retriev'd Amina sings,
Copious as stars and glad as morning light the torrents of her joy.

(The teeming lady comes,
The lustrious orb, Venus contralto, the blooming mother,
Sister of loftiest gods, Alboni's self I hear.)

4

I hear those odes, symphonies, operas,
I hear in the *William Tell* the music of an arous'd and angry
    people,
I hear Meyerbeer's *Huguenots*, the *Prophet*, or *Robert*,
Gounod's *Faust*, or Mozart's *Don Juan*.

I hear the dance-music of all nations,
The waltz, some delicious measure, lapsing, bathing me in bliss,
The bolero to tinkling guitars and clattering castanets.

I see religious dances old and new,
I hear the sound of the Hebrew lyre,
I see the crusaders marching bearing the cross on high, to the
    martial clang of cymbals,
I hear dervishes monotonously chanting, interspers'd with frantic
    shouts, as they spin around turning always towards Mecca,
I see the rapt religious dances of the Persians and the Arabs,
Again, at Eleusis, home of Ceres, I see the modern Greeks dancing,
I hear them clapping their hands as they bend their bodies,
I hear the metrical shuffling of their feet.

I see again the wild old Corybantian dance, the performers
    wounding each other,
I see the Roman youth to the shrill sound of flageolets throwing
    and catching their weapons,
As they fall on their knees and rise again.

I hear from the Mussulman mosque the muezzin calling,
I see the worshippers within, nor form nor sermon, argument nor
    word,
But silent, strange, devout, rais'd, glowing heads, ecstatic faces.

I hear the Egyptian harp of many strings,
The primitive chants of the Nile boatmen,
The sacred imperial hymns of China,
To the delicate sounds of the king, (the stricken wood and stone,)
Or to Hindu flutes and the fretting twang of the vina,
A band of bayaderes.

5

Now Asia, Africa leave me, Europe seizing inflates me,
To organs huge and bands I hear as from vast concourses of
    voices,
Luther's strong hymn *Eine feste Burg ist unser Gott,*
Rossini's *Stabat Mater dolorosa,*
Or floating in some high cathedral dim with gorgeous color'd
    windows,
The passionate *Agnus Dei* or *Gloria in Excelsis.*

Composers! mighty maestros!
And you, sweet singers of old lands, soprani, tenori, bassi!
To you a new bard caroling in the West,
Obeisant sends his love.

(Such led to thee O soul,
All senses, shows and objects, lead to thee,
But now it seems to me sound leads o'er all the rest.)

I hear the annual singing of the children in St. Paul's cathedral,
Or, under the high roof of some colossal hall, the symphonies,
    oratorios of Beethoven, Handel, or Haydn,
The *Creation* in billows of godhood laves me.

Give me to hold all sounds, (I madly struggling cry,)
Fill me with all the voices of the universe,
Endow me with their throbbings, Nature's also,
The tempests, waters, winds, operas and chants, marches and
    dances,
Utter, pour in, for I would take them all!

6

Then I woke softly,
And pausing, questioning awhile the music of my dream,
And questioning all those reminiscences, the tempest in its fury,
And all the songs of sopranos and tenors,
And those rapt oriental dances of religious fervor,

And the sweet varied instruments, and the diapason of organs,
And all the artless plaints of love and grief and death,
I said to my silent curious soul out of the bed of the slumber-
 chamber,
Come, for I have found the clew I sought so long,
Let us go forth refresh'd amid the day,
Cheerfully tallying life, walking the world, the real,
Nourish'd henceforth by our celestial dream.

And I said, moreover,
Haply what thou hast heard O soul was not the sound of winds,
Nor dream of raging storm, nor sea-hawk's flapping wings nor
 harsh scream,
Nor vocalism of sun-bright Italy,
Nor German organ majestic, nor vast concourse of voices, nor
 layers of harmonies,
Nor strophes of husbands and wives, nor sound of marching
 soldiers,
Nor flutes, nor harps, nor the bugle-calls of camps,
But to a new rhythmus fitted for thee,
Poems bridging the way from Life to Death, vaguely wafted in
 night air, uncaught, unwritten,
Which let us go forth in the bold day and write.

PASSAGE TO INDIA.

I

SINGING my days,
Singing the great achievements of the present,
Singing the strong light works of engineers,
Our modern wonders, (the antique ponderous Seven outvied,)
In the Old World the east the Suez canal,
The New by its mighty railroad spann'd,
The seas inlaid with eloquent gentle wires ;*
Yet first to sound, and ever sound, the cry with thee O soul,
The Past ! the Past ! the Past !

The Past — the dark unfathom'd retrospect !
The teeming gulf — the sleepers and the shadows !
The past — the infinite greatness of the past !
For what is the present after all but a growth out of the past?

(As a projectile form'd, impell'd, passing a certain line, still keeps
　　　on,
So the present, utterly form'd, impell'd by the past.)

2

Passage O soul to India !
Eclaircise the myths Asiatic, the primitive fables.

Not you alone proud truths of the world,
Nor you alone ye facts of modern science,
But myths and fables of eld, Asia's, Africa's fables,
The far-darting beams of the spirit, the unloos'd dreams,
The deep diving bibles and legends,
The daring plots of the poets, the elder religions ;
O you temples fairer than lilies pour'd over by the rising sun !
O you fables spurning the known, eluding the hold of the known,
　　　mounting to heaven !
You lofty and dazzling towers, pinnacled, red as roses, burnish'd
　　　with gold !
Towers of fables immortal fashion'd from mortal dreams !
You too I welcome and fully the same as the rest !
You too with joy I sing.

Passage to India !
Lo, soul, seest thou not God's purpose from the first?
The earth to be spann'd, connected by network,
The races, neighbors, to marry and be given in marriage,
The oceans to be cross'd, the distant brought near,
The lands to be welded together.

A worship new I sing,
You captains, voyagers, explorers, yours,
You engineers, you architects, machinists, yours,
You, not for trade or transportation only,
But in God's name, and for thy sake O soul.

3

Passage to India !
Lo soul for thee of tableaus twain,
I see in one the Suez canal initiated, open'd,
I see the procession of steamships, the Empress Eugenie's leading
　　　the van,*
I mark from on deck the strange landscape, the pure sky, the
　　　level sand in the distance,
I pass swiftly the picturesque groups, the workmen gather'd,
The gigantic dredging machines.

In one again, different, (yet thine, all thine, O soul, the same,)
I see over my own continent the Pacific railroad surmounting
    every barrier,
I see continual trains of cars winding along the Platte carrying
    freight and passengers,
I hear the locomotives rushing and roaring, and the shrill steam-
    whistle,
I hear the echoes reverberate through the grandest scenery in the
    world,
I cross the Laramie plains, I note the rocks in grotesque shapes,
    the buttes,
I see the plentiful larkspur and wild onions, the barren, colorless,
    sage-deserts,
I see in glimpses afar or towering immediately above me the
    great mountains, I see the Wind river and the Wahsatch
    mountains,
I see the Monument mountain and the Eagle's Nest, I pass the
    Promontory, I ascend the Nevadas,
I scan the noble Elk mountain and wind around its base,
I see the Humboldt range, I thread the valley and cross the river,
I see the clear waters of lake Tahoe, I see forests of majestic
    pines,
Or crossing the great desert, the alkaline plains, I behold enchant-
    ing mirages of waters and meadows,
Marking through these and after all, in duplicate slender lines,
Bridging the three or four thousand miles of land travel,
Tying the Eastern to the Western sea,
The road between Europe and Asia.

(Ah Genoese thy dream ! thy dream !
Centuries after thou art laid in thy grave,
The shore thou foundest verifies thy dream.)

4

Passage to India !
Struggles of many a captain, tales of many a sailor dead,
Over my mood stealing and spreading they come,
Like clouds and cloudlets in the unreach'd sky.

Along all history, down the slopes,
As a rivulet running, sinking now, and now again to the surface
    rising,
A ceaseless thought, a varied train — lo, soul, to thee, thy sight,
    they rise,
The plans, the voyages again, the expeditions ;

Again Vasco de Gama*sails forth,
Again the knowledge gain'd, the mariner's compass,
Lands found and nations born, thou born America,
For purpose vast, man's long probation fill'd,
Thou rondure of the world at last accomplish'd.

5

O vast Rondure, swimming in space,
Cover'd all over with visible power and beauty,
Alternate light and day and the teeming spiritual darkness,
Unspeakable high processions of sun and moon and countless
      stars above,
Below, the manifold grass and waters, animals, mountains, trees,
With inscrutable purpose, some hidden prophetic intention,
Now first it seems my thought begins to span thee.

Down from the gardens of Asia descending radiating,
Adam and Eve appear, then their myriad progeny after them,
Wandering, yearning, curious, with restless explorations,
With questionings, baffled, formless, feverish, with never-happy
      hearts,
With that sad incessant refrain, *Wherefore unsatisfied soul?* and
      Whither O mocking life?

Ah who shall soothe these feverish children?
Who justify these restless explorations?
Who speak the secret of impassive earth?
Who bind it to us? what is this separate Nature so unnatural?
What is this earth to our affections? (unloving earth, without a
      throb to answer ours,
Cold earth, the place of graves.)

Yet soul be sure the first intent remains, and shall be carried out,
Perhaps even now the time has arrived.

After the seas are all cross'd, (as they seem already cross'd,)
After the great captains and engineers have accomplish'd their
      work,
After the noble inventors, after the scientists, the chemist, the
      geologist, ethnologist,
Finally shall come the poet worthy that name,
The true son of God shall come singing his songs.

Then not your deeds only O voyagers, O scientists and inventors,
      shall be justified,

All these hearts as of fretted children shall be sooth'd,
All affection shall be fully responded to, the secret shall be told,
All these separations and gaps shall be taken up and hook'd and
 link'd together,
The whole earth, this cold, impassive, voiceless earth, shall be
 completely justified,
Trinitas divine shall be gloriously accomplish'd and compacted by
 the true son of God, the poet,
(He shall indeed pass the straits and conquer the mountains,
He shall double the cape of Good Hope to some purpose,)
Nature and Man shall be disjoin'd and diffused no more,
The true son of God shall absolutely fuse them.

6

Year at whose wide-flung door I sing !
Year of the purpose accomplish'd !
Year of the marriage of continents, climates and oceans !
(No mere doge of Venice now wedding the Adriatic,)
I see O year in you the vast terraqueous globe given and giving
 all,
Europe to Asia, Africa join'd, and they to the New World,
The lands, geographies, dancing before you, holding a festival
 garland,
As brides and bridegrooms hand in hand.

Passage to India !
Cooling airs from Caucasus far, soothing cradle of man,
The river Euphrates flowing, the past lit up again.

Lo soul, the retrospect brought forward,
The old, most populous, wealthiest of earth's lands,
The streams of the Indus and the Ganges and their many af-
 fluents,
(I my shores of America walking to-day behold, resuming all,)
The tale of Alexander on his warlike marches suddenly dying,
On one side China and on the other side Persia and Arabia,
To the south the great seas and the bay of Bengal,
The flowing literatures, tremendous epics, religions, castes,
Old occult Brahma interminably far back, the tender and junior
 Buddha,
Central and southern empires and all their belongings, possessors,
The wars of Tamerlane, the reign of Aurungzebe,
The traders, rulers, explorers, Moslems, Venetians, Byzantium, the
 Arabs, Portuguese,

The first travelers famous yet, Marco Polo, Batouta the Moor,
Doubts to be solv'd, the map incognita, blanks to be fill'd,
The foot of man unstay'd, the hands never at rest,
Thyself O soul that will not brook a challenge.

The mediæval navigators rise before me,
The world of 1492, with its awaken'd enterprise,
Something swelling in humanity now like the sap of the earth in
          spring,
The sunset splendor of chivalry declining.

And who art thou sad shade?
Gigantic, visionary, thyself a visionary,
With majestic limbs and pious beaming eyes,
Spreading around with every look of thine a golden world,
Enhuing it with gorgeous hues.

As the chief histrion,
Down to the footlights walks in some great scena,
Dominating the rest I see the Admiral himself,
(History's type of courage, action, faith,)
Behold him sail from Palos leading his little fleet,
His voyage behold, his return, his great fame,
His misfortunes, calumniators, behold him a prisoner, chain'd,
Behold his dejection, poverty, death.

(Curious in time I stand, noting the efforts of heroes,
Is the deferment long? bitter the slander, poverty, death?
Lies the seed unreck'd for centuries in the ground? lo, to God's
          due occasion,
Uprising in the night, it sprouts, blooms,
And fills the earth with use and beauty.)

7

Passage indeed O soul to primal thought,
Not lands and seas alone, thy own clear freshness,
The young maturity of brood and bloom,
To realms of budding bibles.

O soul, repressless, I with thee and thou with me,
Thy circumnavigation of the world begin,
Of man, the voyage of his mind's return,
To reason's early paradise,
Back, back to wisdom's birth, to innocent intuitions,
Again with fair creation.

8

O we can wait no longer,
We too take ship O soul,
Joyous we too launch out on trackless seas,
Fearless for unknown shores on waves of ecstasy to sail,
Amid the wafting winds, (thou pressing me to thee, I thee to me,
    O soul,)
Caroling free, singing our song of God,
Chanting our chant of pleasant exploration.

With laugh and many a kiss,
(Let others deprecate, let others weep for sin, remorse, humilia-
    tion,)
O soul thou pleasest me, I thee.

Ah more than any priest O soul we too believe in God,
But with the mystery of God we dare not dally.

O soul thou pleasest me, I thee,
Sailing these seas or on the hills, or waking in the night,
Thoughts, silent thoughts, of Time and Space and Death, like
    waters flowing,
Bear me indeed as through the regions infinite,
Whose air I breathe, whose ripples hear, lave me all over,
Bathe me O God in thee, mounting to thee,
I and my soul to range in range of thee.

O Thou transcendent,
Nameless, the fibre and the breath,
Light of the light, shedding forth universes, thou centre of them,
Thou mightier centre of the true, the good, the loving,
Thou moral, spiritual fountain — affection's source — thou reser-
    voir,
(O pensive soul of me — O thirst unsatisfied — waitest not there?
Waitest not haply for us somewhere there the Comrade perfect?)
Thou pulse — thou motive of the stars, suns, systems,
That, circling, move in order, safe, harmonious,
Athwart the shapeless vastnesses of space,
How should I think, how breathe a single breath, how speak, if,
    out of myself,
I could not launch, to those, superior universes?

Swiftly I shrivel at the thought of God,
At Nature and its wonders, Time and Space and Death,
But that I, turning, call to thee O soul, thou actual Me,

And lo, thou gently masterest the orbs,
Thou matest Time, smilest content at Death,
And fillest, swellest full the vastnesses of Space.

Greater than stars or suns,
Bounding O soul thou journeyest forth;
What love than thine and ours could wider amplify?
What aspirations, wishes, outvie thine and ours O soul?
What dreams of the ideal? what plans of purity, perfection,
    strength?
What cheerful willingness for others' sake to give up all?
For others' sake to suffer all?

Reckoning ahead O soul, when thou, the time achiev'd,
The seas all cross'd, weather'd the capes, the voyage done,
Surrounded, copest, frontest God, yieldest, the aim attain'd,
As fill'd with friendship, love complete, the Elder Brother found,
The Younger melts in fondness in his arms.

9

Passage to more than India!
Are thy wings plumed indeed for such far flights?
O soul, voyagest thou indeed on voyages like those?
Disportest thou on waters such as those?
Soundest below the Sanscrit and the Vedas?
Then have thy bent unleash'd.

Passage to you, your shores, ye aged fierce enigmas!
Passage to you, to mastership of you, ye strangling problems!
You, strew'd with the wrecks of skeletons, that, living, never
    reach'd you.

Passage to more than India!
O secret of the earth and sky!
Of you O waters of the sea! O winding creeks and rivers!
Of you O woods and fields! of you strong mountains of my land!
Of you O prairies! of you gray rocks!
O morning red! O clouds! O rain and snows!
O day and night, passage to you!

O sun and moon and all you stars! Sirius and Jupiter!
Passage to you!

Passage, immediate passage! the blood burns in my veins!
Away O soul! hoist instantly the anchor!

Cut the hawsers — haul out — shake out every sail!
Have we not stood here like trees in the ground long enough?
Have we not grovel'd here long enough, eating and drinking like
    mere brutes?
Have we not darken'd and dazed ourselves with books long enough?

Sail forth — steer for the deep waters only,
Reckless O soul, exploring, I with thee, and thou with me,
For we are bound where mariner has not yet dared to go,
And we will risk the ship, ourselves and all.

O my brave soul!
O farther farther sail!
O daring joy, but safe! are they not all the seas of God?
O farther, farther, farther sail!

PRAYER OF COLUMBUS.

A BATTER'D, wreck'd old man,
Thrown on this savage shore, far, far from home,
Pent by the sea and dark rebellious brows, twelve dreary months,
Sore, stiff with many toils, sicken'd and nigh to death,
I take my way along the island's edge,
Venting a heavy heart.

I am too full of woe!
Haply I may not live another day;
I cannot rest O God, I cannot eat or drink or sleep,
Till I put forth myself, my prayer, once more to Thee,
Breathe, bathe myself once more in Thee, commune with Thee,
Report myself once more to Thee.

Thou knowest my years entire, my life,
My long and crowded life of active work, not adoration merely;
Thou knowest the prayers and vigils of my youth,
Thou knowest my manhood's solemn and visionary meditations,
Thou knowest how before I commenced I devoted all to come to
    Thee,
Thou knowest I have in age ratified all those vows and strictly
    kept them,
Thou knowest I have not once lost nor faith nor ecstasy in Thee,

In shackles, prison'd, in disgrace, repining not,
Accepting all from Thee, as duly come from Thee.

All my emprises have been fill'd with Thee,
My speculations, plans, begun and carried on in thoughts of Thee,
Sailing the deep or journeying the land for Thee ;
Intentions, purports, aspirations mine, leaving results to Thee.

O I am sure they really came from Thee,
The urge, the ardor, the unconquerable will,
The potent, felt, interior command, stronger than words,
A message from the Heavens whispering to me even in sleep,
These sped me on..

By me and these the work so far accomplish'd,
By me earth's elder cloy'd and stifled lands uncloy'd, unloos'd,
By me the hemispheres rounded and tied, the unknown to the known.

The end I know not, it is all in Thee,
Or small or great I know not — haply what broad fields, what lands,
Haply the brutish measureless human undergrowth I know,
Transplanted there may rise to stature, knowledge worthy Thee,
Haply the swords I know may there indeed be turn'd to reaping-
tools,
Haply the lifeless cross I know, Europe's dead cross, may bud and
blossom there.

One effort more, my altar this bleak sand ;
That Thou O God my life hast lighted,
With ray of light, steady, ineffable, vouchsafed of Thee,
Light rare untellable, lighting the very light,
Beyond all signs, descriptions, languages ;
For that O God, be it my latest word, here on my knees,
Old, poor, and paralyzed, I thank Thee.

My terminus near,
The clouds already closing in upon me,
The voyage balk'd, the course disputed, lost,
I yield my ships to Thee.

My hands, my limbs grow nerveless,
My brain feels rack'd, bewilder'd,
Let the old timbers part, I will not part,
I will cling fast to Thee, O God, though the waves buffet me,
Thee, Thee at least I know.

Is it the prophet's thought I speak, or am I raving?
What do I know of life? what of myself?
I know not even my own work past or present,
Dim ever-shifting guesses of it spread before me,
Of newer better worlds, their mighty parturition,
Mocking, perplexing me.

And these things I see suddenly, what mean they?
As if some miracle, some hand divine unseal'd my eyes,
Shadowy vast shapes smile through the air and sky,
And on the distant waves sail countless ships,
And anthems in new tongues I hear saluting me.

THE SLEEPERS.

I

I WANDER all night in my vision,
Stepping with light feet, swiftly and noiselessly stepping and
        stopping,
Bending with open eyes over the shut eyes of sleepers,
Wandering and confused, lost to myself, ill-assorted, contradic-
        tory,
Pausing, gazing, bending, and stopping.

How solemn they look there, stretch'd and still,
How quiet they breathe, the little children in their cradles.

The wretched features of ennuyés, the white features of corpses,
        the livid faces of drunkards, the sick-gray faces of onanists,
The gash'd bodies on battle-fields, the insane in their strong-door'd
        rooms, the sacred idiots, the new-born emerging from
        gates, and the dying emerging from gates,
The night pervades them and infolds them.

The married couple sleep calmly in their bed, he with his palm on
        the hip of the wife, and she with her palm on the hip of
        the husband,
The sisters sleep lovingly side by side in their bed,
The men sleep lovingly side by side in theirs,
And the mother sleeps with her little child carefully wrapt.

The blind sleep, and the deaf and dumb sleep,
The prisoner sleeps well in the prison, the runaway son sleeps,
The murderer that is to be hung next day, how does he sleep?
And the murder'd person, how does he sleep?

The female that loves unrequited sleeps,
And the male that loves unrequited sleeps,
The head of the money-maker that plotted all day sleeps,
And the enraged and treacherous dispositions, all, all sleep.

I stand in the dark with drooping eyes by the worst-suffering and
the most restless,
I pass my hands soothingly to and fro a few inches from them,
The restless sink in their beds, they fitfully sleep.

Now I pierce the darkness, new beings appear,
The earth recedes from me into the night,
I saw that it was beautiful, and I see that what is not the earth is
beautiful.

I go from bedside to bedside, I sleep close with the other sleepers
each in turn,
I dream in my dream all the dreams of the other dreamers,
And I become the other dreamers.

I am a dance — play up there! the fit is whirling me fast!

I am the ever-laughing — it is new moon and twilight,
I see the hiding of douceurs, I see nimble ghosts whichever way
I look,
Cache and cache again deep in the ground and sea, and where it
is neither ground nor sea.

Well do they do their jobs those journeymen divine,
Only from me can they hide nothing, and would not if they could,
I reckon I am their boss and they make me a pet besides,
And surround me and lead me and run ahead when I walk,
To lift their cunning covers to signify me with stretch'd arms, and
resume the way;
Onward we move, a gay gang of blackguards! with mirth-shouting
music and wild-flapping pennants of joy!

I am the actor, the actress, the voter, the politician,
The emigrant and the exile, the criminal that stood in the box,
He who has been famous and he who shall be famous after to-day,
The stammerer, the well-form'd person, the wasted or feeble
person.

I am she who adorn'd herself and folded her hair expectantly,
My truant lover has come, and it is dark.

Double yourself and receive me darkness,
Receive me and my lover too, he will not let me go without
him.

I roll myself upon you as upon a bed, I resign myself to the dusk.

He whom I call answers me and takes the place of my lover,
He rises with me silently from the bed.

Darkness, you are gentler than my lover, his flesh was sweaty and
panting,
I feel the hot moisture yet that he left me.

My hands are spread forth, I pass them in all directions,
I would sound up the shadowy shore to which you are journeying.

Be careful darkness! already what was it touch'd me?
I thought my lover had gone, else darkness and he are one,
I hear the heart-beat, I follow, I fade away.

2

I descend my western course, my sinews are flaccid,
Perfume and youth course through me and I am their wake.

It is my face yellow and wrinkled instead of the old woman's,
I sit low in a straw-bottom chair and carefully darn my grandson's
stockings.

It is I too, the sleepless widow looking out on the winter mid-
night,
I see the sparkles of starshine on the icy and pallid earth.

A shroud I see and I am the shroud, I wrap a body and lie in the
coffin,
It is dark here under ground, it is not evil or pain here, it is blank
here, for reasons.

(It seems to me that every thing in the light and air ought to be
happy,
Whoever is not in his coffin and the dark grave let him know he
has enough.)

3

I see a beautiful gigantic swimmer swimming naked through the
    eddies of the sea,
His brown hair lies close and even to his head, he strikes out with
    courageous arms, he urges himself with his legs,
I see his white body, I see his undaunted eyes,
I hate the swift-running eddies that would dash him head-fore-
    most on the rocks.

What are you doing you ruffianly red-trickled waves?
Will you kill the courageous giant? will you kill him in the prime
    of his middle age?

Steady and long he struggles,
He is baffled, bang'd, bruis'd, he holds out while his strength holds
    out,
The slapping eddies are spotted with his blood, they bear him
    away, they roll him, swing him, turn him,
His beautiful body is borne in the circling eddies, it is continually
    bruis'd on rocks,
Swiftly and out of sight is borne the brave corpse.

4

I turn but do not extricate myself,
Confused, a past-reading, another, but with darkness yet.

The beach is cut by the razory ice-wind, the wreck-guns sound,
The tempest lulls, the moon comes floundering through the drifts.

I look where the ship helplessly heads end on, I hear the burst as
    she strikes, I hear the howls of dismay, they grow fainter
    and fainter.

I cannot aid with my wringing fingers,
I can but rush to the surf and let it drench me and freeze
    upon me.

I search with the crowd, not one of the company is wash'd to us
    alive,
In the morning I help pick up the dead and lay them in rows in
    a barn.

5

Now of the older war-days, the defeat at Brooklyn,*
Washington stands inside the lines, he stands on the intrench'd
    hills amid a crowd of officers,

His face is cold and damp, he cannot repress the weeping drops,
He lifts the glass perpetually to his eyes, the color is blanch'd from
    his cheeks,
He sees the slaughter of the southern braves confided to him by
    their parents.

The same at last and at last when peace is declared,
He stands in the room of the old tavern, the well-belov'd soldiers
    all pass through,
The officers speechless and slow draw near in their turns,
The chief encircles their necks with his arm and kisses them on
    the cheek,
He kisses lightly the wet cheeks one after another, he shakes
    hands and bids good-by to the army.

6

Now what my mother told me one day as we sat at dinner
    together,
Of when she was a nearly grown girl living home with her parents
    on the old homestead.

A red squaw came one breakfast-time to the old homestead,
On her back she carried a bundle of rushes for rush-bottoming
    chairs,
Her hair, straight, shiny, coarse, black, profuse, half-envelop'd her
    face,
Her step was free and elastic, and her voice sounded exquisitely
    as she spoke.

My mother look'd in delight and amazement at the stranger,
She look'd at the freshness of her tall-borne face and full and
    pliant limbs,
The more she look'd upon her she loved her,
Never before had she seen such wonderful beauty and purity,
She made her sit on a bench by the jamb of the fireplace, she
    cook'd food for her,
She had no work to give her, but she gave her remembrance and
    fondness.

The red squaw staid all the forenoon, and toward the middle of
    the afternoon she went away,
O my mother was loth to have her go away,
All the week she thought of her, she watch'd for her many a
    month,
She remember'd her many a winter and many a summer,
But the red squaw never came nor was heard of there again.

7

A show of the summer softness — a contact of something unseen
　　— an amour of the light and air,
I am jealous and overwhelm'd with friendliness,
And will go gallivant with the light and air myself.

O love and summer, you are in the dreams and in me,
Autumn and winter are in the dreams, the farmer goes with his
　　thrift,
The droves and crops increase, the barns are well-fill'd.

Elements merge in the night, ships make tacks in the dreams,
The sailor sails, the exile returns home,
The fugitive returns unharm'd, the immigrant is back beyond
　　months and years,
The poor Irishman lives in the simple house of his childhood
　　with the well-known neighbors and faces,
They warmly welcome him, he is barefoot again, he forgets he is
　　well off,
The Dutchman voyages home, and the Scotchman and Welshman
　　voyage home, and the native of the Mediterranean voy-
　　ages home,
To every port of England, France, Spain, enter well-fill'd ships,
The Swiss foots it toward his hills, the Prussian goes his way, the
　　Hungarian his way, and the Pole his way,
The Swede returns, and the Dane and Norwegian return.

The homeward bound and the outward bound,
The beautiful lost swimmer, the ennuyé, the onanist, the female
　　that loves unrequited, the money-maker,
The actor and actress, those through with their parts and those
　　waiting to commence,
The affectionate boy, the husband and wife, the voter, the nominee
　　that is chosen and the nominee that has fail'd,
The great already known and the great any time after to-day,
The stammerer, the sick, the perfect-form'd, the homely,
The criminal that stood in the box, the judge that sat and sen-
　　tenced him, the fluent lawyers, the jury, the audience,
The laugher and weeper, the dancer, the midnight widow, the red
　　squaw,
The consumptive, the erysipalite, the idiot, he that is wrong'd,
The antipodes, and every one between this and them in the dark,
I swear they are averaged now — one is no better than the other,
The night and sleep have liken'd them and restored them.

I swear they are all beautiful,
Every one that sleeps is beautiful, every thing in the dim light is
    beautiful,
The wildest and bloodiest is over, and all is peace.

Peace is always beautiful,
The myth of heaven indicates peace and night.

The myth of heaven indicates the soul,
The soul is always beautiful, it appears more or it appears less, it
    comes or it lags behind,
It comes from its embower'd garden and looks pleasantly on
    itself and encloses the world,
Perfect and clean the genitals previously jetting, and perfect and
    clean the womb cohering,
The head well-grown proportion'd and plumb, and the bowels and
    joints proportion'd and plumb.

The soul is always beautiful, ·
The universe is duly in order, every thing is in its place,
What has arrived is in its place and what waits shall be in its place,
The twisted skull waits, the watery or rotten blood waits,
The child of the glutton or venerealee waits long, and the child
    of the drunkard waits long, and the drunkard himself waits
    long,
The sleepers that lived and died wait, the far advanced are to go
    on in their turns, and the far behind are to come on in
    their turns,
The diverse shall be no less diverse, but they shall flow and unite
    — they unite now.

8

The sleepers are very beautiful as they lie unclothed,
They flow hand in hand over the whole earth from east to west as
    they lie unclothed,
The Asiatic and African are hand in hand, the European and
    American are hand in hand,
Learn'd and unlearn'd are hand in hand, and male and female are
    hand in hand,
The bare arm of the girl crosses the bare breast of her lover, they
    press close without lust, his lips press her neck,
The father holds his grown or ungrown son in his arms with meas-
    ureless love, and the son holds the father in his arms with
    measureless love,

The white hair of the mother shines on the white wrist of the
   daughter,
The breath of the boy goes with the breath of the man, friend is
   inarm'd by friend,
The scholar kisses the teacher and the teacher kisses the scholar,
   the wrong'd is made right,
The call of the slave is one with the master's call, and the master
   salutes the slave,
The felon steps forth from the prison, the insane becomes sane,
   the suffering of sick persons is reliev'd,
The sweatings and fevers stop, the throat that was unsound is
   sound, the lungs of the consumptive are resumed, the poor
   distress'd head is free,
The joints of the rheumatic move as smoothly as ever, and
   smoother than ever,
Stiflings and passages open, the paralyzed become supple,
The swell'd and convuls'd and congested awake to themselves in
   condition,
They pass the invigoration of the night and the chemistry of the
   night, and awake.

I too pass from the night,
I stay a while away O night, but I return to you again and love you.

Why should I be afraid to trust myself to you?
I am not afraid, I have been well brought forward by you,
I love the rich running day, but I do not desert her in whom I lay
   so long,
I know not how I came of you and I know not where I go with
   you, but I know I came well and shall go well.

I will stop only a time with the night, and rise betimes,
I will duly pass the day O my mother, and duly return to you.

TRANSPOSITIONS.

LET the reformers descend from the stands where they are forever
   bawling — let an idiot or insane person appear on each of
   the stands ;
Let judges and criminals be transposed — let the prison-keepers be
   put in prison — let those that were prisoners take the keys ;
Let them that distrust birth and death lead the rest.

TO THINK OF TIME.

1

To think of time — of all that retrospection,
To think of to-day, and the ages continued henceforward.

Have you guess'd you yourself would not continue?
Have you dreaded these earth-beetles?
Have you fear'd the future would be nothing to you?

Is to-day nothing? is the beginningless past nothing?
If the future is nothing they are just as surely nothing.

To think that the sun rose in the east — that men and women
      were flexible, real, alive — that every thing was alive,
To think that you and I did not see, feel, think, nor bear our part,
To think that we are now here and bear our part.

2

Not a day passes, not a minute or second without an accouche-
      ment,
Not a day passes, not a minute or second without a corpse.

The dull nights go over and the dull days also,
The soreness of lying so much in bed goes over,
The physician after long putting off gives the silent and terrible
      look for an answer,
The children come hurried and weeping, and the brothers and
      sisters are sent for,
Medicines stand unused on the shelf, (the camphor-smell has long
      pervaded the rooms,)
The faithful hand of the living does not desert the hand of the
      dying,
The twitching lips press lightly on the forehead of the dying,
The breath ceases and the pulse of the heart ceases,
The corpse stretches on the bed and the living look upon it,
It is palpable as the living are palpable.

The living look upon the corpse with their eyesight,
But without eyesight lingers a different living and looks curiously
      on the corpse.

3

To think the thought of death merged in the thought of materials,
To think of all these wonders of city and country, and others taking
      great interest in them, and we taking no interest in them.

To think how eager we are in building our houses,
To think others shall be just as eager, and we quite indifferent.

(I see one building the house that serves him a few years, or
    seventy or eighty years at most,
I see one building the house that serves him longer than that.)

Slow-moving and black lines creep over the whole earth — they
    never cease — they are the burial lines,
He that was President was buried, and he that is now President
    shall surely be buried.

4

A reminiscence of the vulgar fate,
A frequent sample of the life and death of workmen,
Each after his kind.

Cold dash of waves at the ferry-wharf, posh and ice in the river,
    half-frozen mud in the streets,
A gray discouraged sky overhead, the short last daylight of
    December,
A hearse and stages, the funeral of an old Broadway stage-driver,
    the cortege mostly drivers.

Steady the trot to the cemetery, duly rattles the death-bell,
The gate is pass'd, the new-dug grave is halted at, the living alight,
    the hearse uncloses,
The coffin is pass'd out, lower'd and settled, the whip is laid on
    the coffin, the earth is swiftly shovel'd in,
The mound above is flatted with the spades — silence,
A minute — no one moves or speaks — it is done,
He is decently put away — is there any thing more?

He was a good fellow, free-mouth'd, quick-temper'd, not bad-
    looking,
Ready with life or death for a friend, fond of women, gambled,
    ate hearty, drank hearty,
Had known what it was to be flush, grew low-spirited toward the
    last, sicken'd, was help'd by a contribution,
Died, aged forty-one years — and that was his funeral.

Thumb extended, finger uplifted, apron, cape, gloves, strap, wet-
    weather clothes, whip carefully chosen,
Boss, spotter, starter, hostler, somebody loafing on you, you loafing
    on somebody, headway, man before and man behind,
Good day's work, bad day's work, pet stock, mean stock, first out,
    last out, turning-in at night,

To think that these are so much and so nigh to other drivers, and he there takes no interest in them.

5

The markets, the government, the working-man's wages, to think what account they are through our nights and days,
To think that other working-men will make just as great account of them, yet we make little or no account.

The vulgar and the refined, what you call sin and what you call goodness, to think how wide a difference,
To think the difference will still continue to others, yet we lie beyond the difference.

To think how much pleasure there is,
Do you enjoy yourself in the city? or engaged in business? or planning a nomination and election? or with your wife and family?
Or with your mother and sisters? or in womanly housework? or the beautiful maternal cares?
These also flow onward to others, you and I flow onward,
But in due time you and I shall take less interest in them.

Your farm, profits, crops — to think how engross'd you are,
To think there will still be farms, profits, crops, yet for you of what avail?

6

What will be will be well, for what is is well,
To take interest is well, and not to take interest shall be well.

The domestic joys, the daily housework or business, the building of houses, are not phantasms, they have weight, form, location,
Farms, profits, crops, markets, wages, government, are none of them phantasms,
The difference between sin and goodness is no delusion,
The earth is not an echo, man and his life and all the things of his life are well-consider'd.

You are not thrown to the winds, you gather certainly and safely around yourself,
Yourself! yourself! yourself, for ever and ever!

7

It is not to diffuse you that you were born of your mother and father, it is to identify you,

It is not that you should be undecided, but that you should be
    decided,
Something long preparing and formless is arrived and form'd in you,
You are henceforth secure, whatever comes or goes.

The threads that were spun are gather'd, the weft crosses the warp,
    the pattern is systematic.

The preparations have every one been justified,
The orchestra have sufficiently tuned their instruments, the baton
    has given the signal.

The guest that was coming, he waited long, he is now housed,
He is one of those who are beautiful and happy, he is one of those
    that to look upon and be with is enough.

The law of the past cannot be eluded,
The law of the present and future cannot be eluded,
The law of the living cannot be eluded, it is eternal,
The law of promotion and transformation cannot be eluded,
The law of heroes and good-doers cannot be eluded,
The law of drunkards, informers, mean persons, not one iota
    thereof can be eluded.

8

Slow moving and black lines go ceaselessly over the earth,
Northerner goes carried and Southerner goes carried, and they on
    the Atlantic side and they on the Pacific,
And they between, and all through the Mississippi country, and
    all over the earth.

The great masters and kosmos are well as they go, the heroes and
    good-doers are well,
The known leaders and inventors and the rich owners and pious
    and distinguish'd may be well,
But there is more account than that, there is strict account of
    all.

The interminable hordes of the ignorant and wicked are not
    nothing,
The barbarians of Africa and Asia are not nothing,
The perpetual successions of shallow people are not nothing as
    they go.

Of and in all these things,
I have dream'd that we are not to be changed so much, nor the
    law of us changed,

I have dream'd that heroes and good-doers shall be under the
present and past law,
And that murderers, drunkards, liars, shall be under the present
and past law,
For I have dream'd that the law they are under now is enough.

And I have dream'd that the purpose and essence of the known
life, the transient,
Is to form and decide identity for the unknown life, the permanent.

If all came but to ashes of dung,
If maggots and rats ended us, then Alarum! for we are betray'd,
Then indeed suspicion of death.

Do you suspect death? if I were to suspect death I should die
now,
Do you think I could walk pleasantly and well-suited toward
annihilation?

Pleasantly and well-suited I walk,
Whither I walk I cannot define, but I know it is good,
The whole universe indicates that it is good,
The past and the present indicate that it is good.

How beautiful and perfect are the animals!
How perfect the earth, and the minutest thing upon it!
What is called good is perfect, and what is called bad is just as
perfect,
The vegetables and minerals are all perfect, and the imponderable
fluids perfect;
Slowly and surely they have pass'd on to this, and slowly and surely
they yet pass on.

9

I swear I think now that every thing without exception has an
eternal soul!
The trees have, rooted in the ground! the weeds of the sea have!
the animals!

I swear I think there is nothing but immortality!
That the exquisite scheme is for it, and the nebulous float is for it,
and the cohering is for it!
And all preparation is for it — and identity is for it — and life and
materials are altogether for it!

WHISPERS OF HEAVENLY DEATH.

DAREST THOU NOW O SOUL.

DAREST thou now O soul,
Walk out with me toward the unknown region,
Where neither ground is for the feet nor any path to follow?

No map there, nor guide,
Nor voice sounding, nor touch of human hand,
Nor face with blooming flesh, nor lips, nor eyes, are in that land.

I know it not O soul,
Nor dost thou, all is a blank before us,
All waits undream'd of in that region, that inaccessible land.

Till when the ties loosen,
All but the ties eternal, Time and Space,
Nor darkness, gravitation, sense, nor any bounds bounding us.

Then we burst forth, we float,
In Time and Space O soul, prepared for them,
Equal, equipt at last, (O joy! O fruit of all!) them to fulfil O
soul.

WHISPERS OF HEAVENLY DEATH.

WHISPERS of heavenly death murmur'd I hear,
Labial gossip of night, sibilant chorals,
Footsteps gently ascending, mystical breezes wafted soft and low,
Ripples of unseen rivers, tides of a current flowing, forever flowing,
(Or is it the plashing of tears? the measureless waters of human
tears?)

I see, just see skyward, great cloud-masses,
Mournfully slowly they roll, silently swelling and mixing,
With at times a half-dimm'd sadden'd far-off star,
Appearing and disappearing.

(Some parturition rather, some solemn immortal birth;
On the frontiers to eyes impenetrable,
Some soul is passing over.)

CHANTING THE SQUARE DEIFIC.

I

CHANTING the square deific, out of the One advancing, out of the sides,
Out of the old and new, out of the square entirely divine,
Solid, four-sided, (all the sides needed,) from this side Jehovah am I,
Old Brahm I, and I Saturnius am ;
Not Time affects me — I am Time, old, modern as any,
Unpersuadable, relentless, executing righteous judgments,
As the Earth, the Father, the brown old Kronos, with laws,
Aged beyond computation, yet ever new, ever with those mighty laws rolling,
Relentless I forgive no man — whoever sins dies — I will have that man's life ;
Therefore let none expect mercy — have the seasons, gravitation, the appointed days, mercy? no more have I,
But as the seasons and gravitation, and as all the appointed days that forgive not,
I dispense from this side judgments inexorable without the least remorse.

2

Consolator most mild, the promis'd one advancing,
With gentle hand extended, the mightier God am I,
Foretold by prophets and poets in their most rapt prophecies and poems,
From this side, lo ! the Lord Christ gazes — lo ! Hermes I — lo ! mine is Hercules' face,
All sorrow, labor, suffering, I, tallying it, absorb in myself,
Many times have I been rejected, taunted, put in prison, and crucified, and many times shall be again,
All the world have I given up for my dear brothers' and sisters' sake, for the soul's sake,
Wending my way through the homes of men, rich or poor, with the kiss of affection,
For I am affection, I am the cheer-bringing God, with hope and all-enclosing charity,
With indulgent words as to children, with fresh and sane words, mine only,
Young and strong I pass knowing well I am destin'd myself to an early death ;
But my charity has no death — my wisdom dies not, neither early nor late,
And my sweet love bequeath'd here and elsewhere never dies.

3

Aloof, dissatisfied, plotting revolt,
Comrade of criminals, brother of slaves,
Crafty, despised, a drudge, ignorant,
With sudra face and worn brow, black, but in the depths of my
heart, proud as any,
Lifted now and always against whoever scorning assumes to rule me,
Morose, full of guile, full of reminiscences, brooding, with many
wiles,
(Though it was thought I was baffled and dispel'd, and my wiles
done, but that will never be,)
Defiant, I, Satan, still live, still utter words, in new lands duly
appearing, (and old ones also,)
Permanent here from my side, warlike, equal with any, real as any,
Nor time nor change shall ever change me or my words.

4

Santa Spirita, breather, life,
Beyond the light, lighter than light,
Beyond the flames of hell, joyous, leaping easily above hell,
Beyond Paradise, perfumed solely with mine own perfume,
Including all life on earth, touching, including God, including
Saviour and Satan,
Ethereal, pervading all, (for without me what were all? what were
God?)
Essence of forms, life of the real identities, permanent, positive,
(namely the unseen,)
Life of the great round world, the sun and stars, and of man,
I, the general soul,
Here the square finishing, the solid, I the most solid,
Breathe my breath also through these songs.

OF HIM I LOVE DAY AND NIGHT.

OF him I love day and night I dream'd I heard he was dead,
And I dream'd I went where they had buried him I love, but he
was not in that place,
And I dream'd I wander'd searching among burial-places to find
him,
And I found that every place was a burial-place;
The houses full of life were equally full of death, (this house is
now,)
The streets, the shipping, the places of amusement, the Chicago,
Boston, Philadelphia, the Mannahatta, were as full of the
dead as of the living,

And fuller, O vastly fuller of the dead than of the living;
And what I dream'd I will henceforth tell to every person and age,
And I stand henceforth bound to what I dream'd,
And now I am willing to disregard burial-places and dispense
    with them,
And if the memorials of the dead were put up indifferently every-
      where, even in the room where I eat or sleep, I should be
      satisfied,
And if the corpse of any one I love, or if my own corpse, be
      duly render'd to powder and pour'd in the sea, I shall be
      satisfied,
Or if it be distributed to the winds I shall be satisfied.

YET, YET, YE DOWNCAST HOURS.

Yet, yet, ye downcast hours, I know ye also,
Weights of lead, how ye clog and cling at my ankles,
Earth to a chamber of mourning turns — I hear the o'erweening,
    mocking voice,
Matter is conqueror — matter, triumphant only, continues onward.

Despairing cries float ceaselessly toward me,
The call of my nearest lover, putting forth, alarm'd, uncertain,
The sea I am quickly to sail, come tell me,
Come tell me where I am speeding, tell me my destination.

I understand your anguish, but I cannot help you,
I approach, hear, behold, the sad mouth, the look out of the eyes,
    your mute inquiry,
Whither I go from the bed I recline on, come tell me;
Old age, alarm'd, uncertain — a young woman's voice, appealing
    to me for comfort;
A young man's voice, *Shall I not escape?*

AS IF A PHANTOM CARESS'D ME.

As if a phantom caress'd me,
I thought I was not alone walking here by the shore;
But the one I thought was with me as now I walk by the shore,
    the one I loved that caress'd me,
As I lean and look through the glimmering light, that one has
    utterly disappear'd,
And those appear that are hateful to me and mock me.

ASSURANCES.

I NEED no assurances, I am a man who is pre-occupied of his
　　own soul;
I do not doubt that from under the feet and beside the hands and
　　face I am cognizant of, are now looking faces I am not
　　cognizant of, calm and actual faces,
I do not doubt but the majesty and beauty of the world are latent
　　in any iota of the world,
I do not doubt I am limitless, and that the universes are limitless,
　　in vain I try to think how limitless,
I do not doubt that the orbs and the systems of orbs play their
　　swift sports through the air on purpose, and that I shall one
　　day be eligible to do as much as they, and more than they,
I do not doubt that temporary affairs keep on and on millions of
　　years,
I do not doubt interiors have their interiors, and exteriors have
　　their exteriors, and that the eyesight has another eyesight,
　　and the hearing another hearing, and the voice another
　　voice,
I do not doubt that the passionately-wept deaths of young men
　　are provided for, and that the deaths of young women and
　　the deaths of little children are provided for,
(Did you think Life was so well provided for, and Death, the pur-
　　port of all Life, is not well provided for?)
I do not doubt that wrecks at sea, no matter what the horrors of
　　them, no matter whose wife, child, husband, father, lover,
　　has gone down, are provided for, to the minutest points,
I do not doubt that whatever can possibly happen anywhere at
　　any time, is provided for in the inherences of things,
I do not think Life provides for all and for Time and Space, but I
　　believe Heavenly Death provides for all.

QUICKSAND YEARS.

QUICKSAND years that whirl me I know not whither,
Your schemes, politics, fail, lines give way, substances mock and
　　elude me,
Only the theme I sing, the great and strong-possess'd soul, eludes
　　not,
One's-self must never give way — that is the final substance —
　　that out of all is sure,
Out of politics, triumphs, battles, life, what at last finally remains?
When shows break up what but One's-Self is sure?

THAT MUSIC ALWAYS ROUND ME.

THAT music always round me, unceasing, unbeginning, yet long
    untaught I did not hear,
But now the chorus I hear and am elated,
A tenor, strong, ascending with power and health, with glad notes
    of daybreak I hear,
A soprano at intervals sailing buoyantly over the tops of immense
    waves,
A transparent base shuddering lusciously under and through the
    universe,
The triumphant tutti, the funeral wailings with sweet flutes and
    violins, all these I fill myself with,
I hear not the volumes of sound merely, I am moved by the
    exquisite meanings,
I listen to the different voices winding in and out, striving, contend-
    ing with fiery vehemence to excel each other in emotion;
I do not think the performers know themselves — but now I think
    I begin to know them.

WHAT SHIP PUZZLED AT SEA.

WHAT ship puzzled at sea, cons for the true reckoning?
Or coming in, to avoid the bars and follow the channel a perfect
    pilot needs?
Here, sailor! here, ship! take aboard the most perfect pilot,
Whom, in a little boat, putting off and rowing, I hailing you offer.

A NOISELESS PATIENT SPIDER.

A NOISELESS patient spider,
I mark'd where on a little promontory it stood isolated,
Mark'd how to explore the vacant vast surrounding,
It launch'd forth filament, filament, filament, out of itself,
Ever unreeling them, ever tirelessly speeding them.

And you O my soul where you stand,
Surrounded, detached, in measureless oceans of space,
Ceaselessly musing, venturing, throwing, seeking the spheres to
    connect them,
Till the bridge you will need be form'd, till the ductile anchor
    hold,
Till the gossamer thread you fling catch somewhere, O my soul.

O LIVING ALWAYS, ALWAYS DYING.

O LIVING always, always dying!
O the burials of me past and present,
O me while I stride ahead, material, visible, imperious as ever;
O me, what I was for years, now dead, (I lament not, I am
    content;)
O to disengage myself from those corpses of me, which I turn
    and look at where I cast them,
To pass on, (O living! always living!) and leave the corpses
    behind.

TO ONE SHORTLY TO DIE.

FROM all the rest I single out you, having a message for you,
You are to die — let others tell you what they please, I cannot
    prevaricate,
I am exact and merciless, but I love you — there is no escape for
    you.

Softly I lay my right hand upon you, you just feel it,
I do not argue, I bend my head close and half envelop it,
I sit quietly by, I remain faithful,
I am more than nurse, more than parent or neighbor,
I absolve you from all except yourself spiritual bodily, that is eter-
    nal, you yourself will surely escape,
The corpse you will leave will be but excrementitious.

The sun bursts through in unlooked-for directions,
Strong thoughts fill you and confidence, you smile,
You forget you are sick, as I forget you are sick,
You do not see the medicines, you do not mind the weeping
    friends, I am with you,
I exclude others from you, there is nothing to be commiserated,
I do not commiserate, I congratulate you.

NIGHT ON THE PRAIRIES.

NIGHT on the prairies,
The supper is over, the fire on the ground burns low,
The wearied emigrants sleep, wrapt in their blankets;
I walk by myself — I stand and look at the stars, which I think now
    I never realized before.

Now I absorb immortality and peace,
I admire death and test propositions.

How plenteous! how spiritual! how resumé!
The same old man and soul — the same old aspirations, and the
    same content.

I was thinking the day most splendid till I saw what the not-day
    exhibited,
I was thinking this globe enough till there sprang out so noiseless
    around me myriads of other globes.

Now while the great thoughts of space and eternity fill me I will
    measure myself by them,
And now touch'd with the lives of other globes arrived as far
    along as those of the earth,
Or waiting to arrive, or pass'd on farther than those of the earth,
I henceforth no more ignore them than I ignore my own life,
Or the lives of the earth arrived as far as mine, or waiting to arrive.

O I see now that life cannot exhibit all to me, as the day cannot,
I see that I am to wait for what will be exhibited by death.

THOUGHT.

As I sit with others at a great feast, suddenly while the music is
    playing,
To my mind, (whence it comes I know not,) spectral in mist of
    a wreck at sea,
Of certain ships, how they sail from port with flying streamers and
    wafted kisses, and that is the last of them,
Of the solemn and murky mystery about the fate of the President,
Of the flower of the marine science of fifty generations founder'd
    off the Northeast coast and going down — of the steamship
    Arctic going down,
Of the veil'd tableau — women gather'd together on deck, pale,
    heroic, waiting the moment that draws so close — O the
    moment!
A huge sob — a few bubbles — the white foam spirting up — and
    then the women gone,
Sinking there while the passionless wet flows on — and I now
    pondering, Are those women indeed gone?
Are souls drown'd and destroy'd so?
Is only matter triumphant?

THE LAST INVOCATION.

AT the last, tenderly,
From the walls of the powerful fortress'd house,
From the clasp of the knitted locks, from the keep of the well-
    closed doors,
Let me be wafted.

Let me glide noiselessly forth;
With the key of softness unlock the locks — with a whisper,
Set ope the doors O soul.

Tenderly — be not impatient,
(Strong is your hold O mortal flesh,
Strong is your hold O love.)

AS I WATCH'D THE PLOUGHMAN PLOUGHING.

As I watch'd the ploughman ploughing,
Or the sower sowing in the fields, or the harvester harvesting,
I saw there too, O life and death, your analogies;
(Life, life is the tillage, and Death is the harvest according.)

PENSIVE AND FALTERING.

PENSIVE and faltering,
The words *the Dead* I write,
For living are the Dead,
(Haply the only living, only real,
And I the apparition, I the spectre.)

THOU MOTHER WITH THY EQUAL BROOD.*

I

THOU Mother with thy equal brood,
Thou varied chain of different States, yet one identity only,
A special song before I go I'd sing o'er all the rest,
For thee, the future.

I'd sow a seed for thee of endless Nationality,
I'd fashion thy ensemble including body and soul,
I'd show away ahead thy real Union, and how it may be accomplish'd.

The paths to the house I seek to make,
But leave to those to come the house itself.

Belief I sing, and preparation ;
As Life and Nature are not great with reference to the present only,
But greater still from what is yet to come,
Out of that formula for thee I sing.

2

As a strong bird on pinions free,
Joyous, the amplest spaces heavenward cleaving,
Such be the thought I'd think of thee America,
Such be the recitative I'd bring for thee.

The conceits of the poets of other lands I'd bring thee not,
Nor the compliments that have served their turn so long,
Nor rhyme, nor the classics, nor perfume of foreign court or indoor library ;
But an odor I'd bring as from forests of pine in Maine, or breath of an Illinois prairie,
With open airs of Virginia or Georgia or Tennessee, or from Texas uplands, or Florida's glades,
Or the Saguenay's black stream,* or the wide blue spread of Huron,
With presentment of Yellowstone's scenes, or Yosemite,
And murmuring under, pervading all, I'd bring the rustling sea-sound,
That endlessly sounds from the two Great Seas of the world.

And for thy subtler sense subtler refrains dread Mother,
Preludes of intellect tallying these and thee, mind-formulas fitted for thee, real and sane and large as these and thee,
Thou ! mounting higher, diving deeper than we knew, thou transcendental Union !
By thee fact to be justified, blended with thought,
Thought of man justified, blended with God,
Through thy idea, lo, the immortal reality !
Through thy reality, lo, the immortal idea !

3

Brain of the New World, what a task is thine,
To formulate the Modern — out of the peerless grandeur of the
modern,
Out of thyself, comprising science, to recast poems, churches, art,
(Recast, may-be discard them, end them — may-be their work is
done, who knows?)
By vision, hand, conception, on the background of the mighty
past, the dead,
To limn with absolute faith the mighty living present.

And yet thou living present brain, heir of the dead, the Old
World brain,
Thou that lay folded like an unborn babe within its folds so long,
Thou carefully prepared by it so long — haply thou but unfoldest
it, only maturest it,
It to eventuate in thee — the essence of the by-gone time contain'd
in thee,
Its poems, churches, arts, unwitting to themselves, destined with
reference to thee ;
Thou but the apples, long, long, long a-growing,
The fruit of all the Old ripening to-day in thee.

4

Sail, sail thy best, ship of Democracy,
Of value is thy freight, 'tis not the Present only,
The Past is also stored in thee,
Thou holdest not the venture of thyself alone, not of the Western
continent alone,
Earth's *résumé* entire floats on thy keel O ship, is steadied by thy
spars,
With thee Time voyages in trust, the antecedent nations sink or
swim with thee,
With all their ancient struggles, martyrs, heroes, epics, wars, thou
bear'st the other continents,
Theirs, theirs as much as thine, the destination-port triumphant ;
Steer then with good strong hand and wary eye O helmsman, thou
carriest great companions,
Venerable priestly Asia sails this day with thee,
And royal feudal Europe sails with thee.

5

Beautiful world of new superber birth that rises to my eyes,
Like a limitless golden cloud filling the western sky,

Emblem of general maternity lifted above all,
Sacred shape of the bearer of daughters and sons,
Out of thy teeming womb thy giant babes in ceaseless procession
    issuing,
Acceding from such gestation, taking and giving continual strength
    and life,
World of the real — world of the twain in one,
World of the soul, born by the world of the real alone, led to
    identity, body, by it alone,
Yet in beginning only, incalculable masses of composite precious
    materials,
By history's cycles forwarded, by every nation, language, hither
    sent;
Ready, collected here, a freer, vast, electric world, to be con-
    structed here,
(The true New World, the world of orbic science, morals, litera-
    tures to come,)
Thou wonder world yet undefined, unform'd, neither do I define
    thee,
How can I pierce the impenetrable blank of the future?
I feel thy ominous greatness evil as well as good,
I watch thee advancing, absorbing the present, transcending the
    past,
I see thy light lighting, and thy shadow shadowing, as if the
    entire globe,
But I do not undertake to define thee, hardly to comprehend thee,
I but thee name, thee prophesy, as now,
I merely thee ejaculate !

Thee in thy future,
Thee in thy only permanent life, career, thy own unloosen'd mind,
    thy soaring spirit,
Thee as another equally needed sun, radiant, ablaze, swift-moving,
    fructifying all,
Thee risen in potent cheerfulness and joy, in endless great
    hilarity,
Scattering for good the cloud that hung so long, that weigh'd so
    long upon the mind of man,
The doubt, suspicion, dread, of gradual, certain decadence of man ;
Thee in thy larger, saner brood of female, male — thee in thy
    athletes, moral, spiritual, South, North, West, East,
(To thy immortal breasts, Mother of All, thy every daughter, son,
    endear'd alike, forever equal,)
Thee in thy own musicians, singers, artists, unborn yet, but cer-
    tain,

Thee in thy moral wealth and civilization, (until which thy proud-
    est material civilization must remain in vain,)
Thee in thy all-supplying, all-enclosing worship — thee in no single
    bible, saviour, merely,
Thy saviours countless, latent within thyself, thy bibles incessant
    within thyself, equal to any, divine as any,
(Thy soaring course thee formulating, not in thy two great wars,
    nor in thy century's visible growth,
But far more in these leaves and chants, thy chants, great Mother !)
Thee in an education grown of thee, in teachers, studies, students,
    born of thee,
Thee in thy democratic fêtes en-masse, thy high original festivals,
    operas, lecturers, preachers,
Thee in thy ultimata, (the preparations only now completed, the
    edifice on sure foundations tied,)
Thee in thy pinnacles, intellect, thought, thy topmost rational joys,
    thy love and godlike aspiration,
In thy resplendent coming literati, thy full-lung'd orators, thy
    sacerdotal bards, kosmic savans,
These ! these in thee, (certain to come,) to-day I prophesy.

6

Land tolerating all, accepting all, not for the good alone, all good
    for thee,
Land in the realms of God to be a realm unto thyself,
Under the rule of God to be a rule unto thyself.

(Lo, where arise three peerless stars,
To be thy natal stars my country, Ensemble, Evolution, Freedom,
Set in the sky of Law.)

Land of unprecedented faith, God's faith,
Thy soil, thy very subsoil, all upheav'd,
The general inner earth so long so sedulously draped over, now
    hence for what it is boldly laid bare,
Open'd by thee to heaven's light for benefit or bale.

Not for success alone,
Not to fair-sail unintermitted always,
The storm shall dash thy face, the murk of war and worse than
    war shall cover thee all over,
(Wert capable of war, its tug and trials ? be capable of peace, its
    trials,
For the tug and mortal strain of nations come at last in prosper-
    ous peace, not war ;)

In many a smiling mask death shall approach beguiling thee, thou
    in disease shalt swelter,
The livid cancer spread its hideous claws, clinging upon thy
    breasts, seeking to strike thee deep within,
Consumption of the worst, moral consumption, shall rouge thy
    face with hectic,
But thou shalt face thy fortunes, thy diseases, and surmount them
    all,
Whatever they are to-day and whatever through time they may be,
They each and all shall lift and pass away and cease from thee,
While thou, Time's spirals rounding, out of thyself, thyself still
    extricating, fusing,
Equable, natural, mystical Union thou, (the mortal with immortal
    blent,)
Shalt soar toward the fulfilment of the future, the spirit of the
    body and the mind,
The soul, its destinies.

The soul, its destinies, the real real,
(Purport of all these apparitions of the real ;)
In thee America, the soul, its destinies,
Thou globe of globes ! thou wonder nebulous !
By many a throe of heat and cold convuls'd, (by these thyself
    solidifying,)
Thou mental, moral orb — thou New, indeed new, Spiritual World !
The Present holds thee not — for such vast growth as thine,
For such unparallel'd flight as thine, such brood as thine,
The FUTURE only holds thee and can hold thee.

A PAUMANOK PICTURE.

Two boats with nets lying off the sea-beach, quite still,
Ten fishermen waiting — they discover a thick school of moss-
    bonkers — they drop the join'd seine-ends in the water,
The boats separate and row off, each on its rounding course to the
    beach, enclosing the mossbonkers,
The net is drawn in by a windlass by those who stop ashore,
Some of the fishermen lounge in their boats, others stand ankle-
    deep in the water, pois'd on strong legs,
The boats partly drawn up, the water slapping against them,
Strew'd on the sand in heaps and windrows, well out from the
    water, the green-back'd spotted mossbonkers.

FROM NOON TO STARRY NIGHT.

THOU ORB ALOFT FULL-DAZZLING.

THOU orb aloft full-dazzling ! thou hot October noon !
Flooding with sheeny light the gray beach sand,
The sibilant near sea with vistas far and foam,
And tawny streaks and shades and spreading blue ;
O sun of noon refulgent ! my special word to thee.

Hear me illustrious !
Thy lover me, for always I have loved thee,
Even as basking babe, then happy boy alone by some wood edge,
        thy touching-distant beams enough,
Or man matured, or young or old, as now to thee I launch my
        invocation.

(Thou canst not with thy dumbness me deceive,
I know before the fitting man all Nature yields,
Though answering not in words, the skies, trees, hear his voice —
        and thou O sun,
As for thy throes, thy perturbations, sudden breaks and shafts of
        flame gigantic,
I understand them, I know those flames, those perturbations well.)

Thou that with fructifying heat and light,
O'er myriad farms, o'er lands and waters North and South,
O'er Mississippi's endless course, o'er Texas' grassy plains, Kana-
        da's woods,
O'er all the globe that turns its face to thee shining in space,
Thou that impartially infoldest all, not only continents, seas,
Thou that to grapes and weeds and little wild flowers givest so
        liberally,
Shed, shed thyself on mine and me, with but a fleeting ray out of
        thy million millions,
Strike through these chants.

Nor only launch thy subtle dazzle and thy strength for these,
Prepare the later afternoon of me myself — prepare my lengthen-
        ing shadows,
Prepare my starry nights.

FACES.

1

SAUNTERING the pavement or riding the country by-road, lo, such faces!
Faces of friendship, precision, caution, suavity, ideality,
The spiritual-prescient face, the always welcome common benevolent face,
The face of the singing of music, the grand faces of natural lawyers and judges broad at the back-top,
The faces of hunters and fishers bulged at the brows, the shaved blanch'd faces of orthodox citizens,
The pure, extravagant, yearning, questioning artist's face,
The ugly face of some beautiful soul, the handsome detested or despised face,
The sacred faces of infants, the illuminated face of the mother of many children,
The face of an amour, the face of veneration,
The face as of a dream, the face of an immobile rock,
The face withdrawn of its good and bad, a castrated face,
A wild hawk, his wings clipp'd by the clipper,
A stallion that yielded at last to the thongs and knife of the gelder.

Sauntering the pavement thus, or crossing the ceaseless ferry, faces and faces and faces,
I see them and complain not, and am content with all.

2

Do you suppose I could be content with all if I thought them their own finalè?

This now is too lamentable a face for a man,
Some abject louse asking leave to be, cringing for it,
Some milk-nosed maggot blessing what lets it wrig to its hole.

This face is a dog's snout sniffing for garbage,
Snakes nest in that mouth, I hear the sibilant threat.

This face is a haze more chill than the arctic sea,
Its sleepy and wabbling icebergs crunch as they go.

This is a face of bitter herbs, this an emetic, they need no label,
And more of the drug-shelf, laudanum, caoutchouc, or hog's-lard.

This face is an epilepsy, its wordless tongue gives out the unearthly
    cry,
Its veins down the neck distend, its eyes roll till they show nothing
    but their whites,
Its teeth grit, the palms of the hands are cut by the turn'd-in
    nails,
The man falls struggling and foaming to the ground, while he
    speculates well.

This face is bitten by vermin and worms,
And this is some murderer's knife with a half-pull'd scabbard.

This face owes to the sexton his dismalest fee,
An unceasing death-bell tolls there.

3

Features of my equals would you trick me with your creas'd and
    cadaverous march?
Well, you cannot trick me.

I see your rounded never-erased flow,
I see 'neath the rims of your haggard and mean disguises.

Splay and twist as you like, poke with the tangling fores of fishes
    or rats,
You'll be unmuzzled, you certainly will.

I saw the face of the most smear'd and slobbering idiot they had
    at the asylum,
And I knew for my consolation what they knew not,
I knew of the agents that emptied and broke my brother,[*]
The same wait to clear the rubbish from the fallen tenement,
And I shall look again in a score or two of ages,
And I shall meet the real landlord perfect and unharm'd, every
    inch as good as myself.

4

The Lord advances, and yet advances,
Always the shadow in front, always the reach'd hand bringing up
    the laggards.

Out of this face emerge banners and horses — O superb! I see
    what is coming,
I see the high pioneer-caps, see staves of runners clearing the way,
I hear victorious drums.

This face is a life-boat,
This is the face commanding and bearded, it asks no odds of the
　　rest,
This face is flavor'd fruit ready for eating,
This face of a healthy honest boy is the programme of all good.

These faces bear testimony slumbering or awake,
They show their descent from the Master himself.

Off the word I have spoken I except not one — red, white, black,
　　are all deific,
In each house is the ovum, it comes forth after a thousand years.

Spots or cracks at the windows do not disturb me,
Tall and sufficient stand behind and make signs to me,
I read the promise and patiently wait.

This is a full-grown lily's face,
She speaks to the limber-hipp'd man near the garden pickets,
Come here she blushingly cries, *Come nigh to me limber-hipp'd
　　man,*
Stand at my side till I lean as high as I can upon you,
Fill me with albescent honey, bend down to me,
*Rub to me with your chafing beard, rub to my breast and
　　shoulders.*

5

The old face of the mother of many children,
Whist ! I am fully content.

Lull'd and late is the smoke of the First-day morning,
It hangs low over the rows of trees by the fences,
It hangs thin by the sassafras and wild-cherry and cat-brier under
　　them.

I saw the rich ladies in full dress at the soiree,
I heard what the singers were singing so long,
Heard who sprang in crimson youth from the white froth and the
　　water-blue.

Behold a woman !*
She looks out from her quaker cap, her face is clearer and more
　　beautiful than the sky.

She sits in an armchair under the shaded porch of the farmhouse,
The sun just shines on her old white head.

Her ample gown is of cream-hued linen,
Her grandsons raised the flax, and her grand-daughters spun it
　　with the distaff and the wheel.

The melodious character of the earth,
The finish beyond which philosophy cannot go and does not wish
　　to go,
The justified mother of men.

THE MYSTIC TRUMPETER.

1

HARK, some wild trumpeter, some strange musician,
Hovering unseen in air, vibrates capricious tunes to-night.

I hear thee trumpeter, listening alert I catch thy notes,
Now pouring, whirling like a tempest round me,
Now low, subdued, now in the distance lost.

2

Come nearer bodiless one, haply in thee resounds
Some dead composer, haply thy pensive life
Was fill'd with aspirations high, unform'd ideals,
Waves, oceans musical, chaotically surging,
That now ecstatic ghost, close to me bending, thy cornet echoing,
　　pealing,
Gives out to no one's ears but mine, but freely gives to mine,
That I may thee translate.

3

Blow trumpeter free and clear, I follow thee,
While at thy liquid prelude, glad, serene,
The fretting world, the streets, the noisy hours of day withdraw,
A holy calm descends like dew upon me,
I walk in cool refreshing night the walks of Paradise,
I scent the grass, the moist air and the roses ;
Thy song expands my numb'd imbonded spirit, thou freest,
　　launchest me,
Floating and basking upon heaven's lake.

4

Blow again trumpeter ! and for my sensuous eyes,
Bring the old pageants, show the feudal world.

What charm thy music works ! thou makest pass before me,
Ladies and cavaliers long dead, barons are in their castle halls, the
    troubadours are singing,
Arm'd knights go forth to redress wrongs, some in quest of the
    holy Graal ;
I see the tournament, I see the contestants incased in heavy
    armor seated on stately champing horses,
I hear the shouts, the sounds of blows and smiting steel ;
I see the Crusaders' tumultuous armies — hark, how the cymbals
    clang,
Lo, where the monks walk in advance, bearing the cross on high.

5

Blow again trumpeter ! and for thy theme,
Take now the enclosing theme of all, the solvent and the setting,
Love, that is pulse of all, the sustenance and the pang,
The heart of man and woman all for love,
No other theme but love — knitting, enclosing, all-diffusing love.

O how the immortal phantoms crowd around me !
I see the vast alembic ever working, I see and know the flames
    that heat the world,
The glow, the blush, the beating hearts of lovers,
So blissful happy some, and some so silent, dark, and nigh to
    death ;
Love, that is all the earth to lovers — love, that mocks time and
    space,
Love, that is day and night — love, that is sun and moon and stars,
Love, that is crimson, sumptuous, sick with perfume,
No other words but words of love, no other thought but love.

6

Blow again trumpeter — conjure war's alarums.

Swift to thy spell a shuddering hum like distant thunder rolls,
Lo, where the arm'd men hasten — lo, mid the clouds of dust the
    glint of bayonets,
I see the grime-faced cannoneers, I mark the rosy flash amid the
    smoke, I hear the cracking of the guns ;
Nor war alone — thy fearful music-song, wild player, brings every
    sight of fear,
The deeds of .ruthless brigands, rapine, murder — I hear the cries
    for help !
I see ships foundering at sea, I behold on deck and below deck
    the terrible tableaus.

7

O trumpeter, methinks I am myself the instrument thou playest,
Thou melt'st my heart, my brain — thou movest, drawest, chan-
      gest them at will ;
And now thy sullen notes send darkness through me,
Thou takest away all cheering light, all hope,
I see the enslaved, the overthrown, the hurt, the opprest of the
      whole earth,
I feel the measureless shame and humiliation of my race, it
      becomes all mine,
Mine too the revenges of humanity, the wrongs of ages, baffled
      feuds and hatreds,
Utter defeat upon me weighs — all lost — the foe victorious,
(Yet 'mid the ruins Pride colossal stands unshaken to the last,
Endurance, resolution to the last.)

8

Now trumpeter for thy close,
Vouchsafe a higher strain than any yet,
Sing to my soul, renew its languishing faith and hope,
Rouse up my slow belief, give me some vision of the future,
Give me for once its prophecy and joy.

O glad, exulting, culminating song !
A vigor more than earth's is in thy notes,
Marches of victory — man disenthral'd — the conqueror at last,
Hymns to the universal God from universal man — all joy !
A reborn race appears — a perfect world, all joy !
Women and men in wisdom innocence and health — all joy !
Riotous laughing bacchanals fill'd with joy !
War, sorrow, suffering gone — the rank earth purged — nothing
      but joy left !
The ocean fill'd with joy — the atmosphere all joy !
Joy ! joy ! in freedom, worship, love ! joy in the ecstasy of life !
Enough to merely be ! enough to breathe !
Joy ! joy ! all over joy !

TO A LOCOMOTIVE IN WINTER.

Thee for my recitative,
Thee in the driving storm even as now, the snow, the winter-day
      declining,
Thee in thy panoply, thy measur'd dual throbbing and thy beat
      convulsive,

Thy black cylindric body, golden brass and silvery steel,
Thy ponderous side-bars, parallel and connecting rods, gyrating,
    shuttling at thy sides,
Thy metrical, now swelling pant and roar, now tapering in the
    distance,
Thy great protruding head-light fix'd in front,
Thy long, pale, floating vapor-pennants, tinged with delicate
    purple,
The dense and murky clouds out-belching from thy smoke-stack,
Thy knitted frame, thy springs and valves, the tremulous twinkle
    of thy wheels,
Thy train of cars behind, obedient, merrily following,
Through gale or calm, now swift, now slack, yet steadily careering;
Type of the modern — emblem of motion and power — pulse of
    the continent,
For once come serve the Muse and merge in verse, even as here
    I see thee,
With storm and buffeting gusts of wind and falling snow,
By day thy warning ringing bell to sound its notes,
By night thy silent signal lamps to swing.

Fierce-throated beauty!
Roll through my chant with all thy lawless music, thy swinging
    lamps at night,
Thy madly-whistled laughter, echoing, rumbling like an earth-
    quake, rousing all,
Law of thyself complete, thine own track firmly holding,
(No sweetness debonair of tearful harp or glib piano thine,)
Thy trills of shrieks by rocks and hills return'd,
Launch'd o'er the prairies wide, across the lakes,
To the free skies unpent and glad and strong.

O MAGNET-SOUTH.

O MAGNET-SOUTH! O glistening perfumed South! my South!
O quick mettle, rich blood, impulse and love! good and evil! O
    all dear to me!
O dear to me my birth-things — all moving things and the trees
    where I was born — the grains, plants, rivers,
Dear to me my own slow sluggish rivers where they flow, distant,
    over flats of silvery sands or through swamps,
Dear to me the Roanoke, the Savannah, the Altamahaw, the
    Pedee, the Tombigbee, the Santee, the Coosa and the
    Sabine,

O pensive, far away wandering, I return with my soul to haunt
    their banks again,
Again in Florida I float on transparent lakes, I float on the Okee-
    chobee, I cross the hummock-land or through pleasant
    openings or dense forests,
I see the parrots in the woods, I see the papaw-tree and the blos-
    soming titi;
Again, sailing in my coaster on deck, I coast off Georgia, I coast
    up the Carolinas,
I see where the live-oak is growing, I see where the yellow-pine,
    the scented bay-tree, the lemon and orange, the cypress,
    the graceful palmetto,
I pass rude sea-headlands and enter Pamlico sound through an
    inlet, and dart my vision inland;
O the cotton plant! the growing fields of rice, sugar, hemp!
The cactus guarded with thorns, the laurel-tree with large white
    flowers,
The range afar, the richness and barrenness, the old woods
    charged with mistletoe and trailing moss,
The piney odor and the gloom, the awful natural stillness, (here
    in these dense swamps the freebooter carries his gun, and
    the fugitive has his conceal'd hut;)
O the strange fascination of these half-known half-impassable
    swamps, infested by reptiles, resounding with the bellow
    of the alligator, the sad noises of the night-owl and the
    wild-cat, and the whirr of the rattlesnake,
The mocking-bird, the American mimic, singing all the forenoon,
    singing through the moon-lit night,
The humming-bird, the wild turkey, the raccoon, the opossum;
A Kentucky corn-field, the tall, graceful, long-leav'd corn, slender,
    flapping, bright green, with tassels, with beautiful ears each
    well-sheath'd in its husk;
O my heart! O tender and fierce pangs, I can stand them not, I
    will depart;
O to be a Virginian where I grew up! O to be a Carolinian!
O longings irrepressible! O I will go back to old Tennessee and
    never wander more.

MANNAHATTA.*

I WAS asking for something specific and perfect for my city,
Whereupon lo! upsprang the aboriginal name.

Now I see what there is in a name, a word, liquid, sane, unruly,
    musical, self-sufficient,

I see that the word of my city is that word from of old,
Because I see that word nested in nests of water-bays, superb,
Rich, hemm'd thick all around with sailships and steamships, an
     island sixteen miles long, solid-founded,
Numberless crowded streets, high growths of iron, slender, strong,
     light, splendidly uprising toward clear skies,
Tides swift and ample, well-loved by me, toward sundown,
The flowing sea-currents, the little islands, larger adjoining islands,
     the heights, the villas,
The countless masts, the white shore-steamers, the lighters, the
     ferry-boats, the black sea-steamers well-model'd,
The down-town streets, the jobbers' houses of business, the houses
     of business of the ship-merchants and money-brokers, the
     river-streets,
Immigrants arriving, fifteen or twenty thousand in a week,
The carts hauling goods, the manly race of drivers of horses, the
     brown-faced sailors,
The summer air, the bright sun shining, and the sailing clouds
     aloft,
The winter snows, the sleigh-bells, the broken ice in the river,
     passing along up or down with the flood-tide or ebb-tide,
The mechanics of the city, the masters, well-form'd, beautiful-
     faced, looking you straight in the eyes,
Trottoirs throng'd, vehicles, Broadway, the women, the shops and
     shows,
A million people — manners free and superb — open voices —
     hospitality — the most courageous and friendly young men,
City of hurried and sparkling waters! city of spires and masts!
City nested in bays! my city!

ALL IS TRUTH.

O ME, man of slack faith so long,
Standing aloof, denying portions so long,
Only aware to-day of compact all-diffused truth,
Discovering to-day there is no lie or form of lie, and can be none,
     but grows as inevitably upon itself as the truth does upon
     itself,
Or as any law of the earth or any natural production of the earth
     does.

(This is curious and may not be realized immediately, but it must
     be realized,
I feel in myself that I represent falsehoods equally with the rest,
And that the universe does.)

Where has fail'd a perfect return indifferent of lies or the truth?
Is it upon the ground, or in water or fire? or in the spirit of man?
     or in the meat and blood?

Meditating among liars and retreating sternly into myself, I see
     that there are really no liars or lies after all,
And that nothing fails its perfect return, and that what are called
     lies are perfect returns,
And that each thing exactly represents itself and what has pre-
     ceded it,
And that the truth includes all, and is compact just as much as
     space is compact,
And that there is no flaw or vacuum in the amount of the truth —
     but that all is truth without exception;
And henceforth I will go celebrate any thing I see or am,
And sing and laugh and deny nothing.

A RIDDLE SONG.

THAT which eludes this verse and any verse,
Unheard by sharpest ear, unform'd in clearest eye or cunningest
     mind,
Nor lore nor fame, nor happiness nor wealth,
And yet the pulse of every heart and life throughout the world
     incessantly,
Which you and I and all pursuing ever ever miss,
Open but still a secret, the real of the real, an illusion,
Costless, vouchsafed to each, yet never man the owner,
Which poets vainly seek to put in rhyme, historians in prose,
Which sculptor never chisel'd yet, nor painter painted,
Which vocalist never sung, nor orator nor actor ever utter'd,
Invoking here and now I challenge for my song.

Indifferently, 'mid public, private haunts, in solitude,
Behind the mountain and the wood,
Companion of the city's busiest streets, through the assemblage,
It and its radiations constantly glide.

In looks of fair unconscious babes,
Or strangely in the coffin'd dead,
Or show of breaking dawn or stars by night,
As some dissolving delicate film of dreams,
Hiding yet lingering.

Two little breaths of words comprising it,
Two words,* yet all from first to last comprised in it.

How ardently for it !
How many ships have sail'd and sunk for it !
How many travelers started from their homes and ne'er return'd !
How much of genius boldly staked and lost for it !
What countless stores of beauty, love, ventur'd for it !
How all superbest deeds since Time began are traceable to it —
    and shall be to the end !
How all heroic martyrdoms to it !
How, justified by it, the horrors, evils, battles of the earth !
How the bright fascinating lambent flames of it, in every age and
    land, have drawn men's eyes,
Rich as a sunset on the Norway coast, the sky, the islands, and the
    cliffs,
Or midnight's silent glowing northern lights unreachable.

Haply God's riddle it, so vague and yet so certain,
The soul for it, and all the visible universe for it,
And heaven at last for it.

EXCELSIOR.

Who has gone farthest ? for I would go farther,
And who has been just ? for I would be the most just person of
    the earth,
And who most cautious ? for I would be more cautious,
And who has been happiest ? O I think it is I — I think no one
    was ever happier than I,
And who has lavish'd all ? for I lavish constantly the best I have,
And who proudest ? for I think I have reason to be the proudest
    son alive — for I am the son of the brawny and tall-topt
    city,
And who has been bold and true ? for I would be the boldest and
    truest being of the universe,
And who benevolent ? for I would show more benevolence than
    all the rest,
And who has receiv'd the love of the most friends ? for I know
    what it is to receive the passionate love of many friends,
And who possesses a perfect and enamour'd body ? for I do not
    believe any one possesses a more perfect or enamour'd
    body than mine,
And who thinks the amplest thoughts ? for I would surround those
    thoughts,
And who has made hymns fit for the earth ? for I am mad with de-
    vouring ecstasy to make joyous hymns for the whole earth.

AH POVERTIES, WINCINGS, AND SULKY RETREATS.

Ah poverties, wincings, and sulky retreats,
Ah you foes that in conflict have overcome me,
(For what is my life or any man's life but a conflict with foes, the
    old, the incessant war?)
You degradations, you tussle with passions and appetites,
You smarts from dissatisfied friendships, (ah wounds the sharpest
    of all!)
You toil of painful and choked articulations, you meannesses,
You shallow tongue-talks at tables, (my tongue the shallowest of
    any;)
You broken resolutions, you racking angers, you smother'd ennuis!
Ah think not you finally triumph, my real self has yet to come
    forth,
It shall yet march forth o'ermastering, till all lies beneath me,
It shall yet stand up the soldier of ultimate victory.

THOUGHTS.

Of public opinion,
Of a calm and cool fiat sooner or later, (how impassive! how
    certain and final!)
Of the President with pale face asking secretly to himself, *What
    will the people say at last?*
Of the frivolous Judge — of the corrupt Congressman, Governor,
    Mayor — of such as these standing helpless and exposed,
Of the mumbling and screaming priest, (soon, soon deserted,)
Of the lessening year by year of venerableness, and of the dicta
    of officers, statutes, pulpits, schools,
Of the rising forever taller and stronger and broader of the intui-
    tions of men and women, and of Self-esteem and Per-
    sonality;
Of the true New World — of the Democracies resplendent en-
    masse,
Of the conformity of politics, armies, navies, to them,
Of the shining sun by them — of the inherent light, greater than
    the rest,
Of the envelopment of all by them, and the effusion of all from
    them.

MEDIUMS.

They shall arise in the States,
They shall report Nature, laws, physiology, and happiness,
They shall illustrate Democracy and the kosmos,

They shall be alimentive, amative,* perceptive,
They shall be complete women and men, their pose brawny and
    supple, their drink water, their blood clean and clear,
They shall fully enjoy materialism and the sight of products, they
    shall enjoy the sight of the beef, lumber, bread-stuffs, of
    Chicago the great city,
They shall train themselves to go in public to become orators and
    oratresses,
Strong and sweet shall their tongues be, poems and materials of
    poems shall come from their lives, they shall be makers
    and finders,
Of them and of their works shall emerge divine conveyers, to
    convey gospels,
Characters, events, retrospections, shall be convey'd in gospels,
    trees, animals, waters, shall be convey'd,
Death, the future, the invisible faith, shall all be convey'd.

WEAVE IN, MY HARDY LIFE.

WEAVE in, weave in, my hardy life,
Weave yet a soldier strong and full for great campaigns to come,
Weave in red blood, weave sinews in like ropes, the senses, sight
    weave in,
Weave lasting sure, weave day and night the weft, the warp,
    incessant weave, tire not,
(We know not what the use O life, nor know the aim, the end,
    nor really aught we know,
But know the work, the need goes on and shall go on, the death-
    envelop'd march of peace as well as war goes on,)
For great campaigns of peace the same the wiry threads to weave,
We know not why or what, yet weave, forever weave.

SPAIN, 1873-74.

OUT of the murk of heaviest clouds,
Out of the feudal wrecks and heap'd-up skeletons of kings,
Out of that old entire European debris, the shatter'd mummeries,
Ruin'd cathedrals, crumble of palaces, tombs of priests,
Lo, Freedom's features fresh undimm'd look forth — the same
    immortal face looks forth ;
(A glimpse as of thy Mother's face Columbia,
A flash significant as of a sword,
Beaming towards thee.)

Nor think we forget thee maternal;
Lag'd'st thou so long? shall the clouds close again upon thee?
Ah, but thou hast thyself now appear'd to us — we know thee,
Thou hast given us a sure proof, the glimpse of thyself,
Thou waitest there as everywhere thy time.

BY BROAD POTOMAC'S SHORE.

By broad Potomac's shore, again old tongue,
(Still uttering, still ejaculating, canst never cease this babble?)
Again old heart so gay, again to you, your sense, the full flush
　　　　spring returning,
Again the freshness and the odors, again Virginia's summer sky,
　　　　pellucid blue and silver,
Again the forenoon purple of the hills,
Again the deathless grass, so noiseless soft and green,
Again the blood-red roses blooming.

Perfume this book of mine O blood-red roses!
Lave subtly with your waters every line Potomac!
Give me of you O spring, before I close, to put between its
　　　　pages!
O forenoon purple of the hills, before I close, of you!
O deathless grass, of you!

FROM FAR DAKOTA'S CAÑONS.

June 25, 1876.

FROM far Dakota's cañons,
Lands of the wild ravine, the dusky Sioux, the lonesome stretch,
　　　　the silence,
Haply to-day a mournful wail, haply a trumpet-note for heroes.

The battle-bulletin,
The Indian ambuscade, the craft, the fatal environment,
The cavalry companies fighting to the last in sternest heroism,
In the midst of their little circle, with their slaughter'd horses for
　　　　breastworks,
The fall of Custer and all his officers and men.

Continues yet the old, old legend of our race,
The loftiest of life upheld by death,
The ancient banner perfectly maintain'd,
O lesson opportune, O how I welcome thee!

As sitting in dark days,
Lone, sulky, through the time's thick murk looking in vain for light,
  for hope,
From unsuspected parts a fierce and momentary proof,
(The sun there at the centre though conceal'd,
Electric life forever at the centre,)
Breaks forth a lightning flash.

Thou of the tawny flowing hair in battle,
I erewhile saw, with erect head, pressing ever in front, bearing a
  bright sword in thy hand,
Now ending well in death the splendid fever of thy deeds,
(I bring no dirge for it or thee, I bring a glad triumphal sonnet,)
Desperate and glorious, aye in defeat most desperate, most glorious,
After thy many battles in which never yielding up a gun or a color,
Leaving behind thee a memory sweet to soldiers,
Thou yieldest up thyself.

OLD WAR-DREAMS.

IN midnight sleep of many a face of anguish,
Of the look at first of the mortally wounded, (of that indescribable
  look,)
Of the dead on their backs with arms extended wide,
   I dream, I dream, I dream.

Of scenes of Nature, fields and mountains,
Of skies so beauteous after a storm, and at night the moon so
  unearthly bright,
Shining sweetly, shining down, where we dig the trenches and
  gather the heaps,
   I dream, I dream, I dream.

Long have they pass'd, faces and trenches and fields,
Where through the carnage I moved with a callous composure,
  or away from the fallen,
Onward I sped at the time — but now of their forms at night,
   I dream, I dream, I dream.

THICK-SPRINKLED BUNTING.

THICK-SPRINKLED bunting! flag of stars!
Long yet your road, fateful flag — long yet your road, and lined
  with bloody death,

For the prize I see at issue at last is the world,
All its ships and shores I see interwoven with your threads greedy
      banner;
Dream'd again the flags of kings, highest borne, to flaunt unrival'd?
O hasten flag of man — O with sure and steady step, passing
      highest flags of kings,
Walk supreme to the heavens mighty symbol — run up above
      them all,
Flag of stars! thick-sprinkled bunting!

WHAT BEST I SEE IN THEE.

To U. S. G. return'd from his World's Tour.

What best I see in thee,
Is not that where thou mov'st down history's great highways,
Ever undimm'd by time shoots warlike victory's dazzle,
Or that thou sat'st where Washington sat, ruling the land in peace,
Or thou the man whom feudal Europe feted, venerable Asia
      swarm'd upon,
Who walk'd with kings with even pace the round world's prome-
      nade;
But that in foreign lands, in all thy walks with kings,
Those prairie sovereigns of the West, Kansas, Missouri, Illinois,
Ohio's, Indiana's millions, comrades, farmers, soldiers, all to the
      front,
Invisibly with thee walking with kings with even pace the round
      world's promenade,
Were all so justified.

SPIRIT THAT FORM'D THIS SCENE.

Written in Platte Cañon, Colorado.

Spirit that form'd this scene,
These tumbled rock-piles grim and red,
These reckless heaven-ambitious peaks,
These gorges, turbulent-clear streams, this naked freshness,
These formless wild arrays, for reasons of their own,
I know thee, savage spirit — we have communed together,
Mine too such wild arrays, for reasons of their own;
Was't charged against my chants they had forgotten art?
To fuse within themselves its rules precise and delicatesse?
The lyrist's measur'd beat, the wrought-out temple's grace —
      column and polish'd arch forgot?
But thou that revelest here — spirit that form'd this scene,
They have remember'd thee.

AS I WALK THESE BROAD MAJESTIC DAYS.

As I walk these broad majestic days of peace,
(For the war, the struggle of blood finish'd, wherein, O terrific Ideal,
Against vast odds erewhile having gloriously won,
Now thou stridest on, yet perhaps in time toward denser wars,
Perhaps to engage in time in still more dreadful contests, dangers,
Longer campaigns and crises, labors beyond all others,)
Around me I hear that eclat of the world, politics, produce,
The announcements of recognized things, science,
The approved growth of cities and the spread of inventions.

I see the ships, (they will last a few years,)
The vast factories with their foremen and workmen,
And hear the indorsement of all, and do not object to it.

But I too announce solid things,
Science, ships, politics, cities, factories, are not nothing,
Like a grand procession to music of distant bugles pouring,
    triumphantly moving, and grander heaving in sight,
They stand for realities — all is as it should be.

Then my realities;
What else is so real as mine?
Libertad and the divine average, freedom to every slave on the
    face of the earth,
The rapt promises and luminè of seers, the spiritual world, these
    centuries-lasting songs,
And our visions, the visions of poets, the most solid announce-
    ments of any.

A CLEAR MIDNIGHT.

This is thy hour O Soul, thy free flight into the wordless,
Away from books, away from art, the day erased, the lesson done,
Thee fully forth emerging, silent, gazing, pondering the themes
    thou lovest best,
Night, sleep, death and the stars.

SONGS OF PARTING.

AS THE TIME DRAWS NIGH.

As the time draws nigh glooming a cloud,
A dread beyond of I know not what darkens me.

I shall go forth,
I shall traverse the States awhile, but I cannot tell whither or how
    long,
Perhaps soon some day or night while I am singing my voice will
    suddenly cease.

O book, O chants ! must all then amount to but this ?
Must we barely arrive at this beginning of us ?— and yet it is
    enough, O soul ;
O soul, we have positively appear'd — that is enough.

YEARS OF THE MODERN.

YEARS of the modern ! years of the unperform'd !
Your horizon rises, I see it parting away for more august dramas,
I see not America only, not only Liberty's nation but other nations
    preparing,
I see tremendous entrances and exits, new combinations, the soli-
    darity of races,
I see that force advancing with irresistible power on the world's
    stage,
(Have the old forces, the old wars, played their parts ? are the
    acts suitable to them closed ?)
I see Freedom, completely arm'd and victorious and very haughty,
    with Law on one side and Peace on the other,
A stupendous trio all issuing forth against the idea of caste ;
What historic denouements are these we so rapidly approach ?
I see men marching and countermarching by swift millions,
I see the frontiers and boundaries of the old aristocracies broken,
I see the landmarks of European kings removed,
I see this day the People beginning their landmarks, (all others
    give way ;)
Never were such sharp questions ask'd as this day,
Never was average man, his soul, more energetic, more like a God,

Lo, how he urges and urges, leaving the masses no rest !

His daring foot is on land and sea everywhere, he colonizes the
    Pacific, the archipelagoes,

With the steamship, the electric telegraph, the newspaper, the
    wholesale engines of war,

With these and the world-spreading factories he interlinks all
    geography, all lands ;

What whispers are these O lands, running ahead of you, passing
    under the seas ?

Are all nations communing ? is there going to be but one heart to
    the globe ?

Is humanity forming en-masse ? for lo, tyrants tremble, crowns
    grow dim,

The earth, restive, confronts a new era, perhaps a general divine war,

No one knows what will happen next, such portents fill the days
    and nights ;

Years prophetical ! the space ahead as I walk, as I vainly try to
    pierce it, is full of phantoms,

Unborn deeds, things soon to be, project their shapes around me,

This incredible rush and heat, this strange ecstatic fever of dreams
    O years !

Your dreams O years, how they penetrate through me ! (I know
    not whether I sleep or wake ;)

The perform'd America and Europe grow dim, retiring in shadow
    behind me,

The unperform'd, more gigantic than ever, advance, advance upon
    me.

ASHES OF SOLDIERS.

ASHES of soldiers South or North,
As I muse retrospective murmuring a chant in thought,
The war resumes, again to my sense your shapes,
And again the advance of the armies.

Noiseless as mists and vapors,
From their graves in the trenches ascending,
From cemeteries all through Virginia and Tennessee,
From every point of the compass out of the countless graves,
In wafted clouds, in myriads large, or squads of twos or threes or
    single ones they come,
And silently gather round me.

Now sound no note O trumpeters,
Not at the head of my cavalry parading on spirited horses,

With sabres drawn and glistening, and carbines by their thighs, (ah
    my brave horsemen !
My handsome tan-faced horsemen ! what life, what joy and pride,
With all the perils were yours.)

Nor you drummers, neither at reveillé at dawn,
Nor the long roll alarming the camp, nor even the muffled beat
    for a burial,
Nothing from you this time O drummers bearing my warlike drums.

But aside from these and the marts of wealth and the crowded
    promenade,
Admitting around me comrades close unseen by the rest and
    voiceless,
The slain elate and alive again, the dust and debris alive,
I chant this chant of my silent soul in the name of all dead
    soldiers.

Faces so pale with wondrous eyes, very dear, gather closer yet,
Draw close, but speak not.

Phantoms of countless lost,
Invisible to the rest henceforth become my companions,
Follow me ever — desert me not while I live.

Sweet are the blooming cheeks of the living — sweet are the musi-
    cal voices sounding,
But sweet, ah sweet, are the dead with their silent eyes.

Dearest comrades, all is over and long gone,
But love is not over — and what love, O comrades !
Perfume from battle-fields rising, up from the fœtor arising.

Perfume therefore my chant, O love, immortal love,
Give me to bathe the memories of all dead soldiers,
Shroud them, embalm them, cover them all over with tender pride.

Perfume all — make all wholesome,
Make these ashes to nourish and blossom,
O love, solve all, fructify all with the last chemistry.

Give me exhaustless, make me a fountain,
That I exhale love from me wherever I go like a moist perennial
    dew,
For the ashes of all dead soldiers South or North.

THOUGHTS.

1

Of these years I sing,

How they pass and have pass'd through convuls'd pains, as through parturitions,

How America illustrates birth, muscular youth, the promise, the sure fulfilment, the absolute success, despite of people — illustrates evil as well as good,

The vehement struggle so fierce for unity in one's-self;

How many hold despairingly yet to the models departed, caste, myths, obedience, compulsion, and to infidelity,

How few see the arrived models, the athletes, the Western States, or see freedom or spirituality, or hold any faith in results,

(But I see the athletes, and I see the results of the war glorious and inevitable, and they again leading to other results.)

How the great cities appear — how the Democratic masses, turbulent, wilful, as I love them,

How the whirl, the contest, the wrestle of evil with good, the sounding and resounding, keep on and on,

How society waits unform'd, and is for a while between things ended and things begun,

How America is the continent of glories, and of the triumph of freedom and of the Democracies, and of the fruits of society, and of all that is begun,

And how the States are complete in themselves — and how all triumphs and glories are complete in themselves, to lead onward,

And how these of mine and of the States will in their turn be convuls'd, and serve other parturitions and transitions,

And how all people, sights, combinations, the democratic masses too, serve — and how every fact, and war itself, with all its horrors, serves,

And how now or at any time each serves the exquisite transition of death.

2

Of seeds dropping into the ground, of births,

Of the steady concentration of America, inland, upward, to impregnable and swarming places,

Of what Indiana, Kentucky, Arkansas, and the rest, are to be,

Of what a few years will show there in Nebraska, Colorado, Nevada, and the rest,

(Or afar, mounting the Northern Pacific to Sitka or Aliaska,)

Of what the feuillage of America is the preparation for — and of
    what all sights, North, South, East and West, are,
Of this Union welded in blood, of the solemn price paid, of the
    unnamed lost ever present in my mind ;
Of the temporary use of materials for identity's sake,
Of the present, passing, departing — of the growth of completer
    men than any yet,
Of all sloping down there where the fresh free giver the mother,
    the Mississippi flows,
Of mighty inland cities yet unsurvey'd and unsuspected,
Of the new and good names, of the modern developments, of
    inalienable homesteads,
Of a free and original life there, of simple diet and clean and
    sweet blood,
Of litheness, majestic faces, clear eyes, and perfect physique there,
Of immense spiritual results future years far West, each side of the
    Anahuacs,*
Of these songs, well understood there, (being made for that area,)
Of the native scorn of grossness and gain there,
(O it lurks in me night and day — what is gain after all to savage-
    ness and freedom?)

SONG AT SUNSET.

Splendor of ended day floating and filling me,
Hour prophetic, hour resuming the past,
Inflating my throat, you divine average,
You earth and life till the last ray gleams I sing.

Open mouth of my soul uttering gladness,
Eyes of my soul seeing perfection,
Natural life of me faithfully praising things,
Corroborating forever the triumph of things.

Illustrious every one !
Illustrious what we name space, sphere of unnumber'd spirits,
Illustrious the mystery of motion in all beings, even the tiniest
    insect,
Illustrious the attribute of speech, the senses, the body,
Illustrious the passing light — illustrious the pale reflection on the
    new moon in the western sky,
Illustrious whatever I see or hear or touch, to the last.

Good in all,
In the satisfaction and aplomb of animals,

In the annual return of the seasons,
In the hilarity of youth,
In the strength and flush of manhood,
In the grandeur and exquisiteness of old age,
In the superb vistas of death.

Wonderful to depart!
Wonderful to be here!
The heart, to jet the all-alike and innocent blood!
To breathe the air, how delicious!
To speak — to walk — to seize something by the hand!
To prepare for sleep, for bed, to look on my rose-color'd flesh!
To be conscious of my body, so satisfied, so large!
To be this incredible God I am!
To have gone forth among other Gods, these men and women I
    love.

Wonderful how I celebrate you and myself!
How my thoughts play subtly at the spectacles around!
How the clouds pass silently overhead!
How the earth darts on and on! and how the sun, moon, stars,
    dart on and on!
How the water sports and sings! (surely it is alive!)
How the trees rise and stand up, with strong trunks, with branches
    and leaves!
(Surely there is something more in each of the trees, some living
    soul.)

O amazement of things — even the least particle!
O spirituality of things!
O strain musical flowing through ages and continents, now reaching
    me and America!
I take your strong chords, intersperse them, and cheerfully pass
    them forward.

I too carol the sun, usher'd or at noon, or as now, setting,
I too throb to the brain and beauty of the earth and of all the
    growths of the earth,
I too have felt the resistless call of myself.

As I steam'd down the Mississippi,
As I wander'd over the prairies,
As I have lived, as I have look'd through my windows my eyes,
As I went forth in the morning, as I beheld the light breaking in
    the east,

As I bathed on the beach of the Eastern Sea, and again on the
      beach of the Western Sea,
As I roam'd the streets of inland Chicago, whatever streets I have
      roam'd,
Or cities or silent woods, or even amid the sights of war,
Wherever I have been I have charged myself with contentment
      and triumph.

I sing to the last the equalities modern or old,
I sing the endless finalés of things,
I say Nature continues, glory continues,
I praise with electric voice,
For I do not see one imperfection in the universe,
And I do not see one cause or result lamentable at last in the
      universe.

O setting sun ! though the time has come,
I still warble under you, if none else does, unmitigated adoration.

AS AT THY PORTALS ALSO DEATH.

As at thy portals also death,
Entering thy sovereign, dim, illimitable grounds,
To memories of my mother, to the divine blending, maternity,
To her, buried and gone, yet buried not, gone not from me,
(I see again the calm benignant face fresh and beautiful still,
I sit by the form in the coffin,
I kiss and kiss convulsively again the sweet old lips, the cheeks,
      the closed eyes in the coffin ;)
To her, the ideal woman, practical, spiritual, of all of earth, life,
      love, to me the best,
I grave a monumental line, before I go, amid these songs,
And set a tombstone here.

MY LEGACY.

THE business man the acquirer vast,
After assiduous years surveying results, preparing for departure,
Devises houses and lands to his children, bequeaths stocks, goods,
      funds for a school or hospital,
Leaves money to certain companions to buy tokens, souvenirs of
      gems and gold.

But I, my life surveying, closing,

With nothing to show to devise from its idle years,
Nor houses nor lands, nor tokens of gems or gold for my friends,
Yet certain remembrances of the war for you, and after you,
And little souvenirs of camps and soldiers, with my love,
I bind together and bequeath in this bundle of songs.

PENSIVE ON HER DEAD GAZING.

PENSIVE on her dead gazing I heard the Mother of All,
Desperate on the torn bodies, on the forms covering the battle-
fields gazing,
(As the last gun ceased, but the scent of the powder-smoke
linger'd,)
As she call'd to her earth with mournful voice while she stalk'd,
Absorb them well O my earth, she cried, I charge you lose not
my sons, lose not an atom,
And you streams absorb them well, taking their dear blood,
And you local spots, and you airs that swim above lightly
impalpable,
And all you essences of soil and growth, and you my rivers' depths,
And you mountain sides, and the woods where my dear children's
blood trickling redden'd,
And you trees down in your roots to bequeath to all future trees,
My dead absorb or South or North — my young men's bodies
absorb, and their precious precious blood,
Which holding in trust for me faithfully back again give me many
a year hence,
In unseen essence and odor of surface and grass, centuries hence,
In blowing airs from the fields back again give me my darlings,
give my immortal heroes,
Exhale me them centuries hence, breathe me their breath, let not
an atom be lost,
O years and graves! O air and soil! O my dead, an aroma sweet!
Exhale them perennial sweet death, years, centuries hence.

CAMPS OF GREEN.

NOT alone those camps of white, old comrades of the wars,
When as order'd forward, after a long march,
Footsore and weary, soon as the light lessens we halt for the night,
Some of us so fatigued carrying the gun and knapsack, dropping
asleep in our tracks,
Others pitching the little tents, and the fires lit up begin to
sparkle,

Outposts of pickets posted surrounding alert through the dark,
And a word provided for countersign, careful for safety,
Till to the call of the drummers at daybreak loudly beating the
    drums,
We rise up refresh'd, the night and sleep pass'd over, and resume
    our journey,
Or proceed to battle.

Lo, the camps of the tents of green,
Which the days of peace keep filling, and the days of war keep
    filling,
With a mystic army, (is it too order'd forward? is it too only halt-
    ing awhile,
Till night and sleep pass over?)

Now in those camps of green, in their tents dotting the world,
In the parents, children, husbands, wives, in them, in the old and
    young,
Sleeping under the sunlight, sleeping under the moonlight, content
    and silent there at last,
Behold the mighty bivouac-field and waiting-camp of all,
Of the corps and generals all, and the President over the corps
    and generals all,
And of each of us O soldiers, and of each and all in the ranks we
    fought,
(There without hatred we all, all meet.)

For presently O soldiers, we too camp in our place in the bivouac-
    camps of green,
But we need not provide for outposts, nor word for the counter-
    sign,
Nor drummer to beat the morning drum.

THE SOBBING OF THE BELLS.*

(*Midnight*, *Sept.* 19-20, 1881.)

THE sobbing of the bells, the sudden death-news everywhere,
The slumberers rouse, the rapport of the People,
(Full well they know that message in the darkness,
Full well return, respond within their breasts, their brains, the sad
    reverberations,)
The passionate toll and clang — city to city, joining, sounding,
    passing,
Those heart-beats of a Nation in the night.

AS THEY DRAW TO A CLOSE.

As they draw to a close,
Of what underlies the precedent songs — of my aims in them,
Of the seed I have sought to plant in them,
Of joy, sweet joy, through many a year, in them,
(For them, for them have I lived, in them my work is done,)
Of many an aspiration fond, of many a dream and plan ;
Through Space and Time fused in a chant, and the flowing eternal
    identity,
To Nature encompassing these, encompassing God — to the joy-
    ous, electric all,
To the sense of Death, and accepting exulting in Death in its
    turn the same as life,
The entrance of man to sing ;
To compact you, ye parted, diverse lives,
To put rapport the mountains and rocks and streams,
And the winds of the north, and the forests of oak and pine,
With you O soul.

JOY, SHIPMATE, JOY!

Joy, shipmate, joy !
(Pleas'd to my soul at death I cry,)
Our life is closed, our life begins,
The long, long anchorage we leave,
The ship is clear at last, she leaps !
She swiftly courses from the shore,
Joy, shipmate, joy.

THE UNTOLD WANT.

THE untold want by life and land ne'er granted,
Now voyager sail thou forth to seek and find.

PORTALS.

WHAT are those of the known but to ascend and enter the
    Unknown?
And what are those of life but for Death?

THESE CAROLS.

THESE carols sung to cheer my passage through the world I see,
For completion I dedicate to the Invisible World.

NOW FINALÈ TO THE SHORE.

Now finalè to the shore,
Now land and life finalè and farewell,
Now Voyager depart, (much, much for thee is yet in store,)
Often enough hast thou adventur'd o'er the seas,
Cautiously cruising, studying the charts,
Duly again to port and hawser's tie returning;
But now obey thy cherish'd secret wish,
Embrace thy friends, leave all in order,
To port and hawser's tie no more returning,
Depart upon thy endless cruise old Sailor.

SO LONG!

To conclude, I announce what comes after me.

I remember I said before my leaves sprang at all,
I would raise my voice jocund and strong with reference to con-
    summations.

When America does what was promis'd,
When through these States walk a hundred millions of superb
    persons,
When the rest part away for superb persons and contribute to them,
When breeds of the most perfect mothers denote America,
Then to me and mine our due fruition.

I have press'd through in my own right,
I have sung the body and the soul, war and peace have I sung,
    and the songs of life and death,
And the songs of birth, and shown that there are many births.

I have offer'd my style to every one, I have journey'd with confi-
    dent step;
While my pleasure is yet at the full I whisper *So long!*
And take the young woman's hand and the young man's hand for
    the last time.

I announce natural persons to arise,
I announce justice triumphant,
I announce uncompromising liberty and equality,
I announce the justification of candor and the justification of
    pride.

I announce that the identity of these States is a single identity
 only,
I announce the Union more and more compact, indissoluble,
I announce splendors and majesties to make all the previous poli-
 tics of the earth insignificant.

I announce adhesiveness, I say it shall be limitless, unloosen'd,
I say you shall yet find the friend you were looking for.

I announce a man or woman coming, perhaps you are the one,
 (*So long!*)
I announce the great individual, fluid as Nature, chaste, affection-
 ate, compassionate, fully arm'd.

I announce a life that shall be copious, vehement, spiritual, bold,
I announce an end that shall lightly and joyfully meet its transla-
 tion.

I announce myriads of youths, beautiful, gigantic, sweet-blooded,
I announce a race of splendid and savage old men.

O thicker and faster — (*So long!*)
O crowding too close upon me,
I foresee too much, it means more than I thought,
It appears to me I am dying.

Hasten throat and sound your last,
Salute me — salute the days once more. Peal the old cry once
 more.

Screaming electric, the atmosphere using,
At random glancing, each as I notice absorbing,
Swiftly on, but a little while alighting,
Curious envelop'd messages delivering,
Sparkles hot, seed ethereal down in the dirt dropping,
Myself unknowing, my commission obeying, to question it never
 daring,
To ages and ages yet the growth of the seed leaving,
To troops out of the war arising, they the tasks I have set promul-
 ging,
To women certain whispers of myself bequeathing, their affection
 me more clearly explaining,
To young men my problems offering — no dallier I — I the mus-
 cle of their brains trying,
So I pass, a little time vocal, visible, contrary,

Afterward a melodious echo, passionately bent for, (death making
    me really undying,)
The best of me then when no longer visible, for toward that I have
    been incessantly preparing.

What is there more, that I lag and pause and crouch extended
    with unshut mouth?
Is there a single final farewell?

My songs cease, I abandon them,
From behind the screen where I hid I advance personally solely
    to you.

Camerado, this is no book,
Who touches this touches a man,
(Is it night? are we here together alone?)
It is I you hold and who holds you,
I spring from the pages into your arms — decease calls me forth.

O how your fingers drowse me,
Your breath falls around me like dew, your pulse lulls the tympans
    of my ears,
I feel immerged from head to foot,
Delicious, enough.

Enough O deed impromptu and secret,
Enough O gliding present — enough O summ'd-up past.

Dear friend whoever you are take this kiss,
I give it especially to you, do not forget me,
I feel like one who has done work for the day to retire awhile,
I receive now again of my many translations, from my avataras as-
    cending, while others doubtless await me,
An unknown sphere more real than I dream'd, more direct, darts
    awakening rays about me, *So long!*
Remember my words, I may again return,
I love you, I depart from materials,
I am as one disembodied, triumphant, dead.

ANNEX

TO PRECEDING PAGES.

SANDS AT SEVENTY.

(See " NOVEMBER BOUGHS.")*

CONTENTS.

(384)

SANDS AT SEVENTY

MANNAHATTA.*

My city's fit and noble name resumed,
Choice aboriginal name, with marvellous beauty, meaning,
*A rocky founded island—shores where ever gayly dash the coming,
going, hurrying sea waves.*

PAUMANOK.*

Sea-beauty! stretch'd and basking!
One side thy inland ocean laving, broad, with copious commerce,
steamers, sails,
And one the Atlantic's wind caressing, fierce or gentle—mighty
hulls dark-gliding in the distance.
Isle of sweet brooks of drinking-water—healthy air and soil!
Isle of the salty shore and breeze and brine!

FROM MONTAUK POINT.*

I stand as on some mighty eagle's beak,
Eastward the sea absorbing, viewing, (nothing but sea and sky,)
The tossing waves, the foam, the ships in the distance,
The wild unrest, the snowy, curling caps—that inbound urge
and urge of waves,
Seeking the shores forever.

TO THOSE WHO'VE FAIL'D.

To those who've fail'd, in aspiration vast,
To unnam'd soldiers fallen in front on the lead,
To calm, devoted engineers—to over-ardent travelers—to pilots
on their ships,
To many a lofty song and picture without recognition—I'd rear
a laurel-cover'd monument,
High, high above the rest—To all cut off before their time,
Possess'd by some strange spirit of fire,
Quench'd by an early death.

A CAROL CLOSING SIXTY-NINE.

A carol closing sixty-nine—a *résumé*—a repetition,
My lines in joy and hope continuing on the same,
Of ye, O God, Life, Nature, Freedom, Poetry ;
Of you, my Land—your rivers, prairies, States—you, mottled
    Flag I love,
Your aggregate retain'd entire—Of north, south, east and west,
    your items all ;
Of me myself—the jocund heart yet beating in my breast,
The body wreck'd, old, poor and paralyzed—the strange inertia
    falling pall-like round me,
The burning fires down in my sluggish blood not yet extinct,
The undiminish'd faith—the groups of loving friends.

THE BRAVEST SOLDIERS.

Brave, brave were the soldiers (high named to-day) who lived
    through the fight ;
But the bravest press'd to the front and fell, unnamed, unknown.

A FONT OF TYPE.

This latent mine—these unlaunch'd voices—passionate powers,
Wrath, argument, or praise, or comic leer, or prayer devout,
(Not nonpareil, brevier, bourgeois, long primer merely,)
These ocean waves arousable to fury and to death,
Or sooth'd to ease and sheeny sun and sleep,
Within the pallid slivers slumbering.

AS I SIT WRITING HERE.

As I sit writing here, sick and grown old,
Not my least burden is that dulness of the years, querilities,
Ungracious glooms, aches, lethargy, constipation, whimpering
    ennui,
May filter in my daily songs.

MY CANARY BIRD.

Did we count great, O soul, to penetrate the themes of mighty
    books,
Absorbing deep and full from thoughts, plays, speculations ?
But now from thee to me, caged bird, to feel thy joyous warble,
Filling the air, the lonesome room, the long forenoon,
Is it not just as great, O soul ?

QUERIES TO MY SEVENTIETH YEAR.

Approaching, nearing, curious,
Thou dim, uncertain spectre—bringest thou life or death?
Strength, weakness, blindness, more paralysis and heavier?
Or placid skies and sun? Wilt stir the waters yet?
Or haply cut me short for good? Or leave me here as now,
Dull, parrot-like and old, with crack'd voice harping, screeching?

THE WALLABOUT MARTYRS.

[In Brooklyn, in an old vault, mark'd by no special recognition, lie huddled at this moment the undoubtedly authentic remains of the stanchest and earliest revolutionary patriots from the British prison ships and prisons of the times of 1776-83, in and around New York, and from all over Long Island; originally buried—many thousands of them—in trenches in the Wallabout sands.]

Greater than memory of Achilles or Ulysses,
More, more by far to thee than tomb of Alexander,
Those cart loads of old charnel ashes, scales and splints of
    mouldy bones,
Once living men—once resolute courage, aspiration, strength,
The stepping stones to thee to-day and here, America.

THE FIRST DANDELION.

Simple and fresh and fair from winter's close emerging,
As if no artifice of fashion, business, politics, had ever been,
Forth from its sunny nook of shelter'd grass—innocent, golden,
    calm as the dawn,
The spring's first dandelion shows its trustful face.

AMERICA.

Centre of equal daughters, equal sons,
All, all alike endear'd, grown, ungrown, young or old,
Strong, ample, fair, enduring, capable, rich,
Perennial with the Earth, with Freedom, Law and Love,
A grand, sane, towering, seated Mother,
Chair'd in the adamant of Time.

MEMORIES.

How sweet the silent backward tracings!
The wanderings as in dreams—the meditation of old times re-
    sumed—their loves, joys, persons, voyages.

TO-DAY AND THEE.

The appointed winners in a long-stretch'd game ;
The course of Time and nations—Egypt, India, Greece and
    Rome ;
The past entire, with all its heroes, histories, arts, experiments,
Its store of songs, inventions, voyages, teachers, books,
Garner'd for now and thee—To think of it !
The heirdom all converged in thee !

AFTER THE DAZZLE OF DAY.

After the dazzle of day is gone,
Only the dark, dark night shows to my eyes the stars ;
After the clangor of organ majestic, or chorus, or perfect band,
Silent, athwart my soul, moves the symphony true.

ABRAHAM LINCOLN, BORN FEB. 12, 1809.

To-day, from each and all, a breath of prayer—a pulse of
    thought,
To memory of Him—to birth of Him.
Publish'd Feb. 12, 1888.

OUT OF MAY'S SHOWS SELECTED.

Apple orchards, the trees all cover'd with blossoms ;
Wheat fields carpeted far and near in vital emerald green ;
The eternal, exhaustless freshness of each early morning ;
The yellow, golden, transparent haze of the warm afternoon sun ;
The aspiring lilac bushes with profuse purple or white flowers.

HALCYON DAYS.

Not from successful love alone,
Nor wealth, nor honor'd middle age, nor victories of politics or
    war ;
But as life wanes, and all the turbulent passions calm,
As gorgeous, vapory, silent hues cover the evening sky,
As softness, fulness, rest, suffuse the frame, like freshier, balmier
    air,
As the days take on a mellower light, and the apple at last hangs
    really finish'd and indolent-ripe on the tree,
Then for the teeming quietest, happiest days of all !
The brooding and blissful halcyon days !

FANCIES AT NAVESINK.

THE PILOT IN THE MIST.

Steaming the northern rapids—(an old St. Lawrence reminis-
cence,
A sudden memory-flash comes back, I know not why,
Here waiting for the sunrise, gazing from this hill;) *
Again 'tis just at morning—a heavy haze contends with day-
break,
Again the trembling, laboring vessel veers me—I press through
foam-dash'd rocks that almost touch me,
Again I mark where aft the small thin Indian helmsman
Looms in the mist, with brow elate and governing hand.

HAD I THE CHOICE.

Had I the choice to tally greatest bards,
To limn their portraits, stately, beautiful, and emulate at will,
Homer with all his wars and warriors—Hector, Achilles, Ajax,
Or Shakspere's woe-entangled Hamlet, Lear, Othello—Tenny-
son's fair ladies,
Metre or wit the best, or choice conceit to wield in perfect
rhyme, delight of singers;
These, these, O sea, all these I'd gladly barter,
Would you the undulation of one wave, its trick to me transfer,
Or breathe one breath of yours upon my verse,
And leave its odor there.

YOU TIDES WITH CEASELESS SWELL.

You tides with ceaseless swell! you power that does this work!
You unseen force, centripetal, centrifugal, through space's
spread,
Rapport of sun, moon, earth, and all the constellations,
What are the messages by you from distant stars to us? what
Sirius'? what Capella's?
What central heart—and you the pulse—vivifies all? what
boundless aggregate of all?
What subtle indirection and significance in you? what clue to
all in you? what fluid, vast identity,
Holding the universe with all its parts as one—as sailing in a ship?

---

* Navesink—a sea-side mountain, lower entrance of New York Bay.

LAST OF EBB, AND DAYLIGHT WANING.

Last of ebb, and daylight waning,
Scented sea-cool landward making, smells of sedge and salt
    incoming,
With many a half-caught voice sent up from the eddies,
Many a muffled confession—many a sob and whisper'd word,
As of speakers far or hid.

How they sweep down and out! how they mutter!
Poets unnamed—artists greatest of any, with cherish'd lost
    designs,
Love's unresponse—a chorus of age's complaints—hope's last
    words,
Some suicide's despairing cry, *Away to the boundless waste, and
    never again return.*

On to oblivion then!
On, on, and do your part, ye burying, ebbing tide!
On for your time, ye furious debouché!

AND YET NOT YOU ALONE.

And yet not you alone, twilight and burying ebb,
Nor you, ye lost designs alone—nor failures, aspirations;
I know, divine deceitful ones, your glamour's seeming;
Duly by you, from you, the tide and light again—duly the
    hinges turning,
Duly the needed discord-parts offsetting, blending,
Weaving from you, from Sleep, Night, Death itself,
The rhythmus of Birth eternal.

PROUDLY THE FLOOD COMES IN.

Proudly the flood comes in, shouting, foaming, advancing,
Long it holds at the high, with bosom broad outswelling,
All throbs, dilates—the farms, woods, streets of cities—workmen
    at work,
Mainsails, topsails, jibs, appear in the offing—steamers' pennants
    of smoke—and under the forenoon sun,
Freighted with human lives, gaily the outward bound, gaily the
    inward bound,
Flaunting from many a spar the flag I love.

BY THAT LONG SCAN OF WAVES.

By that long scan of waves, myself call'd back, resumed upon
    myself,
In every crest some undulating light or shade—some retrospect,

Joys, travels, studies, silent panoramas—scenes ephemeral,
The long past war, the battles, hospital sights, the wounded and
the dead,
Myself through every by-gone phase—my idle youth—old age at
hand,
My three-score years of life summ'd up, and more, and past,
By any grand ideal tried, intentionless, the whole a nothing,
And haply yet some drop within God's scheme's ensemble—some
wave, or part of wave,
Like one of yours, ye multitudinous ocean.

THEN LAST OF ALL.

Then last of all, caught from these shores, this hill,
Of you O tides, the mystic human meaning:
Only by law of you, your swell and ebb, enclosing me the same,
The brain that shapes, the voice that chants this song.

ELECTION DAY, NOVEMBER, 1884.

If I should need to name, O Western World, your powerfulest
scene and show,
'Twould not be you, Niagara—nor you, ye limitless prairies—nor
your huge rifts of canyons, Colorado,
Nor you, Yosemite—nor Yellowstone, with all its spasmic geyser-
loops ascending to the skies, appearing and disappearing,
Nor Oregon's white cones—nor Huron's belt of mighty lakes—
nor Mississippi's stream:
—This seething hemisphere's humanity, as now, I'd name—*the
still small voice* vibrating—America's choosing day,
(The heart of it not in the chosen—the act itself the main, the
quadriennial choosing,)
The stretch of North and South arous'd—sea-board and inland
—Texas to Maine—the Prairie States—Vermont, Virginia,
California,
The final ballot-shower from East to West—the paradox and con-
flict,
The countless snow-flakes falling—(a swordless conflict,
Yet more than all Rome's wars of old, or modern Napoleon's:)
the peaceful choice of all,
Or good or ill humanity—welcoming the darker odds, the dross:
—Foams and ferments the wine? it serves to purify—while the
heart pants, life glows:
These stormy gusts and winds waft precious ships,
Swell'd Washington's, Jefferson's, Lincoln's sails.

WITH HUSKY-HAUGHTY LIPS, O SEA!

With husky-haughty lips, O sea!
Where day and night I wend thy surf-beat shore,
Imaging to my sense thy varied strange suggestions,
(I see and plainly list thy talk and conference here,)
Thy troops of white-maned racers racing to the goal,
Thy ample, smiling face, dash'd with the sparkling dimples of the
     sun,
Thy brooding scowl and murk—thy unloos'd hurricanes,
Thy unsubduedness, caprices, wilfulness;
Great as thou art above the rest, thy many tears—a lack from all
     eternity in thy content,
(Naught but the greatest struggles, wrongs, defeats, could make
     thee greatest—no less could make thee,)
Thy lonely state—something thou ever seek'st and seek'st, yet
     never gain'st,
Surely some right withheld—some voice, in huge monotonous
     rage, of freedom-lover pent,
Some vast heart, like a planet's, chain'd and chafing in those
     breakers,
By lengthen'd swell, and spasm, and panting breath,
And rhythmic rasping of thy sands and waves,
And serpent hiss, and savage peals of laughter,
And undertones of distant lion roar,
(Sounding, appealing to the sky's deaf ear—but now, rapport for
     once,
A phantom in the night thy confidant for once,)
The first and last confession of the globe,
Outsurging, muttering from thy soul's abysms,
The tale of cosmic elemental passion,
Thou tellest to a kindred soul.

DEATH OF GENERAL GRANT.

As one by one withdraw the lofty actors,
From that great play on history's stage eterne,
That lurid, partial act of war and peace—of old and new con-
     tending,
Fought out through wrath, fears, dark dismays, and many a long
     suspense;
All past—and since, in countless graves receding, mellowing,
Victor's and vanquish'd—Lincoln's and Lee's—now thou with
     them,

Man of the mighty days—and equal to the days!
Thou from the prairies!—tangled and many-vein'd and hard has
    been thy part,
To admiration has it been enacted!

RED JACKET (FROM ALOFT.)

[Impromptu on Buffalo City's monument to, and re-burial of the old Iroquois orator, October 9, 1884.]

Upon this scene, this show,
Yielded to-day by fashion, learning, wealth,
(Nor in caprice alone—some grains of deepest meaning,)
Haply, aloft, (who knows?) from distant sky-clouds' blended
    shapes,
As some old tree, or rock or cliff, thrill'd with its soul,
Product of Nature's sun, stars, earth direct—a towering human
    form,
In hunting-shirt of film, arm'd with the rifle, a half-ironical smile
    curving its phantom lips,
Like one of Ossian's ghosts looks down.

WASHINGTON'S MONUMENT, FEBRUARY, 1885.

Ah, not this marble, dead and cold:
Far from its base and shaft expanding—the round zones circling,
    comprehending,
Thou, Washington, art all the world's, the continents' entire—
    not yours alone, America,
Europe's as well, in every part, castle of lord or laborer's cot,
Or frozen North, or sultry South—the African's—the Arab's in
    his tent,
Old Asia's there with venerable smile, seated amid her ruins;
(Greets the antique the hero new? 'tis but the same—the heir
    legitimate, continued ever,
The indomitable heart and arm—proofs of the never-broken
    line,
Courage, alertness, patience, faith, the same—e'en in defeat de-
    feated not, the same:)
Wherever sails a ship, or house is built on land, or day or night,
Through teeming cities' streets, indoors or out, factories or farms,
Now, or to come, or past—where patriot wills existed or exist,
Wherever Freedom, pois'd by Toleration, sway'd by Law,
Stands or is rising thy true monument.

OF THAT BLITHE THROAT OF THINE.

[More than eighty-three degrees north—about a good day's steaming distance to the Pole by one of our fast oceaners in clear water—Greely the explorer heard the song of a single snow-bird merrily sounding over the desolation.]

Of that blithe throat of thine from arctic bleak and blank,
I'll mind the lesson, solitary bird—let me too welcome chilling
    drifts,
E'en the profoundest chill, as now—a torpid pulse, a brain un-
    nerv'd,
Old age land-lock'd within its winter bay—(cold, cold, O cold!)
These snowy hairs, my feeble arm, my frozen feet,
For them thy faith, thy rule I take, and grave it to the last;
Not summer's zones alone—not chants of youth, or south's warm
    tides alone,
But held by sluggish floes, pack'd in the northern ice, the cumulus
    of years,
These with gay heart I also sing.

BROADWAY.

What hurrying human tides, or day or night!
What passions, winnings, losses, ardors, swim thy waters!
What whirls of evil, bliss and sorrow, stem thee!
What curious questioning glances—glints of love!
Leer, envy, scorn, contempt, hope, aspiration!
Thou portal—thou arena—thou of the myriad long-drawn lines
    and groups!
(Could but thy flagstones, curbs, façades, tell their inimitable
    tales;
Thy windows rich, and huge hotels—thy side-walks wide;)
Thou of the endless sliding, mincing, shuffling feet!
Thou, like the parti-colored world itself—like infinite, teeming,
    mocking life!
Thou visor'd, vast, unspeakable show and lesson!

TO GET THE FINAL LILT OF SONGS.

To get the final lilt of songs,
To penetrate the inmost lore of poets—to know the mighty ones,
Job, Homer, Eschylus, Dante, Shakspere, Tennyson, Emerson;
To diagnose the shifting-delicate tints of love and pride and
    doubt—to truly understand,
To encompass these, the last keen faculty and entrance-price,
Old age, and what it brings from all its past experiences.

OLD SALT KOSSABONE.

Far back, related on my mother's side,
Old Salt Kossabone,* I'll tell you how he died:
(Had been a sailor all his life—was nearly 90—lived with his
    married grandchild, Jenny;
House on a hill, with view of bay at hand, and distant cape, and
    stretch to open sea;)
The last of afternoons, the evening hours, for many a year his
    regular custom,
In his great arm chair by the window seated,
(Sometimes, indeed, through half the day,)
Watching the coming, going of the vessels, he mutters to himself
    —And now the close of all:
One struggling outbound brig, one day, baffled for long—cross-
    tides and much wrong going,
At last at nightfall strikes the breeze aright, her whole luck veer-
    ing,
And swiftly bending round the cape, the darkness proudly enter-
    ing, cleaving, as he watches,
"She's free—she's on her destination"—these the last words—
    when Jenny came, he sat there dead,
Dutch Kossabone, Old Salt, related on my mother's side, far
    back.

THE DEAD TENOR.*

As down the stage again,
With Spanish hat and plumes, and gait inimitable,
Back from the fading lessons of the past, I'd call, I'd tell and
    own,
How much from thee! the revelation of the singing voice from
    thee!
(So firm—so liquid-soft—again that tremulous, manly timbre!
The perfect singing voice—deepest of all to me the lesson—trial
    and test of all:)
How through those strains distill'd—how the rapt ears, the soul
    of me, absorbing
Fernando's heart, *Manrico's* passionate call, *Ernani's*, sweet
    Gennaro's,*
I fold thenceforth, or seek to fold, within my chants transmuting,
Freedom's and Love's and Faith's unloos'd cantabile,
(As perfume's, color's, sunlight's correlation:)
From these, for these, with these, a hurried line, dead tenor,
A wafted autumn leaf, dropt in the closing grave, the shovel'd
    earth,
To memory of thee.

CONTINUITIES.

[From a talk I had lately with a German spiritualist.]

Nothing is ever really lost, or can be lost,
No birth, identity, form—no object of the world.
Nor life, nor force, nor any visible thing;
Appearance must not foil, nor shifted sphere confuse thy brain.
Ample are time and space—ample the fields of Nature.
The body, sluggish, aged, cold—the embers left from earlier
    fires,
The light in the eye grown dim, shall duly flame again;
The sun now low in the west rises for mornings and for noons
    continual;
To frozen clods ever the spring's invisible law returns,
With grass and flowers and summer fruits and corn.

YONNONDIO.

[The sense of the word is *lament for the aborigines.* It is an Iroquois
term; and has been used for a personal name.]

A song, a poem of itself—the word itself a dirge,
Amid the wilds, the rocks, the storm and wintry night,
To me such misty, strange tableaux the syllables calling up;
Yonnondio—I see, far in the west or north, a limitless ravine,
    with plains and mountains dark,
I see swarms of stalwart chieftains, medicine-men, and warriors,
As flitting by like clouds of ghosts, they pass and are gone in the
    twilight,
(Race of the woods, the landscapes free, and the falls!
No picture, poem, statement, passing them to the future:)
Yonnondio! Yonnondio!—unlimn'd they disappear;
To-day gives place, and fades—the cities, farms, factories fade;
A muffled sonorous sound, a wailing word is borne through the
    air for a moment,
Then blank and gone and still, and utterly lost.

LIFE.

Ever the undiscouraged, resolute, struggling soul of man;
(Have former armies fail'd? then we send fresh armies—and
    fresh again;)
Ever the grappled mystery of all earth's ages old or new;
Ever the eager eyes, hurrahs, the welcome-clapping hands, the
    loud applause;
Ever the soul dissatisfied, curious, unconvinced at last;
Struggling to-day the same—battling the same.

"GOING SOMEWHERE."

My science-friend, my noblest woman-friend,*
(Now buried in an English grave—and this a memory-leaf for
    her dear sake,)
Ended our talk—"The sum, concluding all we know of old or
    modern learning, intuitions deep,
"Of all Geologies—Histories—of all Astronomy—of Evolution,
    Metaphysics all,
"Is, that we all are onward, onward, speeding slowly, surely
    bettering,
'Life, life an endless march, an endless army, (no halt, but it is
    duly over,)
"The world, the race, the soul—in space and time the universes,
"All bound as is befitting each—all surely going somewhere.''

From the 1867 edition L. of G.
SMALL THE THEME OF MY CHANT.

Small the theme of my Chant, yet the greatest—namely, One's-
    Self—a simple, separate person. That, for the use of the
    New World, I sing.
Man's physiology complete, from top to toe, I sing. Not physi-
    ognomy alone, nor brain alone, is worthy for the Muse ;—I
    say the Form complete is worthier far. The Female equally
    with the Male, I sing.
Nor cease at the theme of One's-Self. I speak the word of the
    modern, the word En-Masse.
My Days I sing, and the Lands—with interstice I knew of hap-
    less War.
(O friend, whoe'er you are, at last arriving hither to commence,
    I feel through every leaf the pressure of your hand, which I
    return,
And thus upon our journey, footing the road, and more than
    once, and link'd together let us go.)

TRUE CONQUERORS.

Old farmers, travelers, workmen (no matter how crippled or
    bent,)
Old sailors, out of many a perilous voyage, storm and wreck,
Old soldiers from campaigns, with all their wounds, defeats and
    scars;
Enough that they've survived at all—long life's unflinching ones !
Forth from their struggles, trials, fights, to have emerged at all
    —in that alone,
True conquerors o'er all the rest.

THE UNITED STATES TO OLD WORLD CRITICS.

Here first the duties of to-day, the lessons of the concrete,
Wealth, order, travel, shelter, products, plenty;
As of the building of some varied, vast, perpetual edifice,
Whence to arise inevitable in time, the towering roofs, the lamps,
The solid-planted spires tall shooting to the stars.

THE CALMING THOUGHT OF ALL.

That coursing on, whate'er men's speculations,
Amid the changing schools, theologies, philosophies,
Amid the bawling presentations new and old,
The round earth's silent vital laws, facts, modes continue.

THANKS IN OLD AGE.

Thanks in old age—thanks ere I go,
For health, the midday sun, the impalpable air—for life, mere
    life,
For precious ever-lingering memories, (of you my mother dear
    —you, father—you, brothers, sisters, friends,)
For all my days—not those of peace alone—the days of war the
    same,
For gentle words, caresses, gifts from foreign lands,
For shelter, wine and meat—for sweet appreciation,
(You distant, dim unknown—or young or old—countless, un-
    specified, readers belov'd,
We never met, and ne'er shall meet—and yet our souls embrace,
    long, close and long;)
For beings, groups, love, deeds, words, books—for colors, forms,
For all the brave strong men—devoted, hardy men—who've for-
    ward sprung in freedom's help, all years, all lands,
For braver, stronger, more devoted men—(a special laurel ere I
    go, to life's war's chosen ones,
The cannoneers of song and thought—the great artillerists—the
    foremost leaders, captains of the soul:)
As soldier from an ended war return'd—As traveler out of
    myriads, to the long procession retrospective,
Thanks—joyful thanks!—a soldier's, traveler's thanks.

LIFE AND DEATH.

The two old, simple problems ever intertwined,
Close home, elusive, present, baffled, grappled.
By each successive age insoluble, pass'd on,
To ours to-day—and we pass on the same.

THE VOICE OF THE RAIN.

And who art thou? said I to the soft-falling shower,
Which, strange to tell, gave me an answer, as here translated:
I am the Poem of Earth, said the voice of the rain,
Eternal I rise impalpable out of the land and the bottomless sea,
Upward to heaven, whence, vaguely form'd, altogether changed,
 and yet the same,
I descend to lave the drouths, atomies, dust-layers of the globe,
And all that in them without me were seeds only, latent, unborn;
And forever, by day and night, I give back life to my own
 origin, and make pure and beautify it:
(For song, issuing from its birth-place, after fulfilment, wander-
 ing,
Reck'd or unreck'd. duly with love returns.)

SOON SHALL THE WINTER'S FOIL BE HERE.

Soon shall the winter's foil be here;
Soon shall these icy ligatures unbind and melt—A little while,
And air, soil, wave, suffused shall be in softness, bloom and
 growth—a thousand forms shall rise
From these dead clods and chills as from low burial graves.
Thine eyes, ears—all thy best attributes—all that takes cognizance
 of natural beauty,
Shall wake and fill. Thou shalt perceive the simple shows, the
 delicate miracles of earth,
Dandelions, clover, the emerald grass, the early scents and flow-
 ers,
The arbutus under foot, the willow's yellow-green, the blossom-
 ing plum and cherry;
With these the robin, lark and thrush, singing their songs—the
 flitting bluebird;
For such the scenes the annual play brings on.

WHILE NOT THE PAST FORGETTING.

While not the past forgetting,
To-day, at least, contention sunk entire—peace, brotherhood up-
 risen;
For sign reciprocal our Northern, Southern hands,
Lay on the graves of all dead soldiers, North or South,
(Nor for the past alone—for meanings to the future,)
Wreaths of roses and branches of palm.

 Publish'd May 30, 1888

THE DYING VETERAN.

[A Long Island incident—early part of the present century.]

Amid these days of order, ease, prosperity,
Amid the current songs of beauty, peace, decorum,
I cast a reminiscence—(likely 'twill offend you,
I heard it in my boyhood ;)—More than a generation since,
A queer old savage man, a fighter under Washington himself,
(Large, brave, cleanly, hot-blooded, no talker, rather spiritual-
    istic,
Had fought in the ranks—fought well—had been all through the
    Revolutionary war,)
Lay dying—sons, daughters, church-deacons, lovingly tending
    him,
Sharping their sense, their ears, towards his murmuring, half-
    caught words :
" Let me return again to my war-days,
To the sights and scenes—to forming the line of battle,
To the scouts ahead reconnoitering,
To the cannons, the grim artillery,
To the galloping aids, carrying orders,
To the wounded, the fallen, the heat, the suspense,
The perfume strong, the smoke, the deafening noise ;
Away with your life of peace !—your joys of peace !
Give me my old wild battle-life again ! ''

STRONGER LESSONS.

Have you learn'd lessons only of those who admired you, and
    were tender with you, and stood aside for you?
Have you not learn'd great lessons from those who reject you,
    and brace themselves against you? or who treat you with
    contempt, or dispute the passage with you?

A PRAIRIE SUNSET.

Shot gold, maroon and violet, dazzling silver, emerald, fawn,
The earth's whole amplitude and Nature's multiform power con-
    sign'd for once to colors ;
The light, the general air possess'd by them—colors till now un-
    known,
No limit, confine—not the Western sky alone—the high meri-
    dian—North, South, all,
Pure luminous color fighting the silent shadows to the last.

TWENTY YEARS.

Down on the ancient wharf, the sand, I sit, with a new-comer
    chatting:
He shipp'd as green-hand boy, and sail'd away, (took some sud-
    den, vehement notion;)
Since, twenty years and more have circled round and round,
While he the globe was circling round and round,—and now
    returns:
How changed the place—all the old land-marks gone—the
    parents dead;
(Yes, he comes back *to lay in port for good—to settle*—has a well-
    fill'd purse—no spot will do but this;)
The little boat that scull'd him from the sloop, now held in
    leash I see,
I hear the slapping waves, the restless keel, the rocking in the
    sand,
I see the sailor kit, the canvas bag, the great box bound with
    brass,
I scan the face all berry-brown and bearded—the stout-strong
    frame,
Dress'd in its russet suit of good Scotch cloth:
(Then what the told-out story of those twenty years? What of
    the future?)

ORANGE BUDS BY MAIL FROM FLORIDA.

[Voltaire closed a famous argument by claiming that a ship of war and the grand opera were proofs enough of civilization's and France's progress, in his day.]

A lesser proof than old Voltaire's, yet greater,
Proof of this present time, and thee, thy broad expanse,
    America,
To my plain Northern hut, in outside clouds and snow,
Brought safely for a thousand miles o'er land and tide,
Some three days since on their own soil live-sprouting,
Now here their sweetness through my room unfolding,
A bunch of orange buds by mail from Florida.

TWILIGHT.

The soft voluptuous opiate shades,
The sun just gone, the eager light dispell'd—(I too will soon be
    gone, dispell'd,)
A haze—nirwana—rest and night—oblivion.

YOU LINGERING SPARSE LEAVES OF ME.

You lingering sparse leaves of me on winter-nearing boughs,
And I some well-shorn tree of field or orchard-row;
You tokens diminute and lorn—(not now the flush of May, or
  July clover-bloom—no grain of August now ;)
You pallid banner-staves—you pennants valueless—you over-
  stay'd of time,
Yet my soul-dearest leaves confirming all the rest,
The faithfulest—hardiest—last.

NOT MEAGRE, LATENT BOUGHS ALONE.

Not meagre, latent boughs alone, O songs! (scaly and bare,
  like eagles' talons,)
But haply for some sunny day (who knows?) some future spring,
  some summer—bursting forth,
To verdant leaves, or sheltering shade—to nourishing fruit,
Apples and grapes—the stalwart limbs of trees emerging—the
  fresh, free, open air,
And love and faith, like scented roses blooming.

THE DEAD EMPEROR.*

To-day, with bending head and eyes, thou, too, Columbia,
Less for the mighty crown laid low in sorrow—less for the
  Emperor,
Thy true condolence breathest, sendest out o'er many a salt sea
  mile,
Mourning a good old man—a faithful shepherd, patriot.

  Publish'd March 10, 1888.

AS THE GREEK'S SIGNAL FLAME.

[For Whittier's eightieth birthday, December 17, 1887.]

As the Greek's signal flame, by antique records told,
Rose from the hill-top, like applause and glory,
Welcoming in fame some special veteran, hero,
With rosy tinge reddening the land he'd served,
So I aloft from Mannahatta's ship-fringed shore,
Lift high a kindled brand for thee, Old Poet.

THE DISMANTLED SHIP.

In some unused lagoon, some nameless bay,
On sluggish, lonesome waters, anchor'd near the shore,
An old, dismasted, gray and batter'd ship, disabled, done,
After free voyages to all the seas of earth, haul'd up at last and
      hawser'd tight,
Lies rusting, mouldering.

NOW PRECEDENT SONGS, FAREWELL.

Now precedent songs, farewell—by every name farewell,
(Trains of a staggering line in many a strange procession,
      waggons,
From ups and downs—with intervals—from elder years, mid-age,
      or youth,)
"In Cabin'd Ships," or "Thee Old Cause" or "Poets to Come"
Or "Paumanok," "Song of Myself," "Calamus," or "Adam,"
Or "Beat! Beat! Drums!" or "To the Leaven'd Soil they
      Trod,"
Or "Captain! My Captain!" "Kosmos," "Quicksand Years,"
      or "Thoughts,"
"Thou Mother with thy Equal Brood," and many, many more
      unspecified,
From fibre heart of mine—from throat and tongue—(My life's
      hot pulsing blood,
The personal urge and form for me—not merely paper, automatic
      type and ink,)
Each song of mine—each utterance in the past—having its long,
      long history,
Of life or death, or soldier's wound, of country's loss or safety,
(O heaven! what flash and started endless train of all! com-
      pared indeed to that!
What wretched shred e'en at the best of all!)

AN EVENING LULL.

After a week of physical anguish,
Unrest and pain, and feverish heat,
Toward the ending day a calm and lull comes on,
Three hours of peace and soothing rest of brain.*

---

   * The two songs on this page are eked out during an afternoon, June, 1888,
in my seventieth year, at a critical spell of illness. Of course no reader and
probably no human being at any time will ever have such phases of emotional
and solemn action as these involve to me. I feel in them an end and close
of all.

OLD AGE'S LAMBENT PEAKS.

The touch of flame—the illuminating fire—the loftiest look at last,
O'er city, passion, sea—o'er prairie, mountain, wood—the earth itself;
The airy, different, changing hues of all, in falling twilight,
Objects and groups, bearings, faces, reminiscences;
The calmer sight—the golden setting, clear and broad:
So much i' the atmosphere, the points of view, the situations whence we scan,
Bro't out by them alone—so much (perhaps the best) unreck'd before;
The lights indeed from them—old age's lambent peaks.

AFTER THE SUPPER AND TALK.

After the supper and talk—after the day is done,
As a friend from friends his final withdrawal prolonging,
Good-bye and Good-bye with emotional lips repeating,
(So hard for his hand to release those hands—no more will they meet,
No more for communion of sorrow and joy, of old and young,
A far-stretching journey awaits him, to return no more,)
Shunning, postponing severance—seeking to ward off the last word ever so little,
E'en at the exit-door turning—charges superfluous calling back— e'en as he descends the steps,
Something to eke out a minute additional—shadows of nighttall deepening,
Farewells, messages lessening—dimmer the forthgoer's visage and form,
Soon to be lost for aye in the darkness—loth, O so loth to depart!
Garrulous to the very last.

2D ANNEX.

GOOD-BYE MY FANCY.

CONTENTS.

———

(406)

PREFACE NOTE TO 2d ANNEX,

CONCLUDING L. OF G.—1891.

HAD I not better withhold (in this old age and paralysis of me) such little tags and fringe-dots (maybe specks, stains,) as follow a long dusty journey, and witness it afterward? I have probably not been enough afraid of careless touches, from the first—and am not now—nor of parrot-like repetitions—nor platitudes and the commonplace. Perhaps I am too democratic for such avoidances. Besides, is not the verse-field, as originally plann'd by my theory, now sufficiently illustrated—and full time for me to silently retire?—(indeed amid no loud call or market for my sort of poetic utterance.)

In answer, or rather defiance, to that kind of well-put interrogation, here comes this little cluster, and conclusion of my preceding clusters. Though not at all clear that, as here collated, it is worth printing (certainly I have nothing fresh to write)—I while away the hours of my 72d year—hours of forced confinement in my den—by putting in shape this small old age collation:

Last droplets of and after spontaneous rain,
From many limpid distillations and past showers;
(Will they germinate anything? mere exhalations as they all are—
    the land's and sea's—America's;
Will they filter to any deep emotion? any heart and brain?)

However that may be, I feel like improving to-day's opportunity and wind up. During the last two years I have sent out, in the lulls of illness and exhaustion, certain chirps—lingering-dying ones probably (undoubtedly)—which now I may as well gather and put in fair type while able to see correctly—(for my eyes plainly warn me they are dimming, and my brain more and more palpably neglects or refuses, month after month, even slight tasks or revisions.)

In fact, here I am these current years 1890 and '91, (each successive fortnight getting stiffer and stuck deeper) much like some hard-cased dilapidated grim ancient shell-fish or time-bang'd conch (no legs, utterly non-locomotive) cast up high and dry on the shore-sands, helpless to move anywhere—nothing left but behave myself quiet, and while away the days yet assign'd, and discover if there is anything for the said grim and time-bang'd conch to be got at last out of inherited good spirits and primal buoyant centre-pulses down there deep somewhere within his gray-blurr'd old shell............(Reader, you must allow a little fun here—for one reason there are too many of the following poemets about death, &c., and for another the passing hours (July 5, 1890) are so sunny-fine. And old as I am I feel to-day almost a part of some frolicsome wave, or for sporting yet like a kid or kitten—probably a streak of physical adjustment and per-fection here and now. I believe I have it in me perennially anyhow.)

Then behind all, the deep-down consolation (it is a glum one, but I dare not be sorry for the fact of it in the past, nor refrain from dwelling, even vaunting here at the end) that this late-years palsied old shorn and shell-fish condition of me is the indubitable outcome and growth, now near for 20 years along, of too over-zealous, over-continued bodily and emotional excitement and action through the times of 1862, '3, '4 and '5, visiting and waiting on wounded and sick army volunteers, both sides, in campaigns or contests, or after them, or in hospitals or fields south of Washington City, or in that place and elsewhere—those hot, sad, wrenching times—the army volunteers, all States,—or North or South—the wounded, suffering, dying—the exhausting, sweat-ing summers, marches, battles, carnage—those trenches hurriedly heap'd by the corpse-thousands, mainly unknown—Will the America of the future—will this vast rich Union ever realize what itself cost, back there after all?—those hecatombs of bat-tle-deaths—Those times of which, O far-off reader, this whole book is indeed finally but a reminiscent memorial from thence by me to you?

GOOD-BYE MY FANCY.

SAIL OUT FOR GOOD, EIDÓLON YACHT!

HEAVE the anchor short !
Raise main-sail and jib—steer forth,
O little white-hull'd sloop, now speed on really deep waters,
(I will not call it our concluding voyage,
But outset and sure entrance to the truest, best, maturest ;)
Depart, depart from solid earth—no more returning to these
    shores,
Now on for aye our infinite free venture wending,
Spurning all yet tried ports, seas, hawsers, densities, gravitation,
Sail out for good, eidólon* yacht of me !

LINGERING LAST DROPS.

AND whence and why come you?

We know not whence, (was the answer,)
We only know that we drift here with the rest,
That we linger'd and lagg'd—but were wafted at last, and are
    now here,
To make the passing shower's concluding drops.

GOOD-BYE MY FANCY.

GOOD-BYE* my fancy—(I had a word to say,
But 'tis not quite the time—The best of any man's word or say,
Is when its proper place arrives—and for its meaning,
I keep mine till the last.)

  * Behind a Good-bye there lurks much of the salutation of another be-
ginning—to me, Development, Continuity, Immortality, Transformation, are
the chiefest life-meanings of Nature and Humanity, and are the *sine qua
non* of all facts, and each fact.
  Why do folks dwell so fondly on the last words, advice, appearance, of the
departing? Those last words are not samples of the best, which involve
vitality at its full, and balance, and perfect control and scope. But they are
valuable beyond measure to confirm and endorse the varied train, facts, theo-
ries and faith of the whole preceding life.

ON, ON THE SAME, YE JOCUND TWAIN!

On, on the same, ye jocund twain!
My life and recitative, containing birth, youth, mid-age years,
Fitful as motley-tongues of flame, inseparably twined and merged
    in one—combining all,
My single soul—aims, confirmations, failures, joys—Nor single
    soul alone,
I chant my nation's crucial stage, (America's, haply humanity's)
    —the trial great, the victory great,
A strange *eclaircissement* of all the masses past, the eastern
    world, the ancient, medieval,
Here, here from wanderings, strayings, lessons, wars, defeats—
    here at the west a voice triumphant—justifying all,
A gladsome pealing cry—a song for once of utmost pride and
    satisfaction;
I chant from it the common bulk, the general average horde,
    (the best no sooner than the worst)—And now I chant old
    age,
(My verses, written first for forenoon life, and for the summer's,
    autumn's spread,
I pass to snow-white hairs the same, and give to pulses winter-
    cool'd the same;)
As here in careless trill, I and my recitatives, with faith and
    love,
Wafting to other work, to unknown songs, conditions,
On, on, ye jocund twain! continue on the same!

MY 71st YEAR.

After surmounting three-score and ten,
With all their chances, changes, losses, sorrows,
My parents' deaths, the vagaries of my life, the many tearing
    passions of me, the war of '63 and '4,
As some old broken soldier, after a long, hot, wearying march,
    or haply after battle,
To-day at twilight, hobbling, answering company roll-call, *Here*,
    with vital voice,
Reporting yet, saluting yet the Officer over all.

APPARITIONS.

A vague mist hanging 'round half the pages:
(Sometimes how strange and clear to the soul,
That all these solid things are indeed but apparitions, concepts,
    non-realities.)

THE PALLID WREATH.

SOMEHOW I cannot let it go yet, funeral though it is,
Let it remain back there on its nail suspended,
With pink, blue, yellow, all blanch'd, and the white now gray
    and ashy,
One wither'd rose put years ago for thee, dear friend ;
But I do not forget thee.   Hast thou then faded ?
Is the odor exhaled ?   Are the colors, vitalities, dead ?
No, while memories subtly play—the past vivid as ever ;
For but last night I woke, and in that spectral ring saw thee,
Thy smile, eyes, face, calm, silent, loving as ever :
So let the wreath hang still awhile within my eye-reach,
It is not yet dead to me, nor even pallid.

AN ENDED DAY.

THE soothing sanity and blitheness of completion,
The pomp and hurried contest-glare and rush are done ;
Now triumph ! transformation ! jubilate ! *

---

*✻ NOTE.—*Summer country life.—Several years.*—In my rambles and explo-
rations I found a woody place near the creek, where for some reason the birds
in happy mood seem'd to resort in unusual numbers. Especially at the
beginning of the day, and again at the ending, I was sure to get there the
most copious bird-concerts. I repair'd there frequently at sunrise—and also
at sunset, or just before . . . Once the question arose in me : Which is the best
singing, the first or the lattermost? The first always exhilarated, and perhaps
seem'd more joyous and stronger; but I always felt the sunset or late after-
noon sounds more penetrating and sweeter—seem'd to touch the soul—often
the evening thrushes, two or three of them, responding and perhaps blending.
Though I miss'd some of the mornings, I found myself getting to be quite
strictly punctual at the evening utterances.*

*ANOTHER NOTE.—"He went out with the tide and the sunset," was a
phrase I heard from a surgeon describing an old sailor's death under pecu-
liarly gentle conditions.*

*During the Secession War, 1863 and '4, visiting the Army Hospitals around
Washington, I form'd the habit, and continued it to the end, whenever the ebb
or flood tide began the latter part of day, of punctually visiting those at
that time populous wards of suffering men. Somehow (or I thought so) the
effect of the hour was palpable. The badly wounded would get some ease,
and would like to talk a little, or be talk'd to. Intellectual and emotional
natures would be at their best : Deaths were always easier; medicines seem'd
to have better effect when given then, and a lulling atmosphere would
pervade the wards.*

*Similar influences, similar circumstances and hours, day-close, after great
battles, even with all their horrors. I had more than once the same expe-
rience on the fields cover'd with fallen or dead.*

OLD AGE'S SHIP & CRAFTY DEATH'S.

FROM east and west across the horizon's edge,
Two mighty masterful vessels sailers steal upon us:
But we 'll make race a-time upon the seas—a battle-contest yet!
    bear lively there!
(Our joys of strife and derring-do to the last!)
Put on the old ship all her power to-day!
Crowd top-sail, top-gallant and royal studding-sails,
Out challenge and defiance—flags and flaunting pennants added,
As we take to the open—take to the deepest, freest waters.

TO THE PENDING YEAR.

HAVE I no weapon-word for thee — some message brief and
    fierce?
(Have I fought out and done indeed the battle?) Is there no shot
    left,
For all thy affectations, lisps, scorns, manifold silliness?
Nor for myself—my own rebellious self in thee?

Down, down, proud gorge!—though choking thee;
Thy bearded throat and high-borne forehead to the gutter;
Crouch low thy neck to eleemosynary gifts.

SHAKSPERE-BACON'S CIPHER.*

I DOUBT it not—then more, far more;
In each old song bequeath'd—in every noble page or text,
(Different — something unreck'd before — some unsuspected
    author,)
In every object, mountain, tree, and star—in every birth and
    life,
As part of each—evolv'd from each—meaning, behind the os-
    tent,
A mystic cipher waits infolded.

LONG, LONG HENCE.

AFTER a long, long course, hundreds of years, denials,
Accumulations, rous'd love and joy and thought,
Hopes, wishes, aspirations, ponderings, victories, myriads of
    readers,
Coating, compassing, covering—after ages' and ages' encrus-
    tations,
Then only may these songs reach fruition.

BRAVO, PARIS EXPOSITION!*

ADD to your show, before you close it, France,
With all the rest, visible, concrete, temples, towers, goods, ma-
  chines and ores,
Our sentiment wafted from many million heart-throbs, ethereal
  but solid,
(We grand-sons and great-grand-sons do not forget your grand-
  sires,)
From fifty Nations and nebulous Nations, compacted, sent over-
  sea to-day,
America's applause, love, memories and good-will.

INTERPOLATION SOUNDS.

[General Philip Sheridan was buried at the Cathedral, Washington, D. C.,
August, 1888, with all the pomp, music and ceremonies of the Roman Catholic
service.]

OVER and through the burial chant,
Organ and solemn service, sermon, bending priests,
To me come interpolation sounds not in the show—plainly to
  me, crowding up the aisle and from the window,
Of sudden battle's hurry and harsh noises—war's grim game to
  sight and ear in earnest ;
The scout call'd up and forward—the general mounted and his
  aids around him—the new-brought word—the instantaneous
  order issued ;
The rifle crack—the cannon thud—the rushing forth of men
  from their tents ;
The clank of cavalry—the strange celerity of forming ranks—
  the slender bugle note ;
The sound of horses' hoofs departing—saddles, arms, accoutre-
  ments.

NOTE.—CAMDEN, N. J., August 7, 1888.—Walt Whitman asks the *New
York Herald* "to add his tribute to Sheridan : "

"In the grand constellation of five or six names, under Lincoln's Presi-
dency, that history will bear for ages in her firmament as marking the last
life-throbs of secession, and beaming on its dying gasps, Sheridan's will be
bright. One consideration rising out of the now dead soldier's example as
it passes my mind, is worth taking notice of. If the war had continued any
long time these States, in my opinion, would have shown and proved the
most conclusive military talents ever evinced by any nation on earth. That
they possess'd a rank and file ahead of all other known in points of quality
and limitlessness of number are easily admitted. But we have, too, the eligi-
bility of organizing, handling and officering equal to the other. These two,
with modern arms, transportation, and inventive American genius, would make
the United States, with earnestness, not only able to stand the whole world,
but conquer that world united against us."

TO THE SUN-SET BREEZE.

Ah, whispering, something again, unseen,
Where late this heated day thou enterest at my window, door,
Thou, laving, tempering all, cool-freshing, gently vitalizing
Me, old, alone, sick, weak-down, melted-worn with sweat;
Thou, nestling, folding close and firm yet soft, companion bet-
    ter than talk, book, art,
(Thou hast, O Nature! elements! utterance to my heart beyond
    the rest—and this is of them,)
So sweet thy primitive taste to breathe within—thy soothing
    fingers on my face and hands,
Thou, messenger-magical strange bringer to body and spirit of
    me,
(Distances balk'd—occult medicines penetrating me from head
    to foot,)
I feel the sky, the prairies vast—I feel the mighty northern
    lakes,
I feel the ocean and the forest—somehow I feel the globe itself
    swift-swimming in space;
Thou blown from lips so loved, now gone—haply from endless
    store, God-sent,
(For thou art spiritual, Godly, most of all known to my
    sense,)
Minister to speak to me, here and now, what word has never
    told, and cannot tell,
Art thou not universal concrete's distillation? Law's, all As-
    tronomy's last refinement?
Hast thou no soul? Can I not know, identify thee?

OLD CHANTS.

An ancient song, reciting, ending,
Once gazing toward thee, Mother of All,
Musing, seeking themes fitted for thee,
Accept for me, thou saidst, *the elder ballads*,
And name for me before thou goest each ancient poet.

(Of many debts incalculable,
Haply our New World's chiefest debt is to old poems.)

Ever so far back, preluding thee, America,
Old chants, Egyptian priests, and those of Ethiopia,
The Hindu epics, the Grecian, Chinese, Persian,
The Biblic books and prophets, and deep idyls of the Naza-
    rene,

The Iliad, Odyssey, plots, doings, wanderings of Eneas,
Hesiod, Eschylus, Sophocles, Merlin, Arthur,
The Cid, Roland at Roncesvalles, the Nibelungen,
The troubadours, minstrels, minnesingers, skalds,
Chaucer, Dante, flocks of singing birds,
The Border Minstrelsy, the bye-gone ballads, feudal tales, essays,
    plays,
Shakspere, Schiller, Walter Scott, Tennyson,
As some vast wondrous weird dream-presences,
The great shadowy groups gathering around,
Darting their mighty masterful eyes forward at thee,
Thou ! with as now thy bending neck and head, with courteous
    hand and word, ascending,
Thou ! pausing a moment, drooping thine eyes upon them, blent
    with their music,
Well pleased, accepting all, curiously prepared for by them,
Thou enterest at thy entrance porch.

A CHRISTMAS GREETING.

From a Northern Star-Group to a Southern. 1889-'90.

WELCOME, Brazilian brother*—thy ample place is ready ;
A loving hand—a smile from the north—a sunny instant hail !
(Let the future care for itself, where it reveals its troubles, im-
    pedimentas,
Ours, ours the present throe, the democratic aim, the acceptance
    and the faith ;)
To thee to-day our reaching arm, our turning neck—to thee
    from us the expectant eye,
Thou cluster free ! thou brilliant lustrous one ! thou, learning well,
The true lesson of a nation's light in the sky,
(More shining than the Cross, more than the Crown,)
The height to be superb humanity.

SOUNDS OF THE WINTER.

SOUNDS of the winter too,
Sunshine upon the mountains—many a distant strain
From cheery railroad train—from nearer field, barn, house,
The whispering air—even the mute crops, garner'd apples, corn,
Children's and women's tones—rhythm of many a farmer and
    of flail,
An old man's garrulous lips among the rest, *Think not we give
    out yet,*
Forth from these snowy hairs we keep up yet the lilt.

A TWILIGHT SONG.

As I sit in twilight late alone by the flickering oak-flame,
Musing on long-pass'd war-scenes—of the countless buried un-
    known soldiers,
Of the vacant names, as unindented air's and sea's—the un-
    return'd,
The brief truce after battle, with grim burial-squads, and the
    deep-fill'd trenches
Of gather'd dead from all America, North, South, East, West,
    whence they came up,
From wooded Maine, New-England's farms, from fertile Penn-
    sylvania, Illinois, Ohio,
From the measureless West, Virginia, the South, the Carolinas,
    Texas,
(Even here in my room-shadows and half-lights in the noiseless
    flickering flames,
Again I see the stalwart ranks on-filing, rising—I hear the
    rhythmic tramp of the armies ;)
You million unwrit names all, all—you dark bequest from all the
    war,
A special verse for you—a flash of duty long neglected—your
    mystic roll strangely gather'd here,
Each name recall'd by me from out the darkness and death's
    ashes,
Henceforth to be, deep, deep within my heart recording, for
    many a future year,
Your mystic roll entire of unknown names, or North or
    South,
Embalm'd with love in this twilight song.

WHEN THE FULL-GROWN POET CAME.

When the full-grown poet came,
Out spake pleased Nature (the round impassive globe, with all
    its shows of day and night,) saying, *He is mine;*
But out spake too the Soul of man, proud, jealous and unrec-
    onciled, *Nay, he is mine alone;*
—Then the full-grown poet stood between the two, and took
    each by the hand ;
And to-day and ever so stands, as blender, uniter, tightly hold-
    ing hands,
Which he will never release until he reconciles the two,
And wholly and joyously blends them.

OSCEOLA.

[When I was nearly grown to manhood in Brooklyn, New York, (middle of 1838,) I met one of the return'd U. S. Marines from Fort Moultrie, S. C., and had long talks with him—learn'd the occurrence below described—death of Osceola. The latter was a young, brave, leading Seminole in the Florida war of that time—was surrender'd to our troops, imprison'd and literally died of "a broken heart," at Fort Moultrie. He sicken'd of his confinement—the doctor and officers made every allowance and kindness possible for him; then the close :]

WHEN his hour for death had come,
He slowly rais'd himself from the bed on the floor,
Drew on his war-dress, shirt, leggings, and girdled the belt
    around his waist,
Call'd for vermilion paint (his looking-glass was held before
    him,)
Painted half his face and neck, his wrists, and back-hands,
Put the scalp-knife carefully in his belt—then lying down, resting
    a moment,
Rose again, half sitting, smiled, gave in silence his extended
    hand to each and all,
Sank faintly low to the floor (tightly grasping the tomahawk
    handle,)
Fix'd his look on wife and little children—the last :

(And here a line in memory of his name and death.)

A VOICE FROM DEATH.

(The Johnstown, Penn., cataclysm, May 31, 1889.)

A VOICE from Death, solemn and strange, in all his sweep and
    power,
With sudden, indescribable blow—towns drown'd—humanity by
    thousands slain,
The vaunted work of thrift, goods, dwellings, forge, street, iron
    bridge,
Dash'd pell-mell by the blow—yet usher'd life continuing on,
(Amid the rest, amid the rushing, whirling, wild debris,
A suffering woman saved—a baby safely born !)

Although I come and unannounc'd, in horror and in pang,
In pouring flood and fire, and wholesale elemental crash, (this
    voice so solemn, strange,)
I too a minister of Deity.

Yea, Death, we bow our faces, veil our eyes to thee,
We mourn the old, the young untimely drawn to thee,
The fair, the strong, the good, the capable,

The household wreck'd, the husband and the wife, the engulf'd
    forger in his forge,
The corpses in the whelming waters and the mud,
The gather'd thousands to their funeral mounds, and thousands
    never found or gather'd.

Then after burying, mourning the dead,
(Faithful to them found or unfound, forgetting not, bearing the
    past, here new musing,)
A day—a passing moment or an hour—America itself bends low,
Silent, resign'd, submissive.

War, death, cataclysm like this, America,
Take deep to thy proud prosperous heart.

E'en as I chant, lo! out of death, and out of ooze and slime,
The blossoms rapidly blooming, sympathy, help, love,
From West and East, from South and North and over sea,
Its hot-spurr'd hearts and hands humanity to human aid moves on;
And from within a thought and lesson yet.

Thou ever-darting Globe! through Space and Air!
Thou waters that encompass us!
Thou that in all the life and death of us, in action or in sleep!
Thou laws invisible that permeate them and all,
Thou that in all, and over all, and through and under all,
    incessant!
Thou! thou! the vital, universal, giant force resistless, sleepless,
    calm,
Holding Humanity as in thy open hand, as some ephemeral toy,
How ill to e'er forget thee!

For I too have forgotten,
(Wrapt in these little potencies of progress, politics, culture,
    wealth, inventions, civilization,)
Have lost my recognition of your silent ever-swaying power,
    ye mighty, elemental throes,
In which and upon which we float, and every one of us is
    buoy'd.

A PERSIAN LESSON.

For his o'erarching and last lesson the greybeard sufi,
In the fresh scent of the morning in the open air,
On the slope of a teeming Persian rose-garden,
Under an ancient chestnut-tree wide spreading its branches,
Spoke to the young priests and students.

"Finally my children, to envelop each word, each part of the
    rest,
Allah is all, all, all—is immanent in every life and object,
May-be at many and many-a-more removes—yet Allah, Allah,
    Allah is there.

"Has the estray wander'd far ? Is the reason-why strangely
    hidden ?
Would you sound below the restless ocean of the entire world ?
Would you know the dissatisfaction ? the urge and spur of every
    life ;
The something never still'd—never entirely gone? the invisible
    need of every seed ?

"It is the central urge in every atom,
(Often unconscious, often evil, downfallen,)
To return to its divine source and origin, however distant,
Latent the same in subject and in object, without one exception."

THE COMMONPLACE.

THE commonplace I sing ;
How cheap is health ! how cheap nobility !
Abstinence, no falsehood, no gluttony, lust ;
The open air I sing, freedom, toleration,
(Take here the mainest lesson—less from books—less from the
    schools,)
The common day and night—the common earth and waters,
Your farm—your work, trade, occupation,
The democratic wisdom underneath, like solid ground for all.

"THE ROUNDED CATALOGUE DIVINE COMPLETE."

[Sunday, —— — ——.—Went this forenoon to church. A college profes-
sor, Rev. Dr. ———, gave us a fine sermon, during which I caught the above
words ; but the minister included in his " rounded catalogue " letter and spirit,
only the esthetic things, and entirely ignored what I name in the following :]

THE devilish and the dark, the dying and diseas'd,
The countless (nineteen-twentieths) low and evil, crude and
    savage,
The crazed, prisoners in jail, the horrible, rank, malignant,
Venom and filth, serpents, the ravenous sharks, liars, the disso-
    lute ;
(What is the part the wicked and the loathesome bear within
    earth's orbic scheme ?)
Newts, crawling things in slime and mud, poisons,
The barren soil, the evil men, the slag and hideous rot.

MIRAGES.

(*Noted verbatim after a supper-talk out doors in Nevada with two old miners.*)

MORE experiences and sights, stranger, than you'd think for;
Times again, now mostly just after sunrise or before sunset,
Sometimes in spring, oftener in autumn, perfectly clear weather,
    in plain sight,
Camps far or near, the crowded streets of cities and the shop-
    fronts,
(Account for it or not—credit or not—it is all true,
And my mate there could tell you the like—we have often con-
    fab'd about it,)
People and scenes, animals, trees, colors and lines, plain as could
    be,
Farms and dooryards of home, paths border'd with box, lilacs
    in corners,
Weddings in churches, thanksgiving dinners, returns of long-
    absent sons,
Glum funerals, the crape-veil'd mother and the daughters,
Trials in courts, jury and judge, the accused in the box,
Contestants, battles, crowds, bridges, wharves,
Now and then mark'd faces of sorrow or joy,
(I could pick them out this moment if I saw them again,)
Show'd to me just aloft to the right in the sky-edge,
Or plainly there to the left on the hill-tops.

L. OF G.'S PURPORT.

NOT to exclude or demarcate, or pick out evils from their formid-
    able masses (even to expose them,)
But add, fuse, complete, extend—and celebrate the immortal and
    the good.

Haughty this song, its words and scope,
To span vast realms of space and time,
Evolution—the cumulative—growths and generations.

Begun in ripen'd youth and steadily pursued,
Wandering, peering, dallying with all—war, peace, day and
    night absorbing,
Never even for one brief hour abandoning my task,
I end it here in sickness, poverty, and old age.

I sing of life, yet mind me well of death:
To-day shadowy Death dogs my steps, my seated shape, and
    has for years—
Draws sometimes close to me, as face to face.

THE UNEXPRESS'D.

How dare one say it?
After the cycles, poems, singers, plays,
Vaunted Ionia's, India's—Homer, Shakspere—the long, long
    times' thick dotted roads, areas,
The shining clusters and the Milky Ways of stars—Nature's
    pulses reap'd,
All retrospective passions, heroes, war, love, adoration,
All ages' plummets dropt to their utmost depths,
All human lives, throats, wishes, brains—all experiences' utter-
    ance;
After the countless songs, or long or short, all tongues, all lands,
Still something not yet told in poesy's voice or print—something
    lacking,
(Who knows? the best yet unexpress'd and lacking.)

GRAND IS THE SEEN.

GRAND is the seen, the light, to me—grand are the sky and
    stars,
Grand is the earth, and grand are lasting time and space,
And grand their laws, so multiform, puzzling, evolutionary;
But grander far the unseen soul of me, comprehending, endow-
    ing all those,
Lighting the light, the sky and stars, delving the earth, sailing
    the sea,
(What were all those, indeed, without thee, unseen soul? of
    what amount without thee?)
More evolutionary, vast, puzzling, O my soul!
More multiform far—more lasting thou than they.

UNSEEN BUDS.

UNSEEN buds, infinite, hidden well,
Under the snow and ice, under the darkness, in every square or
    cubic inch,
Germinal, exquisite, in delicate lace, microscopic, unborn,
Like babes in wombs, latent, folded, compact, sleeping;
Billions of billions, and trillions of trillions of them waiting,
(On earth and in the sea—the universe—the stars there in the
    heavens,)
Urging slowly, surely forward, forming endless,
And waiting ever more, forever more behind.

GOOD-BYE MY FANCY!

GOOD-BYE my Fancy!
Farewell dear mate, dear love!
I'm going away, I know not where,
Or to what fortune, or whether I may ever see you again,
So Good-bye my Fancy.

Now for my last—let me look back a moment;
The slower fainter ticking of the clock is in me,
Exit, nightfall, and soon the heart-thud stopping.

Long have we lived, joy'd, caress'd together;
Delightful!—now separation—Good-bye my Fancy.

Yet let me not be too hasty,
Long indeed have we lived, slept, filter'd, become really blended
    into one;
Then if we die we die together, (yes, we'll remain one,)
If we go anywhere we'll go together to meet what happens,
May-be we'll be better off and blither, and learn something,
May-be it is yourself now really ushering me to the true songs,
    (who knows?)
May-be it is you the mortal knob really undoing, turning—so
    now finally,
Good-bye—and hail! my Fancy.

A

BACKWARD GLANCE

O'ER

TRAVEL'D ROADS.

A BACKWARD GLANCE O'ER
TRAVEL'D ROADS.

PERHAPS the best of songs heard, or of any and all true love, or
life's fairest episodes, or sailors', soldiers' trying scenes on land
or sea, is the *résumé* of them, or any of them, long afterwards,
looking at the actualities away back past, with all their practical
excitations gone. How the soul loves to float amid such reminis-
cences!

So here I sit gossiping in the early candle-light of old age—I
and my book—casting backward glances over our travel'd road.
After completing, as it were, the journey—(a varied jaunt of
years, with many halts and gaps of intervals—or some lengthen'd
ship-voyage, wherein more than once the last hour had apparently
arrived, and we seem'd certainly going down—yet reaching port
in a sufficient way through all discomfitures at last)—After com-
pleting my poems, I am curious to review them in the light of
their own (at the time unconscious, or mostly unconscious) inten-
tions, with certain unfoldings of the thirty years they seek to
embody. These lines, therefore, will probably blend the weft
of first purposes and speculations, with the warp of that expe-
rience afterwards, always bringing strange developments.

Result of seven or eight stages and struggles extending through
nearly thirty years, (as I nigh my three-score-and-ten I live
largely on memory,) I look upon "Leaves of Grass," now fin-
ish'd to the end of its opportunities and powers, as my definitive
carte visite to the coming generations of the New World,* if I
may assume to say so. That I have not gain'd the acceptance of
my own time, but have fallen back on fond dreams of the future
—anticipations—("still lives the song, though Regnar dies")—
That from a worldly and business point of view "Leaves of
Grass" has been worse than a failure—that public criticism on
the book and myself as author of it yet shows mark'd anger and
contempt more than anything else—("I find a solid line of ene-

---

* When Champollion, on his death-bed, handed to the printer the revised
proof of his "Egyptian Grammar," he said gayly, "Be careful of this—it is
my *carte de visite* to posterity."

mies to you everywhere,"—letter from W. S. K., Boston, May 28, 1884)—And that solely for publishing it I have been the object of two or three pretty serious special official buffetings—is all probably no more than I ought to have expected. I had my choice when I commenc'd. I bid neither for soft eulogies, big money returns, nor the approbation of existing schools and conventions. As fulfill'd, or partially fulfill'd, the best comfort of the whole business (after a small band of the dearest friends and upholders ever vouchsafed to man or cause—doubtless all the more faithful and uncompromising—this little phalanx!—for being so few) is that, unstopp'd and unwarp'd by any influence outside the soul within me, I have had my say entirely my own way, and put it unerringly on record—the value thereof to be decided by time.

In calculating that decision, William O'Connor*and Dr. Bucke are far more peremptory than I am. Behind all else that can be said, I consider "Leaves of Grass" and its theory experimental —as, in the deepest sense, I consider our American republic itself to be, with its theory. (I think I have at least enough philosophy not to be too absolutely certain of any thing, or any results.) In the second place, the volume is a *sortie*—whether to prove triumphant, and conquer its field of aim and escape and construction, nothing less than a hundred years from now can fully answer. I consider the point that I have positively gain'd a hearing, to far more than make up for any and all other lacks and witholdings. Essentially, *that* was from the first, and has remain'd throughout, the main object. Now it seems to be achiev'd, I am certainly contented to waive any otherwise momentous drawbacks, as of little account. Candidly and dispassionately reviewing all my intentions, I feel that they were creditable—and I accept the result, whatever it may be.

After continued personal ambition and effort, as a young fellow, to enter with the rest into competition for the usual rewards, business, political, literary, &c.—to take part in the great *mêlée*, both for victory's prize itself and to do some good—After years of those aims and pursuits, I found myself remaining possess'd, at the age of thirty-one to thirty-three, with a special desire and conviction. Or rather, to be quite exact, a desire that had been flitting through my previous life, or hovering on the flanks, mostly indefinite hitherto, had steadily advanced to the front, defined itself, and finally dominated everything else. This was a feeling or ambition to articulate and faithfully express in literary or poetic form, and uncompromisingly, my own physical, emotional, moral, intellectual, and æsthetic Personality, in the midst of, and tallying, the momentous spirit and facts of its immediate days, and of current America—and to exploit that Personality, identified with place and date, in a far more candid and comprehensive sense than any hitherto poem or book.

Perhaps this is in brief, or suggests, all I have sought to do. Given the Nineteenth Century, with the United States, and what they furnish as area and points of view, "Leaves of Grass" is, or seeks to be, simply a faithful and doubtless self-will'd record. In the midst of all, it gives one man's—the author's—identity, ardors, observations, faiths, and thoughts, color'd hardly at all with any decided coloring from other faiths or other identities. Plenty of songs had been sung—beautiful, matchless songs—adjusted to other lands than these—another spirit and stage of evolution; but I would sing, and leave out or put in, quite solely with reference to America and to-day. Modern science and democracy seem'd to be throwing out their challenge to poetry to put them in its statements in contradistinction to the songs and myths of the past. As I see it now (perhaps too late,) I have unwittingly taken up that challenge and made an attempt at such statements—which I certainly would not assume to do now, knowing more clearly what it means.

For grounds for "Leaves of Grass," as a poem, I abandon'd the conventional themes, which do not appear in it: none of the stock ornamentation, or choice plots of love or war, or high, exceptional personages of Old-World song; nothing, as I may say, for beauty's sake—no legend, or myth, or romance, nor euphemism, nor rhyme. But the broadest average of humanity and its identities in the now ripening Nineteenth Century, and especially in each of their countless examples and practical occupations in the United States to-day.

One main contrast of the ideas behind every page of my verses, compared with establish'd poems, is their different relative attitude towards God, towards the objective universe, and still more (by reflection, confession, assumption, &c.) the quite changed attitude of the ego, the one chanting or talking, towards himself and towards his fellow-humanity. It is certainly time for America, above all, to begin this readjustment in the scope and basic point of view of verse; for everything else has changed. As I write, I see in an article on Wordsworth, in one of the current English magazines, the lines, "A few weeks ago an eminent French critic said that, owing to the special tendency to science and to its all-devouring force, poetry would cease to be read in fifty years." But I anticipate the very contrary. Only a firmer, vastly broader, new area begins to exist—nay, is already form'd —to which the poetic genius must emigrate. Whatever may have been the case in years gone by, the true use for the imaginative faculty of modern times is to give ultimate vivification to facts, to science, and to common lives, endowing them with the glows and glories and final illustriousness which belong to every real thing, and to real things only. Without that ultimate vivification—which the poet or other artist alone can give—reality would seem incomplete, and science, democracy, and life itself, finally in vain.

Few appreciate the moral revolutions, our age, which have been profounder far than the material or inventive or war-produced ones. The Nineteenth Century, now well towards its close (and ripening into fruit the seeds of the two preceding centuries*)—the uprisings of national masses and shiftings of boundary-lines—the historical and other prominent facts of the United States—the war of attempted Secession—the stormy rush and haste of nebulous forces—never can future years witness more excitement and din of action—never completer change of army front along the whole line, the whole civilized world. For all these new and evolutionary facts, meanings, purposes, new poetic messages, new forms and expressions, are inevitable.

My Book and I—what a period we have presumed to span! those thirty years from 1850 to '80—and America in them! Proud, proud indeed may we be, if we have cull'd enough of that period in its own spirit to worthily waft a few live breaths of it to the future!

Let me not dare, here or anywhere, for my own purposes, or any purposes, to attempt the definition of Poetry, nor answer the question what it is. Like Religion, Love, Nature, while those terms are indispensable, and we all give a sufficiently accurate meaning to them, in my opinion no definition that has ever been made sufficiently encloses the name Poetry; nor can any rule or convention ever so absolutely obtain but some great exception may arise and disregard and overturn it.

Also it must be carefully remember'd that first-class literature does not shine by any luminosity of its own; nor do its poems. They grow of circumstances, and are evolutionary. The actual living light is always curiously from elsewhere—follows unaccountable sources, and is lunar and relative at the best. There are, I know, certain controling themes that seem endlessly appropriated to the poets—as war, in the past—in the Bible, religious rapture and adoration—always love, beauty, some fine plot,

---

* The ferment and germination even of the United States to-day, dating back to, and in my opinion mainly founded on, the Elizabethan age in English history, the age of Francis Bacon and Shakspere. Indeed, when we pursue it, what growth or advent is there that does not date back, back, until lost—perhaps its most tantalizing clues lost—in the receded horizons of the past?

or pensive or other emotion. But, strange as it may sound at first, I will say there is something striking far deeper and towering far higher than those themes for the best elements of modern song.

Just as all the old imaginative works rest, after their kind, on long trains of presuppositions, often entirely unmention'd by themselves, yet supplying the most important bases of them, and without which they could have had no reason for being, so "Leaves of Grass," before a line was written, presupposed something different from any other, and, as it stands, is the result of such presupposition. I should say, indeed, it were useless to attempt reading the book without first carefully tallying that preparatory background and quality in the mind. Think of the United States to-day—the facts of these thirty-eight or forty empires solder'd in one—sixty or seventy millions of equals, with their lives, their passions, their future—these incalculable, modern, American, seething multitudes around us, of which we are inseparable parts! Think, in comparison, of the petty environage and limited area of the poets of past or present Europe, no matter how great their genius. Think of the absence and ignorance, in all cases hitherto, of the multitudinousness, vitality, and the unprecedented stimulants of to-day and here. It almost seems as if a poetry with cosmic and dynamic features of magnitude and limitlessness suitable to the human soul, were never possible before. It is certain that a poetry of absolute faith and equality for the use of the democratic masses never was.

In estimating first-class song, a sufficient Nationality, or, on the other hand, what may be call'd the negative and lack of it, (as in Goethe's case, it sometimes seems to me,) is often, if not always, the first element. One needs only a little penetration to see, at more or less removes, the material facts of their country and radius, with the coloring of the moods of humanity at the time, and its gloomy or hopeful prospects, behind all poets and each poet, and forming their birth-marks. I know very well that my "Leaves" could not possibly have emerged or been fashion'd or completed, from any other era than the latter half of the Nineteenth Century, nor any other land than democratic America, and from the absolute triumph of the National Union arms.

And whether my friends claim it for me or not, I know well enough, too, that in respect to pictorial talent, dramatic situations, and especially in verbal melody and all the conventional technique of poetry, not only the divine works that to-day stand ahead in the world's reading, but dozens more, transcend (some of them immeasurably transcend) all I have done, or could do.

But it seem'd to me, as the objects in Nature, the themes of æstheticism, and all special exploitations of the mind and soul, involve not only their own inherent quality, but the quality, just as inherent and important, of *their point of view*,* the time had come to reflect all themes and things, old and new, in the lights thrown on them by the advent of America and democracy—to chant those themes through the utterance of one, not only the grateful and reverent legatee of the past, but the born child of the New World—to illustrate all through the genesis and ensemble of to-day; and that such illustration and ensemble are the chief demands of America's prospective imaginative literature. Not to carry out, in the approved style, some choice plot of fortune or misfortune, or fancy, or fine thoughts, or incidents, or courtesies—all of which has been done overwhelmingly and well, probably never to be excell'd—but that while in such æsthetic presentation of objects, passions, plots, thoughts, &c., our lands and days do not want, and probably will never have, anything better than they already possess from the bequests of the past, it still remains to be said that there is even towards all those a subjective and contemporary point of view appropriate to ourselves alone, and to our new genius and environments, different from anything hitherto; and that such conception of current or gone-by life and art is for us the only means of their assimilation consistent with the Western world.

Indeed, and anyhow, to put it specifically, has not the time arrived when, (if it must be plainly said, for democratic America's sake, if for no other) there must imperatively come a readjustment of the whole theory and nature of Poetry? The question is important, and I may turn the argument over and repeat it: Does not the best thought of our day and Republic conceive of a birth and spirit of song superior to anything past or present? To the effectual and moral consolidation of our lands (already, as materially establish'd, the greatest factors in known history, and far, far greater through what they prelude and necessitate, and are to be in future)—to conform with and build on the concrete realities and theories of the universe furnish'd by science, and henceforth the only irrefragable basis for anything, verse included—to root both influences in the emotional and imaginative action of the modern time, and dominate all that precedes or opposes them—is not either a radical advance and step forward, or a new verteber of the best song indispensable?

---

* According to Immanuel Kant, the last essential reality, giving shape and significance to all the rest.

The New World receives with joy the poems of the antique, with European feudalism's rich fund of epics, plays, ballads—seeks not in the least to deaden or displace those voices from our ear and area—holds them indeed as indispensable studies, influences, records, comparisons. But though the dawn-dazzle of the sun of literature is in those poems for us of to-day—though perhaps the best parts of current character in nations, social groups, or any man's or woman's individuality, Old World or New, are from them—and though if I were ask'd to name the most precious bequest to current American civilization from all the hitherto ages, I am not sure but I would name those old and less old songs ferried hither from east and west—some serious words and debits remain ; some acrid considerations demand a hearing. Of the great poems receiv'd from abroad and from the ages, and to-day enveloping and penetrating America, is there one that is consistent with these United States, or essentially applicable to them as they are and are to be ? Is there one whose underlying basis is not a denial and insult to democracy? What a comment it forms, anyhow, on this era of literary fulfilment, with the splendid day-rise of science and resuscitation of history, that our chief religious and poetical works are not our own, nor adapted to our light, but have been furnish'd by far-back ages out of their arriere and darkness, or, at most, twilight dimness ! What is there in those works that so imperiously and scornfully dominates all our advanced civilization, and culture?

Even Shakspere, who so suffuses current letters and art (which indeed have in most degrees grown out of him,) belongs essentially to the buried past. Only he holds the proud distinction for certain important phases of that past, of being the loftiest of the singers life has yet given voice to. All, however, relate to and rest upon conditions, standards, politics, sociologies, ranges of belief, that have been quite eliminated from the Eastern hemisphere, and never existed at all in the Western. As authoritative types of song they belong in America just about as much as the persons and institutes they depict. True, it may be said, the emotional, moral, and æsthetic natures of humanity have not radically changed—that in these the old poems apply to our times and all times, irrespective of date; and that they are of incalculable value as pictures of the past. I willingly make those admissions, and to their fullest extent; then advance the points herewith as of serious, even paramount importance.

I have indeed put on record elsewhere my reverence and eulogy for those never-to-be-excell'd poetic bequests, and their indescribable preciousness as heirlooms for America. Another and separate point must now be candidly stated. If I had not stood before those poems with uncover'd head, fully aware of their colossal grandeur and beauty of form and spirit, I could not have written "Leaves of Grass." My verdict and conclusions as illustrated in its pages are arrived at through the temper and inculcation of the old works as much as through anything else— perhaps more than through anything else. As America fully and fairly construed is the legitimate result and evolutionary outcome of the past, so I would dare to claim for my verse. Without stopping to qualify the averment, the Old World has had the poems of myths, fictions, feudalism, conquest, caste, dynastic wars, and splendid exceptional characters and affairs, which have been great; but the New World needs the poems of realities and science and of the democratic average and basic equality, which shall be greater. In the centre of all, and object of all, stands the Human Being, towards whose heroic and spiritual evolution poems and everything directly or indirectly tend, Old World or New.

Continuing the subject, my friends have more than once suggested—or may be the garrulity of advancing age is possessing me—some further embryonic facts of "Leaves of Grass," and especially how I enter'd upon them. Dr. Bucke has, in his volume, already fully and fairly described the preparation of my poetic field, with the particular and general plowing, planting, seeding, and occupation of the ground, till everything was fertilized, rooted, and ready to start its own way for good or bad. Not till after all this, did I attempt any serious acquaintance with poetic literature. Along in my sixteenth year I had become possessor of a stout, well-cramm'd one thousand page octavo volume (I have it yet,) containing Walter Scott's poetry entire— an inexhaustible mine and treasury of poetic forage (especially the endless forests and jungles of notes)—has been so to me for fifty years, and remains so to this day.*

Later, at intervals, summers and falls, I used to go off, sometimes for a week at a stretch, down in the country, or to Long Island's seashores—there, in the presence of outdoor influences,

---

* Sir Walter Scott's COMPLETE POEMS; especially including BORDER MINSTRELSY; then Sir Tristrem; Lay of the Last Minstrel; Ballads from the German; Marmion; Lady of the Lake; Vision of Don Roderick; Lord of the Isles; Rokeby; Bridal of Triermain; Field of Waterloo; Harold the Dauntless; all the Dramas; various Introductions, endless interesting Notes, and Essays on Poetry, Romance, &c.

Lockhart's 1833 (or '34) edition with Scott's latest and copious revisions and annotations. (All the poems were thoroughly read by me, but the ballads of the Border Minstrelsy over and over again.)

I went over thoroughly the Old and New Testaments, and ab-
sorb'd (probably to better advantage for me than in any library
or indoor room—it makes such difference *where* you read,) Shak-
spere, Ossian, the best translated versions I could get of Homer,
Æschylus, Sophocles, the old German Nibelungen, the ancient
Hindoo poems, and one or two other masterpieces, Dante's
among them. As it happen'd, I read the latter mostly in an old
wood. The Iliad (Buckley's prose version,) I read first thor-
oughly on the peninsula of Orient, northeast end of Long Island,
in a shelter'd hollow of rocks and sand, with the sea on each side.
(I have wonder'd since why I was not overwhelm'd by those
mighty masters. Likely because I read them, as described, in
the full presence of Nature, under the sun, with the far-spreading
landscape and vistas, or the sea rolling in.)

Toward the last I had among much else look'd over Edgar
Poe's poems—of which I was not an admirer, tho' I always
saw that beyond their limited range of melody (like perpetual
chimes of music bells, ringing from lower *b* flat up to *g*) they
were melodious expressions, and perhaps never excell'd ones, of
certain pronounc'd phases of human morbidity. (The Poetic
area is very spacious—has room for all—has so many mansions !)
But I was repaid in Poe's prose by the idea that (at any rate for
our occasions, our day) there can be no such thing as a long
poem. The same thought had been haunting my mind before,
but Poe's argument, though short, work'd the sum out and proved
it to me.

Another point had an early settlement, clearing the ground
greatly. I saw, from the time my enterprise and questionings
positively shaped themselves (how best can I express my own
distinctive era and surroundings, America, Democracy?) that the
trunk and centre whence the answer was to radiate, and to which
all should return from straying however far a distance, must be
an identical body and soul, a personality—which personality,
after many considerations and ponderings I deliberately settled
should be myself—indeed could not be any other. I also felt
strongly (whether I have shown it or not) that to the true and
full estimate of the Present both the Past and the Future are main
considerations.

These, however, and much more might have gone on and come
to naught (almost positively would have come to naught,) if a
sudden, vast, terrible, direct and indirect stimulus for new and
national declamatory expression had not been given to me. It
is certain, I say, that, although I had made a start before, only
from the occurrence of the Secession War, and what it show'd
me as by flashes of lightning, with the emotional depths it sounded

and arous'd (of course, I don't mean in my own heart only, I saw it just as plainly in others, in millions)—that only from the strong flare and provocation of that war's sights and scenes the final reasons-for-being of an autochthonic and passionate song definitely came forth.

I went down to the war fields in Virginia (end of 1862), lived thenceforward in camp—saw great battles and the days and nights afterward—partook of all the fluctuations, gloom, despair, hopes again arous'd, courage evoked—death readily risk'd—*the cause*, too—along and filling those agonistic and lurid following years, 1863-'64-'65—the real parturition years (more than 1776-'83) of this henceforth homogeneous Union. Without those three or four years and the experiences they gave, "Leaves of Grass" would not now be existing.

But I set out with the intention also of indicating or hinting some point-characteristics which I since see (though I did not then, at least not definitely) were bases and object-urgings toward those "Leaves" from the first. The word I myself put primarily for the description of them as they stand at last, is the word Suggestiveness. I round and finish little, if anything; and could not, consistently with my scheme. The reader will always have his or her part to do, just as much as I have had mine. I seek less to state or display any theme or thought, and more to bring you, reader, into the atmosphere of the theme or thought—there to pursue your own flight. Another impetus-word is Comradeship as for all lands, and in a more commanding and acknowledg'd sense than hitherto. Other word-signs would be Good Cheer, Content, and Hope.

The chief trait of any given poet is always the spirit he brings to the observation of Humanity and Nature—the mood out of which he contemplates his subjects. What kind of temper and what amount of faith report these things? Up to how recent a date is the song carried? What the equipment, and special raciness of the singer—what his tinge of coloring? The last value of artistic expressers, past and present—Greek æsthetes, Shakspere—or in our own day Tennyson, Victor Hugo, Carlyle, Emerson—is certainly involv'd in such questions. I say the profoundest service that poems or any other writings can do for their reader is not merely to satisfy the intellect, or supply something polish'd and interesting, nor even to depict great passions, or persons or events, but to fill him with vigorous and clean manliness, religiousness, and give him *good heart* as a radical possession and habit. The educated world seems to have been growing more and more ennuyed for ages, leaving to our time the inheritance of it all. Fortunately there is the original inexhaustible fund of buoyancy, normally resident in the race, forever eligible to be appeal'd to and relied on.

As for native American individuality, though certain to come, and on a large scale, the distinctive and ideal type of Western character (as consistent with the operative political and even money-making features of United States' humanity in the Nineteenth Century as chosen knights, gentlemen and warriors were the ideals of the centuries of European feudalism) it has not yet appear'd. I have allow'd the stress of my poems from beginning to end to bear upon American individuality and assist it—not only because that is a great lesson in Nature, amid all her generalizing laws, but as counterpoise to the leveling tendencies of Democracy—and for other reasons. Defiant of ostensible literary and other conventions, I avowedly chant "the great pride of man in himself," and permit it to be more or less a *motif* of nearly all my verse. I think this pride indispensable to an American. I think it not inconsistent with obedience, humility, deference, and self-questioning.

Democracy has been so retarded and jeopardized by powerful personalities, that its first instincts are fain to clip, conform, bring in stragglers, and reduce everything to a dead level. While the ambitious thought of my song is to help the forming of a great aggregate Nation, it is, perhaps, altogether through the forming of myriads of fully develop'd and enclosing individuals. Welcome as are equality's and fraternity's doctrines and popular education, a certain liability accompanies them all, as we see. That primal and interior something in man, in his soul's abysms, coloring all, and, by exceptional fruitions, giving the last majesty to him—something continually touch'd upon and attain'd by the old poems and ballads of feudalism, and often the principal foundation of them—modern science and democracy appear to be endangering, perhaps eliminating. But that forms an appearance only; the reality is quite different. The new influences, upon the whole, are surely preparing the way for grander individualities than ever. To-day and here personal force is behind everything, just the same. The times and depictions from the Iliad to Shakspere inclusive can happily never again be realized—but the elements of courageous and lofty manhood are unchanged.

Without yielding an inch the working-man and working-woman were to be in my pages from first to last. The ranges of heroism and loftiness with which Greek and feudal poets endow'd their god-like or lordly born characters—indeed prouder and better based and with fuller ranges than those—I was to endow the democratic averages of America. I was to show that we, here and to-day, are eligible to the grandest and the best—more eligible now than any times of old were. I will also want my utterances (I said to myself before beginning) to be in spirit the poems of the morning. (They have been founded and mainly written in the sunny forenoon and early midday of my life.) I will want them to be the poems of women entirely as much as men. I have wish'd to put the complete Union of the States in my songs without any preference or partiality whatever. Henceforth, if they live and are read, it must be just as much South as North—just as much along the Pacific as Atlantic—in the valley of the Mississippi, in Canada, up in Maine, down in Texas, and on the shores of Puget Sound.

From another point of view "Leaves of Grass" is avowedly the song of Sex and Amativeness, and even Animality—though meanings that do not usually go along with those words are behind all, and will duly emerge; and all are sought to be lifted into a different light and atmosphere. Of this feature, intentionally palpable in a few lines, I shall only say the espousing principle of those lines so gives breath of life to my whole scheme that the bulk of the pieces might as well have been left unwritten were those lines omitted. Difficult as it will be, it has become, in my opinion, imperative to achieve a shifted attitude from superior men and women towards the thought and fact of sexuality, as an element in character, personality, the emotions, and a theme in literature. I am not going to argue the question by itself; it does not stand by itself. The vitality of it is altogether in its relations, bearings, significance—like the clef of a symphony. At last analogy the lines I allude to, and the spirit in which they are spoken, permeate all "Leaves of Grass," and the work must stand or fall with them, as the human body and soul must remain as an entirety.

Universal as are certain facts and symptoms of communities or individuals all times, there is nothing so rare in modern conventions and poetry as their normal recognizance. Literature is always calling in the doctor for consultation and confession, and always giving evasions and swathing suppressions in place of that "heroic nudity" * on which only a genuine diagnosis of serious cases can be built. And in respect to editions of "Leaves of Grass" in time to come (if there should be such) I take occasion now to confirm those lines with the settled convictions and deliberate renewals of thirty years, and to hereby prohibit, as far as word of mine can do so, any elision of them.

---

* "Nineteenth Century," July, 1883.

Then still a purpose enclosing all, and over and beneath all. Ever since what might be call'd thought, or the budding of thought, fairly began in my youthful mind, I had had a desire to attempt some worthy record of that entire faith and acceptance ("to justify the ways of God to man" is Milton's well-known and ambitious phrase) which is the foundation of moral America. I felt it all as positively then in my young days as I do now in my old ones; to formulate a poem whose every thought or fact should directly or indirectly be or connive at an implicit belief in the wisdom, health, mystery, beauty of every process, every concrete object, every human or other existence, not only consider'd from the point of view of all, but of each.

While I can not understand it or argue it out, I fully believe in a clue and purpose in Nature, entire and several; and that invisible spiritual results, just as real and definite as the visible, eventuate all concrete life and all materialism, through Time. My book ought to emanate buoyancy and gladness legitimately enough, for it was grown out of those elements, and has been the comfort of my life since it was originally commenced.

One main genesis-motive of the "Leaves" was my conviction (just as strong to-day as ever) that the crowning growth of the United States is to be spiritual and heroic. To help start and favor that growth—or even to call attention to it, or the need of it—is the beginning, middle and final purpose of the poems. (In fact, when really cipher'd out and summ'd to the last, plowing up in earnest the interminable average fallows of humanity—not "good government" merely, in the common sense—is the justification and main purpose of these United States.)

Isolated advantages in any rank or grace or fortune—the direct or indirect threads of all the poetry of the past—are in my opinion distasteful to the republican genius, and offer no foundation for its fitting verse. Establish'd poems, I know, have the very great advantage of chanting the already perform'd, so full of glories, reminiscences dear to the minds of men. But my volume is a candidate for the future. "All original art," says Taine, anyhow, "is self-regulated, and no original art can be regulated from without; it carries its own counterpoise, and does not receive it from elsewhere—lives on its own blood"—a solace to my frequent bruises and sulky vanity.

As the present is perhaps mainly an attempt at personal statement or illustration, I will allow myself as further help to extract the following anecdote from a book, "Annals of Old Painters," conn'd by me in youth. Rubens, the Flemish painter, in one of his wanderings through the galleries of old convents, came across a singular work. After looking at it thoughtfully for a good while, and listening to the criticisms of his suite of students, he said to the latter, in answer to their questions (as to what school the work implied or belong'd,) "I do not believe the artist, unknown and perhaps no longer living, who has given the world this legacy, ever belong'd to any school, or ever painted anything but this one picture, which is a personal affair—a piece out of a man's life."

"Leaves of Grass" indeed (I cannot too often reiterate) has mainly been the outcropping of my own emotional and other personal nature—an attempt, from first to last, to put *a Person,* a human being (myself, in the latter half of the Nineteenth Century, in America,) freely, fully and truly on record. I could not find any similar personal record in current literature that satisfied me. But it is not on "Leaves of Grass" distinctively as *literature,* or a specimen thereof, that I feel to dwell, or advance claims. No one will get at my verses who insists upon viewing them as a literary performance, or attempt at such performance, or as aiming mainly toward art or æstheticism.

I say no land or people or circumstances ever existed so needing a race of singers and poems differing from all others, and rigidly their own, as the land and people and circumstances of our United States need such singers and poems to-day, and for the future. Still further, as long as the States continue to absorb and be dominated by the poetry of the Old World, and remain unsupplied with autochthonous song, to express, vitalize and give color to and define their material and political success, and minister to them distinctively, so long will they stop short of first-class Nationality and remain defective.

In the free evening of my day I give to you, reader, the foregoing garrulous talk, thoughts, reminiscences,

> As idly drifting down the ebb,
> Such ripples, half-caught voices, echo from the shore.

Concluding with two items for the imaginative genius of the West, when it worthily rises—First, what Herder taught to the young Goethe, that really great poetry is always (like the Homeric or Biblical canticles) the result of a national spirit, and not the privilege of a polish'd and select few; Second, that the strongest and sweetest songs yet remain to be sung.

APPENDIX A
PREFACE TO THE 1855 *LEAVES OF GRASS*

There is evidence to suggest that Whitman wrote the preface in haste after he had written the twelve poems which make up the first edition. The ellipses are Whitman's and may have been intended as elocutionary marks to indicate appropriate pauses in a speech. Many of the ideas and images of the 1855 Preface were subsequently absorbed into 'By Blue Ontario's Shore' (1856) and other poems.

AMERICA does not repel the past or what it has produced under its forms or amid other politics or the idea of casts or the old religions. . . . accepts the lesson with calmness . . . is not so impatient as has been supposed that the slough still sticks to opinions and manners and literature while the life which served its requirements has passed into the new life of the new forms . . . perceives that the corpse is slowly borne from the eating and sleeping rooms of the house . . . perceives that it waits a little while in the door . . . that it was fittest for its days . . . that its action has descended to the stalwart and wellshaped heir who approaches . . . and that he shall be fittest for his days.

The Americans of all nations at any time upon the earth have probably the fullest poetical nature. The United States themselves are essentially the greatest poem. In the history of the earth hitherto the largest and most stirring appear tame and orderly to their ampler largeness and stir. Here at last is something in the doings of man that corresponds with the broadcast doings of the day and night. Here is not merely a nation but a teeming nation of nations. Here is action untied from strings necessarily blind to particulars and details magnificently moving in vast masses. Here is the hospitality which forever indicates heroes. . . . Here are the roughs and beards and space and ruggedness and nonchalance that the soul loves. Here the performance disdaining the trivial unapproached in the tremendous audacity of its crowds and groupings and the push of its perspective spreads with crampless and flowing breadth and showers its prolific and splendid extravagance. One sees it must indeed own the riches of the summer and winter, and need never be bankrupt while corn grows from the ground or the orchards drop apples or the bays contain fish or men beget children upon women.

Other states indicate themselves in their deputies. . . . but the genius of the United States is not best or most in its executives or legislatures, nor in its ambassadors or authors or colleges or churches or parlors, nor even in its newspapers or inventors . . . but always most in the common people. Their manners speech dress friendships—the freshness and candor of their physiognomy—the picturesque looseness of their carriage . . . their deathless attachment to freedom— their aversion to anything indecorous or soft or mean—the practical acknowledgment of the citizens of one state by the citizens of all other states—the fierceness of their roused resentment—their curiosity and welcome of novelty—their self-esteem and wonderful sympathy—their susceptibility to a slight—the air they have of persons who never knew how it felt to stand in the presence of superiors—the fluency of their speech—their delight in music, the sure symptom of manly tenderness and native elegance of soul . . . their good temper and openhandedness—the terrible significance of their elections—the President's taking off his hat to them not they to him—these too are unrhymed poetry. It awaits the gigantic and generous treatment worthy of it.

The largeness of nature or the nation were monstrous without a corresponding largeness and generosity of the spirit of the citizen. Not nature nor swarming states nor streets and steamships nor prosperous business nor farms nor capital nor learning may suffice for the ideal of man . . . nor suffice the poet. No reminiscences may suffice either. A live nation can always cut a deep mark and can have the best authority the cheapest . . . namely from its own soul. This is the sum of the profitable uses of individuals or states and of present action and grandeur and of the subjects of poets.—As if it were necessary to trot back generation after generation to the eastern records! As if the beauty and sacredness of the demonstrable must fall behind that of the mythical! As if men do not make their mark out of any times! As if the opening of the western continent by discovery and what has transpired since in North and South America were less than the small theatre of the antique or the aimless sleep-walking of the middle ages! The pride of the United States leaves the wealth and finesse of the cities and all returns of commerce and agriculture and all the magnitude of geography or shows of exterior victory to enjoy the breed of fullsized men or one fullsized man unconquerable and simple.

The American poets are to enclose old and new for America is the race of races. Of them a bard is to be commensurate with a people. To him the other continents arrive as contributions . . . he gives them reception for their sake and his own sake. His spirit responds to his country's spirit . . . . he incarnates its geography and natural life and rivers and lakes. Mississippi with annual freshets and changing chutes, Missouri and Columbia and Ohio and Saint Lawrence with the falls and beautiful masculine Hudson, do not embouchure where they spend themselves more then they embouchure into him. The blue breadth over the inland sea of Virginia and Maryland and the sea off Massachusetts and Maine and over Manhattan bay and over Champlain and Erie and over Ontario and Huron and Michigan and Superior, and over the Texan and Mexican and Floridian and Cuban seas and over the seas off California and Oregon, is not tallied by the blue breadth of the waters below more than the breadth of above and below is tallied by him. When the long Atlantic coast stretches longer and the Pacific coast stretches longer he easily stretches with them north or south. He spans between them also from east to west and reflects what is between them. On him rise solid growths that offset the growths of pine and cedar and hemlock and liveoak and locusts and chestnut and cypress and hickory and limetree and cotton-wood and tuliptree and cactus and wildvine and tamarind and persimmon . . . . and tangles as tangled as any canebrake or swamp . . . . and forests coated with transparent ice and icicles hanging from the boughs and crackling in the wind. . . . and sides and peaks of mountains. . . . and pasturage sweet and free as savannah or upland or prairie . . . . with flights and songs and screams that answer those of the wildpigeon and highhold and orchard oriole and coot and surf-duck and redshouldered-hawk and fish-hawk and white-ibis and indian-hen and cat-owl and water-pheasant and qua-bird and pied-sheldrake and blackbird and mockingbird and buzzard and condor and night-heron and eagle. To him the hereditary countenance descends both mother's and father's. To him enter the essences of the real things and past and present events—of the enormous diversity of temperature and agriculture and mines—the tribes of red aborigines—the weatherbeaten vessels entering new ports or making landings on rocky coasts—the first settlements north or south—the rapid stature and muscle—the haughty defiance of '76, and the war and peace and formation of the constitution. . . . the union always surrounded by blatherers and always calm and impregnable—the perpetual coming of immigrants—the wharf hem'd cities and superior marine—the unsurveyed interior—the loghouses and clearings and wild animals and hunters and trappers. . . . the free commerce—the fisheries and whaling and golddigging—the endless gestation of new states—the convening of Congress every December, the members duly coming up from all climates and the uttermost parts. . . . the noble character of the young mechanics and of all free American workmen and workwomen. . . . the general ardor and friendliness and enterprise—the perfect equality of the female with the male. . . . the large amativeness—the fluid movement of the population—the factories and mercantile life and laborsaving machinery—the Yankee swap—the New York firemen and the target excursion—the southern plantation life—the character of the northeast and of the northwest and southwest—slavery and the tremulous spreading of hands to protect it, and the stern opposition to it which shall never cease till it ceases or the speaking of tongues and the moving

of lips cease. For such the expression of the American poet
is to be transcendant and new. It is to be indirect and not
direct or descriptive or epic. Its quality goes through these
to much more. Let the age and wars of other nations be
chanted and their eras and characters be illustrated and
that finish the verse. Not so the great psalm of the republic.
Here the theme is creative and has vista. Here comes one
among the wellbeloved stonecutters and plans with decision
and science and sees the solid and beautiful forms of the
future where there are now no solid forms.

Of all nations the United States with veins full of poetical
stuff most need poets and will doubtless have the greatest
and use them the greatest. Their Presidents shall not be
their common referee so much as their poets shall. Of all
mankind the great poet is the equable man. Not in him but
off from him things are grotesque or eccentric or fail of their
sanity. Nothing out of its place is good and nothing in its
place is bad. He bestows on every object or quality its fit
proportions neither more or less. He is the arbiter of the
diverse and he is the key. He is the equalizer of his age and
land. . . . he supplies what wants supplying and checks
what wants checking. If peace is the routine out of him
speaks the spirit of peace, large, rich, thrifty, building vast
and populous cities, encouraging agriculture and the arts
and commerce—lighting the study of man, the soul,
immortality—federal, state or municipal government,
marriage, health, freetrade, intertravel by land and sea. . . .
nothing too close, nothing too far off . . . the stars not too far
off. In war he is the most deadly force of the war. Who
recruits him recruits horse and foot . . . he fetches parks of
artillery the best that engineer ever knew. If the time
becomes slothful and heavy he knows how to arouse it . . .
he can make every word he speaks draw blood. Whatever
stagnates in the flat of custom or obedience or legislation he
never stagnates. Obedience does not master him, he masters
it. High up out of reach he stands turning a concentrated
light . . . he turns the pivot with his finger . . . he baffles the
swiftest runners as he stands and easily overtakes and
envelops them. The time straying toward infidelity and

confections and persiflage he withholds by his steady faith
. . . he spreads out his dishes . . . he offers the sweet
firmfibred meat that grows men and women. His brain is
the ultimate brain. He is no arguer . . . he is judgment. He
judges not as the judge judges but as the sun falling around
a helpless thing. As he sees the farthest he has the most
faith. His thoughts are the hymns of the praise of things. In
the talk on the soul and eternity and God off of his equal
plane he is silent. He sees eternity less like a play with a
prologue and denouement. . . . he sees eternity in men and
women . . . he does not see men and women as dreams or
dots. Faith is the antiseptic of the soul . . . it pervades the
common people and preserves them . . . they never give up
believing and expecting and trusting. There is that indes-
cribable freshness and unconsciousness about an illiterate
person that humbles and mocks the power of the noblest
expressive genius. The poet sees for a certainty how one not
a great artist may be just as sacred and perfect as the
greatest artist. . . . . . The power to destroy or remould is
freely used by him but never the power of attack. What is
past is past. If he does not expose superior models and
prove himself by every step he takes he is not what is
wanted. The presence of the greatest poet conquers . . . not
parleying or struggling or any prepared attempts. Now he
has passed that way see after him! there is not left any
vestige of despair or misanthropy or cunning or exclusive-
ness or the ignominy of a nativity or color or delusion of hell
or the necessity of hell. . . . . and no man thenceforward
shall be degraded for ignorance or weakness or sin.

The greatest poet hardly knows pettiness or triviality. If
he breathes into any thing that was before thought small it
dilates with the grandeur and life of the universe. He is a
seer. . . . he is individual . . . he is complete in himself. . . .
the others are as good as he, only he sees it and they do not.
He is not one of the chorus. . . . he does not stop for any
regulation . . . he is the president of regulation. What the
eyesight does to the rest he does to the rest. Who knows the
curious mystery of the eyesight? The other senses corroborate
themselves, but this is removed from any proof but its own

and foreruns the identities of the spiritual world. A single glance of it mocks all the investigations of man and all the instruments and books of the earth and all reasoning. What is marvellous? what is unlikely? what is impossible or baseless or vague? after you have once just opened the space of a peachpit and given audience to far and near and to the sunset and had all things enter with electric swiftness softly and duly without confusion or jostling or jam.

The land and sea, the animals fishes and birds, the sky of heaven and the orbs, the forests mountains and rivers, are not small themes . . . but folks expect of the poet to indicate more than the beauty and dignity which always attach to dumb real objects . . . . they expect him to indicate the path between reality and their souls. Men and women perceive the beauty well enough . . probably as well as he. The passionate tenacity of hunters, woodmen, early risers, cultivators of gardens and orchards and fields, the love of healthy women for the manly form, seafaring persons, drivers of horses, the passion for light and the open air, all is an old varied sign of the unfailing perception of beauty and of a residence of the poetic in outdoor people. They can never be assisted by poets to perceive . . . some may but they never can. The poetic quality is not marshalled in rhyme or uniformity or abstract addresses to things nor in melancholy complaints or good precepts, but is the life of these and much else and is in the soul. The profit of rhyme is that it drops seeds of a sweeter and more luxuriant rhyme, and of uniformity that it conveys itself into its own roots in the ground out of sight. The rhyme and uniformity of perfect poems show the free growth of metrical laws and bud from them as unerringly and loosely as lilacs or roses on a bush, and take shapes as compact as the shapes of chestnuts and oranges and melons and pears, and shed the perfume impalpable to form. The fluency and ornaments of the finest poems or music or orations or recitations are not independent but dependent. All beauty comes from beautiful blood and a beautiful brain. If the greatnesses are in conjunction in a man or woman it is enough . . . . the fact will prevail through the universe . . . . but the gaggery and gilt of a million years will not prevail. Who troubles himself about his ornaments or fluency is lost. This is what you shall do: Love the earth and sun and the animals, despise riches, give alms to every one that asks, stand up for the stupid and crazy, devote your income and labor to others, hate tyrants, argue not concerning God, have patience and indulgence toward the people, take off your hat to nothing known or unknown or to any man or number of men, go freely with powerful uneducated persons and with the young and with the mothers of families, read these leaves in the open air every season of every year of your life, re-examine all you have been told at school or church or in any book, dismiss whatever insults your own soul, and your very flesh shall be a great poem and have the richest fluency not only in its words but in the silent lines of its lips and face and between the lashes of your eyes and in every motion and joint of your body. . . . . The poet shall not spend his time in unneeded work. He shall know that the ground is always ready ploughed and manured . . . . others may not know it but he shall. He shall go directly to the creation. His trust shall master the trust of everything he touches . . . . and shall master all attachment.

The known universe has one complete lover and that is the greatest poet. He consumes an eternal passion and is indifferent which chance happens and which possible contingency of fortune or misfortune and persuades daily and hourly his delicious pay. What balks or breaks others is fuel for his burning progress to contact and amorous joy. Other proportions of the reception of pleasure dwindle to nothing to his proportions. All expected from heaven or from the highest he is rapport with in the sight of the daybreak or a scene of the winter woods or the presence of children playing or with his arm round the neck of a man or woman. His love above all love has leisure and expanse . . . . he leaves room ahead of himself. He is no irresolute or suspicious lover . . . he is sure . . . he scorns intervals. His experience and the showers l thrills are not for nothing. Nothing can jar him . . . . suffering and darkness cannot— death and fear cannot. To him complaint and jealousy and envy are corpses buried and rotten in the earth . . . . he saw them buried. The sea is not surer of the shore or the shore of the sea than he is of the fruition of his love and of all perfection and beauty.

The fruition of beauty is no chance of hit or miss . . . it is inevitable as life . . . . it is exact and plumb as gravitation. From the eyesight proceeds another eyesight and from the hearing proceeds another hearing and from the voice proceeds another voice eternally curious of the harmony of things with man. To these respond perfections not only in the committees that were supposed to stand for the rest but in the rest themselves just the same. These understand the law of perfection in masses and floods . . . that its finish is to each for itself and onward from itself . . . that it is profuse and impartial . . . that there is not a minute of the light or dark nor an acre of the earth or sea without it—nor any direction of the sky nor any trade or employment nor any turn of events. This is the reason that about the proper expression of beauty there is precision and balance . . . one part does not need to be thrust above another. The best singer is not the one who has the most lithe and powerful organ . . . the pleasure of poems is not in them that take the handsomest measure and similes and sound.

Without effort and without exposing in the least how it is done the greatest poet brings the spirit of any or all events and passions and scenes and persons some more and some less to bear on your individual character as you hear or read. To do this well is to compete with the laws that pursue and follow time. What is the purpose must surely be there and the clue of it must be there . . . . and the faintest indication is the indication of the best and then becomes the clearest indication. Past and present and future are not disjoined but joined. The greatest poet forms the consistence of what is to be from what has been and is. He drags the dead out of their coffins and stands them again on their feet . . . . he says to the past, Rise and walk before me that I may realize you. He learns the lesson . . . . he places himself where the future becomes present. The greatest poet does not only dazzle his rays over character and scenes and passions ... he finally ascends and finishes all ... he exhibits the pinnacles that no man can tell what they are for or what is beyond .... he glows a moment on the extremest verge. He is most wonderful in his last half-hidden smile or frown ... by that flash of the moment of parting the one that sees it shall be encouraged or terrified afterward for many years. The greatest poet does not moralize or make applications of morals ... he knows the soul. The soul has that measureless pride which consists in never acknowledging any lessons but its own. But it has sympathy as measureless as its pride and the one balances the other and neither can stretch too far while it stretches in company with the other. The inmost secrets of art sleep with the twain. The greatest poet has lain close betwixt both and they are vital in his style and thoughts.

The art of art, the glory of expression and the sunshine of the light of letters is simplicity. Nothing is better than simplicity .... nothing can make up for excess or for the lack of definiteness. To carry on the heave of impulse and pierce intellectual depths and give all subjects their articulations are powers neither common nor very uncommon. But to speak in literature with the perfect rectitude and insousiance of the movements of animals and the unimpeachableness of the sentiment of trees in the woods and grass by the roadside is the flawless triumph of art. If you have looked on him who has achieved it you have looked on one of the masters of the artists of all nations and times. You shall not contemplate the flight of the graygull over the bay or the mettlesome action of the blood horse or the tall leaning of sunflowers on their stalk or the appearance of the sun journeying through heaven or the appearance of the moon afterward with any more satisfaction than you shall contemplate him. The greatest poet has less a marked style and is more the channel of thoughts and things without increase or diminution, and is the free channel of himself. He swears to his art, I will not be meddlesome, I will not have in my writing any elegance or effect or originality to hang in the way between me and the rest like curtains. I will have nothing hang in the way, not the richest curtains. What I tell I tell for precisely what it is. Let who may exalt or startle or fascinate or sooth I will have purposes as health or heat or snow has and be as regardless of observation. What I experience or portray shall go from my composition without a shred of my composition. You shall stand by my side and look in the mirror with me.

The old red blood and stainless gentility of great poets will be proved by their unconstraint. A heroic person walks at his ease through and out of that custom or precedent or authority that suits him not. Of the traits of the brotherhood of writers savans musicians inventors and artists nothing is finer than silent defiance advancing from new free forms. In the need of poems philosophy politics mechanism science behaviour, the craft of art, an appropriate native grand-opera, shipcraft, or any craft, he is greatest forever and forever who contributes the greatest original practical example. The cleanest expression is that which finds no sphere worthy of itself and makes one.

The messages of great poets to each man and woman are, Come to us on equal terms, Only then can you understand us, We are no better than you, What we enclose you enclose, What we enjoy you may enjoy. Did you suppose there could be only one Supreme? We affirm there can be unnumbered Supremes, and that one does not countervail another any more than one eyesight countervails another .. and that men can be good or grand only of the consciousness of their supremacy within them. What do you think is the grandeur of storms and dismemberments and the deadliest battles and wrecks and the wildest fury of the elements and the power of the sea and the motion of nature and of the throes of human desires and dignity and hate and love? It is that something in the soul which says, Rage on, Whirl on, I tread master here and everywhere, Master of the spasms of the sky and of the shatter of the sea, Master of nature and passion and death, and of all terror and all pain.

The American bards shall be marked for generosity and affection and for encouraging competitors . They shall be kosmos . without monopoly or secresy . glad to pass any thing to any one   hungry for equals night and day They shall not be careful of riches and privilege . . . . they shall be riches and privilege . . . . they shall perceive who the most affluent man is. The most affluent man is he that confronts all the shows he sees by equivalents out of the stronger wealth of himself. The American bard shall delineate no class of persons nor one or two out of the strata of interests nor love most nor truth most nor the soul most nor the body most . . . . and not be for the eastern states more than the western or the northern states more than the southern.

Exact science and its practical movements are no checks on the greatest poet but always his encouragement and support. The outset and remembrance are there . . there the arms that lifted him first and brace him best . . . . there he returns after all his goings and comings. The sailor and traveler . . the anatomist, chemist, astronomer, geologist, phrenologist, spiritualist, mathematician, historian and lexicographer are not poets, but they are the lawgivers of poets and their construction underlies the structure of every perfect poem. No matter what rises or is uttered they sent the seed of the conception of it . . . of them and by them stand the visible proofs of souls . . . . . always of their fatherstuff must be begotten the sinewy races of bards. If there shall be love and content between the father and the son and if the greatness of the son is the exuding of the greatness of the father there shall be love between the poet and the man of demonstrable science. In the beauty of poems are the tuft and final applause of science.

Great is the faith of the flush of knowledge and of the investigation of the depths of qualities and things. Cleaving and circling here swells the soul of the poet yet it president of itself always. The depths are fathomless and therefore calm. The innocence and nakedness are resumed . . . they are neither modest nor immodest. The whole theory of the special and supernatural and all that was twined with it or educed out of it departs as a dream. What has ever happened . . . . what happens and whatever may or shall happen, the vital laws enclose all . . . . they are sufficient for any case and for all cases . . . none to be hurried or retarded . . . . any miracle of affairs or persons inadmissible in the vast clear scheme where every motion and every spear of grass and the frames and spirits of men and women and all that concerns them are unspeakably perfect miracles all referring to all and each distinct and in its place. It is also not consistent with the reality of the soul to admit that there is anything in the known universe more divine than men and women.

Men and women and the earth and all upon it are simply to be taken as they are, and the investigation of their past and present and future shall be unintermitted and shall be done with perfect candor. Upon this basis philosophy speculates ever looking toward the poet, ever regarding the eternal tendencies of all toward happiness never inconsistent with what is clear to the senses and to the soul. For the eternal tendencies of all toward happiness make the only point of sane philosophy. Whatever comprehends less than that ... whatever is less than the laws of light and of astronomical motion ... or less than the laws that follow the thief the liar the glutton and the drunkard through this life and doubtless afterward ...... or less than vast stretches of time or the slow formation of density or the patient upheaving of strata—is of no account. Whatever would put God in a poem or system of philosophy as contending against some being or influence is also of no account. Sanity and ensemble characterise the great master ... spoilt in one principle all is spoilt. The great master has nothing to do with miracles. He sees health for himself in being one of the mass .... he sees the hiatus in singular eminence. To the perfect shape comes common ground. To be under the general law is great for that is to correspond with it. The master knows that he is unspeakably great and that all are unspeakably great .... that nothing for instance is greater than to conceive children and bring them up well ... that to be is just as great as to perceive or tell.

In the make of the great masters the idea of political liberty is indispensible. Liberty takes the adherence of heroes wherever men and women exist .... but never takes any adherence or welcome from the rest more than from poets. They are the voice and exposition of liberty. They out of ages are worthy the grand idea . . . . to them it is confided and they must sustain it. Nothing has precedence of it and nothing can warp or degrade it. The attitude of great poets is to cheer up slaves and horrify despots. The turn of their necks, the sound of their feet, the motions of their wrists, are full of hazard to the one and hope to the other. Come nigh them awhile and though they neither speak or advise you shall learn the faithful American lesson. Liberty is poorly served by men whose good intent is quelled from one failure or two failures or any number of failures, or from the casual indifference or ingratitude of the people, or from the sharp show of the tushes of power, or the bringing to bear soldiers and cannon or any penal statutes. Liberty relies upon itself, invites no one, promises nothing, sits in calmness and light, is positive and composed, and knows no discouragement. The battle rages with many a loud alarm and frequent advance and retreat . . . . the enemy triumphs . . . . the prison, the handcuffs, the iron necklace and anklet, the scaffold, garrote and leadballs do their work . . . . the cause is asleep . . . . the strong throats are choked with their own blood . . . . the young men drop their eyelashes toward the ground when they pass each other . . . . and is liberty gone out of that place? No never. When liberty goes it is not the first to go nor the second or third to go . . it waits for all the rest to go . . it is the last. . . When the memories of the old martyrs are faded utterly away . . . . when the large names of patriots are laughed at in the public halls from the lips of the orators . . . . when the boys are no more christened after the same but christened after tyrants and traitors instead . . . . when the laws of the free are grudgingly permitted and laws for informers and bloodmoney are sweet to the taste of the people . . . . when I and you walk abroad upon the earth stung with compassion at the sight of numberless brothers answering our equal friendship and calling no man master— and when we are elated with noble joy at the sight of slaves . . . . when the soul retires in the cool communion of the night and surveys its experience and has much extasy over the word and deed that put back a helpless innocent person into the gripe of the gripers or into any cruel inferiority . . . .

when those in all parts of these states who could easier realize the true American character but do not yet—when the swarms of cringers, suckers, doughfaces, lice of politics, planners of sly involutions for their own preferment to city offices or state legislatures or the judiciary or congress or the presidency, obtain a response of love and natural deference from the people whether they get the offices or no . . . . when it is better to be a bound booby and rogue in office at a high salary than the poorest free mechanic or farmer with his hat unmoved from his head and firm eyes and a candid and generous heart . . . . and when servility by town or state or the federal government or any oppression on a large scale or small scale can be tried on without its own punishment following duly after in exact proportion against the smallest chance of escape . . . . or rather when all life and all the souls of men and women are discharged from any part of the earth—then only shall the instinct of liberty be discharged from that part of the earth.

As the attributes of the poets of the kosmos concentre in the real body and soul and in the pleasure of things they possess the superiority of genuineness over all fiction and romance. As they emit themselves facts are showered over with light . . . . the daylight is lit with more volatile light . . . . also the deep between the setting rising sun goes deeper many fold. Each precise object or condition or combination or process exhibits a beauty . . . . the multiplication table its—old age its—the carpenter's trade its—the grand-opera its . . . . the hugehulled cleanshaped New-York clipper at sea under steam or full sail gleams with unmatched beauty . . . . the American circles and large harmonies of government gleam with theirs . . . . and the commonest definite intentions and actions with theirs. The poets of the kosmos advance through all interpositions and coverings and turmoils and strategems to first principles. They are of use . . . . they dissolve poverty from its need and riches from its conceit. You large proprietor they say shall not realize or perceive more than any one else. The owner of the library is not he who holds a legal title to it having bought and paid for it. Any one and every one is owner of the library who can read the same through all the varieties of tongues and subjects and styles, and in whom they enter with ease and take residence and force toward paternity and maternity, and make supple and powerful and rich and large. . . . . These American states strong and healthy and accomplished shall receive no pleasure from violations of natural models and must not permit them. In paintings or mouldings or carvings in mineral or wood, or in the illustrations of books or newspapers, or in any comic or tragic prints, or in the patterns of woven stuffs or any thing to beautify rooms or furniture or costumes, or to put upon cornices or monuments or on the prows or sterns of ships, or to put anywhere before the human eye indoors or out, that which distorts honest shapes or which creates unearthly beings or places or contingencies is a nuisance and revolt. Of the human form especially it is so great it must never be made ridiculous. Of ornaments to a work nothing outre can be allowed . . but those ornaments can be allowed that conform to the perfect facts of the open air and that flow out of the nature of the work and come irrepressibly from it and are necessary to the completion of the work. Most works are most beautiful without ornament. . . Exaggerations will be revenged in human physiology. Clean and vigorous children are jetted and conceived only in those communities where the models of natural forms are public every day. . . . . . Great genius and the people of these states must never be demeaned to romances. As soon as histories are properly told there is no more need of romances.

The great poets are also to be known by the absence in them of tricks and by the justification of perfect personal candor. Then folks echo a new cheap joy and a divine voice leaping from their brains: How beautiful is candor! All faults may be forgiven of him who has perfect candor. Henceforth let no man of us lie, for we have seen that openness wins the inner and outer world and that there is no single exception, and that never since our earth gathered itself in a mass have deceit or subterfuge or prevarication attracted its smallest particle or the faintest tinge of a shade—and that through the enveloping wealth and rank of a state or the whole republic of states a sneak or sly person shall be discovered and despised . . . . and that the soul has never been once fooled and never can be fooled . . . . and thrift without the loving nod of the soul is only a fœtid puff . . . . and there never grew up in any of the continents of the globe nor upon any planet or satellite or star, nor upon the asteroids, nor in any part of ethereal space, nor in the midst of density, nor under the fluid wet of the sea, nor in that condition which precedes them the birth of babes, nor at any time during the changes of life, nor in that condition that follows what we term death, nor in any stretch of abeyance or action afterward of vitality, nor in any process of formation or reformation anywhere, a being whose instinct hated the truth.

Extreme caution or prudence, the soundest organic health, large hope and comparison and fondness for women and children, large alimentiveness and destructiveness and causality, with a perfect sense of the oneness of nature and the propriety of the same spirit applied to human affairs . . these are called up of the float of the brain of the world to be parts of the greatest poet from his birth out of his mother's womb and from her birth out of her mother's. Caution seldom goes far enough. It has been thought that the prudent citizen was the citizen who applied himself to solid gains and did well for himself and his family and completed a lawful life without debt or crime. The greatest poet sees and admits these economies as he sees the economies of food and sleep, but has higher notions of prudence than to think he gives much when he gives a few slight attentions at the latch of the gate. The premises of the prudence of life are not the hospitality of it or the ripeness and harvest of it. Beyond the independence of a little sum laid aside for burial-money, and of a few clapboards around and shingles overhead on a lot of American soil owned, and the easy dollars that supply the year's plain clothing and meals, the melancholy prudence of the abandonment of such a great being as a man is to the toss and pallor of years of moneymaking with all their scorching days and icy nights and all their stifling deceits and underhanded dodgings, or infinitessimals of parlors, or shameless stuffing while others starve . . and all the loss of the bloom and odor of the earth and of the flowers and atmosphere and of the sea and of the true taste of the women and men you pass or have to do with in youth or middle age, and the issuing sickness and desperate revolt at the close of a life without elevation or naivete, and the ghastly chatter of a death without serenity or majesty, is the great fraud upon modern civilization and forethought, blotching the surface and system which civilization undeniably drafts, and moistening with tears the immense features it spreads and spreads with such velocity before the reached kisses of the soul. . . Still the right explanation remains to be made about prudence. The prudence of the mere wealth and respectability of the most esteemed life appears too faint for the eye to observe at all when little and large alike drop quietly aside at the thought of the prudence suitable for immortality. What is wisdom that fills the thinness of a year or seventy or eighty years to wisdom spaced out by ages and coming back at a certain time with strong reinforcements and rich presents and the clear faces of wedding-guests as far as you can look in every direction running gaily toward you? Only the soul is of itself . . . . all else has reference to what ensues. All that a person does or thinks is of consequence. Not a move can a man or woman make that affects him or her in a day or a month or any part of the direct lifetime or the hour of death but the same affects him or her onward afterward through the indirect lifetime. The indirect is always as great and real as the direct. The spirit receives from the body just as much as it gives to the body. Not one name of word or deed . . not of venereal sores or discolorations . . not the privacy of the onanist . . not of the putrid veins of gluttons or rumdrinkers . . . not peculation or cunning or betrayal or murder . . no serpentine poison of those that seduce women . . not the foolish yielding of women . . not prostitution . . not of any depravity of young men . . not of the attainment of gain by discreditable means . . not any nastiness of appetite . . not any harshness of officers to men or judges to prisoners or fathers to sons or sons to fathers or of husbands to wives or bosses to their boys . . not of greedy looks or malignant wishes . . . nor any of the wiles practised by people upon themselves . . . ever is or ever can be stamped on the programme but it is duly realized and returned, and that returned in further performances . . . and they returned again. Nor can the push of charity or personal force ever be any thing else than the profoundest reason, whether it bring arguments to hand or no. No specification is necessary . . to add or subtract or divide is in vain. Little or big, learned or unlearned, white or black, legal or illegal, sick or well, from the first inspiration down the windpipe to the last expiration out of it, all that a male or female does that is vigorous and benevolent and clean is so much sure profit to him or her in the unshakable order of the universe and through the whole scope of it forever. If the savage or felon is wise it is well . . . . if the greatest poet or savan is wise it is simply the same . . if the President or chief justice is wise it is the same . . . if the young mechanic or farmer is wise it is no more or less . . if the prostitute is wise it is no more nor less. The interest will come round . . all will come round. All the best actions of war and peace . . . all help given to relatives and strangers and the poor and old and sorrowful and young children and widows and the sick, and to all shunned persons . . all furtherance of fugitives and of the escape of slaves . . all the self-denial that stood steady and aloof on wrecks and saw others take the seats of the boats . . . all offering of substance or life for the good old cause, or for a friend's sake or opinion's sake . . . all pains of enthusiasts scoffed at by their neighbors . . all the vast sweet love and precious suffering of mothers . . . all honest men baffled in strifes recorded or unrecorded . . . . all the grandeur and good of the few ancient nations whose fragments of annals we inherit . . and all the good of the hundreds of far mightier and more ancient nations unknown to us by name or date or location . . . . all that was ever manfully begun, whether it succeeded or no . . . . all that has at any time been well suggested out of the divine heart of man or by the divinity of his mouth or by the shaping of his great hands . . and all that is well thought or done this day on any part of the surface of the globe . . or on any of the wandering stars or fixed stars by those there as we are here . . or that is henceforth to be well thought or done by you whoever you are, or by any one—these singly and wholly inured at their time and inure now and will inure always to the identities from which they sprung or shall spring. . . Did you guess any of them lived only its moment? The world does not so exist . . no parts palpable or impalpable so exist . . . no result exists now without being from its long antecedent result, and that from its antecedent, and so backward without the farthest mentionable spot coming a bit nearer the beginning than any other spot. . . . . Whatever satisfies the soul is truth. The prudence of the greatest poet answers at last the craving and glut of the soul, is not contemptuous of less ways of prudence if they conform to its ways, puts off nothing, permits no let-up for its own case or any case, has no particular sabbath or judgmentday, divides not the living from the dead or the righteous from the unrighteous, is satisfied with the present, matches every thought or act by its correlative, knows no possible forgiveness or deputed atonement . . knows that the young man who composedly periled his life and lost it has done exceeding well for himself, while the man who has not periled his life and retains it to old age in riches and ease has perhaps achieved nothing for himself worth mentioning . . and that only that person has no great prudence to learn who has learnt to prefer real longlived things, and favors body and soul the same, and perceives the indirect assuredly following the direct, and what evil or good he does leaping onward and waiting to meet him again—and who in his spirit in any emergency whatever neither hurries or avoids death.

The direct trial of him who would be the greatest poet is today. If he does not flood himself with the immediate age as with vast oceanic tides . . . . . and if he does not attract his own land body and soul to himself and hang on its neck with incomparable love and plunge his semitic muscle into its merits and demerits . . . and if he be not himself the age transfigured . . . . and if to him is not opened the eternity which gives similitude to all periods and locations and

processes and animate and inanimate forms, and which is
the bond of time, and rises up from its inconceivable
vagueness and infiniteness in the swimming shape of today,
and is held by the ductile anchors of life, and makes the
present spot the passage from what was to what shall be,
and commits itself to the representation of this wave of an
hour and this one of the sixty beautiful children of the
wave—let him merge in the general run and wait his
development. . . . . . . Still the final test of poems or any
character or work remains. The prescient poet projects
himself centuries ahead and judges performer or perform-
ance after the changes of time. Does it live through them?
Does it still hold on untired? Will the same style and the
direction of genius to similar points be satisfactory now?
Has no new discovery in science or arrival at superior
planes of thought and judgment and behaviour fixed him or
his so that either can be looked down upon? Have the
marches of tens and hundreds and thousands of years made
willing detours to the right hand and the left hand for his
sake? Is he beloved long and long after he is buried? Does
the young man think often of him? and the young woman
think often of him? and do the middleaged and the old think
of him?

A great poem is for ages and ages in common and for all
degrees and complexions and all departments and sects and
for a woman as much as a man and a man as much as a
woman. A great poem is no finish to a man or woman but
rather a beginning. Has any one fancied he could sit at last
under some due authority and rest satisfied with explana-
tions and realize and be content and full? To no such
terminus does the great poet bring . . . he brings neither
cessation or sheltered fatness and ease. The touch of him
tells in action. Whom he takes he takes with firm sure grasp
into live regions previously unattained . . . . thenceforward
is no rest . . . . they see the space and ineffable sheen that
turn the old spots and lights into dead vacuums. The
companion of him beholds the birth and progress of stars
and learns one of the meanings. Now there shall be a man
cohered out of tumult and chaos . . . . the elder encourages

the younger and shows him how . . . they two shall launch off fearlessly together till the new world fits an orbit for itself and looks unabashed on the lesser orbits of the stars and sweeps through the ceaseless rings and shall never be quiet again.

There will soon be no more priests. Their work is done. They may wait awhile . . perhaps a generation or two . . dropping off by degrees. A superior breed shall take their place . . . . the gangs of kosmos and prophets en masse shall take their place. A new order shall arise and they shall be the priests of man, and every man shall be his own priest. The churches built under their umbrage shall be the churches of men and women. Through the divinity of themselves shall the kosmos and the new breed of poets be interpreters of men and women and of all events and things. They shall find their inspiration in real objects today, symptoms of the past and future. . . . They shall not deign to defend immortality or God or the perfection of things or liberty or the exquisite beauty and reality of the soul. They shall arise in America and be responded to from the remainder of the earth.

The English language befriends the grand American expression . . . . it is brawny enough and limber and full enough. On the tough stock of a race who through all change of circumstance was never without the idea of political liberty, which is the animus of all liberty, it has attracted the terms of daintier and gayer and subtler and more elegant tongues. It is the powerful language of resistance . . . it is the dialect of common sense. It is the speech of the proud and melancholy races and of all who aspire. It is the chosen tongue to express growth faith self-esteem freedom justice equality friendliness amplitude prudence decision and courage. It is the medium that shall well nigh express the inexpressible.

No great literature nor any like style of behaviour or oratory or social intercourse or household arrangements or public institutions or the treatment by bosses of employed people, nor executive detail or detail of the army or navy, nor spirit of legislation or courts or police or tuition or architecture or songs or amusements or the costumes of young men, can long elude the jealous and passionate instinct of American standards. Whether or no the sign appears from the mouths of the people, it throbs a live interrogation in every freeman's and freewoman's heart after that which passes by, or this built to remain. Is it uniform with my country? Are its disposals without ignominious distinctions? Is it for the evergrowing communes of brothers and lovers, large, well-united, proud beyond the old models, generous beyond all models? Is it something grown fresh out of the fields or drawn from the sea for use to me today here? I know that what answers for me an American must answer for any individual or nation that serves for a part of my materials. Does this answer? or is it without reference to universal needs? or sprung of the needs of the less developed society of special ranks? or old needs of pleasure overlaid by modern science and forms? Does this acknowledge liberty with audible and absolute acknowledgment, and set slavery at nought for life and death? Will it help breed one goodshaped and wellhung man, and a woman to be his perfect and independent mate? Does it improve manners? Is it for the nursing of the young of the republic? Does it solve readily with the sweet milk of the nipples of the breasts of the mother of many children? Has it too the old ever-fresh forbearance and impartiality? Does it look with the same love on the last born and on those hardening toward stature, and on the errant, and on those who disdain all strength of assault outside of their own?

The poems distilled from other poems will probably pass away. The coward will surely pass away. The expectation of the vital and great can only be satisfied by the demeanor of the vital and great. The swarms of the polished deprecating and reflectors and the polite float off and leave no remembrance. America prepares with composure and goodwill for the visitors that have sent word. It is not intellect that is to be their warrant and welcome. The talented, the artist, the ingenious, the editor, the statesman, the erudite .. they are not unappreciated .. they fall in their place and do their work. The soul of the nation also does it work. No disguise can pass on it . . no disguise can conceal it. It rejects none, it permits all. Only toward as good as itself and toward the like of itself will it advance half-way. An individual is as superb as a nation when he has the qualities which make a superb nation. The soul of the largest and wealthiest and proudest nation may well go half-way to meet that of its poets. The signs are effectual. There is no fear of mistake. If the one is true the other is true. The proof of a poet is that his country absorbs him as affectionately as he has absorbed it.

APPENDIX B
EMERSON TO WHITMAN
21 JULY 1855

Although this now-famous letter was sent from Concord to New York in July, it may not have reached Whitman until late September. Without asking Emerson's permission, the poet had the letter published in the New York Tribune *of 10 October 1855 and as an appendix to his 1856 edition to* Leaves of Grass.

Concord, Massachusetts, 21 July 1855.

Dear Sir,

I am not blind to the worth of the wonderful gift of 'Leaves of Grass'. I find it the most extraordinary piece of wit and wisdom that America has yet contributed. I am very happy in reading it, as great power makes us happy. It meets the demand I am always making of what seemed the sterile and stingy nature, as if too much handiwork or too much lymph in the temperament were making our western wits fat and mean. I give you joy of your free and brave thought. I have great joy in it. I find incomparable things said incomparably well, as they must be. I find the courage of *treatment*, which so delights us, and which large perception only can inspire. I greet you at the beginning of a great career, which yet must have had a long foreground somewhere, for such a start. I rubbed my eyes a little to see if this sunbeam were no illusion; but the solid sense of the book is a sober certainty. It has the best merits, namely, of fortifying and encouraging.

I did not know until I, last night, saw the book advertised in a newspaper, that I could trust the name as real and available for a post-office. I wish to see my benefactor, and have felt much like striking my tasks, and visiting New York to pay you my respects.

R. W. Emerson

Mr Walter Whitman.

EXPLANATORY NOTES

The current edition is annotated primarily with the general reader in mind. The Notes define terms peculiar to Whitman's vernacular, remote allusions, and references not suggested by their poetic context. A more complete annotation of Leaves of Grass *is found in the* Comprehensive Reader's Edition, *edited by Harold W. Blodgett and Sculley Bradley (New York University Press, 1965). The Notes do include, however, instances where the present editor disagrees with the* Reader's Edition.

11 *old cause*: democracy, liberty.

12 *eidólons*: the spiritual realm which stands part for part behind the physical. Whitman pronounced this Greek word 'ei*dolons*'.

14 *For him I sing*: that is, the reader.

15 *Beginners*: the great innovators.

16 *Kanada*: Whitman's spelling for Canada.

17 *the one I sing*: liberty.

18 *Paumanok*: Indian name for Long Island, meaning 'fish-shaped.'

19 *Fifth-month*: Quaker term for May

23 *camerado*: Whitman's own coinage.

It, magnificent: possibly religion.

28 *Kaw*: a river in Kansas.

31 *the hugging and loving bed-fellow*: God.

33 *Kanuck*: French Canadian.

Tuckahoe: Tidewater Virginian.

Cuff: the then-current slang term for African-American.

38 *sluing*: twisting.

gamut: the musical scale.

39 *First-day loafe*: Sunday.

jour printer: journeyman printer.

40 *Wolverine*: resident of Michigan.

41 *fourth of Seventh-month*: US Independence Day.

Chattahooche[e] or Altamahaw: American rivers.

42 *Nation of many nations*: that is, one of the American states.

Hoosier, Badger, Buckeye: individuals from Indiana, Wisconsin, Ohio, respectively.

fancy-man: pimp.

43 *embouchures*: mouthpieces for wind instruments.

This is the meal equally set: life.

44 *Fourth-month showers*: April showers.

45 *a child's carlacue [curlicue]*: an arc of light made by the rapid movement of a 'burnt stick at night.' In using 'carlacue,' however, Whitman may have also intended 'a caper on a boyish trick'; see Annetta Kelley, 'Whitman's "Song of Myself",' *Explicator*, 46 (Fall, 1987), 22–3.

47 *cartouches*: oval frames containing hieroglyphics.

50 *plenum*: fullness.

52 *quahaug*: an edible clam found off the Atlantic coast.

54 *auk*: a seabird.

57 *katy-did*: insect.

61 *Alamo*: site of the most famous Texan defeat during the Mexican War (1846–8). Whitman, however, is referring to a similar massacre at Goliad, Texas, on 27 Mar. 1836.

second First-day morning: second Sunday morning of the month.

62 *sea-fight*: battle between John Paul Jones's *Bonhomme Richard* and the British warship *Serapis* (23 Sept. 1779).

66 *scarf'd chops*: jaws around which a scarf is tied during illness.

67 *Kronos*: (Greek mythology) variant of Cronus, Titan son of Uranus, whom he castrated.

Manito: variant of Manitou, a spirit of nature (good or bad) to the Algonquin Indians.

68 *bandage under the chin*: see note to p. 66.

dimes on the eyes: coins used to keep the eyes of a dead person shut.

69 *fetich*: variant of fetish.

circle of obis: reference to African-American sorcery.

gymnosophist: a member of the ancient sect of Hindu ascetics (the 'naked philosophers').

skull-cup: reference to the ancient Druids.

70 *mass-kneeling . . . puritan's prayer . . . sitting patiently in a pew*: the Roman catholic, the Protestant, and the Quaker, respectively.

insane crisis: a reference to the 'Holy Rollers', a derogatory term describing fundamentalist religious sects whose spiritual fervor is expressed by shouts and violent bodily movements.

waiting dead-like: another reference to the Quaker practice of passively waiting for the 'Inner Light' of inspiration.

circuits: possibly a reference to the 'circuits' or itineraries of evangelical preachers in the United States.

bloody flukes: that is, harpooned whales.

bad disorder: venereal disease.

koboo: a savage people, possibly from the island of Sumatra, who do not subscribe to the idea of a supreme being.

72 *sauroids*: prehistoric lizards.

promulges: promulgates.

74 *chuff*: palm.

91 *bunch*: the seminal seed or fluid. The piece was originally entitled 'Bunch Poem.'

93 *how long we were fool'd*: that is, repressed by a social sense of abstinence.

95 *Calamus*: Whitman told his English editor, William Michael Rossetti, that the Calamus root or leaf 'is a very large and aromatic grass.' Having a phallic shape (see the illustration in Justin Kaplan, *Walt Whitman; A Life*), it symbolized 'the love of comrades.'

114 *Elbruz . . . Bazardjusi*: mountains in Russia.

Styrian . . . Karnac: the Austrian and Italian alps.

cape of Storms: Cape of Good Hope.

115 *Saukara*: Whitman's spelling for Sankara (Shankara) in Hindu literature.

135 *He is the Answerer*: that is, the poet. The first section of the poem appeared as 'Poem of the Poet' in the second (1856) edition of *Leaves of Grass*.

136 *Cudge*: slang term then current for African-American.

137 *tuft*: an ornithological reference meaning 'crown.'

139 *tylandria*: variant of tillandria, or Spanish moss.

140 *Paumanok's fields*: see note to 'Starting from Paumanok,' p. 18 ff.

142 *clew*: variant of clue.

151 *Mizra*: Egyptian.

 lictors: officials.

154 *Albic*: English.

161 *Hoe press*: a rotary printing press invented in 1846 and on display at the 1871 American Institute in New York City. This poem was written on the occasion of the exhibition.

163 *longeve*: long-lasting.

166 *Mendocino*: a county in nothern California.

188 *The 18th Year of these States*: that is, 1794, the climactic year of the French Revolution (1789–95) and eighteen years after the beginning of the American Revolution.

189 *ma femme*: that is, democracy.

190 *19th Presidentiad*: the presidential competition that elected Abraham Lincoln in 1860.

 Old man . . . scaffold: John Brown, the abolitionist, who was executed in 1859 for his raid at Harper's Ferry, Virginia.

191 *Young prince of England*: the Prince of Wales, who visited America in 1860.

 Great Eastern: the largest steamship in the world during the second half of the nineteenth century.

 Alb: Albion, or Englishman.

193 *Niphon*: variant of Nippon, or Japan.

195 *eldest son*: the Prince of Wales, ultimately Edward VII, who visited American in 1860. Whitman also alludes to him in 'Year of Meteors.'

196 *Ninth-month*: Quaker term for September.

197 *Paumanok*: Indian name for Long Island, where the poet was born; see 'Starting from Paumanok,' (p. 18).

202 *Paumanok*: see note above.

203 *father*: that is, Paumanok; the land symbolizes the Father, whereas the sea represents the Mother. Cf. note below.

207 *old mother*: the sea.

209 *see the show*: Anthony Burns, a fugitive slave, was being

delivered to a ship in Boston harbor which would return him to his owner in the South. He required a police escort to the ship because of the Abolitionist sentiment against his return and the Fugitive Slave Act (1850) that required it.

Jonathan: term used to denote the average American in the nineteenth century—from Royall Tyler's comic drama, *The Contrast* (1787).

211 *cute*: acute.

72d and 73d Years of These States: a reference to the various revolutions in Europe in 1848 and 1849.

215 *President*: probably James Buchanan, US president between 1857 and 1861 and an opponent of anti-slavery legislation.

217 *adhesiveness*: phrenological term for same-sex or parental attachment, friendship, or fraternal love.

218 *16th, 17th, or 18th Presidentiad*: allusions to the administrations of Millard Fillmore, Franklin Pierce, and James Buchanan, presidents whose policies Whitman scorned; see note for 'To a President' (p. 215).

222 *Paumanok*: see note to p. 197.

230 *noble sire*: the state of Virginia upon its secession from the Union at the beginning of the Civil War.

232 *Declaration*: the Declaration of Independence, signed six weeks after the Battle of Long Island, which the Centenarian recalls and contrasts with the optimistic expectations of untested soldiers on the eve of the Revolutionary War.

General: George Washington.

234 *27th of August [1776]*: the date of the Battle of Long Island.

241 *Wound-Dresser*: during the Civil War and after, Whitman lived in Washington, D.C., and devoted virtually all his spare time (from the government job he held) visiting and cheering up sick and wounded soldiers from both sides of the conflict. Often, he would assist the surgeon in an operation when no regular nurse was in attendance.

250 *Coals thirty-eight*: indicating the thirty-eight states in the Union by 1881 when this poem was last revised. In earlier versions, the number corresponded to the current number of states.

268 *Phantom*: see note to p. 12.

270 *the great Idea*: the 'good cause' of liberty; see note to p. 11.

282 *Third-month*: March in the Quaker vernacular.

290 *good old cause*: see note to p. 11.

294 *high-hole*: Long Island term for the flicker or North American woodpecker.

   G.P.: George Peabody (1795–1869), American philanthropist, so famous at his death that Queen Victoria sent his body back from England in a British warship.

304 *quits and quits*: 'even and even,' or equally.

306 *1870–71*: dates for the Franco-Prussian War, out of which came the Third Republic of France.

308 *George Fox*: founder of the Quakers.

   evil times: the financial panic of 1873, the year in which this poem was composed.

310 *little house*: that is, the poet's mind or memory.

311 *cantabile*: operatic term for a smooth, lyrical style.

   diapason: musical term for either of the two foundation stops on a pipe organ.

312 *Norma*: a referene to Vincenzo Bellini's opera of the same name.

   Lucia's eyes: a reference to *Lucia di Lammermoor* by Gaetano Donizetti.

   Ernani: see Giuseppi Verdi's opera of the same name.

313 *Fernando's heart*: a reference to Donizetti's opera *La Favorita*.

   Amina: see Bellini's *La Sonnambula*.

   Alboni's self: Marietta Alboni, one of Whitman's favorite opera stars.

315 *Suez canal . . . gentle wires*: the ostensible occasion for this poem is the completion of the Suez Canal, the junction of the Union and Pacific railroads, and the laying of the Atlantic Cable.

316 *Empress Eugenie's leading the van*: wife of Napoleon III, who was on the leading ship during the opening ceremonies of the Suez Canal in 1869.

317 *Genoese*: Christopher Columbus (1451–1506), who was born in Genoa, Italy. Columbus's historic voyage to 'India' and discovery of America were probably the seeds for the idea of this poem.

318 *Vasco de Gama*: Portuguese explorer, the first to reach India by sea.

320 *the Admiral himself*: Columbus.

328 *Brooklyn*: Battle of Brooklyn Heights, 27 Aug. 1776.

346 *Brood*: this poem was originally entitled 'As a Strong Bird on Pinions Free,' when it was read by the poet at Dartmouth College on 26 June 1872.

347 *Saguenay's black stream*: river in south-central Quebec that flows into the St Lawrence.

354 *brother*: Whitman's youngest brother Edward was mentally retarded.

355 *Behold a woman*: very possibly a description of the poet's maternal grandmother, Naomi Van Velsor.

360 *Mannahatta*: Indian name for New York; Whitman objected to the Duke of York.

362 *Two words*: possibly the 'good cause' of liberty. See 'To Thee Old Cause,' p. 11.

365 *alimentive, amative*: phrenological terms for the appetites relating to food and sex.

368 *U.S.G.*: Ulysses S. Grant, who went on a world tour in 1877, following his tenure as president.

374 *Anahuacs*: reference to the lake bed on which Mexico City rests.

376 *mother*: the poet's mother, Louisa Van Velsor Whitman, died on 23 May 1873.

378 *Bells*: written on the death of President James A. Garfield, whom Whitman had known since the 1860s in Washington, DC.

383 *November Boughs*: the title under which this cluster of poems was originally published in 1888.

385 *Mannahatta*: see note to p. 360.

  Paumanok: see note to p. 18.

  Montauk Point: the most eastern tip of Long Island.

386 *nonpareil . . . primer*: standard kinds of types. Whitman was a printer in his earlier days and even set the type to part of the first edition of *Leaves of Grass*.

395   *Kossabone*: 'Dutch' Kossabone was the great-great grandfather of the poet.

      Tenor: Signor Pasquala Brignole, who died in 1884, the year this poem was written.

      Fernando's . . . Gennaro's: references to operas by Donizetti and Verdi.

397   *woman-friend*: Anne Gilchrist (1828–85), one of the first women to write in praise of *Leaves of Grass*. See the Introduction.

399   *To-day*: Memorial Day, 1888—though there is some question the poem was actually published on this day.

402   *Emperor*: William I of Germany, who died in 1888.

409   *eidólon*: see note to p. 12.

412   *Cipher*: see Ignatius Donnelly's *The Great Cryptogram: Francis Bacon's Cipher in the So-Called Shakespeare Plays* (1888), a book championed by the poet's friend, William Douglas O'Connor.

413   *Paris Exposition*: of 1889, at which the Eiffel Tower was exhibited.

415   *Brazilian brother*: on 15 Nov. 1889 (the year of the composition of this poem) a military revolt led to the founding of a republic styled after the U.S.

426   *O'Connor*: see note to p. 412. O'Connor (1832–89) wrote *The Good Gray Poet* (1866), which defended Whitman against censorship. See Jerome Loving, *Walt Whitman's Champion: William Douglas O'Connor* (1978).

      Bucke: Richard Maurice Bucke (1837–1902), Canadian alienist, who was one of Whitman's literary executors. His 1883 biography was partially written by Whitman. See *Richard Maurice Bucke, Medical Mystic: Letters of Dr Bucke to Walt Whitman and His Friends*, ed. Artem Lozynsky (1977).

INDEX
BY TITLE

THE WORLD'S CLASSICS

A Select List

HANS ANDERSEN: Fairy Tales
Translated by L. W. Kingsland
Introduction by Naomi Lewis
Illustrated by Vilhelm Pedersen and Lorenz Frølich

JANE AUSTEN: Emma
Edited by James Kinsley and David Lodge

Mansfield Park
Edited by James Kinsley and John Lucas

J. M. BARRIE: Peter Pan in Kensington Gardens & Peter and Wendy
Edited by Peter Hollindale

WILLIAM BECKFORD: Vathek
Edited by Roger Lonsdale

CHARLOTTE BRONTË: Jane Eyre
Edited by Margaret Smith

THOMAS CARLYLE: The French Revolution
Edited by K. J. Fielding and David Sorensen

LEWIS CARROLL: Alice's Adventures in Wonderland
and Through the Looking Glass
Edited by Roger Lancelyn Green
Illustrated by John Tenniel

MIGUEL DE CERVANTES: Don Quixote
Translated by Charles Jarvis
Edited by E. C. Riley

GEOFFREY CHAUCER: The Canterbury Tales
Translated by David Wright

ANTON CHEKHOV: The Russian Master and Other Stories
Translated by Ronald Hingley

JOSEPH CONRAD: Victory
Edited by John Batchelor
Introduction by Tony Tanner

DANTE ALIGHIERI: The Divine Comedy
Translated by C. H. Sisson
Edited by David Higgins